JAZZ
AMONG
THE
DISCOURSES

JAZZ

AMONG

THE

DISCOURSES

Edited by Krin Gabbard

DUKE UNIVERSITY PRESS *Durham and London 1995*

© 1995 Duke University Press
All rights reserved
Printed in the United States of America on acid-free paper ∞
Typeset in Trump Mediaeval by Keystone Typesetting, Inc.
Library of Congress Cataloging-in-Publication Data and
permissions appear on the last printed page of this book.

Contents

THE JAZZ ARTIST AMONG THE DISCOURSES

THE ESSENTIAL CONTEXT: JAZZ AND POLITICS

Acknowledgments

This anthology began to take shape at the December 1990 meeting of the Modern Language Association in Chicago, where I chaired a session entitled "Representing Jazz." One of the panelists was Fred Garber, a professor of comparative literature with a passion for new projects that is as rare as it is inspiring. It was Fred who urged me to assemble essays about jazz into what he thought could become the first jazz book to adopt the critical theory that has transformed literary studies over the past two decades. Before long, I had located a fascinating assortment of jazz scholars, practically none of whom regularly taught music or jazz. Their work with the music was a passion they cultivated within, outside, or around their work in departments of English, philosophy, African American studies, history, American studies, comparative literature, and film studies as well as music.

Wired in to several mini-networks of jazz scholars, I eventually found so many kindred spirits that the number of potential contributors to the anthology soon numbered more than twenty. I was now faced with the depressing task of paring down the contributions to ten or twelve— the canonical number for anthologies at university presses. Fortunately, I had already contacted Bernard Gendron, whose original work on Negrophilia in French modernism had convinced me that he was someone I ought to get to know. When I complained to Professor Gendron that I had too many essays for a single collection, he consoled me by suggesting that I edit two anthologies. By happy accident, my large stack of contributions fell neatly into two equal stacks of manageable proportions. In one pile were the essays that dealt with film, literature, photography, and dance; in the other were those concerned primarily with jazz history and aesthetics or with specific jazz artists. You are now holding the second of these volumes; the first one, also published by Duke University Press, became *Representing Jazz.*

My sincere thanks go to Professors Garber and Gendron for the crucial roles they played in the genesis of these two books. I also thank the contributors to these anthologies who patiently waited, in some cases as long as five years, to see their work in print. I also thank them for constantly revising their essays to comply with each new round of readers' reports and editorial suggestions. Happily, they always made these revisions with dispatch and without complaint.

Ken Wissoker of Duke University Press will always have my respect and gratitude for his devotion to this project and for the professional manner in which he has shepherded it through to completion. The two jazz scholars commissioned by the press as anonymous readers made essential suggestions for improving the anthologies and were, I am relieved to say, sympathetic to the more heretical aspects of these anthologies. Lewis Porter provided me with ancient issues of *Down Beat* and with less tangible but no less valuable items of jazz scholarship and wisdom. The Comparative Studies Program at the State University of New York at Stony Brook, especially departmental secretary Lee Peters, cheerfully provided logistical support, and Federal Express never let me down when deadlines became tight. Finally, I thank my patient and loving wife, Paula, who, one night in 1973, asked if I would play her some more Eric Dolphy records.

JAZZ
AMONG
THE
DISCOURSES

Introduction: The Jazz Canon
and Its Consequences

irectly or indirectly, all the essays in this book and its companion volume *Representing Jazz* strongly argue that jazz has entered the mainstreams of the American academy. The institutionalization of jazz is consistent with current demystifications of the distinctions between high and low culture, with the growing trend toward multiculturalism in university curricula, and with the postmodernist cachet now enjoyed by marginal arts and artists. Signs of jazz's ascendancy can be found in such peri-academic phenomena as the proliferation of jazz titles now being published by university presses, the birth of jazz repertory orchestras, and the new jazz division at New York's Lincoln Center. For several years Lincoln Center has also run a series of "Classical Jazz" concerts under the artistic directorship of Wynton Marsalis, himself an eminent if controversial symbol of jazz's new legitimacy.

Even television commercials testify to the music's rising cultural capital. In an advertisement a few years ago a well-heeled white gentleman cited a Mozart concerto as the sound most appropriate for the total appreciation of his Mercedes-Benz; more recently, a cool, Milesian trumpet performed a similar function by providing elegant background music in a commercial for the Infiniti, a new luxury car. Concurrent with the Infiniti spot, a faithful re-creation of the Duke Ellington orchestra's 1941 recording of "Chelsea Bridge" played behind a scene of casual affluence in a commercial for the American Express card; more recently, Benny Goodman's 1952 recording of "How Am I to Know?" graces a series of spots for the Chase Manhattan Bank. Advertisers no longer use jazz to connote the nightlife and slumming that can be purchased along with their products—jazz can now signify refinement and upper-class status, once the exclusive province of classical music.[1]

This new parity of jazz with classical music in the sign systems of popular media is an important breakthrough. Because jazz has histor- ically been treated as a stepchild of "serious" music, the music's value is usually established with appeals to standards developed for classical music. The project is explicit, for example, in the title of Grover Sales's book, *Jazz: America's Classical Music*.[2] All jazz writers are richly aware of the various strains of prejudice that place classical music in a loftier position in the cultural hierarchy. A great deal of jazz writing implicitly or explicitly expresses the demand that jazz musicians be given the same legitimacy as practitioners of the canonical arts.

And yet the legitimization of jazz studies takes place at a peculiar moment in the history of academic institutions. Conditions that appear to bode well for jazz scholarship also conceal difficulties for the disci- pline. The canonization of jazz—or more precisely, the canonization of certain jazz artists and styles—would seem to be inescapable if the music is to claim its place within the academy, where an array of organizations such as grant-giving institutions support and further legitimize subjects of research and teaching. At the same time, however, humanistic disci- plines are being re-canonized if not de-canonized, while the entire pro- cess by which texts come under scrutiny is itself being scrutinized. And in spite of the occasional jazz group that called itself an "orchestra" or the jazz writer who composed a "fantasy," the music almost from the begin- ning has placed itself at odds with the canonizing language of high culture. The entry of jazz discourse into the dialogues of the university can only result in the transformation of that discourse. Scott DeVeaux has suggested that the term "jazz concert" once ran the risk of being an oxymoron ("Emergence" 7). Much the same can now be said for "the jazz canon."

My argument here is arranged around two themes that complicate the attempt to establish a jazz canon: (1) the resistance of jazz writing to the protocols of contemporary theory that follow canon-building wherever it takes place, and (2) the conviction on the part of many theorists that ideological forces masquerade as disinterested aesthetics in the discourse around *all* canonical works. I will make regular references to debates within other disciplines—film studies, most prominently—that offer instructive models for the imminent institutionalization of jazz. The creation of a jazz canon, I will argue, is as self-defeating as it is inevitable, especially as jazz studies move toward professionalization and autonomy.

Although people inside and outside academia are now less inclined than ever to subscribe to the concept of the "masterpiece," canonical works of Western literature, classical music, and European painting still bear traces of the Benjaminian aura. Likewise, the term "canon" still carries the marks of its religious origins: the Oxford English Dictionary defines *canon* as "The collection or list of books of the Bible as accepted by the Christian Church as genuine and inspired. . . . Any set of sacred books."[3] Although the sacral antecedents of canons are usually ignored in discussions of great art, music and literature, those works that appear to have endured for centuries possess a mystifying sense of inevitability, as if they had been handed down by God. Like the books of the Bible, "great" works of art are "universal" and "timeless."

In stark contrast to the sacral haze that surrounds canonical texts, the actual path a work takes to "masterpiece" status has little to do with religion. In fact, canonization is usually determined by the likes and dislikes of the last few generations of university professors.[4] If nothing else, professors are more comfortable teaching the material once inflicted upon them in graduate school, if not in college and high school. Teachers can become self-conscious about the hidden politics of canon formation and cease referring to works as immortal masterpieces, even choosing to teach them anticanonically. Still, texts that are repeatedly inscribed in course syllabi possess a largely unquestioned claim upon the attention of scholars and students. This aura of inevitability masks the often tortuous paths such texts may have taken on their way to canonization. Lawrence Levine's account of Shakespeare's fortunes in mid-nineteenth century America provides a particularly revealing example of how texts can be wrested from a popular canon and sequestered within the academy for an educated elite. But at least in part because English professors seldom teach the history of reception, Shakespeare is widely regarded as an eternally stable fixture of the high-art canon. We can also chart the ups and downs of novelists, painters, sculptors, and composers who now occupy equally unquestioned positions in our cultural hierarchies. In spite of the Infiniti and Chase Manhattan Bank commercials, few Americans today regard anything in jazz history as the auratic equal of, say, Faulkner, Copland, or Andrew Wyeth. Consequently, the disciplines that attend to these works carry a legitimacy that jazz studies lack, if only because the music has not been around long enough to acquire real canonical status.

The progress of a youthful discipline such as film studies may offer a better model for contemplating the future of jazz studies. Cinema stood just outside the classroom door in the early 1960s, a position not unlike the one currently occupied by jazz. Colleges and universities had for many years provided meeting places for film societies and buffs, just as "hot record societies" and student jazz bands have long been fixtures at universities. Amid the clutter of fanzines, a bare handful of journals published scholarly articles on movies; a few intellectuals had begun writing on the history and aesthetics of the cinema, in the case of the German-born psychiatrist Hugo Münsterberg as early as 1916. Serious jazz criticism has historically lagged behind film criticism; although jazz was already a popular topic in newspapers and magazines by the second decade of the century, thoughtful jazz articles did not begin to appear in the United States and Europe until the 1930s.[5] In the academy, many universities developed professional schools for filmmakers; in the case of film history and criticism, some faculty members in language and history departments showed feature films in their classrooms to supplement more conventional pedagogical tools, and at a few schools, students could even take a course devoted entirely to cinema. Such courses, however, were usually ghettoized in departments of English or theater. Much the same can be said for jazz today: while there are a number of schools that train young musicians to play the music (Berklee College of Music, William Paterson College, the University of North Texas, etc.), these must be distinguished from schools where jazz is most often taught by musicologists more secure with Eurocentric forms or by a lone jazz musician retreating to the security of academia after some years of paying dues on the road. Institutes and archives such as those at Rutgers and Tulane are the exception, not the rule.

Cinema, on the other hand, has been more successful in gaining acceptance at American colleges and universities. The first doctorate in film studies was granted by New York University in 1971. According to the latest survey by the American Film Institute, more than three hundred colleges and universities offered degrees in film and film-related areas of study in 1990 (Horrigan xviii). By contrast, in the same year, only one hundred colleges and universities in the United States offered degree programs in jazz, almost all of them undergraduate (Miller). The success of cinema in becoming a recognized academic discipline might be attributed in part to the importation from France of *la politique des auteurs* in the 1960s. Andrew Sarris deserves substantial credit for Americanizing an auteur theory of cinema that identifies the director as the true author of a film.[6] The more romantic auteurists created an agonistic model of filmmaking, casting the director as a serious artist imprinting a unique vision on his films in spite of the arbitrary demands of studio bosses, star egos, and the Production Code. Anything that was aesthetically weak or unsavory in a film could be blamed on someone else so long as the auteur's signature was visible in the film's "privileged moments."

By authorizing the reading of a film around a single artist's work, auteurism gave a new aesthetic legitimacy to movies. In universities, films "by" Ford or Welles or Bergman or Antonioni could be collected and interpreted according to many of the same methods developed for, say, the novels of Henry James. Evidence of order and thematic unity, once the sole possession of high culture, was also found in works of cinematic auteurs, and canonized filmmakers were said to possess transcendent artistic visions that spoke to all humanity (Staiger). As the university was being transformed by the sea changes of the 1960s, auteurism helped clear room in the university for film study, bringing with it an aesthetics and a canonical list of director/authors. Sarris eventually became a professor of film studies at Columbia University in spite of his lack of conventional academic credentials.

Auteurism still has force today, even among the filmgoing public who now recognize a large variety of brand-name directors—Spike Lee and David Lynch as well as Steven Spielberg and Woody Allen. In academic film studies any number of theories from the 1970s and 1980s can be cited as refutations, revisions, or rethinkings of auteurism. In general, the mainstream of the discipline has moved away from extolling the transcendent vision of a director and toward what Paul Ricoeur has called "a hermeneutics of suspicion" (29–33). Film theoreticians now rely on Marxist, psychoanalytic, semiotic, and poststructuralist methodologies to connect forces outside the text with meanings that lie beneath the film's smooth narrative surface. These meanings are usually uncovered through techniques of demystification developed by critics such as Roland Barthes who see bourgeois ideology passing itself off as nature. Canonical directors are still the subject of some research, but many scholars have found that the ideological workings of a film are more accessible to analysis when the director is relatively obscure and the film is more "typical" of the industry's production. As befits a discipline moving rapidly toward professionalization, film scholars have adopted a language that is notoriously remote. Most jazz scholars, for better or worse, still speak a language drawn from other disciplines or from journalism.

As in the more established disciplines, the dominant canons of cinema study have been radically questioned by previously excluded groups, most prominently by women. Recently, however, feminist critics have become concerned that their critique of traditional male canons is equally applicable to the emerging feminist canons. Virginia Wright Wexman's essay on the various interpretations of Alfred Hitchcock's *Vertigo* (1958) is exemplary of a feminism that recognizes its own investment in an institutional dialectic of power that feminism itself has sought to expose. *Vertigo* was singled out by Laura Mulvey in what is undoubtedly the single most influential essay in early feminist film theory. Far from labeling the film a work of genius, Mulvey sees *Vertigo* as a convincing illustration of Hollywood's submission of female characters to the sadistic gaze of the male characters, who function as stand-ins for the men in the audience. Wexman suggests that many feminists— who promote a theory that may be illustrated most completely by the obsessive gaze directed at Kim Novak by James Stewart in *Vertigo*—have effectively secured their place in the discipline by helping to place Hitchcock's film on key lists that define the canons of film study.[7]

Wexman observes that canon formation is essential to the political prestige of groups and subgroups in the academy. Following Gramsci, Wexman distinguishes between "traditional intellectuals," who perpetuate and rationalize the values of a society, and "organic intellectuals," who advocate new value systems, in essence theorizing themselves into the society's structures of power. Institutionally established critics have insisted that *Vertigo* is a work of "pure cinema," and, by extension, that as a work of art it transcends commerce. For Wexman, the interpretations of these traditional intellectuals promote bourgeois notions of the autonomy of art. She debunks these readings of the film by demonstrating that large portions of *Vertigo* are endorsements for the touristic delights of San Francisco as well as for the classical beauty of its star Kim Novak. Wexman also finds alternatives to readings of *Vertigo* by certain feminist critics, "organic intellectuals" who have advanced their own cause by holding up the film as an important document for which they offer the most compelling interpretation. By laying claim to a film such as *Vertigo*, feminist scholars have hastened that film's rise to canonical status at the same time that they have rationalized their own ascent in American universities.[8] In much the same way, Sarris promoted himself by creating a pantheon of exclusively male auteur/directors in the 1960s.

The history of film studies suggests that a postcanonical study such as Wexman's is possible only after the discipline has built a foundation around key works. The current demystification and deconstruction of cinematic texts by film theorists might not have become so prominent without canonizing discourses to oppose. The concept of authorship, in both film and literary studies, has been under assault for some years now, most notably in the works of Barthes and Michel Foucault.[9] Coincidental with the collapse of the author has been the ascent of the critic. No longer required to pay tribute to infallible creators, critics gain autonomy and authority of their own. The privileged position of Jacques Derrida in today's critical canon is surely related to his liberation of the critic from subordination to literary texts. Critics establish autonomy most effectively by creating a metalanguage and a series of methodologies that exclude the amateur. Anyone can engage in evaluation and express an opinion about a book, a play or a film. Only a professional can speak a language and brandish a paradigm understood only by a coterie of specialists with mastery over the same language and paradigm.[10]

Turning at last to jazz studies, I would argue that the discipline has for a long time been in a phase comparable to the auteurist era of film studies in the 1960s and 1970s: ever since the first serious writings about jazz appeared, critics have sought to become organic intellectuals, who would theorize themselves and the music into positions of importance. Although a number of writers have ascended to stations with some power, they have not yet been able to carve their canon into the granite of American culture or to install their discipline in the structure of the university. If I am right that jazz may follow the path of film studies in becoming a stable fixture in constantly mutating university curricula, a number of its scholars will become more self-conscious about the problematic nature of canon-formation even as they continue to write about the key artists of their discipline.[11] It is also likely that jazz scholars will develop a professional discourse that may at first draw on the vocabularies of musicology, sociology, critical theory, and other disciplines but that ultimately will be unique to jazz studies.

In doing so, jazz scholars run the risk of losing touch with a group of critics who do not have conventional academic credentials but who nevertheless play a large role in the professional life of the discipline by reading grant proposals and evaluating manuscripts for university presses. In addition, the new metalanguage of the field may strike most jazz enthusiasts as impenetrable. This is the trade-off that professionals in other disciplines have accepted as they have gradually but inexorably separated themselves from the general public. For some time now, the vast majority of poetry lovers have *not* consulted *PMLA* and *Modern Philology* to supplement their enjoyment, just as few movie buffs today expend the effort necessary to read the articles in *Cinema Journal* and *Camera Obscura*. Most academics regret this situation; some of the most eminent among them even bemoan their isolation in speeches at plenary sessions during professional conferences.[12] Tenure, promotion and job mobility, however, are based not on professors' fortunes with general readers but on their reputations among a handful of professional colleagues. Similarly, as the work of jazz studies expands, something more than the straightforward celebration of canonical artists is required if the field is to stand alongside established disciplines that have long since ceased making appeals to outsiders.

The actual development of a jazz canon—not to mention the critic's role in the process—is complex and multidetermined, caught in a complicated web of changing conditions. In the 1920s, for example, the entry of Louis Armstrong's recording of "West End Blues" into a jazz artist's canon can be documented at least in part by a King Oliver recording of the tune that appeared six months after Armstrong's version: on Oliver's record of "West End Blues," trumpeter Louis Metcalf attempted a note-for-note re-creation of Armstrong's opening cadenza.[13] There are a number of reasons why Metcalf may have chosen to duplicate Armstrong's solo, just as Oliver—who in fact wrote "West End Blues" and considered Armstrong his protégé—may have had reasons of his own for directing Metcalf to re-create the difficult solo. We might also interrogate the processes that brought Armstrong and later Oliver into the recording studio as well as those forces that made their records available to large audiences. Basically, however, we have a case of canon-formation through a somewhat uncomplicated process of communication by phonograph record. Today, this kind of homage paid by one artist to another is only one among numerous phenomena that contribute to the creation of a jazz canon; a partial list would include grant-giving agencies, recording contracts and sales, collections issued by mail-order companies and the Book-of-the-Month Club, public appearances by artists, academic appointments, the political structures of universities, roles for jazz musicians in movies (Dexter Gordon in *Round Midnight*, for example), record reviews, "ten best lists" in the popular press, promotions by disc jockeys, Grammy awards, film scores, and faces on postage stamps.

In the academy, however, canonizers are more likely to adopt the strategy of romanticizing the artist. The improvising jazz artist is, after all, a composer as well as a performer, not unlike the mythologized composer/performers of the Romantic Era such as Liszt and Paganini who improvised on well-known works. Although this equation is seldom explicit in jazz writings, its traces can usually be found, hinting at why a music associated with prostitution and drug addiction is as valid as the music associated with landed gentry in premodern Europe. A disproportionate amount of jazz scholarship is and has been devoted to finding the most effective means for identifying and exalting favored artists.

Consider, for example, jazz discography. The practice has long been the almost sole province of an international network of devoted record collectors, largely uninterested in profits and often with careers outside music.[14] From the beginning, discographers have been intimately and unavoidably involved with the work of canon-building. When Charles Delaunay published his first *Hot Discography* in 1938, he created a guidebook for those who agreed with him that the music had more than ephemeral value. He was also committing an act of exclusion, declining to catalog certain performers from "race records," blues, ragtime, and dance music whom he considered to be outside the charmed circle of jazz. Like the auteurists of cinema studies, he built the discography on a model that centered great artists: Delaunay would combine, for example, all the recordings of Armstrong in one section of his book even when titles had not been recorded under Armstrong's name or when the trumpeter was only a sideperson at someone else's recording session. Delaunay did the same with Bix Beiderbecke, even less likely to be listed as leader during his recording history. Just as auteurist critics attributed an entire film to the director rather than to the producer, the screenwriter, the cinematographer, the stars, or some combination of coworkers, Delaunay in effect credited Armstrong or Beiderbecke with a recording even when the trumpeter was essentially an accompanist.[15] For Delaunay, the centrality of Armstrong and Beiderbecke was more consistent with an idealized jazz history than were the pedestrian blues singers and sweet dance bands with whom the two trumpeters had recorded. His view of jazz history was reflected in the very arrangement of his discography.

Delaunay's catalog laid the groundwork for several generations of discographers, who fall into two categories: (1) single-artist discographers who fetishize the recordings of specific musicians, almost always to the point of detailing those sessions in which the artist is present but undetectable in a large ensemble; (2) Orin Blackstone, Dave Carey, Brian Rust, Jørgen Jepsen, Walter Bruyninckx, Erik Raben, and Tom Lord who have, like Delaunay, inventoried the music in large historical sweeps that inevitably suppress artists who do not play in appropriate styles. While the discographers in the first category might be considered inclusionists, tracking down every recorded scrap by specific artists, those in the second are primarily exclusionists.[16] Walter Bruyninckx, surely the most catholic of all jazz catalogers, provides a good illustration of the exclusionist at work. His regularly updated discography, currently known as *Seventy Years of Recorded Jazz*, is an international inventory of jazz as well as gospel, blues, and jazz-inflected pop that fills several feet of shelf space. Nevertheless, even Bruyninckx is likely to truncate the

listings for an artist if he believes that at some moment the recordings
cease to have jazz content. He also frequently writes statements such as:
"Although negroid in origin this group recorded mainly for the white
audiences and their recordings have very little of the sincerity and enthusiasm that is to be found in other negro recordings of religious oriented
music" (F110a).[17] Bruyninckx's candor becomes him well, but his didactic criterion for banishing one group instead of another is characteristic
of any and all enterprises that seek to sort out the real from the ersatz.
Discographers such as Bruyninckx unavoidably participate in the formation of a jazz canon, a project that is scarcely value-free. Single artist discographies appear because a cataloger has responded to a variety
of forces that make an artist worthy of complete documentation. The
methodologies operating in the larger, exclusionary discographies are
invariably grounded in critically sanctioned judgments that discographers are seldom interested in interrogating. For example, Erik Raben,
one of the more recent exclusionists, devotes two sentences to the issue:
"In many cases it has been difficult to decide where the boundaries to
blues, R&B, dance-oriented big band music, pop-vocal music, jazz/rock
fusion music and Latin music should be drawn. In some cases non-jazz
recordings are included to 'complete' the discography of a musician or a
group/band" (iii). Like his predecessors, Raben does not reveal how he
drew the boundaries between jazz and nonjazz.[18]

The canonization of jazz artists has almost always been the major
thrust of jazz scholarship, regardless of whether the writers take their
methodology from traditional musicology or from social science. Two
articles from the Austrian journal *Jazzforschung/Jazz Research* provide
extreme examples of both approaches. Stewart's essay on Clifford Brown
begins with the following paragraph:

> It is now twenty-two years since the passing of Clifford Brown, yet
> his loss is felt today almost as much as it was in the late summer of
> 1956. Musicians and fans alike, some of them too young to have
> heard him in person, pay tribute to this creative person. For many
> people, there is something amazing about the way that beautifully
> developed musical structures flowed from his horn with ease and
> joy. There is something phenomenal about the way that his im-
> provisations are understood and appreciated even by those who or-
> dinarily are not jazz lovers. Clifford Brown was possibly the rare
> musician who comes along only once in a generation.

The body of the essay, however, is devoted to a highly technical, Schenk-
erian analysis of Brown's improvisations, devoid of the adulatory tone

that opens the essay. Here is a representative sample: "The middleground structure of the original piece includes the neighbornote, $b\flat^1$, which serves to prolong a^1, and the movement d^1 in measure 8 which serves to provide acoustical support for a^1 by virtue of the fifth relationship" (136). At this point, the rhetoric of jazz studies is indistinguishable from that of academic music theory.

An article on Lester Young, also published in *Jazzforschung*, grafts the history of racist violence against African American people onto a biographical sketch of Young (Daniels). Here is the conclusion of the article:

> The sensibilities of Lester Young and other Black artists assume even more impressive significance when compared to the callow, materialistic, and often violent nature of the world they inhabited. Young's humanistic, benevolent, and non-materialistic values set him apart from both businessmen and conformist consumers. He represents an ideal example of the qualities allegedly treasured by the people whose actions suggested the very opposite.

Without in any way rejecting the judgments of these two writers, I would point out that both insist on the value of their subjects even when it means speaking with two voices: each scholar writes almost entirely in the professional language of a canonical discipline, but at the beginning or end of his piece, he switches to the vocabulary of the fan and the record collector. Their praise for jazz artists is not and cannot be documented by their use of traditional scholarly apparatus. Footnotes and musical examples disappear when the scholar becomes essentially indistinguishable from the fan. The collapsing of these two categories has run through a great deal of jazz writing ever since the appearance of the first books that dealt with the music.

By contrast, scholarly writing today in literature, music, and art is increasingly less likely to be built around the unequivocal glorification of the artist or the bald valorizing of one artist over another. In literary studies Northrop Frye was calling such evaluative criticism "debaucheries of judiciousness" in the 1950s (18). Hyperbolic praise for the auteur has been largely abandoned by film scholars during the past two decades and is now left almost entirely to critics in the popular press. If a discipline can be considered "professionalized" when it develops its own metalanguage and a self-consciousness about its canon, then jazz study is still in its infancy. The discipline's lingering preprofessionalism is especially evident in Gunther Schuller's *The Swing Era*, doubtlessly one of the most important jazz texts in recent years. Schuller brings impressive credentials to this and his already canonical study of early jazz. In both books, however, he rejects scholarly prose in favor of journalistic terms such as "truly magnificent," "totally unredeemable," and "heartrendingly moving." Because Schuller is also devoted to the myth of jazz's autonomy, he seldom considers the music's contextual and historical relationships.[19] His consistent reluctance in *The Swing Era* to press his analyses beyond his own impressions is most explicit when he states, for example, that Billie Holiday's talent is "in the deepest sense inexplicable" (528), or when he writes of Ben Webster, "as with most truly great art, Webster's cannot be fully explained" (590), or when, after a few words on Lester Young's mastery of understatement, he calls Young "The Gandhi of American jazz" (562). These passages are likely to become increasingly uncharacteristic of jazz writing as the subject advances into the academy. No assistant professor in any discipline is tenured today for declaring a phenomenon to be "in the deepest sense inexplicable" (unless that professor is a deconstructionist, and Schuller is no deconstructionist).

Even when jazz writers perform close analysis of the music, many engage in a kind of canon-building based on paradigms that have been radically questioned in other disciplines. One historically prominent strategy for canonizing the jazz artist is based in an aesthetic of unity and coherence. Few writers employed this strategy as persuasively as Martin Williams, who studied the New Criticism in the 1950s while working on a graduate degree in English at Columbia University. A striking but not atypical example of Williams's application of formalist literary principles to jazz is his discussion of Charlie Parker's 1947 improvisation on the first take of his Dial recording of "Embraceable You":

> In his one-chorus improvisation on "Embraceable You," Parker barely glances at Gershwin's melody. He begins with an interesting six-note phrase which he then uses five times in a row, pronouncing it variously and moving it around to fit the harmonic contours of Gershwin's piece. On its fifth appearance the six-note motive forms the beginning of a delicate thrust of melody which dances along, pauses momentarily, resumes, and finally comes to rest balanced at the end with a variant of that same six-note phrase. . . . [I]t is the core of his improvisation, and, speaking personally, I have seldom listened to this chorus without realizing how ingeniously that phrase is echoed in Parker's remarkable melody. (137)[20]

As many theorists have pointed out, a work's value is not simply a function of how well its artist understands internalist principles of unity and coherence. Jonathan Culler has written, "The notion that the task of criticism is to reveal thematic unity is a post-Romantic concept, whose roots in the theory of organic form are, at the very least, ambiguous" (119). Parker's work might just as easily be discussed in terms of how he *destroys* the illusion of organic unity in his solos by inserting easily recognizable fragments from other musical traditions such as the Habanera from Bizet's *Carmen*, "The Campbells Are Coming," and Alphonse Picou's clarinet solo from "High Society" (Gabbard, "The Quoter and His Culture"). Williams overlooked the ways in which Parker resisted recuperation into a Eurocentric aesthetic by in fact "Signifyin(g)" upon it, as Henry Louis Gates, Jr., might suggest.

Because of the music's youth, jazz writers have gone about the business of canon-building without having to look over their shoulders at those who would demand alternative canons. The infamous battle between the ancients and the moderns in the 1940s was easily resolved by making room in the canon for bebop alongside older forms associated with New Orleans and Chicago. No legitimate history of jazz today can afford to omit either one.[21] In other disciplines, however, canons have faced powerful challenges from women, minorities, and those working with various poststructuralisms (and more recently from resurgent white males such as Allan Bloom, William Bennett, and Roger Kimball). The progress of various teaching anthologies is a good index to canon struggles in literature departments. In the 1970s newly acquired female and minority editors began to effect the contents of W. W. Norton's well-established anthologies of English and world literature. For some time Norton had invested in the belief that single, two-volume anthologies could present coherent canons for an entire discipline. Other presses subscribed to the same proposition and published their own one- and two-volume selections from the canon. Today, however, in addition to more pluralistic anthologies of English and world literatures, Norton has published an anthology of women writers, and Henry Louis Gates, Jr., perhaps the single most articulate critic of the old canon, is currently editing a Norton anthology of African American literature (Gates, "Canon-Formation"). Although Gates is clearly ambivalent about his new role as canonizer (Gates, *Loose Canons*), he has taken the original step of including in the anthology a sound recording of African American writers reading from their work. Not only has Gates emphasized the performative dimensions of a great deal of black literature, but he has changed the rules for canon-formation. By contrast, *The Smithsonian Collection of Classic Jazz*, now in its second edition and available on compact discs, still stands as the only major listening text for an introductory course in jazz history. Many critics have second-guessed Martin Williams's choices for what ought to be included in the set of recordings,

but as of early 1995 no one has undertaken to replace it with a comparable anthology of favored recordings.[22]

Although jazz scholars may need a canon to establish their legitimacy,
there are other consequences of acquiring one. Like feminists who have
found themselves in the uncomfortable position of deploying an institutional politics not unlike the one that had once been used to exclude
women, jazz canonizers may find it difficult to be true to the full range of
jazz culture at the same time that they rely on Eurocentric traditions.
Bernard Gendron has broached the subject of what is at stake as the
discipline solidifies around a canon. In discussing André Hodeir's prefer-
ence for Igor Stravinsky's appropriation of jazz over that of Darius Milhaud, Gendron refers to Hodeir's "inadmissibly essentialist construction
of 'authentic' jazz" (13). Milhaud most likely understood jazz as anything
influenced by the rhythms of African American music. Gendron argues
that Hodeir and other historians have defined jazz more narrowly as an
art music with specific qualities that they have then "read back" into
earlier, amorphous forms of the music.

> We can understand this exclusionary re-reading of history as part of a
> decades-old struggle to establish jazz as a genuine art music, indeed
> as "America's classical music." Recent histories of jazz have by-
> passed those early types of nominal jazz which do not fit into the
> trajectory leading to modern jazz or give sense to its aesthetics; it is
> not that they have succeeded in separating the genuine from the
> counterfeit. . . . Much of what [Milhaud] called "jazz" is no longer
> part of the canon of jazz history. (14)

The tendency of jazz historians to search for predecessors of the more
ambitious modernists may in part explain the inordinate amount of
attention afforded Jelly Roll Morton, whose 1920s recordings are said to
anticipate the "orchestral" aspects of swing and modern jazz. Schuller
has called him "The First Great Composer" (*Early Jazz* 134). The centrality of Morton in many jazz histories is consistent with a "masterpieces only" approach that tends to create a series of museum pieces
alleged to possess universal meanings that travel with the work beyond
its time and place.

   The exclusion of anything not consistent with the "art" of jazz is
complemented by the somewhat opposite phenomenon of celebrating
the down-and-out, subcultural appeal of a repressed art form. This tradition in jazz criticism dates back at least to the various critical uproars in
the 1930s and 1940s that accompanied each stage in Duke Ellington's

progress toward concert music and away from his titillating "jungle music." Ellington perfected his jungle style in the late 1920s while his band was in residence at the Cotton Club playing behind gyrating, light-skinned, African American female dancers.[23] A comparable fascination with the sordid aspects of substance abuse and mental illness has surely enhanced the charisma of artists such as Beiderbecke, Holiday, Young, Parker, Chet Baker, and Bud Powell (and perhaps detracted from the amount of attention devoted to the clean-living Clifford Brown). The trend has culminated most recently in documentary and fiction films, such as *Round Midnight* (1988), *Bird* (1989), and *Let's Get Lost* (1989), that center on the broken lives of jazz artists.[24] In the academy, however, the ideology of jazz criticism has tended away from pathobiography and toward explicit or implicit connections between jazz and canonical aesthetics. Although a jazz musicologist influenced by Hodeir may not overtly argue that Ellington is the equal of Brahms, his use of analytical methods designed for Brahms makes the argument all the same.

In this context, few jazz scholars have yet to grapple with the critique of canons that has become central in many humanistic disciplines.[25] A consensus is now emerging that canon-formation is a discourse of power, reinforcing the values of the canonizers. Groups that have been marginalized by generations of Eurocentric, mostly male academics can legitimately question the claim that certain works speak to us across the ages and possess universal truths. Barbara Herrnstein Smith has argued that any value attributed to a work of art "is radically contingent, being neither a fixed attribute, an inherent quality, or an objective property of things but, rather, an effect of multiple, continuously changing, and continuously interacting variables or, to put this another way, the product of the dynamics of a system, specifically an *economic* system" (30). Smith does not adopt a vulgar Marxist concept of an economic system driven by monopolistic forces, urging instead that we understand how certain works perform desired or desirable functions for certain groups at certain moments in history. A work that continues to provide these functions over extended periods of time becomes amenable to new generations with new economies largely because it has been carefully transmitted and preserved and is thus most easily discovered by a new generation searching for its central texts. Once canonized, a work need not answer to all the demands of a newer culture because its guardians will find reasons why objectionable features—Smith lists "incidents or sentiments of brutality, bigotry, and racial, sexual, or national chauvinism" (49)—ought to be overlooked in favor of other features, usually those that accommodate themselves comfortably to humanist ideologies. Those people in whose economy the canonical authors of the West have little or no value are frequently characterized as primitive or culturally deprived by canonizers who are reluctant to acknowledge that other cultures find value in activities bearing little resemblance to Western conceptions of art.

Smith goes to lengths to rebut the "axiological logic" of writers such as Hume and Kant who have explicitly argued that aesthetic judgments can have objective value. In deconstructing the prose of Hume's "On the Standard of Taste," she finds a pattern of qualifications and hedges that ultimately undermines his claim for universal standards of judgment:

> Hume's claim is that there is empirical, factual evidence for a natural norm of taste. When restated with the conceded qualifications, however, the foundation of that norm, the alleged fact that some objects, by the very structure of the mind, are naturally calculated to please and others to displease, becomes the limp truism, *some objects tend to please or displease some people under some conditions.* . . . (63) (emphasis in text)

Kant's argument in *The Critique of Judgment* for the objective validity of some judgments is rooted in the premise that we are capable of putting aside all stimuli that distract from a direct appreciation of "the beautiful." Once subjects achieve this uncontaminated state, they will, according to Kant, invariably arrive at the same judgments. Smith points out that Kant's list of what one must put aside to become uncontaminated amounts to the sum total of one's humanness.

> Contrary to the key requirements of Kant's analysis, then, our interactions with our environments are always and inevitably multiply contingent and highly individuated for every subject: our "sensations" and "perceptions" of "forms" or of anything else are inseparable from—or, as it might be said, thoroughly contaminated by—exactly who we are, where we are, and all that has already happened to us, and there is therefore nothing in any aspect of our experience of anything that could ever be, in the required sense, pure. (69)

I have quoted Smith at length because her work is especially persuasive and systematic in refuting the notion that one work of art can be declared intrinsically superior to another. By appropriating her work, jazz scholars need no longer argue with those who find classical music more valuable, more beautiful, or—as a colleague of mine once phrased it— "more interesting" than jazz. Although Smith bases her work in rigorously philosophical procedures, she is nevertheless working within the hermeneutics of suspicion that has yet to cast a significant shadow over jazz studies. Once jazz scholars have followed out her arguments in order to dispose of the assertion that Brahms is intrinsically superior to Ellington, they must then face up to the equally valid proposition that Ellington is not necessarily superior to Brahms, nor for that matter that Ellington is necessarily superior to Jimi Hendrix or even to Kenny G. They must also confront the possibility that a solo by a canonical jazz artist in no way communicates universal emotions but rather communicates to both the initiated and uninitiated listener through highly mediated complexes of cultural forces. Jazz studies will come of age only when these cultural forces have been thoroughly investigated.

Of course, jazz scholars may choose to resist Smith's gambit and continue to build their canon with preprofessional professions of faith in the transcendent value of favored artists. Ironically, the impulses that have driven jazz writers to avoid a rhetoric based in suspicion share many of the same radical aspects that have led to the recent transformation of other disciplines. Literary critics today who *attack* the old white canon for marginalizing minority authors have a good deal in common with jazz critics who *defend* what could soon become the old canon in their discipline. Since the vocation of the jazz scholar is intimately bound up with highly charged issues of race, a large group of scholars has almost always shied away from positions that might in some way suggest white-against-black racism. A white critic, for example, may feel more secure in simply praising the achievements of an African American artist than in coming to terms with the forces that may have affected what the artist played and how that playing was received. Any number of jazz writers have continued to write laudatory interpretive criticism even after musicians such as Archie Shepp and critics such as Frank Kofsky have accused the critics of paternalism and of pretending to speak for black artists.[26]

The need to find tortuous paths around or through the currents of racism is only one factor that inhibits a thorough interrogation of canonizing traditions in the study of jazz.[27] A hermeneutics of suspicion has much less raw material when the subject is music. Catherine Clément and Carolyn Abbate have both written feminist critiques of opera, but the uncovering of sexism and racism or the deconstruction of false binarisms is substantially more difficult when the music is attached to no program or literary text. Perhaps as a result, traditional musicology has only recently begun to develop feminist, ideological, and metacritical practices.[28]

There may also be a psychological dimension to musicology's resistance to contemporary critical theory. In an argument that can be applied to the work of musicologists, Donald Kuspit has offered reasons why many art historians react negatively to the introduction of structuralist and poststructuralist theories into their discipline. He lists four assumptions that account for what he calls "the peculiarly hermetic, cult-like character of so-called traditional art history" (346): (1) the artwork possesses a sacral quality that distinguishes it from ordinary objects and that induces the critic to explain why it is special; (2) the visual is closer to the "madness of inner life" than the verbal—to reduce the visual artwork to a series of linguistic gestures is to repress its sensual, libidinous, and/or transgressive character; (3) correlatively, the visual has more to do with "bodiliness," the gut feelings that affect the spectator more profoundly than can anything expressed in words; (4) and, finally, the activity of the critic is secondary to the activity of the artist—to suggest otherwise is to embrace the profane over the sacred.

Most of what Kuspit says about "traditional art history" can be adapted to jazz studies in particular and to musicology in general. Like almost everyone else, disciples of jazz respond to the sensual, libidinous dimensions of their music. If jazz has few conventionally sacral dimensions, it may have an even greater agonistic appeal as its advocates resist the class and racial prejudices of society at large that regularly stigmatize their work. With jazz in particular, strong emotional attachments of youth can persist throughout the devotee's life, especially when that attachment signifies a crucial developmental moment such as the willful rejection of bourgeois values. In addition, what Kuspit calls the "bodiliness" of the visual may have its equivalent in the gut feelings of jazz that seem to render words impotent: "If you have to ask, you'll never know." The jazz writer's corresponding discomfort with words takes many forms. One is the critical trope of privileging the experience of musicians—even when unarticulated—over any written statement by outsiders, that is, other writers and critics.[29]

I must make it clear that I am not unequivocally valorizing terms such as "theory" and "professionalism" in these remarks. I have no illusions about the jargon-mongering that passes itself off as theory in many quarters of academia today. I am also ambivalent about the trade-offs that seem to be necessary as disciplines move away from public concerns and into a sequestered world of professionalism. As DeVeaux has suggested, it may be a little unfair to deconstruct a canonical view of jazz history so soon after it has been constructed ("Constructing" 553). My goal has been to take a long view of jazz studies as it makes its way along the arduous path to institutionalization.

The first section of this book, "Rethinking Jazz History," provides essential background reading for *any* long view of jazz studies. The essays by Bernard Gendron and Steven Elworth both undertake an "archaeology" of the jazz press, a project that has until now been almost completely neglected by historians. Relying on a Foucauldian model of power and knowledge, Gendron charts the evolution of a genuine art discourse within the jazz press of the 1940s. After "the moldy figs," who insisted that the only pure jazz was the "hot" music of New Orleans in the 1920s, had done battle with the proponents of swing in the early years of the decade, the same basic arguments were invoked a few years later when the beboppers were at war with the traditionalists. Gendron convincingly argues that the two conflicts were based in the same discursive formations that constituted jazz as a modernist art form.

Having extensively read through the jazz press of the late 1940s and early 1950s, Elworth charts the rise of bop and the responses of journalists who had committed themselves to a revolution that ultimately failed to win the sizable audiences that had previously supported the big bands. Elworth considers this crisis in the jazz press on several fronts, including the changing articulations of masculinity within jazz, the metacritical tendencies of the writers, the attempts to configure jazz as art, and the strange career of Stan Kenton, considered by many fans and critics to be the solution to the crisis. Elworth's account of bop and its aftermath is framed within a consideration of Wynton Marsalis and the current generation of young, conventionally well-dressed musicians who have abandoned the conventional view of jazz as an ever-progressing moment by singling out the bop of the 1950s as the true form of jazz as art.

Like Elworth, Nathaniel Mackey is concerned about the new traditionalism that marginalizes much of what is most critical to African American experience in general and to jazz in particular. Mackey takes his title, "Other: From Noun to Verb," from Amiri Baraka, who described in *Blues People* how "swing" became commodified in the 1930s and 1940s as it moved from black music to white music—from verb to noun. For Mackey, the concept of otherness must be regarded as a process, as a verb, rather than as a noun, a stable entity without vitality or subversive potential. Among many musical examples, Mackey cites the way that the boppers repeatedly "othered" the music of the mainstream in their musical practice.

William Howland Kenney also argues for a more extensive contextualizing of jazz within African American experience. He finds the definitions of jazz proposed by critics such as Williams and Schuller as well as by discographers such as Brian Rust to be ahistorical and internalist. Relying on his substantial expertise in the history of Chicago jazz in its earliest decades, Kenney cites numerous examples of musicians, dance bands, and changing styles that each in their own way problematize the methods with which jazz has traditionally been defined, and he strongly argues for accounts that are more historically specific.

In "Oral Histories of Jazz Musicians: The NEA Transcripts as Texts in Context," Burton W. Peretti takes a critical look at what is often considered to be a privileged locus of jazz history, the interviews with jazz musicians sponsored by the National Endowment for the Arts in the 1970s and 1980s. Although Peretti finds these interviews to be "deeply illuminating," he urges us to read them with a great deal of caution: we must confront their limited scholarly goals, the bewildering range of interviewer/subject pairings, and the purely technical limitations of the transcription process. According to Peretti, the transcripts are much more valuable when read with the less purely empirical research methodologies of folklorists and poststructuralist critics.

Closing out "Rethinking Jazz History," Jed Rasula contemplates the primacy of recordings in writing the history of the music. In a theoretically sophisticated reevaluation of the recording as artifact, Rasula asks, for example, "what is the epistemological status of a technologically primitive artifact like a 1923 acoustic recording of King Oliver's Jazz Band?" Acknowledging that recordings can give insights into how the music actually sounded, he proposes that the many artificial aspects of sound recording can also provide obstacles to finding this knowledge. But Rasula further points out that written jazz histories are just as likely to provide obstacles, given the fact that historians in a sense *compete* with recordings to establish themselves as the true voice of jazz history.

The next three articles directly address the musical practices of specific jazz artists. Robert Walser's "'Out of Notes': Signification, Interpretation, and the Problem of Miles Davis" is primarily devoted to a close analysis of the trumpeter's solo on his 1964 recording, "My Funny Valentine." Unlike most critics who have dealt with the supposed lack of technical perfection in Davis's work, Walser examines the means by which Davis achieved his sound as well as the various strategies that demanded it. Walser finds the key to Davis's "missed notes" in the theories of African American signification developed by Henry Louis Gates, Jr., finally observing that jazz musicologists need to look beyond limiting concepts such as notes and more directly at "the real-life dialogic flux" of jazz expression.

Ronald M. Radano also considers the extraordinary career of Miles

Davis as he opens his account of Anthony Braxton's rise and fall within the jazz press. Hailed as the solution to the crisis resulting from the "defection" to fusion by Davis and the many who followed him (Hancock, Shorter, Corea, etc.), Braxton was seen as an intellectual black radical on the cutting edge of avant-garde jazz. But Braxton's idiosyncratic image often proved too much for jazz writers, who were especially uncomfortable with the artist's desire to be something more than a jazz artist, even comparing himself at one point to Bach and Webern rather than to the canonical names in jazz. Like Miles Davis, Braxton was "signifying" on dominant culture in an attempt to preserve his artistic integrity. Like many of the contributors to this anthology, Radano has exhaustively read through jazz magazines in his wide-ranging assessments of the discourses that promoted, condemned, and ultimately marginalized Braxton.

With John Corbett's "Ephemera Underscored: Writing Around Free Improvisation," the anthology moves toward the contemporary jazz avant-garde as well as the current avant-garde of critical theory. Concentrating primarily on artists such as Derek Bailey, Evan Parker, John Zorn, and Davey Williams, Corbett asks some fundamental questions about the nature of free improvisation, such as, "what does it mean to suggest an 'outside'?" He also asks if there can be any conventions for free improvisation, and if so, which conventions are most likely to limit true improvisatory freedom. Writing in the neologizing and aphoristic traditions of Barthes, Derrida, and Umberto Eco, Corbett employs the neologism "paradoxy" to describe free improvisation and defines it aphoristically as "the orthodox use of paradox."

The final two essays take direct aim at the relationship between jazz and political struggle, an issue that is essential if not always central to most of the other essays in this volume. In his essay on bebop and politics, Eric Lott argues that the music of Parker, Gillespie, Monk, et al., "was about making disciplined imagination alive and answerable to the social change of its time." Lott aligns bebop with the upheavals of the war years, including the 1941 strike at Ford Motors, the Harlem riots of 1943, and the massive relocation of blacks toward northern cities. Demanding that we listen to bebop with new ears unaffected by contemporary jazz language that would make it safe, Lott argues that bop "attempted to resolve at the level of style what the militancy combatted in the streets."

The last essay in this collection, "Ascension: Music and the Black Arts Movement," was written by a participant in the revolution of the 1960s that was at least as intense as the bop revolution chronicled by Lott. One major difference, as Lorenzo Thomas points out, was the move by black artists and intellectuals to control the *criticism* of the music as well as the music itself. Amiri Baraka attempted to do exactly that, and Thomas devotes a large portion of his essay to Baraka's career, recounting the profound influence that jazz musicians, many of them poets themselves (Charles Mingus, Sun Ra), had on his writings. Throughout his essay, Thomas juxtaposes the work of Baraka and the Black Arts Movement with the Harlem Renaissance, observing that while both can be considered failures, the Black Arts Movement did in fact set the terms for crucial debates still taking place today, including the current controversy regarding rap music.

I close these introductory remarks by returning once again to the paradigm of film studies to conceptualize the course of jazz studies. The late Charles Eckert, a film theorist of some prescience, wrote in 1974 of the new methods entering his discipline: "there is a stiff, cold wind blowing against partial, outmoded, or theoretically unsound forms of film criticism—and it just might blow many of them away" (65). Having boarded up the windows against the winds for some time now, jazz scholarship now faces two significant choices: it may continue developing and protecting its canon, or it may take the consequences of letting in some fresh, if chilling, air. The essays in this volume strongly argue that jazz studies is now being transformed and invigorated by new ideas and approaches.

Notes

1   Since I will be attributing a number of qualities to "jazz" throughout this essay, I feel obliged to offer a definition of the term that distinguishes it from "classical music." Realizing that numerous artists complicate any such distinction (James Reese Europe, Duke Ellington, Benny Goodman, John Lewis, Anthony Davis, John Zorn, Anthony Braxton, Willem Breuker, and many others), I would define jazz as a music that is rooted primarily in the confrontation between African American traditions and European music, involving some improvisation and syncopation, and performed more often in nightclubs and dance halls than in concert halls. The music has changed too quickly throughout its history to accommodate a more precise definition. I am convinced that any attempt to arrive at such a definition must be based on a sociocultural analysis of jazz rather than on its internal aesthetics. In this sense, I am in almost total disagreement with assumptions underlying the otherwise convincing essay by Brown. In his rigorous analysis of André Hodeir's writings, Brown never questions the purely formalist criteria that Hodeir and others employ in their attempts to define jazz. Nowhere does he ask crucial questions about who is listening, what the listener expects, or under what conditions the listening is taking place. Nor does Brown

ask what cultural and ideological forces lay behind Hodeir's decision to write a definition of jazz in France in the 1950s.

2   Also see Taylor. On the other hand, a number of critics have made claims for jazz as the *antithesis* of classical music, most notably Hugues Panassié. In *The Real Jazz,* Panassié effectively redefines music in order to privilege jazz and to reverse the familiar musical hierarchies: "For music is, above all, the cry of the heart, the natural, spontaneous song expressing what man feels within himself" (6). He is thus in a strong position to denigrate the environment in which classical music is consumed: "Likewise many feel that it is ridiculous for Negroes to clap their hands, dance in their seats, sing and cry when listening to an orchestra. . . . But to me the most ridiculous spectacle is the sight of a concert hall filled with hundreds of spectators who sit statue-like in their seats listening with a lugubrious expression to solemn music which is served up to them in massive doses" (29).

3   *Oxford English Dictionary,* s.v. "canon, 4." In addition, canon is a rule, law, or decree from the church or from the pope, as in canonical law. The portion of the Catholic mass between the Preface and the *Pater,* containing the words of the consecration, is also known as the canon. Finally, a canon is a clergyman or anyone living a canonical life, that is, one devoted to the canons of the church.

4   John Guillory has written, "The problem of the canon is a problem of syllabus and curriculum, the institutional forms by which works are preserved as *great* works. One might contrast this institutional function of the school with the function of the library, where ideally *everything* is preserved and where the system of preservation makes no distinction at all between good books and bad" (240).

5   For a good deal of original research on the earliest jazz criticism, see Collier, *The Reception of Jazz in America: A New View,* and Welburn.

6   Sarris's seminal essay, "Notes on the Auteur Theory in 1962," first appeared in *Film Culture* in 1963. It is collected along with responses by Peter Wollen and Pauline Kael in Mast and Cohen. The bible of American auteurism is still Sarris's *The American Cinema: Directors and Directions, 1929–1968.*

7   Perhaps the best place to look for a scholar's film canon is the ten-best list published every decade in the British journal *Sight and Sound.* Although *Vertigo* did not appear on previous editions of the list, it was on both the 1982 and 1992 lists. Significantly, *Vertigo* was also on the first list of twenty-five protected American films established by the Librarian of Congress in 1989.

8   Wexman has not had the last word on the feminist canonization of *Vertigo.* Susan White, an eminent feminist film theorist in her own right, has responded to Wexman's assertion that feminists have been "blind" to the vested interests of their critical positions on key films. In her "Allegory and Referentiality: *Vertigo* and Feminist Criticism," White asks first "how it is that Wexman, a white, feminist, academic critic, is *not* blinded by her own position" (923). Employing a strategy developed by Paul de Man, White then deconstructs the opposition "blindness/insight," suggesting that blindness is in fact what makes insight possible. She concludes by arguing against the claim that *Vertigo* or any other text can be read "from a single, dominating reality that knows itself, knows its priority, comes from a position that knows no blindness and seems to have no vested interest . . . " (931).

9   Roland Barthes's "The Death of the Author" and Michel Foucault's "What Is an Author" are collected with other relevant material in Caughie.

10   For an extended critique of "the professional" in English studies, see McCrea, esp. chaps. 7 and 8. For a more polemical but compatible argument, see Fiedler.

11   DeVeaux's essay, "Constructing the Jazz Tradition," has extensively and convincingly confronted many of these issues. In particular, DeVeaux addresses problems in jazz writing such as a chronic insistence on the music's autonomy from social praxis, the "romance" paradigms promoted by its historians, and the need for canonical figures. Ultimately, he calls for "an approach that is less invested in the ideology of jazz as aesthetic object and more responsive to issues of historical particularity" (553).

12   McCrea describes the typical presidential address at the annual meeting of the Modern Language Association as "the address in which a man or a woman who has achieved eminence on the basis of publications and holds an endowed chair at a major research university laments our failure to pay enough attention to introductory classes and the task of bringing undergraduates to know the joys of studying literature" (147). McCrea, however, observes that "all such talk is nostalgic and largely empty" (147). The demands of professionalism take precedence over goals expressed in the official rhetoric.

13   There is also a 1929 recording by a territory band, Zach Whyte's Chocolate Beau Brummels, that includes a passage for two unison trumpets and rhythm based on Armstrong's cadenza in "West End Blues."

14   Recently, however, discography has begun to move into the academy. The Institute of Jazz Studies in Newark, New Jersey, has begun publishing exhaustive discographies of artists such as Benny Carter, Duke Ellington, Art Tatum, Erroll Garner, James P. Johnson, and Benny Goodman. As a participant in this project, Ed Berger has written on the problems of compiling a complete listing for Benny Carter, who has recorded as a multi-instrumentalist and an arranger in conventional jazz formats but also as the composer and arranger of movie scores and television soundtracks. In fact, the *Journal of Jazz Studies* itself was effectively inaugurated by the single issue of *Studies in Jazz Discography* (1971), also published by the Institute of Jazz Studies and with the same cover design as *JJS*.

15   The work of Gary Giddins, who regularly reviews movies as well as jazz, provides an equally revealing parallel between cinema auteurism and jazz criticism. Auteurist critics transformed previously neglected films into significant texts if they happened to appear in the filmography of a "pantheon" director such as John Ford or Orson Welles. In particular, the late works of the auteur were extolled in spite of previously received notions of his decline. Similarly, Giddins has responded to negative judgments of aging jazz artists (in André Hodeir's writings, most prominently) by celebrating the later phases of their work. In his book on Louis Armstrong, for example, Giddins confronts critical commonplaces about the trumpeter's decline by bestowing praise on Armstrong's recording of "Hello Dolly" (1963) as well as on his 1968 album of songs featured in Walt Disney films (191, 203).

16   The label discographies of Michel Ruppli ought to be considered inclusionist rather than exclusionist. Ruppli's inventories of canonical jazz labels such as Blue Note, Prestige, Savoy, Chess, and Clef/Verve are meant to be complete, even when this necessitates the inclusion of whatever blues, folk, pop or comedy acts the labels recorded along with the jazz material.

17   The group is "Fiske (*sic*) Jubilee Singers."

18 Naoki Suzuki's catalog of Herbie Hancock's early recordings is a rare example of a single-artist discography that is also profoundly exclusionist. By ending with the year 1969—when Hancock's recordings began tilting toward fusion—Suzuki follows the example of exclusionist discographers such as Bruyninckx who refuse to catalog artists after they cease to record in sanctioned styles.

19 In "Constructing the Jazz Tradition," DeVeaux calls Schuller's work "a monument to the ideal of jazz as an autonomous art" (542). For a thorough analysis of *The Swing Era* and the problems it raises, see Porter.

20 The passage appeared with the exact same wording in the first edition of *The Jazz Tradition* (1970).

21 DeVeaux has identified the notion that jazz has undergone an *organic* growth process as the legitimating force behind the eventual reconciliation between bebop and older forms: "In the long run, it proved as much in the interests of the modernists to have their music legitimated as the latest phase of a (now) long and distinguished tradition, as it was in the interests of the proponents of earlier jazz styles (whether New Orleans jazz or swing) not to be swept aside as merely antiquarian" (539).

22 For a survey of anthologies of jazz recordings that *preceded* the *Smithsonian Collection*, see Hasse. Creating real competition for the *Smithsonian Collection* has always been complicated by legal issues related to acquiring permissions from a wide variety of record companies. Now that the major jazz catalogs are owned by Japanese (Columbia, Decca) and European (RCA, Verve) corporations, the opportunities for a competing anthology may be even more diminished.

23 James Lincoln Collier is especially sensitive to the tension between Ellington and his critics in his *Duke Ellington*.

24 Self-destructive artists are not, of course, the sole province of jazz history. Americans are especially fond of crash-and-burn legends among their poets (Lowell, Berryman, Plath), painters (Rothko, Pollock) and rock stars (Joplin, Hendrix, Morrison). Spike Lee has claimed that his film *Mo' Better Blues* (1990) corrected the myth of the doomed jazz artist promoted in *Bird* and *Round Midnight*. I have argued to the contrary that, although the trumpeter-hero of Lee's film is not a drug addict or an alcoholic, he can only be "saved" when at the end he gives up the jazz life with its attendant dangers. See Gabbard, "Signifyin(g) the Phallus."

25 See, for example, the papers published in various issues of *Critical Inquiry* and collected by von Hallberg.

26 Ronald M. Radano's book on Anthony Braxton—a portion of which appears in this anthology—has much to say about the artist's struggle to make himself heard above the voices of critics, many of them well intentioned and supportive if ultimately unhelpful.

27 The many African Americans writing about jazz and related subjects (Stanley Crouch, Albert Murray, Amiri Baraka, Gates, Houston Baker, etc.) will undoubtedly continue to have much to say about jazz canons in years to come. In a personal communication, Burton W. Peretti has suggested that jazz is most likely to be grouped with other black musics and with the study of African American oral traditions as it moves into the academy: Gates and Baker in particular have regularly made implicit and explicit arguments for the inseparability of jazz from African American traditions that long preceded its emergence.

28 Perhaps the most widely heard call for a new hermeneutics in musicology was

voiced by Kerman. Although not necessarily writing in response to Kerman's call, a number of writers have brought new methodologies to music history and musicology; see, for example, Treitler; McClary; Bergeron and Bohlman; and Brett, Wood, and Thomas.

29   See, for example, Palmié, who scorns those writers who claim to be "more knowledgeable than the musicians themselves" (43). Ira Gitler and Stanley Dance are two of the most prominent critics who have for decades uncritically reported the utterances of jazz artists.

Works Cited

Abbate, Carolyn. *Unsung Voices: Opera and Musical Narrative in the Nineteenth Century.* Princeton, N.J.: Princeton UP, 1991.

Baraka, Amiri (LeRoi Jones). *Blues People.* New York: Morrow, 1963.

Berger, Ed. "Benny Carter: A Discographical Approach." *Journal of Jazz Studies* 4.1 (1976): 47–64.

Bergeron, Katherine, and Philip V. Bohlman, eds. *Disciplining Music: Musicology and Its Canons.* Chicago: U of Chicago P, 1992.

Brett, Philip, Elizabeth Wood, and Gary C. Thomas, eds. *Queering the Pitch: The New Gay and Lesbian Musicology.* New York: Routledge, 1994.

Brown, Lee B. "The Theory of Jazz Music: 'It Don't Mean a Thing. . . .'" *Journal of Aesthetics and Art Criticism* 49 (1991): 115–27.

Bruyninckx, Walter. *Seventy Years of Recorded Jazz, 1917–1987.* Mechelen, Belgium: Published by the author, 1978–90.

Caughie, John, ed. *Theories of Authorship: A Reader.* London: British Film Institute, 1981.

Clément, Catherine. *Opera, or the Undoing of Women.* Trans. Betsy Wing. Minneapolis: U of Minnesota P, 1988.

Collier, James Lincoln. *Duke Ellington.* New York: Oxford UP, 1987.

——. *The Reception of Jazz in America: A New View.* Brooklyn: Institute for Studies in American Music, 1988.

Culler, Jonathan. *Structuralist Poetics: Structuralism, Linguistics, and the Study of Literature.* Ithaca, N.Y.: Cornell UP, 1975.

Daniels, Douglas Henry. "History, Racism, and Jazz: The Case of Lester Young." *Jazzforschung/Jazz Research* 16 (1984): 87–103.

Delaunay, Charles. *Hot Discography.* Paris, 1938.

DeVeaux, Scott. "Constructing the Jazz Tradition: Jazz Historiography." *Black American Literature Forum* 25.3 (1991): 525–60.

——. "The Emergence of the Jazz Concert, 1935–1945." *American Music* 7 (1989): 6–29.

Eckert, Charles. "Shall We Deport Lévi-Strauss?" *Film Quarterly* 27 (1974): 63–65. Reprinted in Bill Nichols, ed. *Movies and Methods,* vol. 2. Berkeley: U of California P, 1985. 426–29.

Fiedler, Leslie A. "Literature as an Institution: The View From 1980." *English Literature: Opening Up the Canon.* Ed. Leslie A. Fiedler and Houston A. Baker, Jr. Baltimore: Johns Hopkins UP, 1981. 73–91.

Frye, Northrop. "Polemical Introduction." *Anatomy of Criticism.* Princeton, N.J.: Princeton UP, 1957.

Gabbard, Krin. "The Quoter and His Culture." *Jazz in Mind: Essays on the History and Meanings of Jazz.* Ed. Reginald T. Buckner and Steven Weiland. Detroit: Wayne State UP, 1991. 92–111.

———, ed. *Representing Jazz.* Durham, N.C.: Duke UP, 1995.

———. "Signifyin(g) the Phallus: *Mo' Better Blues* and Representations of the Jazz Trumpet." *Representing Jazz.* Durham, N.C.: Duke UP, 1995.

Gates, Henry Louis, Jr. "Canon-Formation, Literary History, and the Afro-American Tradition: From the Seen to the Told." *Afro-American Literary Study in the 1990s.* Ed. Houston A. Baker, Jr., and Patricia Redmond. Chicago: U of Chicago P, 1989. 14–39.

———. *Loose Canons: Notes on the Culture Wars.* New York: Oxford UP, 1992.

———. *The Signifying Monkey: A Theory of Afro-American Literary Criticism.* New York: Oxford UP, 1988.

Gendron, Bernard. "Jamming at Le Boeuf: Jazz and the Paris Avant-Garde." *Discourse* 12.1 (Fall–Winter 1989–90): 3–27.

Giddins, Gary. *Satchmo.* New York: Doubleday, 1988.

Gramsci, Antonio. *Selections from the Prison Notebooks.* Ed. and trans. Quintin Hore and Geoffrey Nowell-Smith. New York: Verso, 1971.

Guillory, John. "Canon." *Critical Terms for Literary Study.* Ed. Frank Lentricchia and Thomas McLaughlin. Chicago: U of Chicago P, 1990. 233–49.

Hasse, John. "*The Smithsonian Collection of Classic Jazz:* A Review-Essay." *Journal of Jazz Studies* 3.1 (Fall 1975): 66–71.

Horrigan, William, ed. *The American Film Institute Guide to College Courses in Film and Television.* New York: Prentice-Hall, 1990.

Kerman, Joseph. *Contemplating Music: Challenges to Musicology.* Cambridge, Mass.: Harvard UP, 1985.

Kuspit, Donald. "Traditional Art History's Complaint Against the Linguistic Analysis of Visual Art." *Journal of Aesthetics and Art Criticism* 45.4 (1987): 345–49.

Levine, Lawrence W. *Highbrow/Lowbrow: The Emergence of Cultural Hierarchy in America.* Cambridge, Mass.: Harvard UP, 1988.

Mast, Gerald, and Marshall Cohen, eds. *Film Theory and Criticism.* 3rd ed. New York: Oxford UP, 1985.

McClary, Susan. *Feminine Endings: Music, Gender, and Sexuality.* Minneapolis: U of Minnesota P, 1990.

McCrea, Brian. *Addison and Steele Are Dead: The English Department, Its Canon, and the Professionalization of Literary Criticism.* Newark, Del.: U of Delaware P, 1990.

Miller, Susanna L. "Classroom Gigs—Funding for Musician/Clinicians." *Down Beat* June 1990: 56.

Mulvey, Laura. "Visual Pleasure and Narrative Cinema." *Screen* 16.3 (Autumn 1975): 6–18. Reprinted with afterthoughts, in Laura Mulvey. *Visual and Other Pleasures.* Bloomington: Indiana UP, 1989.

Münsterberg, Hugo. *The Film: A Psychological Study* (1916). New York: Dover, 1970.

Palmié, Stephan. "Jazz Culture in the Thirties: 'Kansas City, Here I Come!'" *Jazzforschung/Jazz Research* 16 (1984): 43–85.

Panassié, Hugues. *The Real Jazz.* 1942. Trans. Anne Sorelle Williams. Westport, Conn.: Greenwood Press, 1973.

Porter, Lewis. Review of Gunther Schuller, *The Swing Era. Annual Review of Jazz Studies* 5 (1991): 183–200.

Raben, Erik. *Jazz Records, 1942–80: A Discography.* Vol. 1: A–Ba. Copenhagen: Jazz Media, 1989.

Radano, Ronald M. *New Musical Figurations: Anthony Braxton's Cultural Critique.* Chicago: U of Chicago P, 1993.

Ricoeur, Paul. *Freud and Philosophy.* New Haven, Conn.: Yale UP, 1970.

Sales, Grover. *Jazz: America's Classical Music.* Englewood Cliffs, N.J.: Prentice-Hall, 1984.

Sarris, Andrew. *The American Cinema: Directors and Directions, 1929–1968.* New York: Dutton, 1968.

Schuller, Gunther. *Early Jazz: Its Roots and Musical Development.* New York: Oxford UP, 1968.

——. *The Swing Era: The Development of Jazz, 1930–1945.* New York: Oxford UP, 1989.

Smith, Barbara Herrnstein. *Contingencies of Value.* Cambridge, Mass.: Harvard UP, 1988.

Staiger, Janet. "The Politics of Film Canons." *Cinema Journal* 24.3 (Spring 1985): 4–23.

Stewart, Milton L. "Some Characteristics of Clifford Brown's Improvisational Style." *Jazzforschung/Jazz Research* 11 (1979): 135–64.

Suzuki, Naoki. *Herbie Hancock: A Discography.* Shizuoka, Japan: Published by the author, 1988.

Taylor, Billy. "Jazz—America's Classical Music." *Black Perspective in Music* 14.1 (1986): 21–25.

Treitler, Leo. *Music and the Historical Imagination.* Cambridge, Mass.: Harvard UP, 1989.

Von Hallberg, Robert, ed. *Canons.* Chicago: U of Chicago P, 1984.

Welburn, Ron. "The American Jazz Writer/Critic of the 1930s: A Profile." *Jazzforschung/Jazz Research* 21 (1989): 83–94.

Wexman, Virginia Wright. "The Critic as Consumer." *Film Quarterly* 39.3 (1986): 32–41.

White, Susan. "Allegory and Referentiality: *Vertigo* and Feminist Criticism." *MLN* 106.5 (1991): 910–32.

Williams, Martin. *The Jazz Tradition.* Rev. ed. New York: Oxford UP, 1983.

Discography

Armstrong, Louis. "West End Blues." Rec. 28 June 1928. *Louis Armstrong, Vol. IV: Armstrong and Earl Hines.* Columbia CK 45142 (CD).

Oliver, King. "West End Blues." Rec. 16 Jan. 1929. *King Oliver and His Orchestra, 1928–1930.* Classics 607 (CD).

RETHINKING

JAZZ

HISTORY

"Moldy Figs" and Modernists: Jazz at War (1942–1946)

BERNARD GENDRON

The historical transformation of jazz from an entertainment music to an art music, initiated by the bebop revolution in the mid-1940s, represents arguably one of the most significant cultural shifts of this century.

Mass culture and modernist high culture, it is now agreed, have been in constant communication since both their inceptions sometime in the mid-nineteenth century. But, for a long while, this interchange was decidedly one-sided, as modernists eagerly appropriated materials and devices from a more passive mass culture for the purposes of formal experimentation, parody, and shock—such as Dada's exploitation of the cabaret form and Stravinsky's use of ragtime and the tango.[1]

With the bebop revolution, and since, mass culture has been more the aggressor in this interchange. Rock music, films, MTV, and advertisements have liberally scavenged from a whole storehouse of avant-garde devices and practices, though no form of mass culture seems to have crossed the boundary between "entertainment" and "art" as decisively or irreversibly as jazz.

This is the first of three essays that will deal with the bebop revolution as a major nodal point in the history of interchanges between mass culture and modernist art. In this essay I reconstruct the discursive changes in the jazz community that immediately antedated the bebop revolution and made possible its reception as an avant-garde music.[2]

Warring Factions

The jazz world in the 1940s was embroiled in two major factional wars, two schisms in which spokespersons for the new were set off against those for the old. During a period spanning less than a decade the centuries-old battle between ancients and moderns so endemic to Western culture was twice reenacted. Swing music, the music of the big bands which had dominated jazz and the popular sales charts since 1935, was deeply implicated in both disputes, in one case supported by modernists and in the other by traditionalists. The first of these conflicts pitted swing against the newly revitalized New Orleans jazz, which it had supplanted, and the second against the bebop avant-garde movement that threatened to make it obsolescent.

The seeds for the first jazz war were sown in the late 1930s when a few nightclubs, defying the big band boom, began to feature small jazz combos playing in the abandoned New Orleans style of the 1920s, today popularly referred to as "Dixieland." Such a mild turn of events would not have led to a Dixieland revival without the enthusiastic participation of the aficionados and cultists of the old jazz, who collected out-of-print records and exchanged arcane discographical information.

These purists were driven not only by nostalgia but by a revulsion toward the swing music industry, which by shamelessly pandering to the mass markets had in their eyes forsaken the principles of "true" jazz. A spate of small sectarian journals appeared on the scene to give vent to these revivalist views and concerns. They set themselves off as the only authentic alternatives to the two dominant mainstream jazz journals, *Down Beat* and *Metronome,* which were altogether beholden to the swing phenomenon.[3]

In 1942 *Metronome* fired the first shot of the modernist-revivalist war with a vigorous attack on the exclusionary purism and incessant carping of the revivalists, whom it derisively labeled "moldy figs" (Ulanov 1942).[4] Over the next four years, in a continuous barrage of editorials and articles, *Metronome* would castigate New Orleans jazz as technically backward and "corny," and the writers of the revivalist journals as hysterical cultists and musical ignoramuses, against whom it positioned itself as the defender of modernism and progress in jazz. The revivalists counterattacked with charges of crass commercialism, faddism, and Eurocentrism.

By 1946, just as this war was scaling down, a second battle of jazz ancients and moderns was beginning to heat up. Modernism was now being represented by the bebop school—most notably Dizzy Gillespie, Charlie Parker, and Bud Powell—while swing music suddenly found itself relegated to the company of New Orleans jazz, on the side of the traditional and the tried-and-true. Bebop's opponents complained about the inaccessibility and undanceability of the music, the "wrong notes" and excessive musical acrobatics, the elitism, hostility, and avant-garde posturing of the musicians, their unconventional dress and morally suspicious life-styles.

As a jazz movement, bebop triumphed in 1948 and died in 1950, only to be reclaimed later in the canon of jazz history. It was abandoned even by its modernist supporters, who laid in wait for the next phalanx in the triumphal march of modern, experimental jazz.[5]

Aesthetic Discourses and Musical Revolutions

The bebop revolution has since been enshrined in the jazz canon as a contest of epic proportions, occurring at the major fault line of jazz history. Bebop is given credit for having transformed jazz from a popular dance music, firmly ensconced in the Hit Parade, to a demanding, experimental art music, consigned to small clubs and sophisticated audiences. In contrast, the Dixieland war is usually construed as a retrograde sideshow, a rearguard skirmish that temporarily delayed the avant-garde advances initiated by bebop.[6]

I will be contesting this too tidy a view of what admittedly has turned out to be the most significant permutation within jazz history. What will especially have to be rejected is the severe contrast drawn between a backward-looking Dixieland war and a forward-looking bebop war. In point of fact, both contests were fought on much of the same discursive terrain—the same field of concepts, issues, aesthetic standards, and opposing theories. Indeed, the Dixieland war, as it waned, transposed itself so subtly into the bebop war that many contemporaries failed to distinguish between them.

This suggests that the apparently retrograde Dixieland war played a significant role in the transformation of jazz from an entertainment music to an avant-garde music. I am not asserting, however, that the New Orleans revival was, or was ever meant to be, an avant-garde musical movement, nor am I denying that bebop made the key musical innovations that ushered in the era of modern jazz. What I am accentuating, rather, is the crucial role that the Dixieland war played at the level of discourse, of talk and patter in magazines, books, and radio shows, in preparing the way for the emergence and acceptance of a jazz avant-garde.

The debates between swing modernists and New Orleans revivalists sufficiently reconstructed the issues, alternative characterizations, and standards for discoursing about jazz to make it possible, and indeed to make it seem very natural, to refer to jazz as an "art" music and to construe certain genres of jazz as "modernistic," "experimental," "formally complex," and "avant-garde," even before bebop made its appearance. In effect, what was being constructed in these debates was an aesthetic discourse for jazz, which was later to legitimate its breaching of the "great divide" between mass culture and art.[7]

By "aesthetic discourse," I mean here not a set of agreed-on claims about the artistic merit of various jazz styles, but rather a grouping of concepts, distinctions, oppositions, rhetorical ploys, and allowable inferences, which as a whole fixed the limits within which inquiries concerning the aesthetics of jazz could take place, and outside which the claim that jazz is an art form would be merely an abstraction or an incantation. The revivalists and modernists were slowly and collectively shaping and honing this new aesthetic through their acrimonious disagreements rather than in spite of them.

Thus, my purpose is neither to contest the canonical accounts of the revolutionary changes in jazz musical form in the 1940s, nor to rehabilitate the Dixieland revival, but rather to highlight the crucial role of what Michel Foucault has called "discursive formations" in the constitution of jazz modernism. I will show how the Dixieland war, as a war primarily of words, indeed a profusion and superabundance of words, engendered a new mapping of the terrain on which jazz was debated—a new construction of the aesthetic discourses of jazz—which was only to be amended, rather than radically transformed, by the bebop revolution.

The new aesthetic discourses, by no means pure, were laced with the idioms of commerce, politics, gender, and race.[8] These idioms must be treated as integral to the newly emerging jazz aesthetic rather than as mere intrusions or add-ons. Any attempt to extirpate them in order to reveal the "pure" jazz aesthetic of that period would leave us only with a uselessly inchoate and abstract residue, shorn of any historical specificity.

This integral treatment applies especially to the issue of race, which constantly surfaced in jazz writing during the 1940s, despite, or because of, the fact that virtually all jazz journals in that period were owned, edited, and composed by whites and were sold primarily to a white readership. At this time, blacks entered into the revivalist-modernist field of discourse primarily in the role of musician-subjects, interviewed to settle some score between white critics. Clearly, the newly emerging "official" discourses of jazz aesthetics only codified the preferences, styles, and practices of the primarily white sector of the jazz world. But these codifications were nonetheless skewed, in very intricate ways, by the pressing anxieties of racial contact.

In the following sections I will reconstruct the new discursive formations generated in the Dixieland-swing debates—in effect, the new official jazz aesthetic—by examining in sequence the following clusters of concepts, networks of arguments, and groups of oppositional terms that played key roles in these debates: (1) genres and brand names; (2) art and commerce; (3) folklore and European high culture; (3) progress and the new; (4) technique and schooling; (5) affect and antics; (6) fascists and communists; (7) black and white.

Genres and Brand Names

Wanting the word "jazz" all to themselves, the revivalists sought to hammer out a precise formula that would clearly oppose jazz to swing. Though the revivalists bickered incessantly about the fine details of the proper definition, they agreed that no music could be called "jazz" that was not collectively improvised and whose melodies, rhythms, phrasings, and timbres were not primarily derived from Afro-American sources. The not-so-subtle upshot of this definition was virtually to identify jazz with the New Orleans style of the 1920s and to treat it as the very antithesis of swing, which replaced collective improvisation by written arrangements or by head arrangements, and African American folk themes by "poorly invented" Tin Pan Alley tunes (Borneman, 1944a: 38).[9]

Metronome's two ideologues of swing, Leonard Feather and Barry Ulanov, responded to this "moldy fig" charge in a surprising manner, by saying, not that the umbrella of jazz is broad enough to cover the admittedly distinct genres of New Orleans and swing music, but that the two terms "jazz" and "swing" actually refer to the same thing, "the same musical idiom, the same rhythmic and harmonic characteristics, the same use of syncopation." In short, "swing" is "just a different word" and "not a different music from jazz" (The Two Deuces 22; Feather, 1944a).

In a deft tactical ploy they interviewed a number of musicians who concurred with their view—most notably Louis Armstrong, a favorite of the revivalists, who jocularly entered the fray (Feather, 1945a: 26–27): "To me as far as I could see it all my life—Jazz and Swing is the same thing. . . . In the good old days of Buddy Bolden. . . . it was called Rag Time Music. . . . Later on in the years it was called Jazz Music—Hot Music—Gut Bucket—and now they've poured a little gravy over it, called it Swing Music. . . . Haw Haw haw. . . . No matter how you slice it—it's still the same music."

This strange debate—with one side claiming that swing and jazz are completely *identical* and the other that they are completely *opposite*—

was rooted, not in any factual dispute, but in two very different construals of the semantics of the term "swing." For the revivalists, "swing" was a generic term denoting an easily definable species of popular music. The *Metronome* modernists, on the other hand, seem unreflectively to have been using it as a brand name.

Brand names differ from generic names in not being susceptible to definitions, because their meanings are determined less by the class of objects they refer to than by the necessarily hazy, unarticulated, and frequently revised imagery with which they are irretrievably associated in advertisements and promotions. The word "swing," in its 1930s' beginnings, also exhibited the nebulous, inarticulable suggestiveness typical of brand names.

Even before Benny Goodman's legendary performance at the Palomar Ballroom in December 1935, which inaugurated the Age of Swing, the word "swing" was already gaining currency in the midst of hype and euphoria as an oblique signifier for the anticipated boom in the music industry that would follow the already achieved repeal of prohibition and the anticipated upswing out of the depression. In a somewhat convoluted and inchoate way, "swing" was the new word being associated with a revival, and modern updating, of the more "torrid" and "brassy" "hot jazz" of the past, to suit the lively and fun-loving urges of a new affluent generation, who in their "celebrating mood" would naturally "want to pep things up" ("Is Dixieland Stuff Coming Back?" 25).

At the peak of the swing craze, the media were predictably seeking, but failing to find, a definition for this elusive brand name. From musicians and aficionados they elicited answers to the question "What is swing?" that ranged from the silly to the empty, such as, "syncopated syncopation," "rhythmically integrated improvisation," and "two-thirds rhythm and one-third soul."[10]

Meanwhile, the word "jazz" fell into temporary disuse, stigmatized as a "corny word" standing for a music whose "time had passed" (The Two Deuces 33). Indeed, what had previously been called "jazz" was now being reclassified as "early swing."[11]

Thus, like a brand name, the word "swing" originally had no clear denotation, being associated with a whole variety of hazy images and allusions about markets, fashions, attitudes, emotions, entertainment, *Weltanschauungen*, musical tradition, and musical innovation. But the brand name would soon evolve, at least partly, into a definable generic name. For, at the same time that the music industry was pursuing change in its incessant attempts to tailor the product to new audiences, it was also attempting to stabilize these new consumption patterns by seeking to standardize and congeal the new musical styles. As standardization gradually overcame change, the generic functions of "swing" would overtake its brand-name functions, making it more open to definition and categorization.

The revivalists would contribute to this process of standardization and codification by reintroducing the word "jazz" in the discursive stream as a definitional counterpoise to "swing." Meanwhile, the *Metronome* modernists, harking back to the days when "swing" functioned more as a brand-name replacement for "jazz," resisted any such attempts at definition, precise categorization, and conceptual contrast.

However, the revivalist-modernist debate over the question, "Is swing jazz?"—though floundering on semantic confusions—did reflect real differences. Whereas the revivalist "moldy figs" wanted to identify jazz with particular musical structures and practices that would set the standards for all its future developments and evaluations, the swing partisans, in their unremitting commitment to the new and up-to-date, did not want to be associated with any particular genre or style and expressed no particular undying commitment to big bands over small combos, or arrangements over improvisations. *Metronome* was first and foremost committed to "modern" jazz, and to swing only so long as it remained modern.

Art and Commerce

Nothing seemed to offend the sensitivities of revivalists more than the enormous commercial success of the swing bands and the blatant spirit of commercialism with which *Down Beat* and *Metronome* happily contributed to this success. No previous form of jazz had come even close to the immense popularity of the swing bands, which thoroughly dominated the hit charts during the years 1936 through 1945, to an extent rarely if ever equaled by any other subgenre of popular music.[12]

For the "moldy figs," this was a sure sign of the impurity, corruption, and mediocrity of swing as a jazz form. They further looked upon the modernist critics as mere "stooges" of this commercial music, who could not help acquiring the "crass and callous" values of the "whole stinking commercial structure." *Metronome*, in particular, despite its pretensions, had "no more critical significance than a publicity blurb."[13]

The modernists made no apologies about either the commercial success of swing or their own complicity with it. In a 1944 editorial, *Metronome* admitted that indeed it is "commercially minded" and asserted "furthermore that the best in jazz has been and always will be successful, commercial" ("Jazz of Yesteryear" 8). This happy coincidence between art and commerce means that "much music that finds popular approval will find critical acclaim in *Metronome* and that by critical acclaim in *Metronome* more jazz will meet with popular approval" (Ulanov 1944: 31).

Under the pressure of criticism, the modernists soon had to qualify their facile claims about the convergence of art and commerce. Denying that he ever said that "music pays off according to its merit," Ulanov (1944: 19) admitted only to asserting that "good jazz as all good music will find a supporting box office level several notches above starvation and subsistence living."

With this qualification, the *Metronome* modernists were implicitly distinguishing between two jazz markets, a primary market constituted by the most commercially successful jazz hits, normally of a lower quality, and a secondary market of higher-quality jazz with less, though still significant, commercial success. This enabled them to allow for some discrepancy between artistic and commercial achievement, while asserting that good art is normally commercially viable. Thus, Feather (1944a: 35) could distinguish between those swing bands that "make minor concessions to popular taste"—the secondary market—from those who "devote seventy-five per cent or ninety per cent of their time to straight melody, conventional crooning, vocal groups, comedy routines, and novelty numbers."

However, this text, written in 1944, was already betraying a certain malaise about the sphere of commerce, and about the future of jazz, absent from the boosterism of earlier articles. For we are warned that "even among the best currently active swing bands . . . practically none can be relied upon to offer real jazz, or swing music, at any given time." He might also have been sensing the end of the boom era for swing, and indeed for jazz in general.[14]

Folk Culture/European Culture

If the modernists were forced to allow some distinction between art and commerce—admittedly a distinction existing within the sphere of commerce—the revivalists would be at pains to successfully construct a notion of the *noncommercial* that applied to the original New Orleans music and its current reincarnations. The opposition of art to commerce, in this case, could not be interpreted in the usual way as the opposition of elite culture to mass culture, of "high" versus "low," "refined" versus "vulgar." The revivalist writers were unhesitant, and indeed proud, to admit that the music of Jelly Roll Morton and Louis Armstrong was, in an important sense, a "vulgar" and "low" art. Indeed, it was as important for them to oppose Dixieland to high art as well as to the hit parade and to attack swing for its symphonic pretensions as well as for its commercialism.

Not surprisingly, some revivalists turned to the then fashionable concept of folk music, to distinguish Dixieland both from swing and European art music—not surprisingly, because the ternary opposition of folk/mass/high culture had already become one of the clichés of twentieth-century aesthetic discourse and because the political left of the 1930s, with which many of the revivalists were associated, had already appropriated the notion of folk music to mark off truly progressive music from its bourgeois counterparts.

It was thus easy for many "moldy figs" to slip into the assertion that "real" jazz "is instrumental folk music"—"the music of the American proletariat"—that "began as a folk culture of the illiterate negro." For them, the transition from New Orleans jazz to swing represented the disintegration of an authentic folk culture into a "cliché culture of the masses."[15]

Nonetheless, the claim that New Orleans jazz is folk music could not be maintained without trivializing the very notion of the folkloric. A particular cultural product counts as "folk music," in the strong sense of that expression, if it has been produced and transformed anonymously over generations, outside any modern culture industry, by artists or craftspersons unschooled in any prevailing academy. Of these three criteria, only the latter seems to be satisfied by early jazz.

With its own stars and auteurs, New Orleans jazz and its midwestern derivatives were hardly produced anonymously. Showcased in nightclubs, disbursed through records, and promoted in newspaper advertisements, this brand of jazz was clearly produced within the confines of, and transmitted by, the culture industry—and thus incontrovertibly a commercial music, though admittedly belonging to a less successful secondary market.

Advisedly, some proponents of the folkloric paradigm settled for the less ambitious claim that New Orleans jazz is *based* on, rather than *is*, a folk music, that it is rooted in a "whole store of Negro folk music[s] from spirituals and folk songs, to hollers, street cries, play party songs, and nursery rhymes" (Borneman, 1944a: 5, 38–39).

But, in so doing, these revivalists were shifting the issue away from commerce and art, production and consumption, to that of musical content and training. That is, the implied critique of swing was no longer that it was too commercial, but that it was too European, too much a "dilution" of the "traditional framework" with "foreign elements" (36–37). It was alleged that, by abandoning the blues for Tin Pan Alley tunes as the primary source of melodic material, the swing musician turned away from the "folk ancestry of the jazz idiom" toward the "alien" devices "of vaudeville, music hall, music comedy, and synagogue" (37–39).

But nothing sabotaged the African American tradition in jazz more, it was argued, than the replacement of simultaneous improvisation by the European artifact of written arrangements. West Africans, according to the revivalist Ernest Borneman, prefer "circumlocution" to "direct naming," "direct statement," and any "form of abstraction." "What prevented even the highest civilization of Africa from committing its [musical] language to paper was not lack of intelligence," but the taboo against precise denotation and a "deeply rooted faith in ambiguity as the criterion of man's freedom and spontaneity." Thus, any attempt to commit "the jazz idiom" to the "rigidity of written language" would "vitiate" rather than "preserve" it (1944c: 18, 64–65).

Nonetheless, by the mid-1940s, a number of swing musicians were experimenting with new harmonic patterns associated with modern composition and presenting concerts in places previously reserved for symphonic music—most notably the Duke Ellington concerts at Carnegie Hall.[16] The modernist critics were in the forefront in encouraging the new musicians to learn to "read and write music," to inform themselves "about harmony and counterpoint," and to seek "proper" instruction "so that their instrumental technique may become as accurate and reliable as that of academically trained musicians" (Borneman, 1956: 46).

For revivalists, these attempts at "raising jazz to the level of symphonic music" could only result in "lowering it to the level of a musical hybrid," "doomed to look like parodies of the real things," since the European tradition, with its "head start of five centuries," had developed "all alternatives of scored music to such peaks of perfection" (Borneman, 1944a: 37, 38).

Progress/The New

With typical hyperbole, Feather (1944a: 129) proclaimed that "never before has any branch of music made such rapid progress" as jazz, and that "never before have there been so many superlative jazzmen, or so many first-class bands." This, it was emphasized, is no mere incremental progress, resulting from continued refinements in instrumental prowess, but a substantial and sustained advancement in musical style, tone, and harmony, spurred on by "the most emphatic experimentation" and the "most courageous investigation of new sounds" ("Jazz Looks Ahead" 10). The *Metronome* editors seemed to envision wave upon wave of future avant-garde innovations, which they expected to "like even more" than "what is being played today" ("The Jazz of Yesteryear" 8).

For the modernists it was no happenstance, but a matter of historical necessity, that jazz should have progressed so far and so consistently from those "badly dated relics" of "the crude early stages of New Orleans jazz" (Feather, 1944a: 129). This optimism seems to have been occasioned less by reason and evidence than by the sway of "boom euphoria," that unreflective, giddy conviction in the midst of spiraling growth—in this case, the "swing craze"—that there is nowhere to go but up ("So You Want to Read About Jazz," 1944c: 25). This faith in inevitable progress was further buttressed by the expected Europeanization of jazz, which would make available a centuries-old storehouse of musical resources for gradual appropriation.

To "moldy figs," this "euphoric illusion of progress" merely reflected a desperate and "ceaseless search for novelty," which "has kept [swing] faddishly changing, hectically striving to avoid being out of date." In effect, a "reactionary music which [sacrificed] the truly modern tendencies of polyphonic jazz," swing could claim to be "no more modern than styles in women's clothing" (Blesh, *Shining* 190). The historical transformation from New Orleans to swing was "not an evolution" but "a drastic stoppage of the whole evolutionary process" (Borneman, 1946: 12).

The revivalists themselves were in disagreement whether this decline of jazz since the 1920s was reversible. Ralph Gleason (54, 55) had no doubt that it was. He exhorted his revivalist colleagues to stop merely talking to each other and to reach out to the "big, wide audience" by "usurp[ing]" *Look, Esquire,* and other "fountainheads" of mass information. This solution of course did not catch on, being so blatantly at odds with the purist image of the revivalist movement.

According to some revivalists, the decline was inevitable, since the material and cultural conditions that had called forth the "real jazz" in the 1920s no longer existed to sustain it. Appealing to an improvised version of Marxism, Borneman (1944d: 9) argued that the increased "concentration of capital" accompanying "the growing opulence of the music industry" after the depression sealed the fate of New Orleans jazz and led to the rise of swing by dramatically transforming the manner in which jazz was produced and distributed. In the face of this unprecedented "industrialization" of songwriting and "cartelization" of theaters and nightclubs, with its elaborate system of "hanger-ons and go-betweens," the musicians found themselves "enmeshed" in a "closely woven net of financial strings" from which they could hardly escape. To pay for the "vast new overheads," the music "had to be tailored to a much wider public than jazz had ever been able to attract." Swing music provided the ideal solution, based on the "simple recipe" of mixing the heat of the old jazz with the smooth commodified sound of the "sweet" bands (e.g., Guy Lombardo).

The "Marxist" revivalists were not thereby resigned to continued musical decline. There was hope that changing material conditions would lead, not to a "rediscovery of New Orleans music"—"musically speaking, history does not repeat itself"—but to new "forms which would be as rich and satisfying as New Orleans music." The revivalist critics were thus exhorted not only "to write and argue about jazz but to work for a social development that would keep our music alive" (Ertegun, "A Style" 7; Borneman, 1944d: 10).

Standards, Technique, and Literacy

No issue provoked more concentrated energy, or more straining of intellectual resources, than the debate over the proper standards for evaluating jazz. Given their progressivist bent, the modernists opted for standards "as objective as our background and equipment permit," going so far as to say that the "modern standards" in terms of which all musicians, past and present, were to be judged were based on "absolute values" (Ulanov, 1944: 31; "Jazz of Yesteryear" 8). They thought that an objective evaluation would easily come by attending to "the tone [a musician] drew from his instrument, the accuracy of the notes, the originality of the variations played upon the chords or melodic figures at hand." Thus, allegedly, it was primarily because of its superior "precision" and "finished technique" that the work of the younger swing musicians was deemed to be decidedly superior to that of their New Orleans forebears, with its "dull clichés," and "fumbling," "inept," and "uncertain" procedures ("The Jazz of Yesteryear"; Ulanov, 1943: 14; Blesh, *Shining* 289).

In the writings of the "moldy figs," the modernists professed not to see any standards at work, but only an appeal to "vague emotions," "nostalgia," and "historical associations," with "absolutely no analysis," "explanations," or presentation of "actual musical details." The "old time jazz lovers" are only concerned "with the music as part of a cult, a social scene," sometimes "even a political movement," or in its "relation to their own lives."[17]

This absence of musical standards, this "blind prejudice," on the part of the "moldy figs," was allegedly "based on their complete lack of musical education," particularly their inability to read scores. These "irate gentry" would "run promptly for the shelters if you asked them for the chords of the blues, or showed them a chorus on paper taken down from a solo by one of their idols and asked them to identify it," thus proving themselves no more qualified to write about jazz than "a man who knows no grammar, punctuation, or spelling, is qualified to be a book reviewer."[18]

The revivalists responded with a counterattack against the modernists' shallow appeal to technique. "Technique has nothing to do" with jazz, which as "a free art" cannot "be ruled by music books and music teachers" (Hubner 8–9). They maintained that swing musicians, caught up in "the vanities of solo playing," were driven to "develop instrumental bravura techniques" and acrobatics "in precise ratio to the loss of the music's basic structure." Trumpet players now were flaunting their "high notes," saxophone players their "sustained breath and rounded tones," pianists their "speedy runs," and percussionists their "fast and complicated drum solos," played "as loudly as possible on the greatest possible number of side drums" (Borneman, 1944a: 37).

Even worse, the vaunted techniques of the normal swing band, the revivalists asserted, "are largely mythical." What was being packaged as artistic virtuosity was mere "dexterity," "showmanship," and flashy display, on the same level as the "ability to make faces" or "to talk glibly."[19]

No technical device of swing music incurred more opprobrium from the revivalists than the "meaningless," "idiotic," and "empty" riffs (Hubner 8; Blesh, "Armstrong" 5). The riff is a rhythmic melodic fragment, normally used repetitiously in answer to a lead melodic phrase or to another rhythmic fragment. It was perhaps the most pronounced stylistic marker of the swing band, which frequently used riffs to answer other riffs—as in the case of brass instruments answering reeds. With the development of swing and the expansion of its market, the riff became so dominant, that the typical swing piece, for example, "Tuxedo Junction" or "In the Mood," appeared to be nothing but a series of repeated riff patterns.

The riff was, for the revivalists, the most offensive and blatant symptom of the glorification of the "groove beat as an end in itself" and the triumph of arranged music at the expense of "spontaneous improvisation." The "riffing style" is the "definite opposite of pure creative music," since in "riff music," one knows "exactly what is coming next for a whole chorus."[20]

This focus on the riff by the revivalists displayed, at the same time that it concealed, a certain ambivalence in their standards for critiquing swing. On the one hand, the riff, perhaps more than any other musical device, revealed swing to be a simplistic, standardized, consumer package, loaded with hooks, and operating with the imperative insistence of a military march.[21] On the other hand, the swing arranger would sometimes use a wide variety of different riffs in one piece to create a complex musical montage, generating an experimental, avant-garde sound, which glaringly excluded such pop requisites as a recurrent and easily recognizable melody (e.g., Jimmie Lunceford's "Stratosphere").

In criticizing the riff, the revivalists were thus also complaining about swing's "over-elaborate and complicated phrases . . . stripped of all meaning," its "search for out of chord notes" or more recondite chords, in general, its pretensions at modernist experimentation and formal play. They even resorted to the stereotyped lowbrow complaint of their being "no melody at all" (Ulanov, 1943: 21; Modlin 21; Moynahan 7).

Affect and Antics

For their part, the modernists were most irritated with the revivalists' excessive preoccupation with the expressive and emotional side of music. Revivalist writing was replete with claims such as, "Jazz is either the transmission of emotion or it is nothing," and "the deeper and truer the feeling, the deeper the jazz" (Broome 5). The "moldy figs" excoriated the swing musicians for performing "in a slick, mechanical, and unfeeling manner," as if governed by a "slide rule," in contrast to the practitioners of the New Orleans style who valued "simple honest emotional expression" over "conscious intellectual exercise."[22]

The modernists adamantly rejected the use of "emotional symbols," and they were especially repelled by the "emotional ecstacies" or "orgasms" of "nonmusical writers," which served only to express "personal and narrow prejudices." They feared that the explicit glorification of the emotive in jazz was merely a cover for advocating the "merely nostalgic, aphrodisiac, and cheaply melodic" at the expense of musical risk and experimentation (Broome 4; Glotzer 7; Ulanov, 1947b: 50).

This devaluation of affect on the part of the modernists constituted a radical revision of the swing image, which originally had been constructed more around the perceived emotional excesses of the "swing craze" than the dry, formal innovations imputed to swing arrangers. The expression "swing craze" called to mind wild new acrobatic dances, such as the jitterbug, crowds pressed against the bandstand transported by every trumpet high note and drum solo, flashy zoot suits with the attendant body mannerisms, and a new array of slang expressions, such as "corny," "screwball," and "See ya later, alligator." That is, rather than denigrating emotion, the swing movement seemed to outside onlookers to be producing too much of it (Harvey 100; "The Jargon of Jazz" x).

The revivalists, however, dismissed this appearance of unbridled affect among swing fans as merely phony emotionality—a "spurious" and commercially constructed "frenzy," which is merely the "superficial mechanics of an emotion." Swing, to them, was nothing but "a highly organized form of instrumental noise devoted to the super-inducement of a wholly unnatural excitement" deserving "psychiatric study." This excitement, which was "instantaneously" released by "the first notes or the drum blows," quickly took on the form of "mass auto-hypnosis," venting itself in "anarchistic, orgiastic, and dangerous excitement" (Modlin 21; Blesh, *Shining* 290).

Fascists and Communists

Frequently, the revivalist texts were tinged with the metaphors and insinuations of left-wing political discourse. There was a certain self-congratulatory implication of political correctness—a proper mix of nativism, antifascism, and Marxism—that underlaid many of the arguments espousing New Orleans jazz over swing.

It is within this larger political frame that the revivalist construals of Dixieland jazz as noncommercial folk music, or music of the proletariat, can best be viewed anew. We should thus not be surprised, for example, by one revivalist's complaint that "modernist" black musicians have "sold their birthright for a stale mess of European pottage," a clear evocation of Marx's repeated use of this biblical imagery to describe the conditions of the working class (Borneman, 1956: 46).[23] Nor should we be surprised by revivalist proclivities for cultural pessimism, and in particular by their tendency to blame the degradation of popular culture on the monopolization and cartelization of capital—a view then in vogue among other left-wing cultural critics, including Clement Greenberg and Theodor Adorno.

Also, like these theorists, many of the revivalists began to see signs of creeping fascism even in the cultures of the most formally democratic of capitalist countries. When some "moldy figs" claimed to find the imperatives of militarist discipline lurking in the swing riff, or packaged "frenzy" and "mass auto-hypnosis" appearing as swing affect, they were indirectly pointing to fascist tendencies within the confines of swing itself. As it was put, "swing is a form of *rabble rousing* that elicits . . . the same *blind idolatry* the demagogue or the dictator receives from the mob." In short, swing is "nihilistic, cynically destructive, reactionary" (Blesh, *Shining* 291, 290).

The modernists, in keeping with their politically "liberal" posture, tried as much as possible to keep musical discourse separate from political discourse—which explains in part their preoccupation as critics with technique and other internal features of jazz music. When finally goaded by the revivalists into the arena of politically nuanced charges and countercharges, they tried to restrict the discourse of "left" and "right" to the practices of music performance and music criticism alone.

Thus, they imputed to the revivalists a reactionary aesthetics, not a reactionary politics. In their most virulent and inflammatory articles— particularly Leonard Feather's—they went so far as to accuse the "moldy figs" of "musical fascism." They variously vilified them as the "right- wingers of jazz," "the voice of reaction in music," a "lunatic fringe" of musical criticism with its "ill-tempered and abusive outbursts," in ef- fect, the "vanguard of jazz reactionaries."[24]

The "moldy figs," understandably irate, labeled this a form of "yellow journalism" more "raw" than anything achieved by "Hearst in his palm- iest days," which in particular exposed Feather as the real "fascist raving maniac of the music business."[25]

This minicontroversy over "cultural fascism" was situated in a larger network of discourses that constructed jazz as the very negation of fascist culture. These discourses were generated by the banning of jazz in fascist countries and stimulated by war patriotism. *Down Beat* took pleasure in reporting on Nazi attempts to eradicate jazz as a reminder to musicians on the home front of "what you cats are doing to the supermen of the Third Reich" ("Ist Das nicht . . . " 2). The well-known French jazz discographer Charles Delaunay reported to *Down Beat* that the Ger- man occupation stimulated "an overwhelming burst of enthusiasm by Frenchmen for jazz" as a "symbol of" and "last tie with, the outside, free world." Said Delaunay: "By 1941, I was able to lecture on hot music to farm villages" ("Delaunay on . . . " 1).

Black and White

By the mid-1940s the virtually all-white jazz journals were boasting of their progressive racial attitudes, as well as those of white musicians, while denouncing Jim Crow practices in nightclubs, record companies, and the rest of society. *Metronome* argued, for example, that since "musi- cians as artists are traditionally above bigotry and prejudice"—"artists go where bigots fear to tread"—the music business should follow the example of the "rank and file of white musicians" who long ago had "thrown aside prejudice" to "play side by side with their colored brothers."[26]

In 1945 the editors of *Metronome* announced with fanfare that, as a result of their incessant "fight against racial prejudice," their readers were now voting "automatically without regard to color" in the annual balloting for the all-star jazz band ("Duke, Cole Win Band Contests" 9). The numbers did support the editors' euphoria. Some 74 percent of the musicians voted into the all-star band of 1944 were black, contrasting markedly with previous *Metronome* readership polls when African Americans garnered fewer than 25 percent of the positions.

Metronome's Feather had orchestrated a similar breakthrough a year earlier with a group of selected critics in the first annual *Esquire* jazz poll. This poll, however, provoked a surprisingly hostile and racially tainted counterattack from the revivalist press. By convincing *Esquire* to sponsor an annual yearbook on jazz, Feather had scored a major coup that sent ripples throughout the jazz world, it being the first time that a general mass publication, and a "serious" one at that, had devoted such space and attention to jazz music. Since Feather had a major hand in selecting the writers and the critics, the impression quickly circulated that the 1944 *Esquire's Jazz Book* was largely a purveyor of the *Metronome* line—a bias that the revivalist press was quick to try to expose.

None of these responses was as puzzling as Jake Trussell's essay "Jim Crow—Upside Down," (4–5), which accused the *Esquire* poll's critics of reverse racial discrimination because of their excessive preoccupation with the "fight against Jim Crow." Trussell had discovered to his horror that the *Esquire* critics gave only 28 percent of their first- and second-place votes to white musicians in selecting the all-star band—"a most startling case of race prejudice in cold, analytic figures."

This article reflected a split on racial matters within the revivalist community itself. Some were partisans of the classic black jazz of New Orleans (e.g., Louis Armstrong), while others were more partial to the white midwestern derivatives of this tradition (e.g., Eddie Condon). Of course, the revivalist movement, whatever its racial tastes, was initiated and propagated only by whites with an almost exclusively white audience. The overwhelming tendency of younger black musicians to join the swing movement irritated even the most vociferous supporters of black music among the revivalists, like Rudi Blesh (*Shining* 262), who complained: "How tragically the negro trades his own music for only another sort of slavery!" For swing music, he insisted, "is an abandonment of the truly Negroid elements of jazz in favor of white elements more intelligible and acceptable to white society. Thus, swing, outwardly the symbol of [Negro] triumph, is inwardly the failure of emancipation."

However, even *Metronome,* the self-proclaimed champion of "Negro" rights, was not immune from engaging in some racial bullying of its own, when it severely admonished a small and short-lived black jazz magazine, *The Music Dial*—"an ill-spelled, shoddily-printed rag"—for its "strong political line," carried "regardless of its relevance to music," and its "narrow" preoccupation solely "with the interests of the colored musician." "Music magazines should concern themselves with music, and that's all."[27]

The response was swift. While white "progressives" critiqued the *Metronome* editors vaguely for their "snide" and "reactionary" attitude, *Music Dial* pointedly identified a fascist strain in their tendency to treat music as a "fetish" or an "opiate" (Hammond, "Letter" 7+; Eckles 9).

These local, racially defined conflicts in the jazz press were symptoms of a much larger, more generalized anxiety about racial destabilization and violence in the music industry. There was much to feed this anxiety: the movement of southern whites and blacks to northern industrial cities; racial tensions in the armed services; increasing physical attacks on black musicians; the race riots of 1943; continued and sometimes intensified segregation in the music industry; increasing black militancy. This was reflected in recurrent *Down Beat* headlines during the mid-forties, exposing egregious cases of racial discrimination, in voices that expressed outrage, fear, and sometimes puzzled hysteria, such as, "Racial Hatred Rears Ugly Mug in Music," "Jim Crow Stuff Still Spreading," "Vagrant Chicks Blamed in Part for Racial Row," and "Sarah Vaughan Beaten Up by [White] Gang."[28]

Conclusion: From Swing to Bop

In 1944 when *Metronome* first introduced Dizzy Gillespie to its readers, it portrayed him not as part of any movement, but as a somewhat idiosyncratic stylist with an array of imitators, one of many modernists experimenting within the expanding boundaries of swing (Feather 1944a). Only two years later did "bebop" gain currency as the name designating a larger movement to which Gillespie was only one contributor.

By the mid-forties *Metronome,* sensing the demise of swing, was speculating that postwar jazz would be characterized by a profusion of different, and increasingly adventurous, experimental approaches, identified more with individuals than with movements.[29] Even later, in 1948, when bebop appeared to be the heir of swing, it was consistently portrayed by the jazz press as only one of many alternative modernist tendencies, which also included the work of Stan Kenton or Lennie Tristano (Gendron, "Short": 11–12).

In point of fact, during bebop's years in the jazz limelight (1946–1950), and despite the major musical changes that it wrought, the jazz press continued to apply, with only minor modifications, the same self-styled "modernism" discourse to it that it had used, years before, to differenti-ate the more adventurous tendencies in swing from Dixieland. This is none too surprising since virtually all the main defenders of bebop were veterans of the revivalist war and former proponents of swing. They were not saying that bebop was not "new," nor that it was not different from swing, but rather that it was just one of a whole temporal string of "new's" to affect jazz music, just one moment in the search for the "new," as this was implicitly defined by the prevailing discourses. Bebop had no journals of its own, overseen by disciples, to counteract this tendency.

By 1947 the mainstream jazz journals were subtly recasting the "moldy fig" versus "modernist" war as a conflict now pitting New Orleans jazz against bebop, rather than swing, and they were characterizing the reviv-alists, not altogether accurately, as bebop's most natural and unrelenting opponents. *Time* followed suit by explaining to its neophyte readers that "moldy fig" is merely "boppese for 'decadent' Dixieland jazz"—though people had been called "moldy figs" before there was any "boppese."[30]

Not unexpectedly, in the light of these facile conflations, many of the criticisms, once directed against swing by the "anti-modern" revivalists, were now being leveled against bebop, though in different circumstances and with different inflections. Like their swing forebears, bebop musi-cians were accused of fetishizing technique, of introducing excessive harmonic and rhythmic complications, and of being too mesmerized by the devices and concepts of European art music. They were reprimanded for their preoccupation with showmanship, their undignified publicity stunts, their mannerisms and argot.

Thus, the bebop revolutionaries were confronted at the outset not only with a recalcitrant musical legacy, but with a new but already entrenched discursive formation, fashioned and configured during the Dixieland-swing war. Although the bebop movement significantly trans-formed that musical legacy, it made the smallest of dents in the reigning discursive formation. The jazz critics' claims and counterclaims con-cerning bop, however outrageous, were constrained and delimited by a particular configuration of allowed topics, concepts, contrasts, argumen-tative styles—what I have called an "aesthetic discursive formation"—

which was formed in the heat of the revivalist-modernist debates of the swing era.

The unity of this new aesthetic discourse was a "unity in dispersion," to use Foucault's phrase—that is, a unity that propagated discursive opposition, that created points of discursive repulsion. As such, it was organized primarily around a group of interconnected binary oppositions: *art—commerce, authenticity—artificiality, swing—jazz, European—native, folk culture—refined culture, technique—affect, modern—traditional, black—white, fascism—communism,* and *right wing—left wing.*

The centrality of these binaries to the new aesthetic discourses virtually assured the existence of diametrically opposed aesthetic views that nonetheless belonged to the same discursive world. When the revivalist war shaded into the bebop war, the same unified set of binary oppositions was available, with small modifications, to sharply define the conflict of bebop partisans and their enemies. These binaries did not operate separately, but were densely entwined, accounting in part for the remarkable entrenchment of this discursive practice, despite its relative newness. For example, the anticommercial stance of the revivalists played into, and reinforced, their promotion of authenticity, folklorism, tradition, and affect, set against a vaguely left-wing, antifascist background.

Such a tight interconnection is no accident, since the binaries were not created from scratch, but were lifted out of the various European avant-garde and modernist discourses. The jazz aesthetic generated by the revivalist war was not original in its constituent binaries, or its imagery and rhetorical devices—which were by now clichés of aesthetic modernism—but in the way in which these binaries, images, and devices were brought together as a unified whole to satisfy the requirements for legitimating jazz as an art form, and in particular for fueling the revivalist-swing debate through its twists and turns.

This means that, in the broad sense of "modernist" that applies to European art discourse, the revivalists were as much "modernists" as were their swing adversaries. They simply accentuated certain tendencies of the "modernist" impulse at the expense of others. We need to remember, for example, that the concepts of the *folkloric* and the *primitive* were crucially involved in the "modernist" practices of Picasso, Bartók, Milhaud, and the Surrealists, while the notion of *reactionary* and art/commerce dichotomy entered crucially into the avant-garde terminologies of opprobrium.

Finally, to say that bebop was defined, explicated, defended, and criticized—in general, "received" in the jazz world—in terms of the aesthetic discursive formation previously generated by the revivalist war is not to deny that the bebop war did indeed effect some modest changes in the configurations of this discourse. Certainly, as jazz receded from the hit parade into the secondary markets—bebop never entered the hit parade—there would be inevitable changes in the way in which the binary *art/commerce* would enter into the musical debates and connect with the other binaries. Also, the concepts of *argot, ritual,* and *life-style* would loom more centrally and threateningly in the contestations over bebop.

Meanwhile, by the mid-1950s a whole new generation of jazz critics (e.g., Martin Williams, Nat Hentoff, André Hodeir) would bring about a major transformation in the aesthetic discourses of jazz. LeRoi Jones and Ralph Ellison, in particular, would bring African American voices to these new debates, something widely absent from the journals of the 1940s.

Since then, the attention given to the revivalist-swing debates has dwindled to almost nothing—the occasional cursory chapter in a "comprehensive" jazz history book, which typically approaches its topic as if it were an embarrassment, as belonging to a dark age.[31] Even if it were true that the 1940s produced no "great" jazz critics—a highly contestable point—the discursive formation, collectively and unwittingly generated by these allegedly minor voices, had a formative and enduring impact on the way in which jazz history got constructed and jazz as an art form got legitimated. The first jazz war cleared the discursive field for modern jazz.

Notes

I want to thank the staff of the Institute of Jazz Studies, Rutgers University at Newark, and particularly Dan Morgenstern, for their invaluable research assistance, without which this essay would not have been possible.

1 See Crow; Huyssen; Gendron, "Jamming."

2 The second essay (Gendron, "Short") will narrate the rise and fall of bebop, as proclaimed, interpreted, and influenced by the jazz press, and the third will deal with the confusing aftermath of that fall.

3 I have located thirteen revivalist journals operating in this country alone, but there were ten others in Europe as well. The American journals were *H.R.S. Society Rag* (New York, 1938–41), *Jazz Information* (New York, 1939–41), *Jazz* (Forest Hills, N.Y., 1942–43), *Recordiana* (Norwich, Conn., 1943–44), *Jazz Magazine* (New York, 1944–45), *Record Changer* (New York, 1942–55), *Jazz Quarterly* (Kingsville, Tex., 1942–43), *The Jazz Record* (New York, 1943–47), *Jazz Session* (Chicago, 1944–46), *Jazzette* (Boston, 1944–45) *Needle* (Jackson Heights, N.Y., 1944–45), *Jazz Finder* (New Orleans 1948–), *Playback* (New Orleans, 1949–52).

4   This date and metaphor were suggested to me by Dan Morgenstern.

5   By 1948 the pages of the leading jazz journals, in particular *Down Beat*, were flooded with generally positive references to bebop. *Down Beat*, which previously had been somewhat hostile, was now heralding bebop as the successor to swing, as were even such mass publications as *Life* and *Time*. The new night club scene in New York (e.g., the Royal Roost, Bop City) was dominated by bebop, as was Billy Berg's, the leading jazz club of Los Angeles. There were Carnegie Hall Concerts, hugely successful tours of Europe, articles explaining the bop argot or its musical technicalities, and a rash of imitation bop bands on college campuses. Swing musicians, such as Charlie Barnet, Chubby Jackson, and even the formerly hostile Benny Goodman, introduced bop components into their playbooks. The "moldy" journal, *The Record Changer*, fell in line with a series of serious articles on bop instrumentation.

   By 1950, however, as the jazz music business was plummeting, bebop was abandoned en masse by its former supporters (including Barry Ulanov of *Metronome*) and proclaimed dead. References to bebop in the jazz press declined rapidly. By 1951, bebop was hardly referred to in the jazz press as an ongoing movement, although Gillespie, Parker, and Monk continued to be revered as individual musical practitioners (Gendron, "Short" 17–21).

6   See, for example, Stearns 153–54; Collier 280–92; Sales 158–63.

7   I owe this image to Andreas Huyssen, as well as credit for some of the key ideas underlying this project.

8   I plan to discuss separately, in another essay ("Jazz Cheesecake"), the convolutions of gender in 1940s jazz discourse.

9   See also Borneman 1945a: 8; Blesh, "Armstrong"; Berton; and Borneman 1945b. Head arrangements usually were developed in jam sessions and communicated to other musicians through performance and example rather than by written score. The Count Basie band was noted for its head arrangements.

10   "Swing, Swing, Oh Beautiful Swing" and "Fats Waller Demonstrates Swing."

11   In 1936, Marshall Stearns initiated a year-long series of articles on "The History of Swing Music" for *Down Beat*, which covered what today we would call the "history of jazz." See especially *Down Beat* (June 1946): 4. The translation in 1936 of Hugues Panassié's *Le Jazz hot* was subtitled "The Guide to Swing Music," even though the book dealt only with jazz that came before swing, and Panassié was to become one of the most hostile critics of swing.

12   For example, in 1940, Glenn Miller had ten Top 10 hits, and Tommy Dorsey seven. Swing bands in particular had 65 percent of all Top 10 hits that year, while all bands together—"sweet" as well as "hot" (= "swing")—were responsible for 80 percent. Based on Whitburn.

13   Blesh, "Armstrong" 12; "Jazz of Yesteryear" 8; Borneman 1956: 47.

14   By 1943 the percentage of Top 10 hits by swing bands had declined to 29 percent (from 65 percent in 1940), and in 1946 it would be 19 percent. Based on Whitburn.

15   Stepanek 5; "What Is This Thing Called Jazz?" 2; Borneman 1944d: 6–7.

16   For a revivalist response to these "symphonic" tendencies in Ellington, see Hammond, "Is the Duke."

17   "Jazz of Yesteryear"; "So You Want to Read About Jazz" 1944b: 28; Feather 1944b: 26–27.

18   Feather 1944b: 27; McAuliffe 21. See also Feather 1945b: 16; 1945d: 14.

19 Blesh, *Shining* 289; "The Word 'Jazz' Kicked Around Too Freely" 10; Hubner 9; Modlin 21.
20 Modlin 21; Hubner 9; "From One Poll to Another" 27; Moynahan 7.
21 "Everything must be organized. Attention. . . . Present Riffs! Forward Riffs! Riffs Right! . . . Sax Section Riff!—brass riff—piano riff. . . . Scream, louder, scream, higher, riff-scream, LOUDER, HIGHER!" Hodes 16.
22 Hubner 9; Ulanov 1947b: 50; Crawley 38; Modlin 21. See also Echeverria 9.
23 See, for example, Karl Marx, *Capital*, vol. 1 (New York: International Publishers, 1967), 271.
24 Feather 1945b: 16; Ulanov 1943: 14; "So You Want to Read About Jazz" 1944b: 28.
25 "The Moldy Fig in Reverse" 20; editorial in *Jazz* 16. Not everyone took this latest skirmish very seriously. A pseudo-right-wing article in *Record Changer* inveighed against the "new leftist rabble rousers," Barry U. Leninov and William Z. Feather (after William Z. Foster, a founder and longtime leader of the Communist Party, U.S.A.), who were "injecting" modernist musical "poison into the country's veins." It also gave a right-wing inflection to the names of many revivalists, e.g., "Westbrook Blesh," from "Rudi Blesh" plus the vitriolic newspaper columnist "Westbrook Pegler." Brown 34.
26 "Because" 4. See also "Music Can Destroy Our Racial Bigotry" 10.
27 "So You Want to Read About Jazz" 1943: 21; "Our Contemporaries" 4.
28 *Down Beat* 1 Aug. 1944: 1; 29 July 1946: 1; 15 Aug. 1944: 12; 26 Aug. 1946: 12.
29 "Jazz Looks Ahead" 10; "The Cover of *Metronome*" 17.
30 "How Deaf Can You Get?" 76. Also at this time a show pitting New Orleans jazz musicians against beboppers and postswing modernists was publicized as the "first battle of jazz styles," "of moldy figs vs. moderns," to be broadcast live on a national network. Ulanov 1946: 16.
31 A 1991 article on the history of jazz criticism, otherwise highly informative and useful, virtually leaps over the 1940s. Gennari.

Works Cited

Adorno, Theodor. "On Jazz." Trans. Jamie Owen Daniel. *Discourse* Fall–Winter 1989–1990: 45–69.
Arthur, Bob. "The Great Enlightenment." *Jazz Record* Feb. 1944: 4–5.
"Attack Hamid Pier 'Jim Crow' Policy." *Down Beat* 1 Sept. 1944: 1.
"Because!". *Metronome* Apr. 1943: 4.
Berton, Ralph. "Blesh, Jazz, and Metronome." *Jazz Record* Aug. 1945: 6+.
Blesh, Rudi. "Louis Armstrong and *Metronome*." *Jazz Record* July 1945: 4+.
———. *Shining Trumpets*. 1958. New York: Da Capo, 1988.
Borneman, Ernest. 1944a. "The Anthropologist Looks at Jazz." *Record Changer* May 1944: 5+.
———. 1944b. "Responses to Letters." *Record Changer* July 1944: 41.
———. 1944c. "Questions and Answers." *Record Changer* Oct. 1944: 18+.
———. 1944d. "From Jazz to Swing." *Record Changer* Dec. 1944: 6–10.
———. 1945a. "Questions and Answers." *Record Changer* June 1944: 38.
———. 1945b. "The Musician and the Critic." *Jazz Record* Sept. 1945: 9+.
———. 1946. "Questions and Answers." *Record Changer* February 1946: 11–12.

——. 1956. "The Jazz Cult." *Eddie Condon's Treasury of Jazz.* Ed. Eddie Condon and Richard Gehman. New York: Dial, 1956. 33–67.

"Bouquets . . . Brickbats . . . with Due Humility." *Metronome* July 1943: 5.

Broome, John. "On the Feather in *Esquire*'s Bonnet." *Jazz Record* Aug. 1945: 4–5.

Brown, Bilbo (pseud.). "Rebop and Mop Mop." *Record Changer* Oct. 1945: 34.

Cesana, Otto. "Swing Is—Well, It's Here." *Metronome* June 1936: 14.

Collier, James Lincoln. *The Making of Jazz.* New York: Dell, 1987.

"The Cover of Metronome." *Metronome* 1945: 17.

Crow, Thomas. "Modernism and Mass Culture in the Visual Arts." *Pollock and After.* Ed. Francis Frascina. New York: Harper, 1985.

Crawley, Robert. Letter to the Editor. *Metronome* Mar. 1944: 7+.

"Delaunay on First Visit to America." *Down Beat* 26 Aug. 1946: 1.

"Duke, Cole Win Band Contests: Seven New All-Stars Elected." *Metronome* Jan. 1945: 9+.

Echeverria, Tom. Letter to the Editor. *Metronome* May 1944: 9+.

Eckles, Mick. "Too Much Music." *Metronome* Mar. 1944: 9.

Editorial. *Music Dial* July 1943: 3.

Editorial. "Our Contemporaries." *Metronome* Feb. 1944: 4.

Editorial. *Jazz Magazine* Oct. 1945: 16.

Ellison, Ralph. *Shadow and Act.* New York: Random, 1953.

Ertegun, Nesuhi. "Esquire 1945," *Record Changer* Feb. 1945: 3–5.

——. "A Style and a Memory." *Record Changer* July 1947: 7. Reprinted from *Record Changer* Apr. 1943.

"Fats Waller Demonstrates Swing." *Metronome* Feb. 1936: 19+.

Feather, Leonard. 1944a. "Jazz Is Where You Find It." *Esquire* Feb. 1944: 35+.

——. 1944b. "What Makes a Good Jazz Critic?" *Metronome* May 1944: 26–27.

——. 1944c. "Dizzy Is Crazy Like a Fox." *Metronome* July 1944: 15+.

——. 1944d. "Maxie Speaks Up." *Metronome* Sept. 1944: 14.

——. 1945a. "Louis on Jazz and Swing." *Metronome* June 1945: 26–27.

——. 1945b. "On Musical Fascism." *Metronome* Sept. 1945: 16+.

Foucault, Michel. *The Archaeology of Knowledge.* New York: Pantheon, 1972.

"From One Poll to Another." *Jazz Session* May–June 1945: 26–27.

Gendron, Bernard. "Jamming at Le Boeuf: Jazz and the Paris Avant-Garde." *Discourse* Fall–Winter 1989–90: 3–27.

——. "A Short Stay in the Sun: The Reception of Bebop (1944–50)." *Library Chronicle* 24.1–2 (Jan. 1994): 137–59.

Gennari, John. "Jazz Criticism: Its Development and Ideologies." *Black American Literature Forum* 25.3 (Fall 1991): 449–523.

Gleason, Ralph. "Featherbed Ball." *Record Changer* Sept. 1944: 48+.

Glotzer, Fred E. Letter to the Editor. *Metronome* July 1944: 7.

Goffin, Robert. "From the Blues to Swing." *Jazz Record* (Jan. 1946): 12–13.

Greenberg, Clement. "Avant-Garde and Kitsch." *Partisan Review* Fall 1959: 34–49.

Hammond, John. Letter to the Editor. *Metronome* Feb. 1944: 7+.

——. "Is the Duke Deserting Jazz?" *Jazz Record* Feb. 1945: 2–3.

Harrison, Richard G. "Room for Two Schools of Jazz Thought Today." *Down Beat* Jan. 1946: 10+.

Harvey, Holman. "It's Swing." *Reader's Digest* Jan. 1937: 99–102.

Hodes, Art. *Oral History File.* Vol. 2. Newark, N.J.: Institute of Jazz Studies (Rutgers University).

——. Editorial. *Jazz Record* Dec. 1945: 16.

"How Deaf Can You Get?" *Time* 17 May 1948: 76–77.

Hubner, Alma. "Must Jazz Be Progressive?" *Jazz Record* Apr. 1944: 8–9.

Huyssen, Andreas. *After the Great Divide.* Bloomington: Indiana UP, 1986.

"Is Dixieland Stuff Coming Back?" *Metronome* Sept. 1938: 25.

"Ist Das nicht Eine Sad Riff, Himmler?" *Down Beat* 1 May 1944: 2.

"The Jargon of Jazz." *American Mercury* May 1936: x.

"Jazz Looks Ahead." *Metronome* Oct. 1945: 10.

"Jazz of Yesteryear." *Metronome* Apr. 1944: 8.

"Jim Crow Stuff Still Spreading!: Girl Trumpeter Tastes Southern Chivalry and Color Ousts Mab's Men." *Down Beat* 29 July 1946: 1.

Jones, LeRoi. *Blues People,* New York: Morrow, 1963.

"Kansas City Court Makes Just Ruling." *Down Beat* 14 Jan. 1946: 10.

Lucas, John. "More on Semantics," *Jazz Record* Dec. 1944: 5+.

——. "Gettin' the *Esquire* Bounce." *Jazz Session* (Nov.–Dec. 1945): 16+.

McAuliffe, Arthur. "On Moldy Figs." *Metronome* Aug. 1945: 13+.

Modlin, Jules. "Notes Toward a Definition of Jazz." *Needle* June 1944: 20–21.

"The Moldy Fig in Reverse." *Jazz Session* Sept.–Oct. 1945: 20–21.

"Movies Fix Merit by Color of Skin." *Down Beat* 29 July 1946: 10.

Moynahan, Jim. "Jazz—A Vanishing Art." *Jazz Record* July 1944: 6–8.

"Music Can Destroy Our Racial Bigotry." *Down Beat* 15 Sept. 1945: 10.

"Negro Bands Lose "Busses." *Metronome* Feb. 1943: 5.

Panassié, Hugues. *Le Jazz Hot.* Paris: Correa, 1934.

——. *The Real Jazz.* New York: Smith and Durrell, 1942.

"Racial Hatred Rears Ugly Mug in Music." *Down Beat* 1 Aug. 1944: 1.

"Racial Prejudice Crops Out Again." *Down Beat* 1 Dec. 1945: 10.

Sales, Grover. *Jazz: America's Classical Music.* Englewood Cliffs, N.J.: Prentice-Hall, 1984.

"Sarah Vaughan Beaten Up by Gang." *Down Beat* 26 Aug. 1946: 2.

Smith, Charles Edward. *The Jazz Record Book.* New York: Smith, 1942.

——. "The Jazz of Yesteryear." *Metronome* May 1944: 18–19.

"So You Want to Read About Jazz." 1943. *Metronome* Dec. 1943: 21.

——. 1944a. *Metronome* Feb. 1944: 28.

——. 1944b. *Metronome* Mar. 1944: 28.

——. 1944c. *Metronome* June 1944: 25.

"Sop-Pop Celebrity." *Economist* 14–20 Sept. 1991: 75.

Stearns, Marshall. *The Story of Jazz.* London: Oxford UP, 1956.

Stepanek, Anton. "Jazz and Semantics." *Jazz Record* Nov. 1944: 5+.

"Stompin' at the Savoy." *Metronome* June 1943: 5.

"Swing, Swing, Oh Beautiful Swing." *Metronome* Feb. 1936: 19+.

Trussell, Jake, Jr. "Jim Crow—Upside Down." *Jazz Record* Apr. 1944: 4.

——. "The Jazz of Yesteryear." *Metronome* May 1944: 18.

The Two Deuces. "Jazz vs. Swing, Which Is Which? Are They Both the Same? *Metronome* Apr. 1944: 22–23.

"An Ugly Story." *Metronome* Nov. 1943: 4.

Ulanov, Barry. 1942. "It's Not the Book, It's the Attitude." *Metronome* Mar. 1942: 11.

——. 1943. "Panassié Book Draws Reverse Rave." *Metronome* Feb. 1943: 14, 21.

——. 1944. "Jazz of Yesteryear." *Metronome* May 1944: 19+.

——. 1947a. "Moldy Figs vs. Moderns." *Metronome* Jan. 1947: 15, 23.

——. 1947b. "The Heartless Modernists?!" *Metronome* July 1947: 50.

"Vagrant Chicks Blamed in Part for Racial Row." *Down Beat* 15 Aug. 1944: 12.

"What Is This Thing Called Jazz?" *Down Beat* 15 Apr. 1944: 2.

Whitburn, Joel. *Pop Memories, 1890–1954*. Menomonee Falls, Wis. Record Research, 1986.

"Why?" *Metronome* Mar. 1943: 34.

"The Word 'Jazz' Kicked Around Too Freely." *Down Beat* 15 June 1945: 10.

Yaw, Ralph. "What Is Swing?" *Metronome* May 1936: 22+.

Jazz in Crisis, 1948–1958: Ideology and Representation

STEVEN B. ELWORTH

The most common of these false totalities is "tradition," which is seen not as it is, an active and continuous selection and reselection, which even at its latest point in time is always a set of specific choices, but now more conveniently as an object, a projected reality, with which we have to come to terms on its terms, even though its terms are always and must be the valuations, the selections and omissions, of other men.—Raymond Williams, Problems *16*

The problem is no longer one of tradition, of tracing a line, but one of division, of limits; it is no longer one of lasting foundations, but one of transformations that serve as new foundations, the rebuilding of foundations.—Michel Foucault, Archaeology *5*

Time magazine's cover of 22 October 1990 announced another rebirth of jazz in the person of Wynton Marsalis and his generation of bop revivalists. The cover photograph presented a serious young African American musician playing a trumpet and wearing a tie and a sports jacket. Those familiar with the earlier career of Marsalis might have noticed that his glasses were absent: a bookish image had been replaced by a more stylish one. Although fashionable suits had once been an important part of the image of jazz artists such as Duke Ellington and the younger Miles Davis, male dress codes had changed in the jazz of the last thirty years: the importance of clothes as a signifier of upper-class status had become much less significant. This does not at all mean that jazz musicians could not dress with style, but by dressing more casually, musicians such as the later Miles Davis connoted a different kind of image, one of a constantly changing present.[1]

In both dress and musical style Marsalis and his confreres represent a return to the past, most notably the 1950s. If in their aspirations toward an older tradition, these musicians reject inelegant styles of dress, they also reject the more experimental music of the previous generation of jazz artists. Although their movement can be discounted as one more case of massive cultural industry hype in an age of reaction, the era of Reagan-Bush,[2] the musicians are significant because of their emergent skill but also because of their unprecedented cultural acceptance as the first approved acoustic jazz musicians in decades. Their predecessors who pioneered this style, called hard bop or bop, encountered much less success and were mainly denied the major label recording contracts now won by the younger artists.[3]

The recent canonization of bop—once rejected as an extreme style—is a significant cultural shift. Jazz in the last twenty-five years has ceased to be obsessed with an evolutionary teleology: musicians of many different aesthetic models no longer believe in an ever-progressing moment.[4] They instead regard the jazz past as a revered tradition and a field ripe for the picking. In fact, the concept of the jazz tradition has been formulated through moments of crisis. Far from being an unchanging and an easily understood historical field, the jazz tradition is a constantly transforming construction. Like traditions as disparate as those of classical Hollywood and Abstract Expressionist painting, the history of jazz is predominantly constructed in retrospect. The past is constantly rewritten in the present as a prediction of both what is now and what is to be. The crisis in jazz and the jazz press caused by the seeming success of the bebop revolution in the late 1940s and 1950s is an important site for reexamining the recent invention of the canon promulgated as the jazz tradition. I will discuss the creation of the jazz canon within a shifting historical matrix: the jazz press, evolving constructions of masculinity, the strange career of the great white hope Stan Kenton, and the attempt by writers such as Martin Williams to reconfigure jazz as a fine art.

An important place to examine the transformation of jazz from a popular to an art music is the series of changes in the discourse of the jazz press, especially *Down Beat* and *Metronome*. The rise of a generation of young African American beboppers created an image of masculinity and creativity difficult to sell to white society. Bebop could not and was not supposed to replace swing as the popular American dance music. The writers of the jazz press such as Leonard Feather, Nat Hentoff, Michael Levin, and Barry Ulanov wanted jazz to be intellectually accepted, but they had varying degrees of ambivalence about the possibility that the music might lose its vast popular appeal.

The emergence of Marsalis and the current generation of new traditionalists may lead to an acceptance of a stifling tradition in which musicians are ostracized for not following limited and preestablished protocols of both musical and nonmusical styles.[5] The frequent appeals to the tradition as the arbiter of eternal verities inevitably includes elements of totalization. According to Raymond Williams, the concept of the tradition: "moves again and again towards *age-old* and towards ceremony, duty and respect. Considering only how much has been handed down toward us, and how various it actually is, this, in its own way, is both a betrayal and a surrender" (*Keywords* 269).

No one could have predicted that an extremely controversial music of the 1940s and 1950s would be revived by twentysomething musicians from New Orleans and upheld as the most advanced and unchanging form of jazz. A closer look at the period of bop's brief notoriety reveals the radical instability of jazz and its representations of masculinity. The years after World War II were marked by an immense cultural transformation in which established cultural forms became archaic and insignificant. No longer an important element in the dominant pop music of the day, jazz became an art music created primarily by young urban African Americans, part of a subculture with its own somewhat scandalous cultural codes and the use of various illegal drugs. African American youths, one of the most socially repressed groups in postwar America, invented this radically reshaped form of jazz and called it bop. Elsewhere in this volume, Eric Lott writes of the music's codes: "At its hippest (and meanest), such a common language became a closed hermeneutic that had the undeniable effect of alienating the riff-raff and expressing a sense of felt isolation, all the while affirming a collective purpose—even at the expense of other musicians."

Bebop has usually been interpreted as a reaction by younger African American musicians to the dominance of swing as an increasingly corrupted form of jazz. But bop also allowed black musicians to seize their discourse from the white-dominated culture industry and to create something less likely to be appropriated. The various social codes stressed by bop are a part of this creation of a counterdiscourse, a seemingly uncorrupted voice of an isolated subculture. This position is inherently contradictory—once bop became a music performed in public it became commodified if only because the musicians made records for purchase. Some of the same codes that operated to isolate the musicians from the dominant culture industry became a part of the product differentiation of bebop: for example, uninitiated audiences were titillated by tales of strange black musicians with bop ties and jive talk. The importance of style

probably explains why the flamboyant Dizzy Gillespie was more celebrated than the inscrutable Charlie Parker.

Although bebop was recorded sparingly by the major established labels, the music's greatest impetus came from independent record companies originally created to record jazz or other kinds of African American pop music. A major exception was the series of big-band recordings
made by Gillespie for RCA that accommodated, at least on some levels,
the well-established format of the swing era. Gillespie's big band was
popular enough to be voted band of the year and to put Gillespie on the
cover of the January 1948 issue of *Metronome*. But bop had not yet
become the jazz mainstream: the other popular jazz bands of this period
were led by the white bandleaders Stan Kenton and Woody Herman; the
young musicians in the Herman band enthusiastically endorsed and
played the new music, but Kenton's bands, for the most part, were barely
touched by bop's influence.

By the late 1940s the two dominant jazz publications of this period,
Metronome and *Down Beat*, charted one major economic crisis after
another as each of the mighty orchestras of the swing era was first
rumored to be dying and then, with the major exception of Duke Ellington's orchestra, did in fact disband. Even though the new sounds of bop
influenced bands as well-established as Benny Goodman's, its inaccessibility no doubt furthered the constant breaking up of these bands. But
contradictions within the swing bands themselves, most notably the
tension between popularity and art, were just as responsible for the
demise of the big-band era.

The big bands against which the boppers revolted were multiply fac-
eted popular cultural institutions. The commodified white bands of the
earlier forties, such as those led by Jimmy Dorsey, Tommy Dorsey, and
Glenn Miller, were never simply jazz bands, or even dance bands, but
transmitters of various styles of popular music. Along with "hot" and
"sweet" numbers, the bands invariably included male and female vocalists and sometimes a group of singers. During the war several white
swing bands worked with entire string sections. A significant sign of the
commodification of swing was the common practice of a band bankroll-
ing an entire staff of arrangers, occasionally including African Americans
hired away from black bands. One result of the care that went into swing
arrangements was the variety of responses demanded from audiences—
they could listen passively or actively at the same time that they could
practice different forms of dancing. The dancing elicited by the white
bands varied from white appropriation of the erotic freedom of black
dancing to sedate fox-trotting to slow ballads. There was a certain degree

of contestation in this realm of cultural production: black jazz was trivialized at the same time that real structures of feeling from black cultural experience entered the music. For the young white musicians who staffed the swing bands, African American music and dance styles were a source of what was repressed in the dominant culture. Lewis A. Erenberg writes:

> When whites first encountered jazz in the 1920s, it had a dangerous as well as liberating aura, for the new music that first emerged in black urban areas in the early twentieth century had an enormous vitality and spontaneity. Segregated from white society, blacks had created their own expressiveness in the area that was less policed— their music and dance. Jazz bore the free, improvisatory energy of this one realm of freedom and expressed the body as a natural and divine feature of human existence. (223)

If the dance music of the white bands was a commodified trace of this celebration of the body, bop returned to the importance of the dance in only a symbolic sense by centering the bodies of the musicians. The stage antics of Thelonious Monk and the movements evoked by his music represented a negative image of the earlier social dancing. Instead of a community created by the dance, Monk's music created a community of listeners and musicians who expressed themselves in their own restricted movements as they watched Monk's unique physical motions. This type of community is emblematic of bebop's earlier attempt to create a counterpublic sphere apart from the corrupted social sphere.

The male and female singers who invariably traveled with each white swing band present another trace of the music's contradictions. The singers performed the popular songs of the day, but they were also there as objects of visual display. Not fundamentally jazz singers, the vocalists treated songs with more respect than did the arrangers who wrote the bands' instrumental numbers. A split had developed in these bands between a popular commercial music that observed the intentions of the culture industry and a mostly instrumental music that gave improvisatory freedom to both musicians and dancers.

The Tommy Dorsey orchestra from 1940 until 1942 provides an excellent example of the highly bifurcated nature of the white swing bands. By hiring the African American composer and arranger Sy Oliver away from the jazz orchestra led by Jimmie Lunceford, Dorsey bought a style of swing from the black bands at the same time that he was presenting the smoothly crooning Frank Sinatra as his principal male vocalist. Dorsey's recordings from this period that feature Oliver's arrangements are dramatically different from those that feature Sinatra's voice.[6] Sinatra's tremendous popularity during World War II with a massive, predominantly female audience was a significant turning point in the downgrading of swing as the dominant form of popular music.[7] What purpose was served by the balding, bespectacled trombonist Dorsey when the voice of Sinatra was the focus of pleasure? The stardom of Frank Sinatra and other fundamentally nonjazz vocalists eclipsed the bands backing them. Even star sidemen such as Bunny Berigan (1942) and Buddy DeFranco (mid-1940s) of the Dorsey band were largely lost in what became an essentially anonymous backup band. In addition to Sinatra, some of the last significant pop singers produced by the white swing bands included Peggy Lee, Doris Day, and Jo Stafford, all of whom made the transition to becoming popular stars whose faces frequently appeared on the covers of magazines, including *Down Beat.*

One of the more striking phenomena of this era was Sinatra's ability to transform the received image of masculinity. Sinatra was an obvious ethnic type and unusually skinny; to some, he may have appeared both effeminate and masculine. In his account of this oscillation between masculinity and femininity in Sinatra's career, Keir Keightley writes, "Sinatra's persona is continuously being masculinized in order to be re-feminized, and feminized in order to be re-masculinized" (2). His image and sound launched a progression of male and female pop singers who continuously rewrote images of allowable sexuality. What was considered forbidden for one generation is accepted as old hat by the next, as Sinatra is replaced by Elvis Presley, Mick Jagger, David Bowie, and Madonna.

Both *Down Beat* and *Metronome* were intimately involved with the aesthetic and financial crises that transformed jazz in the 1940s from the dominant form of popular music to a more ambitious form with a significantly smaller audience. The two publications shared some of the same contradictions found in swing as it was being replaced by bop, by singers, and by thoroughly commercial bands such as Ray Anthony's. *Down Beat,* edited in Chicago with a New York editorial office, was split between industry news and critical commentary, each with its own somewhat different agenda. Business concerns coexisted with the emerging notion that jazz was an art form. In the late 1940s and early 1950s *Down Beat* was a biweekly newspaper with advertisements and articles addressed to members of the popular music trade: musicians, agents, publicists, and fans. News stories covered such events as the disbanding of major units of the swing era as well as the tantrums of Stan Kenton and

Artie Shaw. Advertisements were predominantly for musical instruments. In 1949, subscriptions for *Down Beat* came with a year's worth of accident insurance after a succession of musicians died on the road.

The split nature of the publication was demonstrated by the dissonance between its covers and its interiors. Cheesecake dominated *Down Beat*'s covers in the late forties; instead of images of major stars of the age such as Charlie Parker and Dizzy Gillespie, the covers featured what were considered to be glamorous closeups of white women. These vary from major stars of the period such as Peggy Lee to pop singer Patti Page to RKO actress Marilyn Maxwell. The men who appeared on the covers sometimes were pictured next to female stars or models. These covers seldom bore any relationship to the magazine's contents. Most significantly absent from the covers were African American musicians. The few covers from 1948 and 1949 that did present images of African Americans stayed with well-known stars such as Lionel Hampton.

In its constant attempt to keep up with the changing business, the magazine eventually became a more general-interest music newspaper. Only in its critical columns did *Down Beat* continuously maintain its interest in jazz. By 1955 it had become a biweekly magazine similar in size to *Metronome,* and the implied audience changed from working musicians to a larger group of fans and amateur musicians. With the rise of the long-playing album in the mid-1950s, the record industry became the magazines' chief advertiser, and the record review sections grew correspondingly. The magazines survived while the big bands they had celebrated did not. The best way to understand *Down Beat* in the late forties is as a version of *Variety* with critical commentary and the photographs normally associated with *Esquire.*

Down Beat's regular columnists from the late 1940s to mid-1950s included Michael Levin, Leonard Feather, Nat Hentoff, and Barry Ulanov. Levin, who disappeared from jazz criticism in the mid-1950s, was also interested in classical music and worked in advertising and classical radio. Feather, a British émigré, was also a professional musician and record producer. Hentoff, a dropout from a graduate program in American studies, later became a general interest reporter and columnist who often focused on constitutional and educational issues. Ulanov was a professor of English at Barnard College with an interest in Christian mysticism and Jungian psychoanalysis. The *Down Beat* columns were mostly written from New York, and unlike the rest of the paper, they were usually about jazz—for example, recent events in New York, new artists on the scene, and the state of the music. There was a shared disinterest in pop vocal music and the commercial big bands, while hopes for a successful future for renewed big bands were regularly voiced into the early fifties.

A somewhat surprising aspect of the commentaries in *Down Beat* was an interest in metacriticism. The critics themselves began to discuss the possibility that their work could solve the crisis in jazz and create a new future for the music. There were calls for and celebration of a new generation of postbop musicians. At the same time, there was a new demand that jazz be taken seriously as an art music, removed from its industrial and socioaesthetic background. *Down Beat*'s project was different from that of bebop, which strove to construct a counterpublic sphere through a vibrant subculture with shared oppositional codes.

The white male critics of *Down Beat* and *Metronome* were strongly attracted to a strange and yet American subculture to which they both did and did not belong. The critics increasingly came to view jazz as a black art form, but they usually resisted the temptation to emulate black musicians who broke racial and cultural barriers. In addition, the critics developed a deep ambivalence toward their fellow traveler, the devoted jazz fan. Barry Ulanov writes of the ways that fans corrupt musicians when they do not have the critical distance of the critic.

> The deeply admiring fan must somehow curb his enthusiasm, too, at least enough to preserve a balanced view of those he admires. It is wonderful to get to know the object of one's musical affections, but not if in the process one ceases to have valid affections, not if as a result one's judgment becomes lost in the spider-web of unthinking adoration, as hopelessly consigned to the dust-heap as yesterday's instruments and the bad notes of the day before. Jazz needs fans but not slaves. ("Morality and Maturity" 17)

Unlike the Beats and some white musicians, the critics had no desire to transform themselves into the Other. They were working journalists with professional codes that allowed them to remain outsiders, looking but not touching. Nat Hentoff shared Ulanov's discomfort with the jazz audience, realizing that the nightclub scene was both prohibitively expensive for many fans and exploitative for the musicians. Hentoff wrote that,

> a jazzman's "live" audience is thereby diminished. What is often left for him to play to are conventioneers; call girls; a nucleus of jazz listeners; boozers; and the curious tabloid readers who are waiting for a man to appear on the stand with a needle in his arm. As a result,

the two-way communication essential to all music is considerably
delimited and distorted for the jazzman in the night club. (329–30)

Missing from Hentoff's argument is a possibility of shifting audience
positions. The audience, which he held largely in contempt, is not allowed to exist as a constantly mutating entity in which its members take
on many roles. This does not mean that the nightclub scene was not
filled with a certain amount of disdain for the musicians. The stories of
exploitation are all too true. Still, Hentoff tended to stereotype the members of the audience with simple labels, reducing them with the same
curious gaze that reduces the creative musician to an exotic junkie. For
Hentoff, nightclubbing had become a search for repressed pleasures in
which jazz is viewed by the audience as a foreign culture not to be taken
seriously.

The major paradox of all writing on culture is how to take seriously a
culture not one's own without reducing it to an ineffable Other. I do not
wish to argue, of course, that one can only write of one's own culture. In
the contemporary moment of constant cultural transformation and commodification, even the definition of one's own culture is exceedingly
contradictory and problematic. Definitions of jazz that limit it to a
specific totalizing meaning pull it out of the varied and shifting inter-
texts of race and aesthetics.[8] This intellectual conundrum is especially
evident in the transformation of jazz and the jazz audience after the rise
of bebop, the first jazz form that stressed the importance of otherness.
Bop was also the motivating force in critics' attempts to have jazz music
be considered an art music while retaining a large audience.

The 1950s were marked by an increased intellectualization in jazz
discourse as the music was beginning to be taken slightly more seriously
as a significant aspect of the culture. The increasing conviction that jazz
was an art emerges in both the careers of musicians and in the critical
discourse. Dave Brubeck, who appeared on the cover of *Time* in 1954,
was one of several jazz figures to aspire to acceptance in the same public
sphere as classical music. The jazz press happily pointed out that he had
studied with the French composer Darius Milhaud. Well-groomed and
well-dressed, Brubeck was extremely popular on the white college circuit, where his image was seen as that of an exemplary white jazz
musician who was also an artist and intellectual.

But the jazz press also faced real difficulties in formulating a critical
approach to jazz as art. Barry Ulanov's prolific writing for *Metronome* in
the late 1940s is a significant illustration of these problems. Less trade-
news oriented than *Down Beat*, *Metronome* possessed an essentially

split nature created by the aesthetic differences of its two longtime editors, Ulanov and George T. Simon. While Simon was a defender and advocate of the big white swing bands and their pop values, Ulanov was both a writer on classical music and a devotee of a modernist aesthetic that included bop. Ulanov shared with his contemporaries an interest in constructing the protocols of criticism, including why they should be believed by their readers. In interrogating the proper relationship between the critic and the audience, he wrote, for example, of the constant attacks on critics who abandoned musicians that they earlier championed: "Our dislikes followed a pattern, a pattern which began with our celebration of an unknown musician, singer or band and ended with our derogation of the same musician, singer or band when he, she or they had achieved popularity" ("Cantankerous?" 15). He also wrote of the way that earlier movements or artists become co-opted by success: "The bulk of beboppers, after having made the largest collective contribution yet made to jazz, become lost in trite formulas in which they find inner and outer security, the certainty that they can make it instrumentally, and that there's always an audience for their work" ("Cantankerous?" 15). This is an interesting argument for a defender of bop: as early as 1949 the music had been already appropriated by an undemanding subculture and rendered insignificant. Ulanov was horrified by the idea that the boppers could be so seduced by gold that their music would become the trash that its cultural enemies had always claimed it to be: "But if it can't be stopped, if it won't be stopped, then jazz will turn out to be what its most carping critics, the boys on the other side of the musical fence, have called it, a decadent form of entertainment, an aphrodisiac designed only to rouse flagging glands and lagging hearts, to set bodies in motion and numb minds and souls" ("Cantankerous?" 15).

Behind the attacks of an unnamed and unspecified cultural elite, Ulanov sees a fear that jazz is a source of a black contagion that will destroy the European intellect. This disaster can be prevented *not* by transforming the social order or by empowering the musicians but by creating standards held by musicians and critics and, implicitly, by the audience. Ulanov believed these standards were upheld by a cast of characters as musically different as Herb Jeffries, Billie Holiday, Lennie Tristano, Duke Ellington, and Charlie Parker. The qualities that unite these "good" artists become clear when they are compared with "the bad of the others who have sacrificed everything for box office survival" ("Cantankerous?" 28). The social dimension of this theory of value was reduced to the purity of individuals who know: they are the priests of jazz.[9]

Ulanov, a few months later, attempted to develop these ineffable criteria with a trinity: freshness, profundity, and skill. Freshness is the process of examining a musician for originality, weighing what is borrowed against what has not been heard before. Profundity is self-evident, "for no clearer description of the process can be found outside of the great works of art themselves, the very greatness of which proscribes description" ("What's Hot" 31). Skill "is the easiest standard to describe, to understand and to recognize. The abundant technical skill of such men as Roy Eldridge, Johnny Hodges, Charlie Parker, Art Tatum, Charlie Shavers, Coleman Hawkins, Benny Goodman, etc. is beyond argument" ("What's Hot" 31). The three criteria must have a productive relationship for the ineffable, real jazz creativity to occur. Jazz strives for an almost unobtainable profundity. For Ulanov, the critic's function is to understand this ineffable. The creative critic is intuitive if "he" can "to some large extent duplicate the intuitive power of the performer" ("Function of the Critic" 17). The critic and musician are fellow acolytes of the first church of jazz. The critic is the high priest whose "perceptions are such that more often than not he can describe the next development in jazz before the musicians have reached it" ("Function of the Critic" 17). The magical mysteries of the universe and the teleology of jazz are decoded by the keepers of the holy secrets of intuition.

Ulanov concludes his series by describing the history of jazz as it progresses from the primitivism of New Orleans to the dignity of Armstrong and Bessie Smith and then to the profound potential of Ellington. The jazz of the 1930s and 1940s translated this potential and made the profound realizable in the work of Goodman, Hawkins, Eldridge, Lester Young, Christian, Parker, and Tristano. The jazz musician stands at a new historical threshold. "No longer then does the jazzman stand alone, uncluttered technically, emotionally constricted. Behind him is a history and a tradition. Before him is an art" ("Function of the Audience" 16). Ulanov is clearly rewriting the past and creating his own canon. The fact that any canon is inevitably a construction should be kept in mind as we explore a controversial and perhaps excised member of the canon, the third inductee voted by readers into the *Down Beat* Jazz Hall of Fame, Stan Kenton.

The bifurcated nature of the earlier white bands is a major factor in the popular but extremely controversial career of Stan Kenton, a tall, commanding, voguishly dressed man who was featured on more *Down Beat* covers than any other bandleader of the late 1940s. Although he essentially continued the traditions of multiple address exhibited by the earlier white swing bands, Kenton also sought the status of the "progressive" with ambitions to European art music and a belief in a teleological argument of cultural advancement. During the late forties and early fifties, Kenton toured with either a dance band or with a mammoth concert orchestra that included a string section. These coexisting ensembles played different repertoires at concert halls and dance halls. The explicit address to the audience was allegedly different for these two venues—to the body in the dance hall, to the intellect in the concert hall. In practice, there were important similarities. The two bands shared many of the same players, and all the featured soloists and vocalists of the dance band were in the concert orchestra. The "hits" originally played by earlier versions of the dance band were included in the concert orchestra's program. By drawing from the same pool of arrangers and composers, Kenton maintained stylistic similarities between his two ensembles, in particular a pronounced interest in loud, brass-ridden arrangements. The longer pieces for the concert orchestra sought to create new forms, borrowed from twentieth-century classical composers such as Stravinsky, Hindemith, Villa-Lobos, and Schoenberg. Newly composed pieces, such as Bob Graettinger's "City of Glass," bear little resemblance to pop, dance music, or preexisting jazz styles, suggesting rather the merger of jazz with elements of modernist classical music.

My own harsh assessment of Kenton's musical project sees it as a white male's hysterical reaction to the ongoing cultural transformations of postwar America, particularly the renewed emergence and significance of African American musicians through the new music of bebop. Kenton's musical progressivism is a reaction to bop, replacing the pyrotechnics of that style with a stress on spectacle for its own sake. Gary Giddins has written of Kenton's aesthetic doctrine: "his response to every fashion in jazz or pop was, mine is bigger than yours" (85). Kenton's project is primarily one of overcompensation, a tendency toward stylistic and rhetorical bombast. A psychoanalytic reading would characterize Kenton's music as a reaction formation of a criticized and diminished white male ego.

A typical Kenton piece such as "Concerto to End All Concertos" is a musical representation of this male hysteria. It was first released as a two-sided 78-rpm recording in 1946 and then remade in 1956. The piece begins like many of Kenton's pieces, with the leader's piano attempting a lyrical style. The differences between this mellow opening and the rest of the piece—in which loud brass climaxes are placed one on top of another—are the key to this aesthetic of hysteria, a tendency to overdo, allegedly for immediately gratifying excitement. The various soloists on the 1956 version of "Concerto" continue this attempt at an overpowering male orgasm, especially Maynard Ferguson, the ultimate hyperphallic trumpeter. Striving consistently for the highest and loudest notes, Ferguson's practice of overcompensation is similar to Kenton's arranging style in "Concerto." The piece concludes with changes of dynamics and volume, frenzied theme, throbbing drums, a thematic recap, and of course loud brass. Striving toward effect for the sake of effect, the piece lacks any real relation to any tradition of classical concerto or to the jazz concerto style of Duke Ellington, who had already parodied Kenton's pretensions in his "Controversial Suite" of 1951.

Kenton created a whiter, more European version of jazz, misunderstanding the significance of jazz as fundamentally a practice of cultural miscegenation. White cultural workers who come to grips with jazz must come to terms with the African American culture that originally nurtured jazz. Since at least the 1920s, white and black musicians have borrowed from each other, creating a music that constantly transgresses borders. Kenton's music was fundamentally made by whites for whites. The interaction between white and black occurred for Kenton at the origins of the music safely in the past. It was now the white man's burden to make a man out of jazz.[10] Bernard Gendron is convinced that the interest of the jazz press in white hopes stems from this repression of the importance of black musicians in the creation of modern jazz.

> Faced with a bebop movement dominated by African American musicians, the virtually all-white jazz journals seemed always to be in search of "great white hopes"—white modernists, like Tristano and Kenton, with whom a mostly white readership would feel more at home. There may indeed have been a racial code operating in the white critics' expressed desire for a more cerebral and European modern jazz, as well as a jazz purified of any association with life-styles, argots, or dress.[11] (141)

This does not at all mean that the musicians in Kenton's band did not take part in this interaction between white and black cultures or could not take part in the subcultures of bebop. Among the early stars of the postwar Kenton band was Art Pepper, who later became widely canonized as the great white bopper. All of Kenton's featured sideman of this period, as disparate as Pepper and Ferguson, were rewarded with high vote totals in the *Down Beat* readers' polls. Being featured with Kenton in this period was tantamount to at least some degree of popular success.[12]

If Kenton's style and manner were not considered hysterical during the height of his career, they were on occasion termed "neurotic." Reviewing the "progressive" band in the February 1948 *Metronome,* Barry Ulanov not only referred to it as neurotic, but added, "There is a danger, one approaching psychopathic proportions, of an entire generation growing up with the idea that jazz and the atom bomb are essentially the same natural phenomenon" ("What's Wrong" 33). In response, Kenton used similar language to defend the band. "Neurotic? Yes—aren't most of us today, to one extent or another?" (Levin 33). When Kenton broke up the "progressive" band in December 1948, he announced that he wanted to become a psychiatrist.[13] He regrouped at the end of the year, however, and never did get to medical school. His choice of a new career was extremely telling, taking place at the height of the American romance with Sigmund Freud. Psychiatrists were considered to be the new exemplars of humanity. The man from Vienna was perhaps the only one who could solve the problems of the age.

Kenton's fall from his already controversial place in the canon probably resulted from racist statements he made in a moment of panic after he felt that his band had been slighted in the 1956 *Down Beat* Critics' Poll. In a telegram to *Down Beat*, he wrote,

> IT'S OBVIOUS THAT THERE IS A NEW MINORITY GROUP, WHITE JAZZ MUSICIANS. THE ONLY THING I GAINED FROM STUDYING THE OPINIONS OF YOUR LITERARY GENIUSES OF JAZZ IS COMPLETE AND UTTER DISGUST. (Feather 122)

Leonard Feather subsequently wrote an open letter to Kenton, telling him to disown the telegram and asking, "Do you feel that first place on piano should have gone to Stan Kenton rather than Art Tatum?" (Feather 123). Disgusted by Kenton's racism, Feather still praised his career and his current band as the best Kenton ensemble. Interestingly, a judgment that might have been offered simply to please Kenton has become the dominant opinion: the band that recorded *Contemporary Concepts* with Bill Holman's arrangements is the only one honored with entry in the Smithsonian Collection's *Big Band Jazz: From the Beginnings to the Fifties*, selected by Gunther Schuller and Martin Williams. The longstanding rumor was that Kenton did not like the record because it swung too much.

If Kenton ended his career in political and critical disgrace as one of the few jazz musicians to publicly embrace the right-wing politics of Barry Goldwater, it is not at all impossible for his music to be reused in some form. The contemporary European trumpeter Franz Koglmann, who is usually aligned with and performs alongside avant-garde musicians such as Paul Bley, Tony Coe, and Steve Lacy, has recorded *A White Line* in order to construct a countertradition for jazz that stresses its "'modern' qualities—considered design, lucid coolness, detached lyricism, a swing that opts for a cautious and artistic approach" (Koglmann). The disc consists of homages to some of the significant white Americans of jazz history, including expected figures such as Gerry Mulligan, Gil Evans, and Lennie Tristano, and somewhat lesser-known figures today such as Red Nichols and Shorty Rogers. The first selection on the disc, "A White Line," includes citations of such Kenton "standards" as "Collaboration," "Artistry in Rhythm," "Intermission Riff," "Painted Rhythm," "Eager Beaver," and "Concerto to End All Concertos."

The ultimate reductionist version of jazz as fine art became dogma in the 1960s in the work of Gunther Schuller and Martin Williams. As coeditor with Nat Hentoff of *The Jazz Review*—one of the short-lived attempts to create a jazz "little magazine" with a pronounced intellectual content—Williams became significant in the later 1950s after jazz and its periodicals had for the most part ceased to concern themselves with popular music and a mass audience. *The Jazz Review* sought to change jazz talk from a journalistic to an intellectual discourse in the late 1950s.[14] Its new argument for jazz is highly problematic, with intellectual roots in New Criticism and an end-of-ideology consensus built around the rejection of the social and the historical. The creation of an almost free-flowing valorization of artistic genius was undertaken primarily by Williams and Schuller, whose attempts to take records and individual musicians out of any kind of historical moment have left a significant if debatable mark on the writing of jazz history. Concepts of the past based on "Great Traditions" have always obstructed an understanding of how history actually works. Great men do not occur in a vacuum, nor do the great records of the age appear as manna from heaven. They are produced within the changing, often contradictory field of the social and historical. For Schuller and Williams, the concept of a great tradition originating in the ideas of F. R. Leavis[15] leads to a true road, with the nonelect sentenced to purgatory.

For many years jazz history was defined as an examination of the exceptional with its real potential in the present and the horizon of the future. This linear view of progress was shared by almost all critics and musicians of the period. Only within the last few years, with the collapse of teleological models at the hands of late capitalism and its attendant poststructuralisms, has this view begun to be critiqued. The construction of images of masculinity has also shifted. Significant women musicians (Marilyn Crispell, Geri Allen, Jane Ira Bloom, Myra Melford, etc.) are being taken seriously and not merely tolerated for their appearance.[16] If admissible standards of appearance have shifted to allow for different styles of dress and behavior, one can see the real reactionary nature of the Marsalis *Time* cover. The suit has become an image of seriousness that props up outworn images of masculinity. The young musicians on the bandstand now look like nervous young job applicants. The African-inspired garb so prevalent in the 1960s is now taboo. I would not argue that musicians should only wear native garb, but I would insist that there is a definite semiotics of band dress. For example, in the 1980s the World Saxophone Quartet wore tuxedos, the dominant costume of European classical music. Their formal appearance destabilized the various meanings produced by four African American male avant-gardists playing saxophones with no rhythm instruments in the background.[17]

Appearance and different images of masculinity have become part of the dividing line[18] in jazz between retrenchment and the continuity of experimentation. The jazz of postmodernity now falls into two distinct strands: a negative attempt to retrieve the best that was ever played—the jazz of Marsalis; and a scrutinizing of the detritus of past pop and jazz to discover new ways to say the already said—the jazz of such contradictory figures as Don Byron,[19] Koglmann, Henry Threadgill, and David Murray.

Notes

I would very much like to thank Krin Gabbard for his constant encouragement and assistance in producing this essay. I would also like to thank the staff of the Institute of Jazz Studies, Rutgers University, Newark, for their help and assistance. Louise Spence has again shown herself to be the ideal reader and commentator.

1   Significantly, *Time* considered no young women musicians worthy to be featured in the Marsalis article. This omission may reflect in part the lack of codified dress styles for female jazz musicians. Certainly the possibility of female jazz musicians as something other than singers has been repressed throughout most of jazz history, yielding a tradition of female artists who made their voices and bodies the object of display.

2   It will be interesting to watch the careers of these musicians develop in a changing cultural and historical moment marked by the election of President Bill Clinton, the first Democrat in a generation. Clinton is, of course, a saxophone player with highly catholic if not contradictory tastes: he has expressed admiration for both Kenny G and Sonny Rollins.

3   Roy Hargrove, an extremely gifted young trumpet player, had an exclusive recording contract at a very young age with RCA. He has since moved to Verve, a division of Polygram, another multinational label. The trumpeters of earlier generations, such as Lee Morgan, for example, never received this level of support. Unlike Hargrove, Morgan never appeared on the cover of a jazz periodical or performed on *The Tonight Show*. I should also point out that Marsalis's own development has included more than a simple embrace of canonical bop styles.

More recently he has rediscovered other earlier forms of jazz associated with Duke Ellington as well as with his native New Orleans.

4   Jed Rasula writes elsewhere in this volume, "It's not only curious, then, but a sign of systematic misconception, that a music celebrated for its improvisatory character is viewed chiefly as an example of developmental progress." Only in the recent past has jazz been configured in terms of an awe-inspiring tradition from which young artists can creatively pick and choose.

5   The recent controversy surrounding Jazz at Lincoln Center is a perfect example of this situation. Led by Wynton Marsalis, Stanley Crouch, and Rob Gibson, the series has become the center of an argument in the jazz press because important jazz artists from the past and present have not been invited to Lincoln Center. Many commentators have objected to the exclusion of musicians as different as Anthony Braxton, Lee Konitz, Joe Lovano, and George Russell.

6   In some of the Dorsey recordings, Sinatra does in fact sing with arrangements by Sy Oliver. These recordings, such as "Blue Skies," put Sinatra in a jazz-based terrain that is dramatically different from records such as "Once in a While" that established his tremendous popularity. That Sinatra performed both kinds of songs does not mean that his smooth style was used in both.

7   Sinatra has become one of the most canonized of American singers, and his fandom makes for strange bedfellows. Anthony Braxton recently told John Corbett, "I'm trying to get tickets to see Sinatra when he comes to Connecticut. I'd do anything to see my man! He's an old guy, he sings like an old guy, but he's a great master who's come to his old and senile period, and I want to hear it! It's past perfect pitch, past all of that. It's got heavy life-experience!" (Corbett 29).

8   In his introductory essay to this volume, Krin Gabbard writes that any definition of jazz "must be based on a sociocultural analysis of jazz rather than on its internal aesthetics." Jazz cannot be defined in terms of abstract forms; it is rather a product of the cultural sphere.

9   This same kind of argument would eventually be expressed in somewhat different terms by Martin Williams. This is one of the central themes of his *Jazz Tradition*, an attempt to codify the jazz canon.

10   Paul Whiteman, who said in the 1920s that he wanted to make a lady out of jazz, is in many ways an earlier, parallel figure to Kenton.

11   I would like to thank Bernard Gendron for making his pioneering work on jazz discourse available to me. Significant parallel work is always invaluable as one works on one's own project. There are, however, significant differences between Kenton and Tristano. A major difference was that Kenton was always more popular with his audience than with critics, while Tristano was a coterie taste. In the late 1940s, Tristano's major critical acolyte was Barry Ulanov. Tristano later became the focal center of what could be considered the longest-running cult in jazz. His white disciples follow a canon created by Tristano that consists of his disciples and very few black musicians. The only post-Charlie Parker black musician that they find of importance is Freddie Hubbard, but only in his early work.

12   Lee Konitz, one of the major disciples of Tristano, reached his first popular and financial success in his short featured stint with Kenton in the early 1950s.

13   This sentiment was repeated in the 1950s by another jazz musician with limited schooling, Stan Getz.

14   *Jazz: A Quarterly* shared many of the same goals as *The Jazz Review* in the 1950s.

It was edited on the West Coast by another refugee from the jazz press, Ralph J. Gleason.

15   F. R. Leavis, who taught English at Cambridge and edited *Scrutiny,* was a major force in a half-hearted social criticism that ended up as a valorization of genius.

16   Cindy Blackman, an extremely talented young drummer, has called into question the codes of proper dress and decorum for young female jazz musicians. In the photographs that appear on both of her CDs and in her appearances on the bandstand, she deliberately makes herself an object of display in order to ac-knowledge the possibilities of feminine desire. Martin Johnson wrote, "Blackman wears some of the most daring outfits ever seen on a jazz bandstand and, because of her flamboyant style, has drawn the wrath of many conservative jazz followers. 'This music is about freedom and possibility,' says Blackman. 'I don't see why I should repress any part of myself to play it' " (Johnson 15). The idea that approved garb is necessary if musicians are to be taken seriously is exploded by the notion that clothing is another parameter of constantly shifting expression.

17   Stanley Crouch, who was at that time still allied with the avant-garde, wrote, "As usual, most of the jazz press missed the point, interpreting the tuxedos and gleaming shoes worn by each player as some sort of superficial commentary or parodic assault, when any examination of bandstand dress by black American musicians prior to the influence of rock and roll will reveal aristocratic modes of dress" (Crouch). Crouch's reading of the World Saxophone Quartet's appearance reveals much of what has made his more recent ideological shift possible. The meaning of clothes is reduced to an unchanging, ahistorical aspect associated with a natural aristocracy of artists. Crouch denies the possibilities of parody and multiple meanings and connects the correct way to dress with the correct way to play jazz. At the same time, Crouch attacked a leading white saxophonist, Phil Woods, for the alleged casualness of his garb. Although I disagree with Crouch's interpretation of the semiotics of jazz clothes, he is right to make this issue a more central facet of jazz criticism.

18   This line is very much a critical construct. Musicians have their own relation-ships and affiliations. Some musicians, such as Geri Allen, are creating their own groupings containing "conservatives," "cultural scavengers," and older players of the avant-garde.

19   Byron is a significant figure for the current discussion. Two years younger than Wynton Marsalis, his hair is in dreadlocks and he wears shorts. Though consid-ered by almost all listeners to be a virtuoso of the clarinet, he is constantly protest-ing and reformulating the canons of the various musics that he plays. Besides jazz, these include klezmer and European classical music. His favored composers include Webern, Schumann, Raymond Scott, and Ellington. Byron is particularly interested in the music of Mickey Katz, an uncanonized klezmer clarinetist who specialized in the pastiche. Stanley Crouch considers Byron to be a great musician but one who is outside the tradition of jazz. He is praised to be criticized. This is the same move that Crouch once used to place Cecil Taylor outside jazz.

Works Cited

Corbett, John. "Of Science and Sinatra: Anthony Braxton." *Down Beat* Apr. 1994: 27–31.

Crouch, Stanley. Liner Notes. *World Saxophone Quartet, Revue.* 1982. Black Saint BSR 0056.

Erenberg, Lewis A. "Things to Come: Swing Bands, Bebop, and the Rise of a Postwar Jazz Scene." *Recasting America: Culture and Politics in the Age of the Cold War.* Ed. Lary May. Chicago: U of Chicago P, 1989. 221–45.

Feather, Leonard. *The Jazz Years: Earwitness to an Era.* New York: Da Capo, 1987.

Foucault, Michel. *The Archaeology of Knowledge.* New York: Harper, 1972.

Gendron, Bernard. "A Short Stay in the Sun: The Reception of Bebop (1944–1950)." *Library Chronicle* 24, no. 1–2 (1994): 137–59.

Giddins, Gary. "Kitschy Kenton." *Village Voice* 13 Oct. 1992: 85.

Hentoff, Nat. "Whose Art Form? Jazz at Mid-Century." *Jazz: New Perspectives on the History of Jazz.* Ed. Nat Hentoff and Albert J. McCarthy. New York: Holt, Rinehart and Winston, 1959. 325–42.

Johnson, Martin. "Ex-Kravitz Drummer Cindy Blackman's *Telepathy.*" *Pulse* June 1994: 15.

Keightley, Keir. "Singing, Suffering, Sinatra: Celebrity and Articulations of Masculinity and Femininity, 1953–62." Paper delivered at Society for Cinema Studies conference, Syracuse University, 1994.

Koglmann, Franz. *A White Line.* 1990. hat ART CD 6048.

Levin, Michael. "Why Fidelity?" *Down Beat* 14 Nov. 1956: 33, 48.

Ulanov, Barry. "What's Wrong with Kenton?" *Metronome* 17 Feb. 1948: 32–33.

——. "Are We Cantankerous?" *Metronome* 15 Apr. 1949: 28.

——. "What's Hot and What's Not." *Metronome* 18 July 1949: 30–31.

——. "The Function of the Critic in Jazz." *Metronome* 16 Aug. 1949: 17.

——. "The Function of the Audience in Jazz." *Metronome* 16 Oct. 1949: 26.

——. "Morality and Maturity in Jazz; Fourteenth in a Series." *Metronome* June 1954: 17.

Williams, Raymond. *Keywords.* Croon Helm: Fontana, 1976.

——. *Problems in Materialism and Culture.* London: Verso, 1980.

Other: From Noun to Verb

NATHANIEL MACKEY

Cultural diversity has become a much-discussed topic. I would like to emphasize that cultural diversity *is* cultural, that it is a consequence of actions and assumptions which are socially—rather than naturally, genetically—instituted and reinforced. The inequities that the recent attention to cultural diversity are meant to redress are in part the outcome of confounding the social with the genetic; so we need to make it clear that when we speak of otherness we are not positing static, intrinsic attributes or characteristics. We need instead to highlight the dynamics of agency and attribution by way of which otherness is brought about and maintained, the fact that *other* is something people do, more importantly a verb than an adjective or a noun. Thus, I would like to look at some instances of and ways of thinking about othering—primarily othering within artistic media, but also othering within the medium of society, touching on relationships between the two. Artistic othering has to do with innovation, invention, and change, on which cultural health and diversity depend and thrive. Social othering has to do with power, exclusion, and privilege, the centralizing of a norm against which otherness is measured, meted out, marginalized. My focus is the practice of the former by people subjected to the latter.

The title "Other: From Noun to Verb" is meant to recall Amiri Baraka's way of describing white appropriation of black music in chapter 10 of *Blues People*. In that chapter he discusses the development of big-band jazz during the twenties and thirties by Fletcher Henderson, Duke Ellington, Jimmie Lunceford, and others and the imitation and commoditization of it by white musicians like Jimmy and Tommy Dorsey, Artie

Shaw, Charlie Barnet, and Benny Goodman (who became known as the "King of Swing"). He calls the chapter "Swing—From Verb to Noun." Typical of the way he uses the verb/noun distinction is this remark: "But for most of America by the twenties, jazz (or *jass*, the noun, not the verb) meant the Original Dixieland Jazz Band (to the hip) and Paul Whiteman (to the square)" (143). Or this one: "*Swing*, the verb, meant a simple reaction to the music (and as it developed in verb usage, a way of reacting to anything in life). As it was formalized, and the term and the music taken further out of context, *swing* became a noun that meant a commercial popular music in cheap imitation of a kind of Afro-American music" (212–13).

"From verb to noun" means the erasure of black inventiveness by white appropriation. As in Georg Lukács's notion of phantom objectivity, the "noun," white commodification, obscures or "disappears" the "verb" it rips off, black agency, black authority, black invention. Benny Goodman bought arrangements from black musicians, later hired Fletcher Henderson as his band's chief arranger, and later still brought black musicians Teddy Wilson, Lionel Hampton, Charlie Christian, Cootie Williams, Sid Catlett, and John Simmons into his band or small groups, but for the most part black musicians were locked out of the enormous commercial success made of the music they had invented. The most popular and best-paid bands were white, and the well-paying studio jobs created by the emergence of radio as the preeminent medium for disseminating the music were almost completely restricted to white musicians.

"From verb to noun" means, on the aesthetic level, a less dynamic, less improvisatory, less blues-inflected music and, on the political level, a containment of black mobility, a containment of the economic and social advances that might accrue to black artistic innovation. The domain of action and the ability to act suggested by *verb* is closed off by the hypostasis, paralysis, and arrest suggested by *noun*, the confinement to a predetermined status Baraka has in mind when he writes: "There should be no cause for wonder that the trumpets of Bix Beiderbecke and Louis Armstrong were so dissimilar. The white middle-class boy from Iowa was the product of a culture which could *place* Louis Armstrong, but could never understand him" (153–54). This confinement to a predetermined status (predetermined stasis), the keeping of black people "in their place," gives rise to the countering, contestatory tendencies I will be talking about as a movement from noun to verb.

My topic, then, is not so much otherness as othering, black linguistic and musical practices that accent variance, variability—what reggae musicians call "versioning." As Dick Hebdige notes: " 'Versioning' is at the heart not only of reggae but of *all* Afro-American and Caribbean musics: jazz, blues, rap, r&b, reggae, calypso, soca, salsa, Afro-Cuban and so on" (12). When Baraka writes of John Coltrane's recording of Billy Eckstine's "I Want to Talk About You," he emphasizes what could be called Trane's versioning of the tune, what I would call his othering of it:

> Instead of the simplistic though touching note-for-note replay of the ballad's line, on this performance each note is tested, given a slight tremolo or emotional vibrato (not to chord to scale reference), which makes it seem as if each one of the notes is given the possibility of "infinite" qualification . . . proving that the ballad as it was written was only the beginning of the story. (Baraka, *Black Music* 66)

Trane himself spoke of his desire to work out a kind of writing that would allow for "more plasticity, more viability, more room for improvisation in the statement of the melody itself" (Hentoff). His lengthy solos caused some listeners to accuse him of practicing in public, which, in a sense that is not at all derogatory, he was—the sense in which Wilson Harris calls one of his novels *The Infinite Rehearsal*.

Such othering practices implicitly react against and reflect critically on the different sort of othering to which their practitioners, denied agency in a society by which they are designated other, have been subjected. The black speaker, writer, or musician whose practice privileges variation subjects the fixed equations which underwrite that denial (including the idea of fixity itself) to an alternative. Zora Neale Hurston writes of the gossipers and storytellers in *Their Eyes Were Watching God*:

> It was the time for sitting on porches beside the road. It was the time to hear things and talk. These sitters had been tongueless, earless, eyeless conveniences all day long. Mules and other brutes had occupied their skins. But now, the sun and the bossman were gone, so the skins felt powerful and human. They became lords of sounds and lesser things. They passed nations through their mouths. (9–10)

Hurston is one of the pioneer expositor-practitioners of a resistant othering found in black vernacular culture. In her essay "Characteristics of Negro Expression," published in the thirties, she writes: "What we really mean by originality is the modification of ideas. . . . So if we look at it squarely, the Negro is a very original being. While he lives and moves in the midst of a white civilization, everything he touches is reinterpreted for his own use" (49). Baraka's valorization of the verb recalls a similar move on Hurston's part thirty years earlier, her discussion of "verbal nouns" as one of black America's contributions to American English. She emphasizes action, dynamism, and kinetics, arguing that black vernacular culture does the same: "Frequently the Negro, even with detached words in his vocabulary—not evolved in him but transplanted on his tongue by contact—must add action to it to make it do. So we have 'chop-axe,' 'sitting-chair,' 'cook-pot' and the like because the speaker has in his mind the picture of the object in use. Action." She goes on to list a number of "verbal nouns," nouns and adjectives made to function as verbs, and "nouns from verbs," verbs masquerading as nouns. *Funeralize, I wouldn't friend with her,* and *uglying away* are among her examples of nouns and adjectives functioning as verbs, *won't stand a broke* and *She won't take a listen* among those verbs masquerading as nouns.

The privileging of the verb, the movement from noun to verb, linguistically accentuates action among a people whose ability to act is curtailed by racist constraints. I prefer to see a connection between such privileging and such curtailment than to attribute the former, as Hurston occasionally does, to black primitivity. Language is symbolic action, frequently compensatory action, addressing deprivations that it helps its users to overcome. The privileging of the verb, the black vernacular investment in what Hurston calls "action words," makes this all the more evident. The sort of analysis found in the passage from *Their Eyes Were Watching God* that I quoted is brought to bear on the movement from noun to verb in a piece that Hurston published in the early forties, "High John de Conquer." The High John the Conqueror root that plays so prominent a role in African American hoodoo is here personified and figured as a key to black endurance and resilience, "the secret of black song and laughter." In the title and throughout the piece, Hurston elides the last syllable of *conqueror,* as is frequently done in black speech. In doing so, honoring the vernacular in more senses than one, she changes *conqueror* to *conquer,* noun to verb, practicing what she expounds on in "Characteristics of Negro Expression."

Hurston presents High John de Conquer as an inner divergence from outward adversity, the ability of enslaved Africans to hold themselves apart from circumstance. "An inside thing to live by," she calls it. She relates High John de Conquer to a propensity for laughter, story, and song, to black liberties taken with music and language. He embodies mastery of sound and mastery through sound, "making a way out of no-way." High John de Conquer moves quickly, as mercurial as he is musical: "His footsteps sounded across the world in a low but musical rhythm as if the world he walked on was a singing-drum. . . . He had come from Africa. He came walking on the waves of sound." He embodies music, storytelling, and laughter as a kind of mobility, a fugitivity that others the slaves' condition:

> He walked on the winds and moved fast. Maybe he was in Texas when the lash fell on a slave in Alabama, but before the blood was dry on the back he was there. A faint pulsing of a drum like a goat-skin stretched over a heart, that came nearer and closer, then some-body in the saddened quarters would feel like laughing and say, "Now, High John de Conquer, Old Massa couldn't get the best of *him*. . . ."

Hurston writes of the song High John de Conquer helps the slaves find: "It had no words. It was a tune that you could bend and shape in most any way you wanted to fit the words and feelings that you had."

The bending and shaping of sound, black liberties taken with music and language, caused Lucy McKim Garrison, one of the editors of *Slave Songs in the United States*, to write in 1862: "It is difficult to express the entire character of these negro ballads by mere musical notes and signs. The odd turns made in the throat, and the curious rhythmic effect produced by single voices chiming in at different irregular intervals, seem almost as impossible to place on the score as the singing of birds or the tones of an Aeolian Harp." Another of its editors, William Allen, likewise wrote:

> What makes it all the harder to unravel a thread of melody out of this strange network is that, like birds, they seem not infrequently to strike sounds that cannot be precisely represented by the gamut, and abound in "slides from one note to another and turns and cadences not in articulated notes. . . . " There are also apparent irregularities in the time, which it is no less difficult to express accurately.

Henry G. Spaulding wrote in 1863: "The most striking of their barbaric airs it would be impossible to write out." The compilers of the Hampton spirituals, M. F. Armstrong and Helen W. Ludlow, wrote similarly a decade later: "Tones are frequently employed which we have no musical characters to represent. . . . The tones are variable in pitch, ranging through an entire octave on different occasions, according to the inspiration of the singer."[1] One could go on and on with similar statements. Western musical notation's inability to capture the tonal and rhythmic mobility and variability such quotes remark on confirms the fugitive spirit Hurston identifies with High John de Conquer. "It is no accident that High John de Conquer has evaded the ears of white people," she writes, punning on while poking fun at the use of accidentals by Garrison, Smith, and others to approximate the flatted or bent notes of the African American's altered scale.

Fugitive spirit has had its impact on African American literary practices as well. As fact, as metaphor, and as formal disposition, the alliance of writing with fugitivity recurs throughout the tradition. One recalls that in 1829 George Moses Horton hoped to buy his freedom with money made from sales of his book of poems, *Hope of Liberty*. One thinks of the role played by literacy in Frederick Douglass's escape, of Harriet Jacobs's denunciations of the Fugitive Slave Law, of the importance of the slave narratives to the antislavery movement. W. E. B. Du Bois referred to the essays in *The Souls of Black Folk* as "fugitive pieces," and the impact of fugitive spirit can also be found in the work of William Melvin Kelley (the mass exodus in *A Different Drummer*, the bending and reshaping of language in *Dunfords Travels Everywheres*), Ishmael Reed (Quickskill in *Flight to Canada*), Toni Morrison (the flying African in *Song of Solomon*, the "lickety-split, lickety-split" at the end of *Tar Baby*, Sethe's escape in *Beloved*), and others. Ed Roberson, for example, in a recent poem called "Taking the Print":

See night in the sunlight's starry reflection
off the water   darkening the water
by contrast.
                    The dark hiding in the water
also hid us in the river at night
Our crossing guided by the internal sight
on our darkness
                    the ancient graphis
and -from this passage of abductions and escapes-
this newer imprimatur of the river
cut deep in the plate.
                    see in the river the ripples'
picture on the surface of the wind the lifting of the
image
has taken at the deeper face
                    the starry freedom
written in the milky rivery line that pours
the brilliance of that image from a depth only black
night fleeing across this land
                    has to voice

An especially good example of the movement from noun to verb's identification or alliance with fugitive spirit is Aimé Césaire's 1955

poem "The Verb 'Marroner' / for René Depestre, Haitian Poet." Written
in response to Louis Aragon and the French Communist party's call for a
return to traditional poetic meters and forms, which Depestre supported
in the journal *Présence africaine,* the poem insists on openness, experimentation, and formal innovation:

> Comrade Depestre
> It is undoubtedly a very serious problem
> the relation between poetry and Revolution
> the content determines the form
>
> and what about keeping in mind as well the dialectical
> backlash by which the form taking its revenge
> chokes the poems like an accursed fig tree (368)

The poem announces and enacts its poetics under the sign of a neologis-
tic verb. Césaire invokes the history of fugitive slaves in the Caribbean,
the runaway Africans known as maroons who escaped the plantations
and set up societies of their own. The French noun for this phenomenon,
marronage, is the basis for the word, the verb *marroner,* Césaire invents,
an act of invention exemplifying the independence for which the poem
calls. The coinage has no English equivalent. Clayton Eshleman and
Annette Smith translate it "escape like slaves":

> Is it true this season that they're polishing up sonnets
> for us to do so would remind me too much of the sugary
> juice drooled over there by the distilleries on the mornes
> when slow skinny oxen make their rounds to the whine
> of mosquitoes
>
> Bah! Depestre the poem is not a mill for
> grinding sugar cane absolutely not
> and if the rhymes are flies on ponds
>   without rhymes
>   for a whole season
> away from ponds
>   under my persuasion
> let's laugh drink and escape like slaves
> (Césaire 368–71)

Such invention in Césaire's work, such othering of and taking of liberties with French, has been referred to as "a politics of neologism" (Clifford 175). A similar practice can be found in the work of another Ca-

ribbean poet, Edward Kamau Brathwaite, who writes of Césaire: "His fabulous long poem *Cahier d'un retour au pays natal* (1939) evolved the concept of *negritude:* that there is a black Caliban Maroon world with its own aesthetics (*sycorax*), contributing to world and Third World consciousness" (Brathwaite, *X/Self* 129–30). Brathwaite's second trilogy, consisting of *Mother Poem, Sun Poem,* and *X/Self,* is characterized by a versioning of English he calls "calibanization," a creolization "which comes into conflict with the cultural imperial authority of Prospero" (*Mother Poem* 121). One of the remarkable features of the work, one of the features any reader will come away from it unable to forget, is its linguistic texture—not only what is done with words but what is done to them. Brathwaite makes greater use of West Indian nation-language (the term he puts in place of "dialect" or "patois") than in the first trilogy, *The Arrivants,* but what he is doing goes further than that. In his use of "standard" English as well, he takes his cue from the vernacular, subjecting words to bends, breaks, deformation, reformation—othering.

Brathwaite concludes the next-to-last poem in *The Arrivants* with the lines, "So on this ground, / write; / . . . on this ground / on this broken ground" (265–66). Nation-language, what some would call broken English, partakes of that ground. "Calibanization" insists that in West Indian folk speech English is not so much broken as broken into, that a struggle for turf is taking place in language. "It was in language," Brathwaite has written, "that the slave was perhaps most successfully imprisoned by his master; and it was in his (mis-)use of it that he perhaps most effectively rebelled. Within the folk tradition, language was (and is) a creative act in itself" (Brathwaite, *Development* 237). This tradition of black liberties taken with language informs *Mother Poem, Sun Poem,* and *X/Self* with the weight of a history of anti-imperial struggle, a weight felt in so small a thing as the word. As in the anagrammatic "derangement" Shakespeare had recourse to in fashioning *Caliban* from *cannibal,* the puns, malapropisms, odd spellings, neologisms, and strained meanings Brathwaite resorts to speak of disturbances outside as well as inside the language, social disruptions the word is thus made to register.

Changing *militia* to *malitia* is one small example (Brathwaite, *Sun Poem* 56). As in this instance, most of Brathwaite's "calibanisms" underscore senses of malice and malaise, emphasize the hurt put on the land and on the people by slavery, the plantation system, colonialism, capitalism. The words partake of that hurt. It shows in the language both as referent and as a telling misuse inflicted on English, an abuse which brings that referent more emphatically to light. *The panes of his eyes* becomes *the pains of his eyes; the games we played* becomes *the games we paid; landscape* becomes *landscrape; the future* becomes *the few-/ture.* Huts becomes *hurts* and *hillsides* turn into *hillslides:*

> but those that drone their lorries all day up the sweating
> hill to the factory of mister massa midas
> those mindless arch
>
> itects that cut the cane
> that built their own hurts on the hillslide
> (Brathwaite, *Sun Poem* 61)

Brathwaite avails himself of and takes part in a revolution of the word that has long been a part of Caribbean folk culture, a reinvention of English of the sort one hears in Rastafarian speech, where *oppressor* gets replaced by *downpressor, livicate* takes the place of *dedicate,* and so forth.

But a revolution of the word can only be a beginning. It initiates a break while remaining overshadowed by the conditions it seeks to go beyond. The shadow such conditions cast makes for a brooding humor that straddles laughter and lament, allows no easy, unequivocal foothold in either. Oppositional speech is only partly oppositional. Cramp and obstruction have to do with it as well. In Brathwaite's trilogy we not only get the sorts of pointed, transparent wordplay I just quoted, but something more opaque and more disconcerting, not resolved as to its tone or intent. Brathwaite revels in a sometimes dizzying mix of parody and pathos, an embrace complicated by a sense of the bizarre and even bordering on embarrassment here and there. His otherings accent fugitive spirit and impediment as well, the predicaments that bring fugitive spirit into being:

> but is like we still start
> where we start/in out start/in out start/in out start/in
> out since menelek was a bwoy & why
> is dat & what is de bess weh to seh so/so it doan sounn like
>
> brigg
> flatts nor hervokitz
> nor de pisan cantos nor de souf sea
> bible
>
> nor like ink. le & de anglo saxon
> chronicles

&

a fine
a cyaan get nutten

write

a cyaan get nutten really
rite
while a stannin up here in me years & like i inside a me shadow
like de man still mekkin i walk up de slope dat e slide
in black down de whole long curve a de arch
i
pell
ago
(Brathwaite, *X/Self* 85–86)

Brathwaite helps impeded speech find its voice, the way Thelonious Monk makes hesitation eloquent, or the way a scat singer makes inarticulacy speak. This places his work in the New World African tradition of troubled eloquence, othered eloquence, I'm here sketching. Here, that is, trouble acts as a threshold. It registers a need for a new world and a new language to go along with it, discontent with the world and the ways of speaking we already have. A revolution of the word can only be a new beginning, "beating," as Brathwaite puts it, "its genesis genesis genesis genesis / out of the stammering world" (*Sun Poem* 97).

My reference to Monk, as Hurston would say, is no accident. Indeed, had Hurston written "Characteristics of Negro Expression" later, she might have included "Rhythm-a-ning" and "Jackie-ing," two Monk titles, in her list of "verbal nouns." In her section on asymmetry ("Asymmetry," she begins it by saying, "is a definite feature of Negro art"), she might have quoted Chico O'Farrill's comments on the advent of bebop in the forties:

It was such a new thing, because here we were confronted for the first time with phrases that wouldn't be symmetrical in the sense that string-music phrasing was symmetrical. Here we were confronted with phrases that were asymmetrical. They would come in into any part of the phrase they felt like, and, at first, also the changes threw us off completely because it was a complete new harmonic—not new, but we'll say unusual harmonic concept that was so alien to what we had been doing. To us it was such a drastic change that I think anything that came afterwards wasn't as drastic as that particular first step from swing to bop. I think in a sense bop probably marks the real cut-off point of the old concept of swinging. I don't mean in the sense of swinging—we were still swinging—but the concept of the square structure of the music as to this new particular way of playing and writing. (Gitler, *Swing to Bop* 153)

The bebop revolution of which Monk was a part—Ellington called it "the Marcus Garvey extension"—was a movement, in its reaction to swing, from noun to verb. It was a revolution that influenced a great number of writers, Brathwaite included, as can be seen, among other places, in his early poem "Blues" (*Other Exiles* 12–16). Its impact on Baraka's work and thought can be seen not only in *Blues People* but in the poetics, the valorization of the verb, in the 1964 essay "Hunting Is Not Those Heads on the Wall" (Baraka, *Home* 173–78). There he espouses a poetics of process, arguing: "The clearest description of now is the present participle. . . . Worship the verb, if you need something." Halfway through the essay he mentions Charlie Parker, having earlier remarked: "I speak of the *verb process*, the doing, the coming into being, the at-the-time-of. Which is why we think there is particular value in live music, contemplating the artifact as it arrives, listening to it emerge." The sense he advances that "this verb value" is an impulse to "make words surprise themselves" recalls the popular description of jazz as "the sound of surprise."

The white appropriation and commercialization of swing resulted in a music that was less improvisatory, less dependent on the inventiveness of soloists, than was the case with music played by African Americans. The increased reliance on arrangements in the Fletcher Henderson mold led to a sameness of sound and style among the various bands. In *Blues People* Baraka quotes Hsio Wen Shih's comments regarding the anthology album *The Great Swing Bands*, a record Shih refers to as "terrifying" because of the indistinguishability of one band from another. It was against this uniformity that bebop revolted. "Benny Goodman," Howard McGhee recalls, "had been named the 'King of Swing'. . . . We figured, what the hell, we can't do no more than what's been done with it, we gotta do somethin' else. We gotta do some other kind of thing" (Gitler, *Swing to Bop* 314). ("Some other stuff," a common expression among black musicians, would become the title of an album by Grachan Moncur III in the sixties.) Mary Lou Williams said of her first meeting with Monk in the thirties: "He told me that he was sick of hearing musicians play the same thing the same way all the time" (Cuscuna). Monk himself summed up his music by saying: "How to use notes differently. That's it. Just how to use notes differently" (Gitler, Liner notes). It is no accident that bebop was typically performed by small combos rather than the big bands that were featured in swing. It accentuated individual expression, bringing the soloist and improvisation once more to the fore.

Baraka emphasizes nonconformity in his treatment of bebop in *Blues People*, stressing what he terms its "willfully harsh, *anti-assimilationist* sound" (181). The cultivation of a unique, individual style of black music encourages, informs, and inspires his attitudes toward writing. In his statement on poetics for the anthology *The New American Poetry, 1945– 1960*, Baraka echoes Louis Armstrong's ad-libbed line on a 1949 recording of "My Sweet Hunk o' Trash" with Billie Holiday, calling it "How You Sound??" The emphasis on self-expression in his work is also an emphasis on self-transformation, an othering or, as Brathwaite has it, an X-ing of the self, the self not as noun but as verb. Of the postbop innovations of such musicians as Albert Ayler and Sun Ra, Baraka writes: "New Black Music is this: Find the self, then kill it" (*Black Music* 176). To kill the self is to show it to be fractured, unfixed. The dismantling of the unified subject found in contemporary critical theory is old news when it comes to black music. I've seen Bukka White break off singing to exhort himself: "Sing it, Bukka!" Charles Mingus's autobiography begins: "In other words, I am three" (7). A recent composition by Muhal Richard Abrams has the title "Conversation with the Three of Me." Craig Harris remarks of the polyrhythmicity of one of his pieces: "It's about cutting yourself in half."

Our interest in cultural diversity—diversity within a culture as well as the diversity of cultures—should lead us to be wary of hypostasis, the risk we take with nouns, a dead end that will get in the way of change unless "other," "self," and such are "given the possibility of 'infinite' qualification."[2] Wilson Harris in his novel *The Infinite Rehearsal* has written of "qualitative and infinite variations of substance clothed in nouns," arguing that "nouns may reveal paradoxically when qualified, that their emphasis on reality and their inner meaning can change as they are inhabited by variable psychic projections" (Harris, *Explorations* 139). In his new novel, *The Four Banks of the River of Space*, Harris speaks of "the instructive bite of music" on the way to suggesting that "breaking a formula of complacency" consists of "becoming a stranger to oneself" (140–41). As Monk's tune "Jackie-ing" tells us, even a so-called proper noun is a verb in disguise—present-participial, provisional, subject to change. John Gilmore, the tenor saxophonist with Sun Ra's band for some thirty years, tells a story about the time he spent with Art Blakey's

Jazz Messengers in 1965. After about a month, he says, the music was at so inventive a level that one night in Los Angeles, following one of his solos, trumpeter Lee Morgan looked over at him and asked: "Is that you, Gilmore?" Morgan then took a solo that caused Gilmore to ask the same thing of him: "Lee, is that you?" (Sato 21).

II

The "nounization" of swing furthered and partook in a commoditization of music that, as Jacques Attali points out, had been developing in the West since the 1700s. "Until the eighteenth century," he writes in *Noise: The Political Economy of Music*, "music was of the order of the 'active'; it then entered the order of the 'exchanged'" (57). The process was completed in the twentieth century, he argues, with the birth of the recording industry and its exploitation of black musicians: "Music did not really become a commodity until a broad market for popular music was created. Such a market did not exist when Edison invented the phonograph; it was produced by the colonization of black music by the American industrial apparatus" (103). The transition from "active" to "exchanged," verb to noun, reflects the channeling of power through music it is the point of the book to insist on:

> Listening to music is . . . realizing that its appropriation and control is a reflection of power, that it is essentially political. . . . With music is born power and its opposite: subversion. . . . Music, the quintessential mass activity, like the crowd, is simultaneously a threat and a necessary source of legitimacy; trying to channel it is a risk that every system of power must run. . . . Thus music localizes and specifies power, because it marks and regiments the rare noises that cultures, in their normalization of behavior, see fit to authorize. (Attali 6, 14, 19–20)

Attali is at all points alive to the shamanic roots of music, its magico-prophetic role, no matter how obscured those roots and that role tend to be by the legal, technological, and social developments he goes to great lengths to analyze and describe.

The idea of music as a conduit of power, a channeler of violence, a regulator of society, is particularly visible—unobscured—among the Carib-speaking Kalapalo of the Upper Xingu Basin in Brazil. Ellen B. Basso, in her study *A Musical View of the Universe: Kalapalo Myth and Ritual Performances*, deals with their ideas regarding sound and what she terms "orders of animacy," a hierarchic taxonomy at the top of which the Kalapalo place entities known as "powerful beings." These beings are nonhuman, though they sometimes appear in human form, and, Basso points out, "they are preeminently and essentially musical":

> Powerful beings are different from concrete historical figures because they and their acts are "always" and everywhere. . . . This multiplicity of essence or "hyperanimacy" is coupled on the one hand with a multiplicity of feeling and consequent unpredictability and on the other with a monstrous intensity of some feeling or trait; hence powerful beings are dangerous beings. . . . Their hyperanimacy and multiplicity of essence are perhaps what is deeply metaphorized by their association with musical invention. (69–70)

Music represents the highest degree or level of animacy, hyperanimacy, and in their musical performances the Kalapalo model themselves on their images of powerful beings, aspiring to the condition of powerful beings. They seek both to endow themselves with and to domesticate hyperanimate power. Basso writes:

> Music (or more exactly, musical performance) is identified by the Kalapalo as having controlling force over aggressive, transformative, and wandering power; it is also a manifestation of that power. The ability of music to control and channel aggression, to limit hyperanimacy in ways that are helpful to people, has further consequences for understanding its importance within ritual contexts. This is because in such contexts of use, political life—the relations of control that some people effect over others—achieves its most concrete and elaborate expression. (246)

I would like to highlight two features of Kalapalo thought and practice concerning music and bring them to bear, by way of analogy, on the minstrel show, a form of theatrical performance unique to the United States that emerged during the 1820s and reached its apex between 1850 and 1870. An appropriation of the slave's music and dance by white men who blackened their faces with burnt cork, going on stage to sing "Negro songs," perform dances derived from those of the slaves, and tell jokes based on plantation life, the minstrel show is an early instance of the cannibalization of black music to which we saw Attali refer. "Minstrelsy," Robert C. Toll observes in *Blacking Up: The Minstrel Show in Nineteenth Century America*, "was the first example of the way American popular culture would exploit and manipulate Afro-Americans and their culture to please and benefit white Americans" (51). The first of the two aspects of Kalapalo thought and practice I would like to highlight is the fact that powerful beings are associated with darkness and with the color black, that for ritual performances the Kalapalo shaman darkens himself with pot black as a way of becoming, Basso explains, "less visibly human and appearing more like a powerful being" (248). Blacking up, the white minstrel practice of donning blackface makeup, amounts to a pseudoshamanic performance in which the power of black musicality is complimented yet simultaneously channeled, caricatured, and contained. As is not the case for the Kalapalo shaman, for the white minstrel "less visibly human" means less than human, even as the appeal and the power of the music are being exploited.

Minstrelsy reveals the ambivalent, duplicitous relationship of nineteenth-century white Americans not only to black people but to music and language. The second aspect of Kalapalo thought and practice I would like to highlight relates to this, having to do with the distinctions the Kalapalo make among calls, speech, and music, and among degrees of animacy. Human beings share with entities of lesser animacy the ability to emit calls and with entities of greater animacy, powerful beings, the ability to speak and to make music, but it is speech that is regarded as quintessentially human. Speech is the form of sound by which humans are characterized and symbolized in the taxonomic order, music the form with which powerful beings are identified. Interestingly, calls as well as music are considered more truthful, more trustworthy than speech:

> Human beings can express truthful and empirically motivated feelings best through *itsu* [calls]. Pain of varying degrees of intensity, deep sadness, shame, joy, sexual passion, frustration with oneself, indeed, the entire range of human emotion is expressed most succinctly (and by implication as truthful feeling) this way.
>
> Human beings are distinguished from other *ago* [living things], however, by their ability to speak, and it is through language that they are most commonly symbolized and distinguished from other categories of entities. . . . But language allows people to do something very different from animals. Human beings were created by a trickster, whose name "Taugi" means "speaks deceptively about himself". . . . Hence human beings are in essence deceitful beings because of their ability to speak. Therefore, people are capable not only of truthfully expressing their feelings, but—and this is the unmarked understanding of human speech for the Kalapalo—of creating an illusory screen of words that conceals their true thoughts. (67–68)

Music, the Kalapalo believe, is more to be trusted than speech because, rather than masking the mental, powerful beings "in J. L. Austin's sense . . . are performative beings, capable of reaching the limits of awareness of meaning by constructing action through a process that is simultaneously mental and physical" (71).

Calls and music both put sound in the service of sentience. In this they differ from speech, which valorizes the sentence, the humanly constructed realm of meaning, grammaticality, predication. The minstrel show, in its recourse to music (the slave's music, moreover, in which calls, cries, and hollers played a prominent part) and in its "translation" of that music into songs of sentiment (Stephen Foster's "Old Folks at Home," "Massa's in de Cold, Cold Ground," and so forth), critiqued even as it exemplified the deceptiveness of language. The implicit critique, the recourse to music and to sentimentality, to songs that advertised themselves as innocent of ambiguity, insincerity, or circumlocution, was accompanied by an explicit critique. This took the form of the stump speech and its malapropisms, the heavy reliance on wordplay and puns in minstrel humor and such routines as the following, called "Modern Language":

> *Bones:* How things have changed of late. A man can't depend on anything. A man must discount his expectations by at least 80 percent.
> *Midman:* In other words, "never count your chickens before they are hatched."
> *Bones:* That sort of language is not up to the four hundred. You should say that this way: Never enumerate your feathered progeny before the process of incubation has been thoroughly realized.
> *Midman:* That does take the rag off the bush.
> *Bones:* Wrong again. You should not say that. You should say: That removes the dilapidated linen from off the shrubbery. (*Complete Minstrel Guide* 49–50)

While the stump speech poked fun at black people's alleged insecure hold on language, such humor as this poked fun at language itself, at language's—especially elevated language's—insecure hold on the world. Minstrelsy, under cover of blackface, was able to vent apprehensions regarding the tenuousness of language, even as it ridiculed its target of choice for a supposed lack of linguistic competence. In regard to language as in other matters, the minstrel show allowed its audience to have it both ways.

One of the reasons for minstrelsy's popularity was what Alexander

Saxton terms "the flexibility of standards which flourished behind the fake façade of blackface presentation" (12). That façade made it permissible to refer to such topics as homosexuality and masturbation, which were taboo on the legitimate stage, in the press, and elsewhere. Sentimental songs and female impersonation, as did the blackface façade, allowed performers and audience alike access to a world of emotion that was otherwise held to be off limits. Minstrelsy's wide appeal had largely to do with the illusion of escape from conventional strictures it afforded, the degree to which it spoke to a white, predominantly male imaginary. Minstrel star George Thatcher's description of his feelings after seeing his first minstrel show as a boy alerts us to the deep psychic forces at work (and also, incidentally, sheds light on the title of John Berryman's *Dream Songs*, which, dedicated to Thomas D. Rice, the "father" of blackface minstrelsy, makes use of the minstrel figure Bones): "I found myself dreaming of minstrels; I would awake with an imaginary tambourine in my hand, and rub my face with my hands to see if I was blacked up. . . . The dream of my life was to see or speak to a performer" (Toll 33).

The influence of blackface minstrelsy extended well into the present century, having an impact on vaudeville, musical comedy, radio, movies, television, and other forms of popular culture. It tells us a great deal regarding the obstacles in the way of a genuine multiculturality or cross-culturality, a genuine, nonexploitative cultural exchange. Toll recounts that in 1877 Bret Harte and Mark Twain wrote a minstrel play based on a poem of Harte's about the "heathen chinee." On opening night, Twain explained to the audience: "The Chinaman is getting to be a pretty frequent figure in the United States and is going to be a great political problem and we thought it well for you to see him on the stage before you had to deal with the problem." Toll goes on to remark that Twain's is a clear and accurate statement of one of minstrelsy's functions: "Although on the surface they just sang songs and told jokes about peculiar people, minstrels actually provided their audiences with one of the only bases that many of them had for understanding America's increasing ethnic diversity" (169). This base, however, was an impediment rather than an aid to cultural diversity, a strategy of containment through caricature designed to consolidate white privilege and power. The minstrel made use of music to channel power in the service of "orders of animacy" in which whites came out on top, to uphold unequally distributed orders of agency in which violence, albeit under control, was never out of the picture. Saxton remarks of a minstrel song: "This 'comic-banjo' piece, as it was described, appeared in a songster published in New York in 1863. Geographically and emotionally, it was only a block or two from a song such as this to the maiming and lynching of blacks on the sidewalks of New York during the draft riots of the same year" (23).

The subject of cultural diversity and the goal of a healthy cross-culturality are haunted by the specter of such appropriation as the minstrel legacy represents. We should not be surprised that not only pop-cultural but also high-cultural and avant-garde venues number among its haunts. I am thinking, for example, of Gertrude Stein's early piece "Melanctha," described by her in "Composition as Explanation" as "a negro story." Katherine Mansfield, reviewing the book in which "Melanctha" appears, *Three Lives*, heard sentences overwhelmed by sound and sentience, much to her alarm. Moreover, she heard it as a minstrel band, a channeling of black musicality into prose:

> Let the reader go warily, warily with *Melanctha*. We confess we read a good page or two before we realised what was happening. Then the dreadful fact dawned. We discovered ourselves reading in *syncopated time*. Gradually we heard in the distance and then coming uncomfortably near, the sound of banjos, drums, bones, cymbals and voices. The page began to rock. To our horror we found ourselves silently singing "Was it true what Melanctha said that night to him" etc. Those who have heard the Syncopated Orchestra sing "It's me—it's me—it's me" or "I got a robe" will understand what we mean. *Melanctha* is negro music with all its maddening monotony done into prose; it is writing in real ragtime. Heaven forbid Miss Stein should become a fashion. (Sprigge 124–25)

The analogue to what Mansfield misapprehends as black musical monotony, Stein's notorious use of repetition advances a critique of language that is not unrelated to the one we see in the minstrel show. Under cover of blackness, she issues an avant-garde caveat regarding the trustworthiness of the linguistic sign and of the discursive, ratiocinative order it promotes. The search for and the nature of "understanding" are pointedly at issue in the story, especially in the relationship between impulsive, sensation-seeking Melanctha and reflective, respectability-minded Jeff:

> "Yes I certainly do understand you when you talk so Dr. Campbell. I certainly do understand now what you mean by what you was always saying to me. I certainly do understand Dr. Campbell that you mean you don't believe it's right to love anybody." "Why sure no, yes I do Miss Melanctha, I certainly do believe strong in loving, and in being good to everybody, and trying to understand what they all need, to help them." "Oh I know all about that way of doing Dr.

> Campbell, but that certainly ain't the kind of love I mean when I am
> talking. I mean real, strong, hot love Dr. Campbell, that makes you
> do anything for somebody that loves you." "I don't know much about
> that kind of love yet Miss Melanctha. You see it's this way with me
> always Miss Melanctha. I am always so busy with my thinking about
> my work I am doing and so I don't have time for just fooling, and then
> too, you see Miss Melanctha, I really certainly don't ever like to get
> excited, and that kind of loving hard does seem always to mean just
> getting all the time excited. That certainly is what I always think
> from what I see of them that have it bad Miss Melanctha, and that
> certainly would never suit a man like me." (85–86)

On a typical page of dialogue between the two, the word *certainly* occurs
as often as twenty times. Such repetition undermines the word, underscoring the uncertainty in which the two of them are immersed. Words
are treated as though, rather than sticking to the real, as Jack Spicer
put it, they were continually slipping from it. Repetition compulsively
moves to make up for that slippage, accenting all the more the words'
insecure grip on the world. Not unlike the Kalapalo, Jeff at one point
complains that "the ordinary kind of holler" would offer "much more
game," much more forthright expression (127). The story strongly suggests that the order of what the Kalapalo term *itsu* is where "understanding" most unproblematically resides:

> And now the pain came hard and harder in Jeff Campbell, he groaned,
> and it hurt him so, he could not bear it. And the tears came, and his
> heart beat, and he was hot and worn and bitter in him.
>   Now Jeff knew very well what it was to love Melanctha. Now Jeff
> Campbell knew he was really understanding. (145)

"Melanctha" recalls minstrelsy in that Stein uses one form of marginality, blackness, to mask another, to mask two others in fact—the
avant-garde linguistic experimentation that we just noted (experimental
writing being relegated to the fringes by middle-brow, if not outright
philistine American predilections) and, albeit much less evident, lesbi-
anism. Janice Doane and Carolyn Copeland argue that "Melanctha," as
Copeland puts it, "is not really a story about the ethnic reality of Negroes" (Copeland 24), that the story reworks material from the earlier
novel *Q.E.D.* "Melanctha" can be said to be *Q.E.D.* done in blackface.
Doane writes that "the lesbian affair of *Q.E.D.* is converted into the
heterosexual affair of the 'Melanctha' story" (52). Copeland says the
same at greater length:

It will be recalled that *Q.E.D.*, written in 1903, concerned three homosexual women involved in a triangle. When one considers the trouble Theodore Dreiser had with *Sister Carrie* during that same period, it is not surprising that Gertrude Stein dropped the homosexual elements from her story before using the material again. Some very important elements of *Q.E.D.*, however, would have become problematic in a simple shift from homosexual to heterosexual in the story, and these elements must be discussed briefly.

Adele and Helen together undergo a full and complete series of sexual experiences, and obviously they are not married when they experience them. It is important to Adele's full realization of how completely "out of rhythm" she and Helen are that they not be married. Adele must be able to walk away from the experience with no ties such as marriage to complicate it. At the turn of this century in America the only background against which a writer could portray premarital sexual relationships without having an outraged white, middle-class public to contend with was one dealing with Negroes. It was part of the white man's view of the black man that they were sexually promiscuous. If Gertrude Stein wished to drop the homosexual elements and make them heterosexual, her choice of Negroes instead of whites allowed her to retain as much as possible of the important extramarital elements involved. And this is exactly what she did. (24–25)

Orders of marginality contend with one another here. It is instructive that blackness is the noun-mask under whose camouflage two other forms of marginality gain an otherwise blocked order of animacy or agency, an otherwise unavailable "verbness." We are at the sacrificial roots of the social order, the ritual murder of which music, Attali argues, is the simulacrum. Under cover of scapegoat blackness, the otherwise marginal cozies up to the center.[3]

I say this not to encourage turf wars among marginalized groups or individuals, but to raise a question. Wilson Harris writes of marginality in a way that is as promising as it is challenging. "Extremity or marginality, in my view," he writes, "lifts the medium or diverse experience to a new angle of possibility. . . . It involves us in a curiously tilted field in which spatial pre-possessions and our pre-possessions are dislodged. . . . Marginality is a raised contour or frontier of habit in the topography of the heart and mind" (Harris, "In the Name" 15). I think of this tilt as arising to contend with another form of tilt—that of unevenly allotted orders of agency, the unfair playing field, as it is commonly put.[4] I think

of the tilt of Edgar Pool's tenor saxophone in John Clellon Holmes's novel
The Horn:

> Edgar Pool blew methodically, eyes beady and open, and he held his
> tenor saxophone almost horizontally extended from his mouth. This
> unusual posture gave it the look of some metallic albatross caught
> insecurely in his two hands, struggling to resume flight. In those
> early days he never brought it down to earth, but followed after
> its isolated passage over all manner of American cities, snaring it
> nightly, fastening his drooping, stony lips to its cruel beak, and
> tapping the song. (8)

The idiosyncratic tilt of "isolated originality," modeled on Lester Young:

> It was only one of many bands he worked those years, the tireless
> jumping colored bands that flourished like a backwash after the
> initial wave of swing. But already he was blowing strange long lines,
> rising out of the section, indrawn and resolute, to stand before the
> circling dancers, tilt the big horn roofward from his body, and play
> his weightless, sharply veering phrases over the chunking of unsub-
> tle drums. In those days, no one heard. (89)

I also, however, think of another tilt we see in the novel, that of a whisky
bottle "tilted into the coffee as he [Pool] spiked it generously" (194)
during the last night of an alcoholic binge, the last night of his life. The
tilt of entropy, exhaustion, disillusionment. Hence, my question: Which
tilt will it be? In order that the latter not prevail, the discourse on cultural
diversity will have to acknowledge both.

By this I mean that we need more than content analyses based on
assumptions of representationality. The dislocating tilt of artistic othering, especially as practiced by African American artists, deserves a great
deal more attention than it has been given. While the regressive racial
views of white writers like Stein and Ezra Pound tend to be regarded (if
they are regarded at all) as secondary to their artistic innovations, black
writers tend to be read racially, primarily at the content level, the noun
level, as responding to racism, representing "the black experience." That
black writers have been experimentally and innovatively engaged with
the medium, addressing issues of form as well as issues of content, tends
to be ignored. The ability to have an impact on and to influence the
course of the medium, to *move* the medium, entails an order of animacy
granted only to whites when it comes to writing. The situation with
regard to music is a bit better, black musicians having been acknowledged to be innovators, even though their white imitators enjoy commer-

cial success and critical acclaim greatly disproportionate to their musical contributions. The nonrecognition of black artistic othering is symptomatic of the social othering to which black people are subjected, particularly in light of the celebration accorded artistic othering practiced by whites. This is a disparity that the discussion of cultural diversity should be addressing.

Perhaps we can increase not only the quantity but also the quality of attention given to African American art and cultural practices. Perhaps we can make it possible for the music of Henry Threadgill or David S. Ware to be as widely known as that of Wynton Marsalis; Ed Roberson's *Lucid Interval as Integral Music* or Will Alexander's *The Black Speech of the Angel* to win the sort of acclaim accorded Rita Dove's *Thomas and Beulah*; Amiri Baraka to be as well known for *The Dead Lecturer* as for *Dutchman*. If we are to do so, we must, à la Césaire, confront the neotraditionalism that has taken hold of late with a countertradition of marronage, divergence, flight, fugitive tilt. Henry Dumas put it well in "Black Trumpeter": "The wing praises the root by taking to the limbs" (52).

Notes

1 Lucy McKim Garrison, William Allen, Henry G. Spaulding, M. F. Armstrong, and Helen W. Ludlow are all quoted in Southern, 191–94.

2 Artistic othering pertains to intracultural as well as intercultural dialectics. The will to change whereby African American culture reflects critically on the dominant white culture is intertwined with its impulse to reflect critically on itself, the will to change whereby it redefines, reinvents, and diversifies itself. Bebop, for example, was a reaction to the datedness of the music played by black swing musicians as well as to its appropriation by white musicians. No last word, no seal of prophecy, bebop in turn became dated, subject to the changes initiated by Ornette Coleman, Cecil Taylor, Albert Ayler, and others during the late fifties and early sixties. An aspect of intracultural dialectics that we should not overlook is the role of eccentric individuals whose contributions come to be identified with the very culture which may have initially rejected them. Think of Ornette Coleman being beaten up outside a Baton Rouge dance hall in 1949 for interjecting "modern" runs into an R&B solo (Spellman 101). The recent ascendancy of cultural studies in academia tends to privilege collectivity and group definition over individual agency and self-expression, to see individual expression as a reflection of group definition. In relating the two, however, we should remember that in matters of artistic othering, individual expression both reflects and redefines the collective, realigns, refracts it. Thus it is that Lester Young was in the habit of calling his saxophone's keys his people. Bill Crow reports that when the keys on Young's horn got bent during a Jazz at the Philharmonic tour, Young went to Flip Phillips for help. "Flip," he said, "my people won't play!" (Crow 272).

3   For a discussion of Stein's racist view of black people and of "Melanctha" as "the signpost of modernism's discourse on the nonwhite," see Nielsen 21–28.

4   Hurston, in "Characteristics of Negro Expression": "After adornment the next most striking manifestation of the Negro is Angularity. Everything that he touches becomes angular."

Works Cited

Attali, Jacques. *Noise: The Political Economy of Music.* Trans. Brian Massumi. Minneapolis: U of Minnesota P, 1985.

Baraka, Amiri [LeRoi Jones]. *Black Music.* New York: Morrow, 1967.

———. *Blues People: Negro Music in White America.* New York: Morrow, 1963.

———. *Home: Social Essays.* New York: Morrow, 1966.

Basso, Ellen B. *A Musical View of the Universe: Kalapalo Myth and Ritual Performances.* Philadelphia: U of Pennsylvania P, 1985.

Brathwaite, Edward Kamau. *The Arrivants: A New World Trilogy.* Oxford: Clarendon, 1973.

———. *The Development of Creole Society in Jamaica, 1770–1820.* Oxford: Clarendon, 1971.

———. *Mother Poem.* Oxford: Oxford UP, 1977.

———. *Other Exiles.* London: Oxford UP, 1975.

———. *Sun Poem.* Oxford: Oxford UP, 1982.

———. *X/Self.* Oxford: Oxford UP, 1987.

Césaire, Aimé. *The Collected Poetry, 1939–1976.* Trans. Clayton Eshleman and Annette Smith. Berkeley: U of California P, 1983.

Clifford, James. *The Predicament of Culture: Twentieth-Century Ethnography, Literature, and Art.* Cambridge, Mass.: Harvard UP, 1988.

Complete Minstrel Guide. Chicago: n.p., n.d.

Copeland, Carolyn. *Language & Time & Gertrude Stein.* Iowa City: U of Iowa P, 1975.

Crow, Bill. *Jazz Anecdotes.* New York: Oxford UP, 1990.

Cuscuna, Michael. Liner notes. *Complete Blue Note Recordings of Thelonious Monk.* 1983. Mosaic MR4-101.

Doane, Janice. *Silence and Narrative: The Early Novels of Gertrude Stein.* Westport, Conn.: Greenwood, 1986.

Dumas, Henry. *Play Ebony, Play Ivory.* New York: Random, 1974.

Gitler, Ira. Liner notes. *Thelonious Monk Live at the It Club.* 1982. Columbia C2-38030.

———. *Swing to Bop: An Oral History of the Transition in Jazz in the 1940s.* New York: Oxford UP, 1985.

Harris, Craig. Liner notes. *Black Bone.* 1984. Soul Note SN 10550.

Harris, Wilson. *Explorations: A Selection of Talks and Articles, 1966–1981.* Mundelstrup, Denmark: Dangaroo P, 1981.

———. *The Four Banks of the River of Space.* London: Faber, 1990.

———. *The Infinite Rehearsal.* London: Faber, 1987.

———. "In the Name of Liberty." *Third Text* 11 (Summer 1990): 8–15.

Hebdige, Dick. *Cut 'n' Mix: Culture, Identity, and Caribbean Music.* London: Methuen, 1987.

Hentoff, Nat. Liner notes. *Coltrane Live at the Village Vanguard Again!* 1966. Impulse AS-9124.

Holmes, John Clellon. *The Horn.* 1958. New York: Thunder's Mouth, 1988.

Hurston, Zora Neale. *Their Eyes Were Watching God.* 1937. Urbana: U of Illinois P, 1978.

——. "Characteristics of Negro Expression." *The Sanctified Church.* Berkeley: Turtle Island, 1981. 49–68.

——. "High John de Conquer." *Sanctified Church.* 69–78.

Mingus, Charles. *Beneath the Underdog.* 1971. New York: Penguin, 1980.

Nielsen, Aldon Lynn. *Reading Race: White American Poets and the Racial Discourse in the Twentieth Century.* Athens: U of Georgia P, 1988.

Roberson, Ed. "Taking the Print." *Hambone* 9 (Winter 1991): 2.

Sato, Art. "Interview with John Gilmore." *Be-Bop and Beyond* 4.2 (Mar.–Apr. 1986): 15–21.

Saxton, Alexander. "Blackface Minstrelsy and Jacksonian Ideology." *American Quarterly* 27.1 (Mar. 1975): 3–28.

Southern, Eileen. *The Music of Black Americans: A History.* New York: Norton, 1983.

Spellman, A. B. *Black Music: Four Lives.* 1966. (Originally published as *Four Lives in the Bebop Business.*) New York: Schocken, 1970.

Sprigge, Elizabeth. *Gertrude Stein: Her Life and Work.* New York: Harper, 1957.

Stein, Gertrude. *Three Lives.* New York: Penguin, 1990.

Toll, Robert C. *Blacking Up: The Minstrel Show in Nineteenth Century America.* New York: Oxford UP, 1974.

Historical Context and the Definition of Jazz: Putting More of the History in "Jazz History"

WILLIAM HOWLAND KENNEY

The beloved hipster maxim that anyone "square" enough to ask what jazz is would never understand it anyway expresses a cultish inner circle perspective unlikely to either impress or assist scholars. Much formative jazz writing, so often what historians would call "primary source" testimony, evidence from first-hand observers, avoided formal definitions. Although the late Martin Williams (*Tradition*), following the lead of André Hodeir, suggested that jazz possessed a definitive rhythmic essence, he otherwise defined it by a series of examples of a musical tradition shaped by selected, musically influential performers and records. Musicologist Gunther Schuller also preferred to define jazz indirectly through musical analysis of what he judged to be its outstanding practitioners and by his manner of organizing them into major stylistic periods. His glossaries of musical and jazz terms have not included the word "jazz."

Several recent writers have more directly addressed the question of how "jazz" can be defined. Three of them, Charles Keil, Mark Gridley, and Lee B. Brown, have reinforced what might be called an essentialist notion by identifying certain characteristics without which music cannot be jazz. Gridley has been the clearest and most precise of the three by describing a large number of musicians, groups, and recordings that fit his definition.

Neither the Williams/Schuller approach nor that of Gridley et al. manages, however, to distinguish jazz from other closely related musical genres. Many have believed it better to leave the boundaries between jazz and nonjazz as vague as possible in order not to define jazz away. Williams and Schuller likely did not mean to suggest that any musician omitted from their analyses should be considered to have played something other than jazz. (They probably were making qualitative musical judgments, however.)

But once the focus of inquiry shifts from the qualitative musical considerations that make jazz greats great to the more historical task of describing the extent and limits of past jazz activity and offering conclusions about its significance in American life, present definitions prove both too narrow and too vague: too narrow because many more musicians played jazz in the past than those select few who made it into the canon of jazz criticism; too vague because some of the musical characteristics of jazz turn up on the records of groups that rejected, sometimes emphatically, the label itself.[1]

Unfortunately, one of the first to pursue a nonmusicological approach that focused on the social and political functions of jazz also bitterly attacked it. German sociologist Theodor Adorno created a sweeping definition of jazz in its social and cultural context.[2] Unlike the American jazz writers and musicologists, who have rather pointedly ignored his work, Adorno attempted to decode its political implications. Defining jazz as a type of entertainment and dance music that first appeared in 1914, Adorno argued that "propagandistic jazz writers" had perpetrated what amounted to an elaborate misrepresentation; they had put forward the false notion of a jazz rebellion against social and political regimentation. Actually, he claimed, jazz functioned as a capitalistic commodity, a form of "pseudo-individualization" disguised in the elaborate trappings of proletarian primitivism and spontaneity. Unlike the other writers mentioned, all of whom have worked on definitions of jazz, Adorno provided no specific historical context (and precious few factual examples) for his definition. He seems to have been writing about jazz in Germany during the interwar years.

Kathy Ogren, departing from a similar sociocultural perspective but achieving a much greater historical depth and racial awareness, has provided the best rebuttal of Adorno. Ogren has defined jazz in 1920s' America as an Afro-American form of communication, both within the black community and between the races. Her focus on the cultural context of black performance practices in the United States during the 1920s suggests an entire level of meaning to which Theodor Adorno was blind.

Ogren's in-depth treatment of jazz in a national-historical and cultural context may be further narrowed so as to focus on specific musicians in particular historical times and places. James Lincoln Collier, for example, has provided instances of valuable historical context in his jazz biographies and, more particularly, his analysis of the reception of jazz in the United States during the 1920s.[3]

As these and other scholars such as Leroy Ostransky and Neil Leonard[4] recognize, musicians as much as everyone else, live and perform within the opportunities and constraints of their time. Jazz styles have manifestly changed over time, sometimes, as in the case of the movement from jazz bands to swing bands and from swing to bebop, with a remarkable abruptness. Current definitions of jazz, however, too often assume that the musicians existed in a historical vacuum. Schuller has made gestures in the direction of historical context (*Swing Era*, 3–5), but the music made by the musicians he discusses remains largely unaffected by any social, economic, and political forces. Musicians form and re-form jazz styles according to musical considerations alone. According to Adorno, who makes much more room for an abstract sort of social context, jazz musicians and jazz itself always function in one particular way in society no matter where or when one looks at them.

The growing interest in re-creating the cultural process that produced jazz has gained impetus from parallel debates stimulated by Lawrence Levine over the creation of cultural hierarchies in the United States.[5] A clearer recognition of the cultural and historical process by which certain art forms received exclusive institutional entitlement in the United States has encouraged a greater recognition of the role of political and historical forces in shaping all of them. At the same time, as Krin Gabbard has shown, some influential jazz writers have tried to discredit the privileged position of European concert-hall music in the United States by creating a jazz canon of superior recorded performances that would, among other things, demonstrate a strong counterclaim that jazz should be enshrined as "America's Classical Music."[6]

Ambiguities affecting both the definition of jazz and of the music's canon in a context lacking historical specificity are reflected in the problematical distinctions drawn by discographer Brian Rust, for example, between jazz records and dance band records. Rust separated the two styles into different discographies, gathering some into *Jazz Records, 1897–1942*, while listing the others in *The American Dance Band Discography*. Rust thought of dance band music as "commercial," "sweet," "romantic," and, of course, music meant for dancing. Jazz, on the other hand, tended to be "hot," and, by implication at least, noncommercial, unsweet, unromantic, and not for dancing. The "sweet romantic styles of Guy Lombardo and Wayne King" provided Rust's example of dance music "which clearly was not Jazz" (*Dance*, i).

Rust nevertheless readily admitted to much overlap between jazz and dance music and selected some dance band recordings for inclusion in his *Jazz Records*. For example, he considered some records by what he called " 'commercial' dance bands, usually made up of white musicians" to be "undeniably excellent," and therefore these were included in his jazz discography. He also incorporated in his definition of jazz those "dance records of the kind described at the time of their original issue as 'hot'" (*Jazz Records* I, i). Thus, he found that he was even forced to include in *Jazz Records* some records made by Guy Lombardo and His Royal Canadians, one of the major examples of a dance band that normally did not play jazz, remarking that although Lombardo had "long been associated with the most saccharine form of dance music," aural analysis of his records revealed that "when required, he and his band could play as 'hot' as any of their contemporaries" (*Jazz Records*, II, 1028). As a host of deceased hipsters writhe in their graves, Guy Lombardo is enshrined in the jazz discography on the strength of a handful of records that he made during a long and productive career devoted to recording sweet dance music.

Uncertainties like these muddy the definition of the jazz canon since the discographer nowhere defined his terms, which, moreover, appear to have proceeded primarily from his personal aesthetic judgments. Would another discographer have produced a different listing of jazz records for the period? How to explain, furthermore, that the "hot" dance band records which Rust selected for inclusion in *Jazz Records* also appeared in the dance band discography? None of the jazz records appear in the dance band discography. Did Rust mean to suggest that from 1897 to 1942, a jazz orchestra could or would only play jazz, whereas a dance band played either dance music or jazz or both? Most importantly from the historian's point of view, did contemporaries of the orchestras in question make the same distinctions in the same way as the midcentury British discographer?

A closer look at a sample of dance records made by Chicago dance bands in the 1920s, less celebrated but still known in jazz circles, will begin to put the historical dimensions of such definitional problems into a clearer perspective. While confirming that jazz functioned as a form of popular music in 1920s' Chicago, this essay will underline the significance of differences in the positions and functions of jazz and dance orchestras within the musical entertainment business at that particular time and place.

All of Chicago's dance bands of the twenties, for example, recorded many records that both reflected and generated nineteenth-century Victorian sensibilities. Rust excluded these from his jazz discography. Moreover, the groups that he included in *Jazz Records* did not record this more overtly sentimental material. For example, even though Guy Lombardo and His Royal Canadians did record hot stomps like "St. Louis Blues," "The Cannon Ball," and "Mama's Gone, Goodbye," records that Rust heard as jazz, they were more likely to record waltzes (the bane of flaming youth in the Roaring Twenties) like "Charmaine," "Ramona," and "Sweet Chewaulka, The Land of Sleepy Water" and a broad range of mawkish vocal numbers like "Sweet Dreams," "Please Let Me Dream in Your Arms," and "You're the Sweetest Girl This Side of Heaven" (*Dance* 1109–11). Without explaining it further, Rust likely felt that sentiment-filled ballads with achingly nostalgic lyrics about the singer's high regard for a genteel white woman somehow did not qualify as jazz.

This lingering Victorian sentiment ("sweetness and light" in Matthew Arnold's famous words), a genteel remnant of an earlier era, survived in prominent sectors of society and characterizes the recorded work of all of the Chicago dance bands that sometimes played jazz.[7] For example, Rust included many records by the Benson Orchestra of Chicago, one of the foremost dance bands of the Windy City's Roaring Twenties, in his jazz discography. Not only did this group record hot jazz tunes like Jelly Roll Morton's "Wolverine Blues" and "King Porter Stomp," but the band sometimes included the highly regarded jazz C-melody saxophone solo-ist Frank Trumbauer (*Jazz Records*, I, 132–34).[8] On the other hand, this group's recorded renditions of waltzes like "Pal of My Cradle Days," "I'm Drifting Back to Dreamland," and "Tears of Happiness" (not to speak of its bathetic immortalization of "Fair One," "Lonely Little Wallflow'r," and "After All, I Adore You") generate genteel sensibilities much more rarely if ever found on the jazz records. A powerful cultural conservatism that Rust may have taken for granted generated the late Victorian sensibilities to which the discographer only eluded in separating jazz from dance band records in 1920s' Chicago.

In some important ways, jazz in Chicago of that day functioned in tension with these often sweetly gentle sensibilities. Dance bands like Guy Lombardo's and Edgar Benson's played in large, racially segregated dance halls or hotel ballrooms. Lombardo, for example, played at Al Quodbach's large, streamlined, segregated Granada Cafe, while Edgar Benson long controlled the dance bands playing at most of the leading Chicago dance halls—the Trianon Ballroom, Merry Gardens, and Guyon's Paradise.[9] That jazz bands were pointedly not hired to play in these prominent dance halls did much to earn them their jazz band name.

Dance band musicians and entrepreneurs worked within Chicago's popular music establishment, while their jazz counterparts were usually relegated to its fringes. Three major differences consequently distinguished dance bands from jazz bands: first, they responded to different performance environments; second, they played distinct roles in the phonograph record business; and third, they often occupied opposite sides of the racial lines that cut across the popular music business.

These differences played important roles in contemporary definitions of jazz. Chicago's large dance halls and hotel ballrooms represented major capital investments in the mass entertainment business. Vast numbers of young blue-collar workers flowed into and through the major neighborhood dance halls: Dreamland Ballroom and Guyon's Paradise on the West Side, White City, the Trianon, and the Midway Ballroom on the South Side, and the Arcadia and Cinderella Ballrooms on the North Side. These institutions built their reputations by catering to divergent elements within the dancing public. White City Ballroom and Guyon's Paradise catered to an older, more conservative clientele; *Variety* characterized the music at Guyon's Paradise as "A service brand of dance music—peppy but not hotsy totsy."[10] *Orchestra World*, a dance band trade paper of the 1920s, reported that "in keeping with the well-known Guyon policy, the band plays none of the real hot music, but . . . 'sweet' or 'snappy.' "[11]

White City Casino and the Midway Gardens, on the other hand, encouraged hot Roaring Twenties dance music for young sheiks and shebas. *Variety* likened the music of Sig Meyers's Casino Druids at White City Casino to "a blast from a furnace"; the band, which included some of the hottest aspiring white Chicago jazzmen such as Danny Altiere, Arnold Loyocano, Wop Waller, and Benny Goodman was "full of sock."[12] But sweeter, more restrained, gentler dance bands performed for the older generation in the White City Ballroom, a larger dance area with a cushioned dance floor for tired feet. Clearly, some dance bands got hotter than others, but they all catered in a particularly open manner to such immense numbers of people that some middle ground had to be fashioned between what the younger set considered stodgy Victorian sentiments and the latest jazz howls.

Chicago's urban reformers contributed to the historical differences between the city's jazz bands and dance bands by encouraging this middle-of-the-road music policy in the dance halls. Deeply concerned about the combined impact of dance halls, alcoholic beverages, and cheap hotels on city youth, Jane Addams, Louise de Koven Bowen, and Jesse Binford spearheaded the Juvenile Protective Association, an organization that exerted pressure on the owners of all of Chicago's major dance halls to ban the sale of alcohol, prohibit lewd dancing, and police the darker corners inside their buildings. Through their paid chaperons, urban reformers policed "obscene" dance steps like the shimmy (in which a woman manipulated her pectoral muscles in time to the rhythm) or the "dip" (during which the man bent his partner backward until her head touched the floor, at which moment the woman would kick up one leg "so that [her] privates were shown").[13] Reform pressure also led to the creation of the National Association of Ballroom Managers and Proprietors, which facilitated voluntary cooperation between the dance halls and urban reformers. The NABMP sponsored chaperons in its member dance halls and policed the music provided by the various dance bands.[14]

By the same token, the major center city (Loop) hotels, located in proximity to major railroad terminals, catered to the relatively affluent among tourists and business travelers. They offered supper clubs and ballrooms in which some of the most prominent dance bands of the twenties performed. In these establishments, a one dollar *"couvert charge"* acted as a "sort of refiner keeping the undesirable element away and attracting the type of patron that a hotel desires" (H. Leonard). So, too, the major urban hotels worked hard to create an atmosphere of elegance and social restraint in their dine-and-dance clubs and ballrooms. In the privacy of their rooms, hotel patrons might drink whatever alcoholic beverages that a bellhop had purchased for them or that they had brought in with them, but the major hotel ballrooms and dine-and-dance clubs were too prominent to openly defy the Volstead Act and function as speakeasies. Orchestra leaders coordinated their music with the maître d'hôtel, playing fifteen-minute (five three-minute dance selections) dance periods followed by twelve-minute intermissions. Special efforts were made to avoid interference with the food service. The dance orchestra musicians were required to be "at all times immaculate in appearance, gentlemanly in conduct, clean-cut, well-bred, and business-like. . . . " They should take care never "to assert authority or assume an attitude of superiority (H. Leonard)."[15]

In Chicago during the twenties, Edgar Benson fashioned exclusive booking arrangements with the Sherman House, Drake, Edgewater Beach, Blackstone, LaSalle, and Bismark hotels. Trade papers alleged that Benson created such bookings through kickback schemes; wealthy hotel patrons would hire his bands for private parties, and Benson "kicked back" to the hotel a percentage of what he earned. Benson's power in the dance band business served to impede the passage of newer jazz sounds into hotel clubs and to promote weaker dilutions of jazz. At one time or another, Benson booked the orchestras of Ben Bernie, Roy Bargy, Paul

Biese, the Oriole Orchestra at Edgewater Beach, Arnold Johnson, Dell Lampe, Don Bestor, Frank Westphal, Jean Goldkette (before he moved to Detroit), and his own Benson Orchestra. These bands moved about, playing long-term contracted runs at the Green Mill Gardens, Trianon Ballroom, Marigold Gardens, Merry Gardens, the Pershing Palace, Crillon, Deauville, the Tent, Silver Slipper, La Boheme, Pantheon, the Senate, Tip Top Room, Rector's, the North American, the Midway Gardens, and Guyon's Paradise. As *Variety* put it: "It is next to impossible for any outside orchestra to come into Chicago at the recognized Benson thresholds. . . ."[16]

By citing certain dance band records in his discography, Brian Rust included in his definition of jazz recordings some records by professional dance band musicians and leaders who refused to embrace the term "jazz" itself. Dance hall and hotel band leaders, even those otherwise fairly favorably disposed to jazz, strove to avoid the label itself. For example, Isham Jones, whose orchestra played for years in the racially exclusive College Inn of the Loop's Sherman Hotel, a major tourist institution, recorded many jazz numbers in the 1920s. Bix Beiderbecke is said to have frequented the College Inn to listen to Jones's trumpeter Louis Panico (Sudhalter et al.). But Jones went on record as denying that his music was jazz, insisting that most dance band musicians considered jazz a " 'down South Negro type' of blues." To better indicate the wider range and more refined sensibilities encouraged by his orchestra, Jones preferred that his music be called "American Dance Music."[17]

Similarly, in the mid-twenties, dance bandleader Meyer Davis had sponsored a contest to rename "jazz" for people who apparently disliked the word's sociological implications. "Synco-Pep" won from a group of sanitizing euphemisms, which included "Rhythmic-reverie," "Rhapsodoon," "Peppo," "Exilera," "Hades Harmonies," "Paradisa," "Glideola," and "Mah Song." Chicago's Edgar Benson exerted a much more negative influence on jazz, letting it be known that he would accept only "novelty and symphonic syncopating combinations without the general noisy effects produced by jazz bands."[18] The hotel dance orchestra often defined itself in contrast to the "rackety, 'blarey' conglomerations of noise makers" of past years, searching for something "softer," with a "fullness of tonal quality . . . decidedly more melodious and symphonic."

The compromises fashioned between urban reformers and the owners and managers of the leading dance halls and ballrooms did not extend to the nightclubs or cabarets in which jazz musicians and jazz bands most often performed. Jazz in Chicago was intimately involved with cabarets and nightclubs, which were financially and morally more marginal institutions than the dance halls and hotel ballrooms. Cabarets usually occupied one or two floors of nondescript city buildings. The cabaret owner's actual investment might stop well short of the building itself and involve only rental of the space structured into a cabaret. Someone else, as Prohibition agents often discovered, might own the building itself.[19] When pressured by Prohibition agents, a clever club owner like Chicago's Mike Fritzel, who owned the popular Friars Inn, easily closed down his celebrated Loop club and kept a step or two ahead of the law thereafter by opening and closing nightclubs faster than municipal and federal agents could follow (Starr; Fritzel).

Moreover, cabarets and nightclubs, by plying their trade in close association with the bootleggers who defied Prohibition, turned their jazz musicians into outlaws. Technically, cabarets were not speakeasies, since the sale of illegal alcoholic beverages was not the overt focus of their business activities. Chicago's Sunset Cafe, Plantation Cafe, Dreamland Cafe, and Friars Inn usually allowed their customers to secure booze from street merchants hanging around the sidewalk out front or from waiters who had been given money to purchase the bottle off the premises. This little shell game made the clubs themselves guilty only of serving glasses, ice, water, and sodas to people they knew to be drinking alcohol. Until 1927 the courts allowed cabarets to remain in business until a federal court interpreted the legality of these activities under the Volstead Act. In 1927 the federal courts ruled that such activities defied the act, and Chicago's leading cabarets were padlocked ("U.S. Wars").[20] Cabaret work, therefore, placed jazz musicians in a morally more marginal position than those who worked only in hotel and dance hall orchestras. Jazz activity participated in the defiance of the Victorian moral sensibilities that fueled Prohibition.

The historical distinctions between jazz and social dance music went beyond their different performance environments. Chicago's dance bands occupied a more established and lucrative position in the phonograph record business than its jazz bands. In the 1920s the dance bands overwhelmingly recorded for the higher-priced record labels—Brunswick, Victor, and Columbia. The jazz bands recorded for specialty labels usually aimed at ethnic and racial audiences—Gennett, Okeh, Paramount, and Vocalion. Prices varied with market conditions, but the higher-priced labels generally retailed for $1.00 or more per record while the smaller specialty labels sold for 75 cents or less in music stores. Paramount race records, a blues and jazz label, actually sold for 27.5 cents per disc to wholesalers who then marked them up to 45 cents apiece for sale to dealers (Rust, *American Record Label*).[21]

But the differing roles and positions of the dance and jazz groups within the record business did not end there. The dance orchestras usually contained twelve musicians, while the jazz bands often used around seven. The recording company's expenses were correspondingly higher in making a dance band record than one by a jazz band. This helps to explain the different pricing levels.

Moreover, because of both copyright and close business associations, the record companies paid royalties to the sheet-music publishers whenever they issued a recording of a published song. This further increased production expenses while cementing business relations between the song publishers and the record company executives. According to *Variety,* recording company studio managers kept lists of numbers they wanted to record and invariably passed the list first to "the[ir] premier orchestra" which picked all the "hit numbers," that is, tunes that had already sold exceptionally well in sheet-music form. The list then moved on to the lesser name orchestras, each of them picking from the most promising numbers left available (Green 37). Thus, under this system Isham Jones likely would have had the first pick of potential hit tunes at Brunswick Records, followed by Russo and Fiorito's Oriole Orchestra from the posh Edgewater Beach Hotel, and Charlie Straight and his [Rendez Vous Cafe] Orchestra.

Jazz polyphonies even endangered the well-established musical arrangements that turned out hit melodies. As the New York *Clipper* put it: "A well written melodious number is so buried under the jazz antics of scores of orchestras that the audience can scarcely recognize the melody. . . . " Dance bands like the Benson Orchestra featured plenty of unadorned melody, emphasizing, as James Lincoln Collier has put it, "smooth exposition of melody, with good tone, clean attack, [and] accurate execution, at the expense of improvised risk-taking" (*Armstrong* 239).

This musical policy assured the continued support of the music publishing houses. Once a likely hit had been recorded, promotional activity could become intense as well-known recording bands appeared in vaudeville, cabarets, hotels, and even music stores, where the windows were decorated with special publicity streamers, hangers, folders, catalogs, and cardboard cutouts. Such arrangements for choosing songs left the "minor bands" to record only "numbers with freaky 'blues' titles . . . or straight fox-trots of only local popularity or passing familiarity."

Jazz bands in Chicago did record some drably conventional popular song material (eminently suitable for dancing), but they tended more often to record original numbers of their own creation. Record companies were looking for racial and novelty music from certain types of musicians during the 1920s. Dave Peyton, the popular music columnist for the *Chicago Defender*, the city's leading black newspaper, tried to establish himself as an orchestra leader of symphonic and refined dance music and complained bitterly about the way black musicians were stereotyped by the recording industry: "In the past the big recording companies have confined our musicians to one style of recording. This style of recording they consider our orchestras are perfected in. They confine us to low jazz and blues. They have an idea that our orchestras cannot play real music for recordings, but they never were so wrong" (10).[22] Clearly, the racial policies of the recording companies in the 1920s effectively encouraged the development of jazz by black musicians. To pair within the definition of jazz those musicians who specifically rejected the label and those who were not allowed to record anything but jazz does a historical injustice to the jazz musicians.

The unthinking assumption that the record companies simply recorded music that had long been "out there" has obscured their power in shaping jazz. Rust even listed black Chicago dance bands like the Doc Cook Dreamland Orchestra and Charles Elgar's Creole Orchestra in *Jazz Records* despite the fact that each performed primarily at Chicago's racially segregated Dreamland Ballroom, where African Americans could work and perform but not dance. Pressure from record company representatives probably forced these orchestras into recording jazz-like material, since South Side Chicago jazz musician Willie Randall recalled that the Elgar band played "good *bona fide* ballroom music" at Harmon's Dreamland. "I don't say you would identify it and tag it as jazz . . . " he said.

The motivations given to black musicians to record original jazz, blues, and novelty numbers did give both bands and record companies something more promising to record, since no one could really predict when some original "novelty" number would catch on with the public. These business relations also held out to the company the possibility of exceptionally high profits, since the corporation usually purchased the original numbers outright for a modest sum and therefore paid no royalties to composers or sheet-music publishers (Calt 17).[23]

Specific historical forces therefore distinguished jazz performance activity from that of the dance bands. The range of musical sensibilities, particularly the influence of late Victorian sentiment, distinguished dance band from jazz records. So, too, the social circumstances of the venues in which they played differed. The company labels that their records wore, the kinds of song material they presented, the prices at which the records were sold, the number of musicians used, and the financial arrangements under which they were made all differentiated jazz from dance records.

In general, Rust appears to have been historically accurate when he distinguished jazz from social dance music. The historical differences between these two types of popular music organizations also need to be kept in mind when we read Theodor Adorno. The influential sociologist frequently elided the two in his definition of jazz, arguing that jazz, as he understood it, functioned like commercial dance music ("On Jazz"). As we can now see, during the 1920s they actually occupied very different positions within the music industry and functioned differently in time and space.

But through all of these distinctions has run the most influential force of all, the role of race in the popular music business of the 1920s. The numerous exceptions that Rust made by including certain white dance band records in his jazz discography merely underlined the strong, indeed, nearly exclusive association of jazz with African American popular musicians. The *New Grove Dictionary of Jazz* defines jazz as a "music created mainly by black Americans . . . " (Kernfeld 580).

Once more, the definition involves musical matters, but the historical activities of jazz musicians in 1920s' Chicago will bear it out. Many of the cabarets in which black popular musicians played—Bill Bottom's Dreamland Cafe, the Sunset Cafe, the Plantation Cafe—were "black-and-tans," nightclubs in black neighborhoods that specialized in presenting black musical entertainment to racially mixed but often predominantly white audiences. Although a small number of influential African Americans owned leading black-and-tan cabarets in Chicago in the late 1910s and early 1920s, whites owned all of them by the end of the decade.

White-owned black-and-tans certainly did underline white control of the marketing of black music, but Adorno goes much too far in concluding that in the urban "manufacture" of jazz, "the skin of the black man functions as much as a coloristic effect as does the silver of the saxophone" ("On Jazz" 53). Since the actual musical process necessary to make jazz was far too esoteric in the 1920s to be understood by white cabaret owners in Chicago, those like Joe Glaser of the Sunset Cafe employed black floor show directors to create and stage musical entertainment. African American cabaret musicians fashioned their own secret musical knowledge and innovations into a small but dynamic sphere of artistic independence. They were hired to play a certain type of music, but white club owners did not know enough to tell them how to do it.

So, too, the companies for which jazz musicians recorded produced what the companies called "race records," gathering them into marketing catalogs of inexpensively produced discs by African American musicians making music intended for black customers. But African American recording directors worked with black musicians in controlling the musical content of race records. Like the black-and-tan cabarets, race records offered the musicians a strictly limited but tangible arena of artistic independence.

What, then, does greater attention to historical context contribute to recent attempts to define "jazz?" First, this less fully developed dimension reveals far better than aural evidence that jazz involved a set of specific social, economic, and racial experiences among those who performed it and those who eagerly listened to it. Jazz performers played in certain clubs that presented certain kinds of entertainment. Jazz performers were infrequently welcome in the leading venues where salaries were most impressive. Jazz performers often were black musicians working in a white-dominated music business, be it in cabarets, recording studios, or dance halls. Whatever their personal or group inclinations, jazz involved the experience of playing a certain type of music that white club and studio managers required of them (and it had to be "spontaneous"). It meant having to strain to hear their efforts through all the surface noise on cheaply made race records.

The irrevocability of the jazz stance for African American musicians could never be fully apprehended by white jazz musicians, but to the extent that white jazzmen in 1920s' Chicago such as Frank Teschemacher, Wild Bill Davison, Bud Freeman, Dave Tough, and Eddie Condon frequented the clubs where black musicians performed, rebelled against the culturally privileged white dance bands, modeled their playing styles on those of blacks, and gave priority to jazz over dance music, they could appreciate the black position and its intimate bearing on jazz.

Jazz experiences produced a cultural sensibility compounded of the repetitive education of working on the margins of the music business. By definition, most dance band musicians, especially those working regularly and happily in the hotel ballrooms and the more conservative dance halls—the Trianon, Aragon, and Guyon's Paradise—could not directly experience the stance of alienation that came so easily to jazz musicians. Contrary to Rust's practice, their "hot" records might be gathered, with more historical accuracy, into a separate Hot Dance Band discography or into a subsection of a dance band discography, even when a recognized jazz musician soloed.

More importantly, the specific historical context that shaped jazz performance and separated it from that of the dance bands changed over time in some significant respects. For example, the stock market crash of 1929, the ensuing economic depression, and the national enforcement of Prohibition destroyed many of the leading cabarets of the Roaring Twenties while leaving the large dance halls and hotel ballrooms in place. In addition to driving many musicians out of the business altogether, these adverse economic developments encouraged the further assimilation of jazz musicians into the surviving commercial dance bands.

The swing era, moreover extended and deepened the care with which Chicago dance band leaders like Edgar Benson, Isham Jones, Russo and Fiorito, and the rest had incorporated elements of jazz into their arrangements and repertoires while refusing to identify themselves directly with it by calling their music "jazz." The desire to fashion some new form of popular music like swing, one appropriate for the dance halls and ballrooms, one that would carry some jazz punch while skirting jazz's special moral and racial connections, would remain much alive from 1935 to 1945.

The stock market crash marked a turning point in the history of jazz and American popular music. Theodor Adorno wrote his first article on jazz in 1936, and his second, which appeared in 1967, refers to things like "jitterbugs" and "crooners." He seems, therefore, to have been reacting to the swing era, which was shaped by a whole new pattern of commercialization facilitated by the earlier bankruptcy and subsequent reorganization of the musical entertainment industry after 1929. Thanks to separate projects in progress by historians Lewis A. Erenberg, Victor Greene, Edward Pessen, and Burton Peretti, we will soon know much more about the cultural history of the swing era. For the moment, however, it appears that the commercial organization of jazz activity underwent such momentous changes during the depression that future discographers, very likely working under the umbrella of American music, will want to consider separating the records into groups that more accurately reflect the contrasting cultural contexts of this history.

Notes

The data in this article on jazz and social dance music in 1920s' Chicago are taken from my book, *Chicago Jazz: A Cultural History, 1904–1930.* I would like to thank Spencer Bennett, James Lincoln Collier, and Victor Greene for reading and criticizing this article.

1   The strong parallels in the cultural process that produced jazz and polka music emerge with a fascinating clarity from Greene. Erenberg builds a model for the rise of the sort of nightclubs in which both jazz and nonjazz musicians played.

2   See Adorno's "Perennial Fashion" and "On Jazz." His chapter on "Popular Music" in *Introduction to the Sociology of Music* should also be read in this context.

3   See Collier's books on Ellington, Armstrong, Goodman, and *The Reception of Jazz in America*. The compulsion to castigate Collier's interpretations without doing the scholarly work necessary to fully develop another point of view comes repeatedly from writers who often have interpreted jazz outside any historical context.

4   Leonard's first book (*Jazz and the White Americans*) did much to draw attention to the rewards of a cultural history of jazz. It also provided more specific historical context than his second work, *Jazz: Myth and Religion*, which focuses on a religious-oriented cultural process.

5   Peretti's *The Creation of Jazz* had not been published when this essay was being written.

6   Also see Williams, *The Smithsonian Collection of Classic Jazz*, and Sales.

7   See Trachtenberg, especially chap. 5. Mussulman analyses the musical ideology of the Gilded Age.

8   Edgar Benson's dominance of the band booking business in Chicago's leading hotels, ballrooms, and major cabarets is reported in *New York Clipper* 5 Apr. 1922: 29.

9   See *Variety* 8 Apr. 1925: 43; 22 Apr. 1925: 34; 6 May 1925: 49; 8 July 1925: 41.

10   *Variety* 16 Dec. 1925: 46. Also see Cressy.

11   *Orchestra World* 1 Dec. 1925: 16.

12   *Variety* 7 Oct. 1925: 50.

13   *New York Clipper* 9 Aug. 1919: 6; 18 May 1921: 12.

14   The refining influence of the NABRPM on dance halls is documented in the files of the Juvenile Protective Association, Special Collections, University Library, University of Illinois at Chicago.

15   *New York Clipper*, 9 May 1923: 18, reports on "a list of do's and don'ts" for musicians working in the large hotels and cafés.

16   Benson's control of Chicago's major hotel and supper club orchestras is documented in *Variety* 8 Apr. 1925: 43; 22 Apr. 1925: 34, 37; 6 May 1925: 49; 8 July 1925: 41; and *New York Clipper* 15 May 1924: 16.

17   The College Inn catered to "the better class of transients" in the Windy City tourist trade. See *New York Clipper* 12 Oct. 1923: 25.

18   *New York Clipper* 5 Apr. 1922: 29.

19   This was the case, for example, with South Side Chicago's famous Royal Garden Cafe. *Chicago Whip* 23 Dec. 1922: 1, 3.

20   Also see *Variety* 22 June 1927: 58; 26 Oct. 1927: 57; 30 Nov. 1927: 56; 8 Feb. 1928: 55; 15 Feb. 1928: 54, 62; 28 Mar. 1928: 37.

21   *New York Clipper*, 17 May 1922: 22, reported that Okeh was thinking of lowering its prices to 50 cents and that Columbia and Victor were interested in the idea. See Calt and Wardlow.

22   Peyton made similar accusations of broader scope in the *Chicago Defender* 21 May 1927: 8 and 13 Oct. 1928: 9.

23   Hennessey argues persuasively that these business practices at the record companies reduced the reliability of jazz records as indicators of the repertoire performed live by jazz bands in the clubs.

Works Cited

Adorno, Theodor W. "On Jazz." Trans. Jamie Owen Daniel. *Discourse* 12.1 (Fall–Winter 1989–90): 45–69.

——. "Perennial Fashion—Jazz." *Prisms.* Trans. Samuel and Shierry Weber. Cambridge, Mass.: MIT P, 1981.

——. "Popular Music." *Introduction to the Sociology of Music.* Trans. E. B. Ashton. New York: Seabury, 1976.

Brown, Lee B. "The Theory of Jazz Music: 'It Don't Mean a Thing. . . . ' " *Journal of Aesthetics and Art Criticism* 49 (1991): 115–27.

Calt, Stephen. "The Anatomy of a 'Race' Label, Part II." *78 Quarterly* 1 (1989): 17.

Calt, Stephen, and Gayle Dean Wardlow. "The Buying and Selling of Paramounts (Part 3)." *78 Quarterly* 1 (1990): 10.

Collier, James Lincoln. *Benny Goodman and the Swing Era.* New York: Oxford UP, 1989.

——. *Duke Ellington.* New York: Oxford UP, 1987.

——. *Louis Armstrong: An American Genius.* New York: Oxford UP, 1983.

——. *The Reception of Jazz in America: A New View.* Brooklyn, N.Y.: Institute for Studies in American Music, 1988.

Cressy, Paul G. *The Taxi-Dance Hall: A Sociological Study in Commercialized Recreation and City Life.* Chicago: U of Chicago P, 1932.

Daniel, Jamie Owen. "Introduction to Adorno's 'On Jazz.' " *Discourse* 12.1 (Fall–Winter 1989–90): 39–44.

Erenberg, Lewis A. *Steppin' Out: New York Nightlife and the Transformation of American Culture, 1890–1930.* Chicago: U of Chicago P, 1981.

Fritzel, Mike. Obituary. *Chicago Daily Tribune* 29 Sept. 1956: sec. 3:12.

Gabbard, Krin. "The Jazz Canon and Its Consequences." *Jazz Among the Discourses.* Ed. Krin Gabbard. Durham, N.C.: Duke UP, 1995. 1–28.

Green, Abel. "Abel's Comment." *Variety* 6 Aug. 1924: 37.

Greene, Victor. *A Passion for Polka: Old-Time Ethnic Music in America.* Berkeley: U of California P, 1992.

Gridley, Mark C. "What Is Jazz?" *Jazz Styles: History and Analysis.* Englewood Cliffs, N.J.: Prentice-Hall, 1988. Chap. 2.

Hennessey, Thomas J. *From Jazz to Swing: African-American Jazz Musicians and Their Music, 1890–1935.* Detroit: Wayne State UP, 1994.

Hodeir, André. *Jazz—Its Evolution and Essence.* Trans. David Noakes. New York: Grove, 1956. Trans. of *Hommes et problèmes du Jazz.* Paris: Parentheses, 1954.

Jones, Isham. "American Dance Music Is Not Jazz." *Etude Music Magazine* 42 (1924): 526.

Keil, Charles M. H. "Motion and Feeling Through Music." *Journal of Aesthetics and Art Criticism* 24 (Spring 1966): 337–49.

Kenney, William Howland. *Chicago Jazz: A Cultural History, 1904–1930.* New York: Oxford UP, 1993.

Kernfeld, Barry, ed. *New Grove Dictionary of Jazz.* New York: Macmillan, 1988.

Leonard, Harold. "The Hotel Dance Orchestra." *Orchestra World* 1 Feb. 1926: 5–6.

Leonard, Neil. *Jazz and the White Americans: The Acceptance of a New Art Form.* Chicago: U of Chicago P, 1962.

——. *Jazz: Myth and Religion.* New York: Oxford UP, 1987.

Levine, Lawrence. *Highbrow/Lowbrow: The Emergence of Cultural Hierarchy in America.* Cambridge, Mass.: Harvard UP, 1988.

Mussulman, Joseph A. *Music in the Cultured Generation: A Social History of Music in America, 1870–1900.* Evanston, Ill.: Northwestern UP, 1971.

Ogren, Kathy. *The Jazz Revolution: Twenties America and the Meaning of Jazz.* New York: Oxford UP, 1989.

Ostransky, Leroy. *Jazz City: The Impact of Our Cities on the Development of Jazz.* Englewood Cliffs, N.J.: Prentice-Hall, 1978.

Peretti, Burton. *The Creation of Jazz.* Urbana: U of Illinois P, 1992.

Peyton, Dave. "Recording Units." *Chicago Defender* 9 Mar. 1929: 10.

Randall, Willie. Interview with John Lax. 28 Dec. 1971. Columbia University Oral History Collection.

Rust, Brian. *American Dance Band Discography, 1917–1942.* New Rochelle, N.Y.: Arlington House, 1975.

——. *American Record Label Book.* New York: Da Capo, 1984.

——. *Jazz Records, 1897–1942.* 2 vols. Chigwell, Eng.: Storyville, 1975.

Sales, Grover. *Jazz: America's Classical Music.* Englewood Cliffs, N.J.: Prentice-Hall, 1984.

Schuller, Gunther. *Early Jazz: Its Roots and Musical Development.* New York: Oxford UP, 1968.

——. *The Swing Era: The Development of Jazz, 1930–1945.* New York: Oxford UP, 1989.

Starr, Louis M. "45 Years of Night Life." *Chicago Sun* 6 June 1943: 47.

Sudhalter, Richard M., and Philip R. Evans, with William Dean-Myatt. *Bix: Man and Legend.* New Rochelle, N.Y.: Arlington House, 1974.

Trachtenberg, Alan. *The Incorporation of America: Culture and Society in the Gilded Age.* New York: Hill and Wang, 1982.

"U.S. Wars on Chicago Night Life." *Chicago Herald and Examiner* 6 Feb. 1928: 1.

Williams, Martin. *The Jazz Tradition.* New York: Oxford UP, 1970.

——. *The Smithsonian Collection of Classic Jazz.* Washington, D.C.: Smithsonian Institution, 1973.

Oral Histories of Jazz Musicians: The NEA
Transcripts as Texts in Context

BURTON W. PERETTI

[Subject]: . . . when I was there in 1942, you needed a pass just to go on the beach. You couldn't go on Miami Beach.

[Interviewer]: This was people who were working there, you know.

[S]: Well, I—

[I]: (Inaudible) hotels had to be out of there by a certain time and if not, they had to have a pass.

[S]: See, I was working—I was there in—when was it I went down there, in '57 I went down there, it was. You had to have a pass then. You had to have a police card. Yeah. But it was a lot different than it was—in '42. But people survived those things, and I think the strongest people survived.

(Laughter)

[I]: Well, you had to be strong to survive. But the thing is, you know—

[S]: I tell the guys, though, when I went to Africa—after I came back from Africa, I said, thank God for slavery.

(Laughter)

I said, if it hadn't been for slavery, I'd still probably—I would be in Africa— Africa's nice, a pretty country, but—I've been all over the world, and there's no place like this country. Even as bad as it is, it's the best place in the world to be.

[I]: Now, you've been in Europe and Africa. How about the Far East? (Barefield 4:12)

Anyone who came to this exchange with no knowledge of the specific subject or participant would casually (or worryingly) notice some striking dynamics. The subject recalls that a pass was needed to walk on the beach in Miami but struggles to remember the precise year he or she was there, haltingly arriving at specific dates. The conversational syntax is repetitive, disturbs the reading eye, and seems wasteful. The interviewer, perhaps with the future reader in mind, supplies information regarding hotels, information that may or may not have had any meaning for the subject. In addition, the former's precise comment is "inaudible." The unknown third party who typed the transcript informs us of this. Other disorienting details of this nature pile up in a few short lines, in the course of which we also discern that the subject is a black American and that he or she was a victim of Jim Crow in Miami. We learn this from the astonishingly ironic payoff of this passage, the subject's declaration, "thank God for slavery." Even if we accept the fairly rational explanation that follows, the remark puzzles and consumes us—is it a joke? Signifyin'? The foundation of his attitude toward race relations in America? An easy laugh-getter from the guys? (If the last, why did they laugh?) After this specific puzzlement, we are more generally bemused by the limitations of the document, with its inaudible passages, mediocre interviewer, and frowsy lack of articulateness and crisp recollection. It is, at best, a dubious source for clues that might convey the meaning of the subject's curious final declaration.

The other two hundred pages of testimony by the subject, a jazz saxophonist named Eddie Barefield, do not appear to be more helpful. None contain an obvious ideological, biographical, or contextual explanation of how Barefield (in his late sixties when interviewed) reached a point of magnanimity toward the United States that some African Americans might equate with self-loathing. The interview transcript, thus, gives us small frustrations, such as garbled words and weak interrogators, as well as large ones, especially regarding an ever-elusive remark that may (or may not) hint at the subject's basic beliefs.

The ambiguity, however, is stimulating. The oral history transcript's equal measure of revelation and obscurity invites us to apply the same kinds of analysis to it that cultural and literary critics now use to explore similar autobiographical sources and other textual artifacts. The fragment of Barefield's testimony reproduced here illustrates problems any reader of oral history transcripts would face in trying to determine a subject's veracity, an interviewer's helpfulness, and the factual content of testimony, and in seeking to interpret a subject's attitudes regarding the great social questions of an era. Such transcripts force us to choose strategies for dealing with the past and its imperfect record. In addition, the fragment suggests the special elusiveness of jazz history. Who else but a successful jazz musician, among African Americans born near the turn of the century, might have made the crack Barefield makes about slavery?

The Barefield interview belongs to a major resource in jazz history: the more than one hundred transcripts of taped oral histories of early jazz musicians created by the Jazz Oral History Project. The project, funded by the National Endowment for the Arts, was run by the Smithsonian Institution and (after 1979) the Institute of Jazz Studies at Rutgers University-Newark. The typed transcripts are kept in a large steel cabinet at the institute, where I have had the privilege of reading about seventy of them while doing research for a book.

The special contributions and problems of the Jazz Oral History Project, or JOHP, is my main concern here. First, I will examine the nature of the JOHP transcripts—both their pleasures and limitations, and how these qualities resulted from the conception and execution of the project. (I discuss the transcripts because I am most familiar with them, having only sampled the actual tapes, and because the interviews will gain a far wider audience in written than in taped form.) Second, I will explore how the interviews can be used as sources for research in twentieth-century U.S. social history. Most academic social historians, dedicated to pursuing factual evidence about the past "as it essentially happened," have found oral histories to be of limited use in certain general ways (Novick; Lummis 133; Abrahams, 6; Neuenschwander 52). The large number of interviews in JOHP, concentrating on the fairly limited subject of jazz music between 1920 and 1945, offer an important test case in the use of extensive oral history as a source for empirical social history. My finding, in short, is that they are deeply illuminating if the researcher takes certain precautions: acknowledging the limited scholarly goals of the project, confronting the bewildering variety of interviewer-subject pairings, and being aware of the problems related to working with written transcripts. Finally, I will consider how the transcripts might yield greater and different kinds of information if the approaches of other, less purely empirical research philosophies of folklorists and poststructuralist critics are applied.

The Jazz Oral History Project originated in 1968 at the NEA, which had learned that older jazz performers were not applying for or receiving support from the three-year-old endowment. It was decided by NEA's jazz advisers that the wealth could be distributed more equitably if these elders were paid to give their oral histories. Each subject would receive $2,000 for a minimum of five hours of speaking. Beginning in 1972, the project was first operated by Jazz Interactions, a New York clearinghouse for the profession, but in 1974 it was transferred to the Smithsonian. In 1979 the Rutgers Institute of Jazz Studies began to supervise the project; the writer and literary scholar Ron Welburn administered JOHP until 1983, when the Reagan-era NEA cut its budget by two-thirds and forced its suspension.[1] Subjects for the oral histories were chosen under very general criteria: they were to be of advanced age (a minimum of sixty years, except for younger subjects in frail health) and to have no memoirs completed or in progress. The musicians chosen were both prominent and obscure, sidemen and leaders, black and white. The goal of reaching frail or aging musicians was fortuitous: almost fifty of the 123 subjects had died by the end of 1991 (Morgenstern; Welburn; Institute of Jazz Studies; Chilton; New York Times 1986–90).

The JOHP's main goal was to capture the reminiscences of older jazz musicians in substantial and serious interviews. Social historians might be disappointed to learn that few other objectives were established at the outset. Beginning in 1981, Welburn did instruct interviewers to seek out details relating to the musicians' ethnic, family, and educational backgrounds. Welburn was inspired in part by the oral history movement's dedication to preserving the stories of previously "unsung" Americans. The academic historian, however, would likely find that many potentially significant topics were not targeted; searches for specific kinds of information (with the exception of birth dates) were not systematically pursued, and no explicit rules governing the interviewing process were ever developed (Welburn 84–86; Lummis 17).

A side issue worth mentioning now is the quality of the written transcriptions created from the tapes—always a monumental task (Dunaway 113–16; Frisch chap. 5; Daniels 152; Morgenstern; Welburn). Transcription was almost completed during Welburn's tenure, but it is still unfinished. Professional transcribers worked for the JOHP, but as Welburn has noted, the quality of transcription from tape to tape varied widely. Amusing transcribing errors abound—one interview tells of the famous Slavic composers "Bartaugh" and "Scrivene," and another referred to the jazz flutist Herbie Mann as "heavy man." There were also serious mishearings, deletions, and even bowdlerization committed by typists, most of which were tirelessly corrected by Welburn, the assistant coordinator Phil Schaap, and others. For present purposes we can accept Welburn and Schaap's painstaking emendations on faith (Freeman, JOHP 85; Welburn 87, 93–94).

The greatest weakness of the project is evident in the Barefield fragment: the interrogators were decidedly of varying quality. Historians will find few interviewers here who were consistently conscientious (whether or not they had received Welburn's guidelines) about exploring the subject's social background and pursuing further questioning about significant opinions, ideas, and activities mentioned by the subject. In the JOHP, the writer Patricia Willard, who conducted more than a dozen oral histories, was the most capable interviewer, maintaining a serious, probing, and yet modest profile, yielding extraordinarily rich results from Lawrence Brown, Juan Tizol, Charlie Barnet, Nellie Lutcher, and others. Compared to the fishing expedition conducted by Eddie Barefield's interlocutor, Willard's series of questions put to Tizol (a longtime Duke Ellington trombonist) are models of thoughtful investigation:

> And what about places to stay? Could the band go to hotels? [Tizol's responses excluded here]
> Was there ever any question down south about your being with the band and your not being black?
> Did anybody ever object in the [S]outh?
> You didn't ever run in to [*sic*] any place that had a law, because once Willie Smith told me once that when Harry's [James's] band, they ran into someplace that had a law that said you couldn't have black and white on the same bandstand. . . . (Tizol 2:10)

Female oral historians (dominated by Willard and the longtime record producer Helen Dance) are well-represented in the JOHP. Among the other female interviewers were Vi Redd (for Andrew Blakeney) and Helene Johnston (Gil Evans, Jimmy McPartland). Black interviewers are much less prominent, an unfortunate fact given that over four-fifths of the subjects are African American. The vocalist Vi Redd's interview with Andrew Blakeney and the bassist Milt Hinton's discussion with Budd Johnson show how helpful it could be to have a black, as well as a musician, as an interrogator (Daniels 153). The dialogues between Hinton and his subjects are professional and often trenchant, such as when he points out to Johnson that Johnson's colleague in Dallas, the saxophonist Booker T. Pittman, "is the grandson of Booker T. Washington" and triggers Johnson's recollection of the prominent Pittman family. Hinton, though, is also sometimes loquacious enough to overshadow his subject. In the Booker Pittman discussion, for example, he makes the unfortunate error of asking Johnson to speculate about Booker's blood ties to Miss Jane Pittman, a fictional character[2] (Johnson 2:4–7).

More generally, even the most capable interviewers, such as Willard, Hinton, and the veteran jazz writers Chris Albertson, Stanley and Helen Dance, and Ira Gitler, might disappoint the academic historian, for the unavoidable reason that they do not ask the questions about jazz that would be of most interest to scholars. The best oral histories are strongest empirically in straight biography, personnel information (of more use to discographers than anyone else), and anecdotes (Lummis 92). Even they do not systematically address issues of intellectual development, social context, and racial conditions, which (as some scholars argue) might place such topics as jazz in the context of more general social history (Frisch chap. 4; Daniels). The historian Douglas Daniels interviewed many older jazz musicians in the 1980s while researching a biography of Lester Young. After four years of oral history fieldwork among Young's former colleagues, Daniels found that the subjects' "views on culture, history, and philosophy might in the long run tell us far more than data on place of birth, record dates, and band personnel." The late sociologist Morroe Berger, who asked the jazz giant Benny Carter about his perceptions of Harlem cultural life in the 1920s, was a very rare JOHP interviewer who directly addressed a major historiographical issue (I discuss Carter's response below) (Daniels 162–64; Carter 2:88).

The problem arose because jazz historians as a group have not made the methodological transition from journalistic interviewing to oral history. Jazz historiography has long been a pleasurable, vaguely discursive enterprise, disconnected from the highly empirical project of the academy, perhaps more interested in a good story than in uncovering the past "as it essentially was" (although discographers are, in a narrow way, exceptions to this). Interviews by journalists, critics, and fans, while often irresistibly entertaining, have also been adulatory and superficial. In book form, many interviews and sketches are often called "jazz history," but they are designed mainly to present uncritically the words of jazz's creators and admirers, as if this task alone resulted in the writing of history (Hentoff and Shapiro; Travis; Gillespie and Fraser). Of course, academic historians themselves share the blame, since they have ignored jazz for decades and have deprived jazz history of their empirical expertise.

All of this does not indicate that the oral histories are useless. On the contrary, used with care, they are almost priceless sources for a crucial chapter in American cultural history.

A few special challenges, once identified and pondered, reveal the peculiar empirical strengths of these documents. In these interviews, ironclad "facts" relating to jazz history cannot be obtained instantly. The main criticism of all oral history, in fact, asks how any testimony presented decades after the fact could possibly "clear up" the historical record. Oral history advocates respond that corroboration of interviews with one another, and with written sources from the period, establish the veracity of interviews. Jazz history, however, is notoriously lacking in hard, written documentation from past periods, and the verbal evidence we are left with is often contradictory. Ever since jazz histories were first published in the 1930s, it has been difficult to separate "facts" from folklore. For example, the JOHP presents conflicting testimony regarding Mezz Mezzrow's "first interracial band" in the early 1930s. Despite discographical evidence which shows that Benny Carter was involved in this band, Carter testified that "that's what I might call an interesting anecdote, but I don't remember it." (Is Carter's lack of memory of this a significant fact?) (Mezzrow and Wolfe 226–32; Rust 1114; Carter 105–7). Another popularly embroidered topic is the struggle of Bix Beiderbecke, the great cornetist of the twenties, with alcohol. While Eddie Condon (in his autobiography) argues and most others imply that Beiderbecke was an alcoholic, Bud Freeman argues in the JOHP that he reacted strongly to small amounts of liquor and always played sober. (The arranger Bill Challis, interestingly, argues in an interview for another project that Bix drank because of the goading and harassment of Condon and other "characters.") (Condon and Sugrue 140, 148; Freeman, JOHP 55, 87, 2:13–15; Freeman, *You Don't* 19; Sudhalter and Evans 324–26). Similarly, it is hard to determine in the JOHP how much socializing went on between white and black musicians in clubs on Chicago's South Side. Musicians generally agree that they never played together in the clubs, but they seem evenly divided on the question of whether whites and blacks fraternized offstage. Mezz Mezzrow, Bill Davison, Ralph Brown, and Pops Foster saw a great deal of contact, while Scoville Browne and Muggsy Spanier noted very little (Mezzrow and Wolfe 3–4; Davison; Brown 36, 39; Foster and Stoddard 124; Browne 9; Spanier 9). Such question will remain open, perhaps even if corroborative evidence from the era is thoroughly researched.

The JOHP's minimum age of sixty inevitably increased the likelihood that memories would be clouded—sometimes more clouded than the musicians were willing to admit. After 1980, Welburn took care not to allow certain memory-impaired musicians to participate, but incorrect memories, misinterpretations of questions, and mishearings hobble a number of the allowed interviews, as they often do in oral history (Brink 93–105; Neuenschwander 46–49).

More typically, though, regardless of their ability to recall the past, subjects eagerly took an active role in the interview process, using the platform of the oral history to define and interact with their pasts (Neuenschwander 49–51; Abrahams 4; Lummis 90; McMahan chap. 1; Daniels 153; Bennett 6). As in many oral history projects, the elderly displayed feeble memory less often than a vigorous desire to get the "authorized" versions of their lives on record. J. R. Taylor of the Smithsonian, and later Ron Welburn, facilitated this by advising interviewers not to constrain subjects unnecessarily to a rigid schedule of topics for

discussion. While this often invited rambling dialogue certain to frustrate students of the oral histories, it also granted authorial powers to
musicians eager to claim them. As one subject, Duke Ellington's drummer Sonny Greer, said, the "JOHP gives the subject a chance to tell all he
knows about his own life and the lives of those he knew. He can fill in
actual detail and interpretation to things, rather than just spout off
names and dates" (Welburn, "Interview"; Institute of Jazz Studies).

It is easy to present many examples of musicians "filling in" or shaping
their interviews. For example, Bud Freeman was determined to use his
interview as an occasion for memorializing his deceased friends Bix
Beiderbecke and the drummer Dave Tough in new and insightful ways.
Freeman stresses that Tough "knew more about this music than any
drummer I had ever heard," and that his "great mentality made him a
great drummer" and "a sensitive artist." Jimmy McPartland uses his
childhood delinquency in the street gangs of Chicago as a recurring motif
as he describes his personality and perceptions in later years. His years in
a reform home, he emphasizes, "affected me throughout my life somehow or another," but "since I started to play [jazz], why, I've never been a
bad boy." Horace Henderson suavely recounts a string of accomplishments and famous friends, probably unaware that several other JOHP
subjects accuse him of stealing arrangements and tunes from his brother,
Fletcher. Benny Carter, by contrast, modestly effaces himself from much
of his story, almost becoming a third-person narrator at times (Freeman,
JOHP, 44, 46, 56; McPartland 2:15, 20; Henderson; Carter).

The transcripts capture the statements of jazz musicians at the end of
their careers, telling us as much (if not more) about their recent experiences and perspective as they do about the past. In a century of upheaval
and mass culture these largely working-class artists rose to achieve fame
and to travel the world (Daniels 146). The oral histories confirm that as
old people, they largely shed the goals, concerns, and confinements of
youth and reworked the materials of their early lives into coherent and
illustrative chronicles. Some musicians disparaged their early selves,
refusing to imbue the past with nostalgia. The white cornetist Wild Bill
Davison's striking gloom regarding his career after 1932, for example,
shows an individual periodizing his life and career into appropriate pre-
and post-Great Depression eras. In that year Davison drove the car in
which the clarinetist Frank Teschemacher was killed, and though Davison was not responsible for the accident, he was quickly suspended by
the musicians' union president on a contract technicality. Davison's
lingering pain is clear from even the transcript: "He was absolutely
wrong to do it and all of my friends said—oh, man—that is—they don't

kick you out of the union for something you didn't do—. . . . " Davison goes on to describe his years of low-level employment in Milwaukee for the rest of the 1930s, and he clearly labels the Teschemacher incident as his rite of passage from a carefree creative early life to a more hazard-filled and bittersweet professional career (Davison 86–91).

Other musicians looked back on the youthful 1920s with unabashed nostalgia. They recall traumatic incidents with chuckles instead of pain, retrieving humor from these incidents that they could not perceive in their youth. Thus Milt Hinton remembered the South Side of the twenties as "paradise," where "everybody's kids are doing fine, everybody's doing fine, all these great jazz musicians are playing in all those places" and "I'm a superstar. Got nice clothes, you know, everything." Cootie Williams noted that as a youth in Mobile he "used to say, 'Dear Lord, please hurry up and let me grow up so I can get to New York'" (where he settled in 1928). In an earlier, independent oral history, the trumpeter Lee Collins noted that after he migrated from New Orleans to Chicago, he "didn't know [his] own power." Bill Davison, Bud Freeman, and other whites saw their first visits to black Chicago clubs as major moments of *conversion* to "a whole way of life" (in Freeman's words), to "a lot of things we had never seen before." The clarinetist Garvin Bushell found new racial pride while playing before cheering crowds in Europe in the 1920s. "We were highly impressed with the people and the attitude and the mannerisms of Europeans and we sort of took on some of that and we assumed some of that air" (Hinton; Williams 61; Davison 79–80; McPart-land 4, 7–11; Bushell 75; Freeman, *You Don't* 7–8; Freeman, JOHP 23; Collins 43).

In interviews with African American musicians (the large majority of JOHP subjects) we observe the "New Negroes" of the 1920s in old age. They note with obvious pride and reflect on how they fulfilled the promise of their early lives and how they confronted injustice. For Milt Hinton, the "paradise" of the twenties gave way to a realization that "there's no place for a black violinist in this world," and the pain of the Great Depression when he "toughed it out" as a bass player. Benny Carter came to the same understanding of his opportunities. He carefully tried "to live within a situation that I know exists, and at the same time, do everything that I can do to change it," but he too learned "that there was no future in being a symphonic musician." Carter notes that young players in Harlem were not inspired by the literary "renaissance": "everybody was just trying to do their thing without a great deal of thought about what was black or Afro-American or jazz . . . without thinking in terms of roots." Most musicians, however, are much less explicit about important social conditions of the past. The testimony of many, including Eddie Durham, Bill Coleman, and Snub Moseley, portray the impact of racism on black musicians in ways that are softened by the passing of years and by a kind of bemused reticence (Hinton 6:13; Carter 2:88, 126; Durham 54–56; Coleman 9, 105, 112; Wintz; Institute of Jazz Studies).

Elder black jazz players were deeply aware of struggles for racial equality that took place in their lifetimes, and, perhaps unavoidably, they use the civil-rights movement as a metaphor for their own personal and career struggles. The tap dancer John Bubbles stressed that as a youth he emulated the mythic black avenger, Stackolee. "I was worse than Luther King, but I'm violent, he ain't. . . . I'm going to be a helluva Negro, man," he thought then, preparing to take on gangs of white boys. Sir Charles Thompson, similarly, portrayed himself as having been militantly opposed to the white power structure virtually from birth. Earl "Fatha" Hines (in his oral history told to Stanley Dance, published as a book) insisted that his 1930s band "was among the first of the Freedom Riders, because we were riding through the South . . . creating all kinds of excitement" (Bubbles 27; Thompson 4–21ff.; Dance 81).

In many oral histories of elderly people, the young person looking ahead is depicted vividly by the old person looking back, and there is some revealing dissonance between the two selves. This dissonance is especially striking in the testimony of black jazz musicians. Drawing on African American oral traditions, they shape their early stories into odysseys of young tricksters. These, however, are recounted often in an elegiac, even detached tone. The calmest retrospective gazes of some subjects are almost eerie in their acceptance of good and evil fortune in a racist America. When Garvin Bushell recalls that Paul Whiteman withdrew a job offer when he learned that Bushell was black, he concludes simply that "the name Bushell tricked him." Similarly, Benny Carter says, recalling the barring of Harlem musicians from downtown jobs, "I don't remember . . . harboring that feeling [of anger] or noting it in anyone else. Maybe we just kind of at that moment . . . sort of resigned ourselves to the situation as it was and feeling maybe that even the white musicians themselves couldn't do anything about it, you know?" (Bushell 79–80; Carter 68–69).

Nostalgia for the old days probably derived more from subjects' more recent experiences and opinions than from their early lives. This is most clearly revealed in many comments regarding the alleged safety and communality of 1920s urban life. According to the singer Alberta Hunter, in Chicago one could "lose . . . $100 or something, they see you drop it, they'd say, 'Hey, fellow, you dropped this money.'" "Nobody bothered anybody," another subject remembers (Hunter 59; Spivey 38, 40). Cities today, in their view, are dangerous, alien, antisocial places. It was probably inconceivable to them that contemporary cities could nurture young jazz musicians and jazz cultures. In addition, the subjects are very sensitive to the fact that they and jazz music, while respected and popular among a devoted small audience today, are also on the margin of American mass culture and are box-office has-beens. Many musicians, in fact, make reference to the waves of new popular music styles that have swept over jazz's beachhead since 1940, and they often despise or lament those innovations that helped to eclipse their careers. Bebop was "Chinese music" to Cab Calloway and "weird chords that don't mean nothin' " to Louis Armstrong, and Bud Freeman doubted strongly that rock musicians had created anything of value. If we carefully observe the ways in which change and innovation in music are depicted by elderly jazz musicians, we may learn something about how people resist the shocks of change by bathing their early surroundings and accomplishments in auras of nostalgia (Dahl 65; Collier 305; Freeman, "Interview"; also Dominique 2; Mezzrow and Wolfe 281).

These are a few of the empirical benefits of the JOHP. From the point of view of the social historian, these benefits are elusive and subtle. It appears that one must work hard to *corroborate* and *contextualize* these statements with great care, finding other written and oral evidence to establish veracity and a vast array of other facts to determine the significance of statements in larger contexts (Neuenschwander 51). There are, however, other ways of approaching these texts, which might draw more meaning out of their words by more fully explaining the elderly musicians' minds and priorities.

In the academy, aside from musicologists, folklorists rather than historians have found the most value in jazz (and in African American music in general). Folklore has always favored oral traditions (in direct opposition to history's penchant for written sources), and additionally, folklorists' interest in performances as "texts" and texts as "performances" leads them to collapse the playing and testimony of the jazz musician into a single phenomenon (Abrahams 9; Dunaway 114). In interviews, what is seen and heard is "truth" of a phenomenological variety, expressed in the cadences, gestures, rhetorical strategies, and statements of the subject (Abrahams 2, 5; Titon 276–92; Dunaway 116–17; Bennett 11; Ostry 9, 12–13). Even lies, willful distortions of the truth, are a form of "truth" expressed in a peculiar way by the performer (Joyner 52). Folklorists and folklore-oriented university presses admire and promote jazz oral history in part because jazz musicians, when speaking, seem more able than others to convey their view of the world and of life through verbal agility, emotional openness, and above all adeptness at "performance" (Abrahams 11; Lomax xv). Jazz devotees, folklorists, and oral historians alike are eager to hear the words of jazz musicians because they hope that these words will be the verbal equivalent of jazz.

The benefits of this approach for evaluation of the JOHP are obvious. The oral histories themselves are the events, and they can be analyzed for their rhetorical and traditional functions as ballads, confessions, petitions, testimony, and other revealing forms of communication. The piquant features of the JOHP I discussed may also receive greater illumination if the focus is on the performer/subject rather than on the empirical value of the testimony.

The folklorists' approach is not the only alternative. It is also tempting to consider recent theories of analysis that question the importance of contextualization and claim that instead ideas and texts must be "interpreted" in a "dialogue" between the historian's suppositions and the text's language. This view animated the June 1989 issue of the *American Historical Review*, in which David Harlan pleaded the case for this kind of poststructuralist analysis of texts. Harlan stated that the traditional method of contextualizing sources—in which historians sought to situate written documents within contexts and debates recently determined by historiography—was a futile attempt to regain the perspective of a past era. Intellectual historians, in actuality, could hope only to interpret the inner content of these sources, their linguistic, structural, and rhetorical strategies. Harlan's position was challenged by David A. Hollinger, who defends traditional empiricism—the placing of a source into a larger context so that both may be better understood—as the necessary epistemological approach to retrieving the past (Harlan; Hollinger; Jay 106).

It takes little imagination for us to consider a text containing a creative artist's reflections to be as problematic as a political or scientific document, in the sense that the transcript too can be considered either self-constituting or demanding contextualization by the historian (McMahan 2–4 and chap. 5). When reading these oral histories it is tempting to avoid the sticky contextual problems that these highly attractive but problematic transcripts raise and to indulge instead in their internal "pleasures." I have noted some of the texts' empirical difficulties. Might the reader not simply explore the inner life of the transcripts' "writerly" details (or "speakerly" details, as students of African American lore might point out), anecdotes, revelations of personality, and flavorful syntax (Bennett 3; Barthes, *Plaisir*, "From Work"; Gates, "Introduction")?

One example might illustrate the benefits of a diverse interpretive approach. In his JOHP interview, the pianist Jay McShann tells a melodramatic story from his days with the Eddie Hill band at a tavern in the hills near Albuquerque, New Mexico, in the 1930s. Jim, the club owner, walked into the sleeping quarters behind the building early one morning and found "Eddie Hill . . . in there with his old lady." "Jim walked on back to the car, went and got his .45 and come back in there." As the woman pleaded with Jim not to shoot, Hill fled into the mountains: "Eddie had some brand new shoes he'd bought. He picked them shoes and clothing up and ran." Jim "shot [the woman] and he run around the club, looking for Eddie, and then he come back and shot her again. Then he pulled the pistol on himself . . . when he shot himself the second time, he fell right over her, you know." McShann seems to tie up this tragic, triangular tale neatly by having Hill wander back in: "Eddie done come by the mountains and Eddie was crying, 'Oh,' and I looked at them shoes and they was wore out."

But the story continues. The town commissioner shows up, views the wastage, and warns the band to get out of town. All band members but McShann and Hill then leave. The woman's father arrives from Denver and asks first, "Who got the money?" The commissioner suspects that the Mexican bartender absconded with the woman's savings. The band's guitarist, though, earlier had told his colleagues that he could pay for their return trip to Oklahoma City, so McShann "knew where the money was." But he was not telling this to the commissioner: "I just told him, ' . . . I'll stand all day and tell you, all night, that Nestor did not get that money.' . . . Now, the other guys, they're gone. But I know Nestor didn't do it." The dead woman's mother, "over [in] the other big house," then "cut her own throat," and finally, the father "went in the bathroom and blew his brains out. I said, 'Well, I done seen everything now.' One, two, three, four" (McShann 70–75).

It is obvious, even in this summary form, that this colorful vignette is exquisitely told. McShann closes both halves of the tale with hilarious flourishes, regarding Hill's new shoes and his own reaction to the four violent deaths. These touches, along with the economy and relish with which the story is told (it takes up only five pages of transcript), suggest that McShann has polished the anecdote for years in front of appreciative auditors. This is further suggested by its gradual, artful process of centering on the dead woman, whose pleadings to Jim, stolen money, and bereaved parents become the focal points of the plot. (McShann's employer Eddie Hill, in his ruined new shoes, becomes a secondary comic figure—indeed, "that first night" McShann puts Hill on a bus to Los Angeles and never sees him again.) Clearly this is a fine example of folk narration, perhaps empirically useless (although the Hill band's stay in Albuquerque, and the deaths, might be corroborated) but speaking volumes about the hazards of visiting engagements, the volatile mixture of personalities in any band, the persistence of both "Western" codes of behavior and African American humor and irony in the jazz discourse, and McShann's own ability to take control of such a situation and negotiate with white authority figures (he went on in the 1930s to become a highly successful bandleader himself, and in early 1995 he was still vigorously pursuing one of jazz's longest careers). The main point is that such evidence invites an interpretive strategy, while also being congenial to folklorists' conceptualizations of oral performance and truth-values. Such attractive stories as these stand on their own, reveal by themselves the speakers' notions of power, will, beauty, and politics, and stimulate readers to confront their own ideology. Poststructuralists might say that these transcripts can do nothing else, and that this might be enough.

These considerations might be open to a wide range of attacks. Traditionalist historians are wont to denigrate jazz history as quotidian, oral history as empirically unsound, folkloristics as ahistorical, and poststructuralism as heretical. These negative opinions, when arrayed together, almost certainly show that many historians still consider jazz oral histories a suspect source. The debate of Harlan and Hollinger and other historians regarding the merits of "the return to literature" and "contextualism" must be kept in mind by those seeking to make the most fruitful use of jazz oral histories. Certainly both approaches contribute to our understanding of (and caution regarding) what the oral histories tell us.

The JOHP transcripts, I argue, are both pleasurable *and* useful texts, valuable both to contextualists and hermeneuticists. Folkloristic-minded scholars will find oral "performances" of uncommon breadth and detail in the JOHP. Historians, too, who hesitate to give up on context and to treat the transcripts as self-constituting, will find them more frustrating, but with some corroboration they yield far more than mere personnel information. They do contribute to the traditional body of knowledge that historians have sought to accumulate about twentieth-century American society. The transcripts help to affirm oral history as a worthy method, and jazz as a worthy subject, for empirical historical study—among other activities.

Notes

1 It should be noted that beginning in 1987, the NEA awarded annually five or six Jazz Masters grants to active jazz veterans, each award amounting to $30,000, for performing and educational ventures.

2 Other veterans of the early jazz eras who interview, such as Stanley and Helen Dance, are garrulous at times, which becomes harmful when the questions are leading and even provide their own "answers." See Welburn, "Toward Theory and Method" 89–90.

Works Cited

Abrahams, Roger D. "Story and History: A Folklorist's View." *Oral History Review* 9 (1981): 1–11.

Barefield, Eddie. JOHP transcript, 1978. Institute of Jazz Studies, Rutgers U-Newark.

Barthes, Roland. *Le Plaisir du texte.* Paris: Editions du Seuil, 1973.

——. "From Work to Text." *Image, Music, Text.* Trans. Stephen Heath. New York: Hill and Wang, 1977.

Bennett, James. "Human Values in Oral History." *Oral History Review* 11 (1983): 1–15.

Brink, T. L. "Oral History and Geriatric Mental Health: Distortions of Testimony Produced by Psychopathology." *Oral History Review* 13 (1985): 93–105.

Brown, Ralph. Transcript, 1971. Columbia U Oral History Collection.

Browne, Scoville. Transcript, 1971. Columbia U Oral History Collection.

Bubbles, John. JOHP transcript, 1979. Institute of Jazz Studies, Rutgers U-Newark.

Bushell, Garvin. JOHP transcript, 1977. Institute of Jazz Studies, Rutgers U-Newark.

Carter, Benny. JOHP transcript, 1976. Institute of Jazz Studies, Rutgers U-Newark.

Chilton, John. *Who's Who of Jazz: From Storyville to Swing Street.* 3rd ed. New York: Da Capo, 1985.

Coleman, Bill. Autobiography typescript, 1981. Institute of Jazz Studies, Rutgers U-Newark.

Collier, James Lincoln. *Louis Armstrong.* New York: Oxford UP, 1984.

Collins, Lee. *Oh, Didn't He Ramble: The Life Story of Lee Collins.* Urbana: U of Illinois P, 1974.

Condon, Eddie, and Thomas Sugrue. *We Called It Music: A Generation of Jazz.* New York: Holt, 1947.

Dahl, Linda. *Stormy Weather: The Music and Lives of a Century of Jazzwomen.* New York: Pantheon, 1984.

Dance, Stanley. *The World of Earl Hines.* New York: Scribner's, 1977.

Daniels, Douglas Henry. Oral History, Masks, and Protocol in the Jazz Community. *Oral History Review* 15 (1987): 143–64.

Davison, Wild Bill. JOHP transcript, 1980. Institute of Jazz Studies, Rutgers U-Newark.

Dominique, Natty. Transcript, 1958. Tulane Jazz Oral History Project, Hogan Jazz Archive, Tulane U.

Dunaway, David King. "Transcription: Shadow or Reality?" *Oral History Review* 12 (1984): 113–17.

Durham, Eddie. JOHP transcript, 1978. Institute of Jazz Studies, Rutgers U-Newark.

Foster, George "Pops," and Tom Stoddard. *Pops Foster: The Autobiography of a New Orleans Jazzman.* Berkeley: U of California P, 1971.

Freeman, Bud. *You Don't Look Like a Musician!* Detroit: Balamp P, 1974.

——. JOHP transcript, 1977. Institute of Jazz Studies, Rutgers U-Newark.

——. Interview with author, 1987.

Frisch, Michael. *A Shared Authority: Essays on the Craft and Meaning of Oral and Public History.* Albany, N.Y.: SUNY Press, 1990.

Gates, Henry Louis, Jr. *The Signifying Monkey: A Theory of African-American Literary Criticism.* New York: Oxford UP, 1988.

Gillespie, Dizzy, and Al Fraser. *To Be or Not . . . to Bop: Memoirs.* New York: Doubleday, 1979.

Harlan, David. "Intellectual History and the Return of Literature and Reply to David Hollinger." *American Historical Review* 94 (1989): 581–609, 622–26.

Henderson, Horace. JOHP transcript, 1975. Institute of Jazz Studies, Rutgers U-Newark.

Hentoff, Nat, and Nat Shapiro. *Hear Me Talkin' to Ya: The Story of Jazz Told By the Men Who Made It.* New York: Holt, Rinehart and Winston, 1955.

Hinton, Milt. JOHP transcript, 1976. Institute of Jazz Studies, Rutgers U-Newark.

Hollinger, David A. "The Return of the Prodigal: The Persistence of Historical Knowing." *American Historical Review* 94 (1989): 3, 610–21.

Hunter, Alberta. JOHP transcript, 1976. Institute of Jazz Studies, Rutgers U-Newark.

Institute of Jazz Studies. Jazz Oral History Project (pamphlet) n.p., 1983.

Jay, Martin. "Should Intellectual History Take a Linguistic Turn? Reflections on the Habermas-Gadamer Debate." *Modern European Intellectual History: Reappraisals and New Perspectives.* Ed. Dominick LaCapra and Steven Kaplan. Ithaca, N.Y.: Cornell UP 1982. 100–117.

Johnson, Budd. JOHP transcript, 1975. Institute of Jazz Studies, Rutgers U-Newark.

Joyner, Charles. "Oral History as Communicative Event: A Folkloristic Perspective." *Oral History Review* (1979): 47–52.

Lomax, Alan. *Mister Jelly Roll.* New York: Grosset and Dunlap, 1950.

Lummis, Trevor. *Listening to History.* London: Hutchinson, 1987.

McMahan, Eva M. *Elite Oral History Discourse: A Study of Cooperation and Coherence.* Tuscaloosa: U of Alabama P, 1989.

McPartland, Jimmy. JOHP transcript, 1973. Institute of Jazz Studies, Rutgers U-Newark.

McShann, Jay. JOHP transcript, 1978. Institute of Jazz Studies, Rutgers U-Newark.

Mezzrow, Mezz, and Bernard Wolfe. *Really the Blues.* New York: Random, 1946.

Morgenstern, Dan. Interview with author. Newark, N.J., 1990.

Neuenschwander, John A. "Remembrance of Things Past: Oral Historians and Long-Term Memory." *Oral History Review* (1978): 45–53.

New York Times. 1986–90. *Index.*

Novick, Peter. *That Noble Dream: The "Objectivity Question" and the American Historical Profession.* New York: Cambridge UP, 1988.

Ostry, Bernard. "The Illusion of Understanding: Making the Ambiguous Intelligible." *Oral History Review* (1977): 7–16.

Rust, Brian. *Jazz Records, 1897–1942.* 2nd ed. London: Storyville, 1978.

Spanier, Muggsy. Transcript, 1957. Tulane Jazz Oral History Project, Hogan Jazz Archive, Tulane U.

Spivey, Donald. *Union and the Black Musician: William Everett Samuels and Chicago Local 208.* Lanham, Md.: UP of America, 1984.

Sudhalter, Richard M., and Philip R. Evans. *Bix: Man and Legend.* New Rochelle, N.Y.: Arlington House, 1974.

Thompson, Sir Charles. JOHP transcript, 1978. Institute of Jazz Studies, Rutgers U-Newark.

Titon, Jeff Todd. "The Life Story." *Journal of American Folklore* 93 (1980): 276–92.

Tizol, Juan. JOHP transcript, 1978. Institute of Jazz Studies, Rutgers U-Newark.

Travis, Dempsey J. *An Autobiography of Black Jazz.* Chicago: Urban Research Institute, 1983.

Welburn, Ron. Telephone interview with author, 1990.

——. "Toward Theory and Method with the Jazz Oral History Project." *Black Music Research Journal* (1986): 79–95.

Williams, Cootie. JOHP transcript, 1976. Institute of Jazz Studies, Rutgers U-Newark.

Wintz, Carey D. *Black Culture and the Harlem Renaissance.* Houston: Rice UP, 1988.

The Media of Memory: The Seductive Menace of Records in Jazz History

JED RASULA

The violence of the body reaches the written page only through absence, through the intermediary of documents that the historian has been able to see on the sands from which a presence has since been washed away, and through a murmur that lets us hear—but from afar—the unknown immensity that seduces and menaces our knowledge.—Certeau 3

Jazz is a unique subject for historians because of the nature and quantity of a certain kind of artifact, the sound recording, a medium that, in Michel de Certeau's image, actually does murmur. Despite their prodigious use of recordings in formulating perspectives on jazz history, historians have tended to avoid theorizing the actual status and function of these artifacts—the very artifacts that constitute what would seem to constitute primary evidence about jazz music. The technological constrictions of the medium have generally been cited as cause for suspicion; drums were not used for early jazz recordings because they made the stylus jump the groove, and the three-minute parameters of 78-rpm obviously imposed a temporal handcuff on a music that legendarily thrived on the ad hoc ingenuity of self-perpetuating performances that could even outlast the stamina of individual musicians.[1]

The tension between legend and fact is central to jazz. The legendary stories recycled in histories of the music have given flavor to the historian's report; at the same time, *as* legends they have been treated as illegitimate testimony. The legends appear in histories to serve as limit-texts, emblems of everything dubious in narrative that the historian will discursively rectify. Legends are the fanciful versions that the history purports to render true.[2] Legend and truth are nonetheless linked as language acts. Conversion of a fictive statement into a truth proposition is a technical possibility, or it is at least approached as if it were by jazz historians. But what of the status of recordings? Are they truth or fiction? What is the epistemological status of a technologically primitive artifact like a 1923 acoustic recording of King Oliver's Jazz Band? Is it a conduit, an acoustic window giving access to how the music really sounded, or is it an obstacle?

Perhaps recordings have not been theorized because the impulse to theorize has been diverted by the myth/history distinction. That is, in place of legends as such, we have "legendary" moments. "Legendary" is an adjective of value applied by historians to singularities of the music; Armstrong's "West End Blues" is customarily cited as a classic, the legendary inauguration of an ongoing legacy.[3] The performance may be legendary, but its medium, the recording, is as spurious as myth for the historian, something to be pillaged for documentary purposes only. Recordings have the status of an impressive testimony that is, regrettably for the historian, a secondary substitute for the "living presence" of actual performance. Inasmuch as recordings can be described as technologically suspect, their role in determining the history of the music is subservient to the historian's role as speaker of the discourse, the discourse of a history that is evidently true because it can dispassionately account for and overcome a variety of technological, cultural, and racial impediments. It is all too obvious that the material constraints of recording have interceded in numerous ways in the development of jazz. I have no interest in prioritizing records or reclaiming some hitherto neglected authority for them; but I am interested in what and how recordings testify, particularly in that evidential scenario which is called history. Critics and historians have always used jazz records as primary sources, while pretending that what they are really talking about is something else, some putative essence of a "living tradition" that cannot be "captured" by the blatant artifice of technology.[4] In Brian Priestley's succinct diagnosis: "In the past, most authors ostensibly treating the history of jazz wrote instead about their favorite records. . . . But what is especially confusing is that such writers did not admit to themselves or to their readers that they were only writing about what had been *recorded*, implying that this was the only jazz worth writing about"[5] (x).

My contention is that recordings are vexatious for historians precisely because they are a medium of inscription; the act of writing a history must covertly contend with a history already in the process of transcribing itself, rendering the historian's account a surrogate act masquerading as authority. By considering the ambiguous function of the recorded legacy in the following pages, I want to accentuate a disturbance at the heart of the historicizing impulse; for the historian setting out to compose a written history of jazz will find that history already composed, and made audible, in recordings. In the place where a history would assert its powers of attorney, an intrusive sound emerges. I will suggest that jazz history, as a practice of writing, is the revenge of words on a wordless but nonetheless highly articulate history, a history that threatens to preempt the written documents that adhere to it. Inasmuch as jazz history has mostly been written by white fans, we should not discount the mystique of jazz as "a vital, and *natural* source of spontaneous, precivilized, antitechnological values . . . " (Ross 74)—values in which recordings clearly straddle conflicting claims, since they are technological mediations of an "authenticity" otherwise unavailable. The writing of jazz history is positioned as a struggle between grapho-centrism and its phono-eccentric phantoms. In effect, the official history of jazz is that which appears in print, taking the form of a coherent story of progress, of "continuity and change," certified by its canonical hierarchy of "major figures" who are compelled to recite a tale of evolutionary destiny.

Occluded by this affirmation of the graphic legend is the sonic legend, inscribed in the obstinately material medium of recordings. It is interesting that historians are virtually incapable of getting a history of jazz under way without using records to provide traction. For convenience, some historians have favored 1917 as a starting block, because the Original Dixieland Jazz Band cut its first record then. Recordings are a methodological convenience for marking the origin of the music. It has also been customary for the historian to augment the motif of genesis by two other means: first, by citing or detailing such prefiguring legends as Buddy Bolden ("legend" in this instance meaning someone who made no recordings), and second, by tracing the African roots of the musical idioms of black Americans.

Before going on to discuss recordings, it is worth pausing at the prospect of origins articulated in the search for African roots. Africans, along with Asians and other so-called marginal people, were until recently regarded as people without history, eccentric to—if not subordinate to— the scheme of an evolutionary destiny with Europe as global capital of "humanity." Is it entirely coincidental that the first serious historical writing about jazz was undertaken by Europeans whose personal welfare was to be threatened by the most notorious advocate of this enterprise, Adolf Hitler? Surely there is subversive intent in Hugues Panassié's celebration of jazz players as archetypes of "primitive man," or Robert Goffin's history of jazz that emphasizes in its subtitle an affront to

Eurocentric dignity: *Jazz: From the Congo to the Metropolitan.*[6] There is, however, an antithetical consequence of a different order in these (and others') ambition to write jazz history, for the ultimate aspiration is to get jazz to coincide with *writing* as such, history-writing. As Marshall Stearns insists several times in his standard history *The Story of Jazz* (1956), West Africans have "no written music" and, indeed, "no literature," their customs and rituals being handed down instead "by example and word of mouth" (4, 17). Stearns notices that African music is played without notation, but he fails to recognize a corollary: namely, that history might already be inscribed in some medium other than writing, that truth might be conveyed by "word of mouth" or even the more fleeting record of rhythmic signatures in music and dance. The precedent established by Panassié and Goffin is continued here by Stearns, and it consists of the silent augmentation of an ongoing (and self-documenting) history, an augmentation that can be performed only by a writer, and not just any writer, but a historian, which is to say, a practitioner of that legacy of writing which declared Africans and their descendants to be a people "without history."

The ambition to write jazz history brings with it the presumption that history is something that must be provided for or added to an otherwise primitive, non- or ahistoric people, as a way of enabling them to attain consciousness of their role in an evolutionary destiny, a master plan. This need not be the conscious purpose of the historian, as the underlying assumptions are not methodological but *ontological.* To undertake even so simple an identification of jazz as the music of African Americans is to posit an essence, to *assign* an identity to people who are eccentric to the authorized centrality of that (Eurocentric) point of view claiming "history" as a neutral exercise in empirical investigation. Liberation theologist Enrique Dussel precisely defines the asymmetry: "Being is; beings are what are seen and controlled" (6). Robert Young in *White Mythologies,* summarizing comparable insights of the Jewish philosopher Emmanuel Levinas, elaborates: "For being is always defined as the appropriation of either difference into identity, or of identities into a greater order, be it absolute knowledge, History, or the state" (13). History is the spotlight shining on the Other, about whom Hélène Cixous asks:

> What is the "Other"? If it is truly the "other," there is nothing to say; it cannot be theorized. The "other" escapes me. It is elsewhere, outside: absolutely other. It doesn't settle down. But in History, of course, what is called "other" is an alterity that does settle down,

that falls into the dialectical circle. It is the other in a hierarchically organized relationship in which the same is what rules, names, defines, and assigns "its" other. (71)

Attendant on claims of historical fidelity are the more pervasive, hidden, and insidious claims of a theory of essence and identity; it is the awareness of how ontology underwrites history that should compel our attention, particularly in the work of jazz historians.

It is admittedly contentious to speak of "jazz historians" to indicate writing by journalists, musicologists, and enthusiasts. Few writers on jazz have had any training in historiography. Consequently, "history" as it pertains to jazz consists in whatever a given writer has inherited as cultural shorthand. This shorthand, in practice, has consistently turned out to be the dominant explanatory device, the viewfinder through which the legacy of the music has been focused and appraised. Commonplace vernacular formulae about history have been picked up by jazz chroniclers as the unexamined tools of their trade. Most conspicuous among these is the nineteenth-century vision (whether Hegelian or Comtean) of history as the concrete and progressive realization of transcendental and universal norms. In this light, even so indigenous and nomadic a practice as jazz playing is validated for its *corroborative* function, for the way it illuminates or is said to contribute to dominant cultural norms—as in the common phrase taken by Grover Sales as the title of his book *Jazz: America's Classical Music.*

The evolutionary suppositions of this shorthand historicism tend to deform the very notion of what the music may be all about. This is implied by Ralph Ellison in "The Golden Age, Time Past" when he explains that "our memory and our identity are ever at odds; our history ever a tall tale told by inattentive idealists"[7] (199). German idealism is of course the major tributary feeding nineteenth-century historicism; and while Ellison is criticizing those who romantically idealize the past, he is correct to notice that it is idealism in some form that retroactively imposes order on "our history." Historian David Lowenthal has put it most explicitly: "To make history intelligible, the historian must reveal a retrospectively immanent structure in past events, creating an illusion that these things happened as they did because they had to" (234). The explanatory power of this model has been so thoroughly absorbed into jazz history that it may be thought of as an *addiction* rather than a theory. Like the narcotics abuse that has been inscribed in the mythos of jazz, the historians' fixation on a progressive "immanent structure" is a serious malady. As Kenneth Burke comments (about Marxism), "Once you have placed your terms in a developmental series, you have an arrangement whereby each can be said to participate, within the limitations of its nature, in the ultimate perfection ('finishedness') of the series" (198). Secured in their developmental niches by the cumulative hierarchy, each individual is in effect *finished off*, mortared into place in a monument that can all too easily function as a mausoleum.

This is precisely what Ernst Bloch takes pains to avoid in theorizing a history of music, for he wants to conceive music as an array of "objects which cannot be transformed into history" (14). Bloch is here using history in its vernacular sense as developmental totality, and what he wants is to avoid "the senseless turbulence within [its] progressive criterion . . . "—a turbulence articulated in jazz in terms of cutting sessions, battles of the bands, and other means by which the musicians have sought new ways of *hearing* what they are about, but which historians have read as a practice intrinsic to the tradition that tidies it up for retrospective overview, in which the commanding figures are the fittest survivors.[8] As a result, an iconoclast like Herbie Nichols has been systematically omitted from the history, a victim not only of the dominant society with its twilight zone of jazz clubs, drugs, and desperation, but of the "senseless turbulence" of the historical overview repackaging the past into a commodified tradition.

The legendary cutting contests are paradigmatic of those colorful aspects of jazz that historians find irresistible. Such legends extend another convenience to the historian, which is narrative order. Since information about them generally derives from oral accounts, there is narrative momentum encoded in the information. Some of the most satisfying publications in the field are compilations (or more accurately: systematized collages) of oral history (Shapiro and Hentoff; Gitler; Meltzer). The extent to which such works simulate an evolutionary perspective reflects the tendency of the musicians to adopt that perspective as a mode of oral storytelling. There are issues of obvious ethnographic pertinence that emerge from such multiple framings of narration, most conspicuous of which is that the "informant" participants tell tales about their lives, not about historical totalities. *Tradition* from such a vantage point appears less an evolutionary process than a congeries of practical options and impractical pressures, with accident and obligation, contingency and necessity, playing equal roles. Biographical detail and social texture not only dominate oral histories, but they become coextensive features of a lifeworld to such a degree one realizes that, to the musician, music is indeed a nutritive esemplastic environment. Music rarely emerges from oral history as a topic as such, and this is clearly attributable to the fact that the music is its own discourse: talk about it is inseparable from it. It is a practiced (and performed) theory.

Existing concepts of tradition and praxis as applied to jazz history are theoretically malnourished to the extent that they fail to credit the music's discursivity. The narratological boundaries fabricated by oral testimony, as Kathy Ogren has shown, are coextensive with performative style. Commenting on jazz autobiographies, Ogren cautions against reading as "objective" that which is performative.[9] That is to say, performance is not text but the context (the discourse) within which narrative episodically recurs. Historians seeking to narrativize jazz into a coherent totality fail to comprehend that all the little stories do not so easily add up to a big story. The megascopic aggregate of all the little stories is not a story at all, but a big *picture,* an image of totality that masquerades as explanation. "Continuity is embodied in the mythic path of narrative, which 'explains' by its very sequential course, even when it merely reports" (Kellner 1). This explains in part why some of the more successful books on jazz favor a synchronic over a diachronic approach, in which the historian—opting to portray the music's context by means of a social history portrait—tacitly forswears the perspectival centrality of the multitemporal overview. There are in fact only a handful of such studies, and these tend to avoid discussion of the music, providing instead much of the raw data and local color that general historians are fond of pillaging to flesh out their commentary on the music.[10]

The customary approach in jazz history has been to submerge discussion of records in a narrativized package of sociological information in ways that obscure the fact that recordings are the actual subject, not the music as such. Brian Priestley's *Jazz on Record,* cited earlier, is unique in its explicitness about using recordings as a means of sketching narrative logic. Gunther Schuller's books *Early Jazz* and *The Swing Era* are monuments to the musical history that *can* be patently derived from recordings alone, as well as showcasing the material liability of a thoroughgoing musicological approach. Other histories that rely almost exclusively on recordings attempt to integrate social history with a descriptive commentary that can all too easily be a variant of record reviews (cf. Gordon; Litweiler; and Rosenthal). Ross Russell's *Jazz Style in Kansas City and the Southwest* is the most proficient of such books, and this is attributable, I think, to the fact that much of the music he documents was not recorded. As a result, Russell consistently uses recordings as a basis for speculating on inaudible phenomena, a position that is intrinsically theoretical, albeit treated as an empirical hindrance by Russell (who was, after all, the record producer of Bird's Dial sessions).

To turn now to recordings, I want to begin by noting the obvious pertinence of records not only as a research tool for the historian but as a prominent factor in the lives of jazz musicians. Yet scanning writings on jazz, a curious tendency emerges: historians are very fond of recounting stories of origins, and these stories are invariably framed as personal encounters. Some jazz historians have a particular fondness for primal torch-passing scenes, like Sonny Rollins loitering around Coleman Hawkins's doorstep; or Charlie Parker being so humiliated at a cutting session he went into a woodshedding retreat to get his act together, after which he returned to the scene with his new, legendary sound; or the sixteen-year-old Johnny Hodges's meeting with his idol, Sidney Bechet. These are the kinds of stories that get repeated, endlessly.

But take a closer look at Johnny Hodges. Born in 1907, he was a scant half-dozen years younger than Armstrong, Bechet's junior by ten years. Old enough in the chronicle of jazz to be there almost from the start, and to receive the personal blessings of his mentor. Yet he did not actually study with Bechet; by the time of their encounter Hodges had already won the respect of local Boston musicians. In a different sense, however, the Rabbit *did* study with the master. Here is Harry Carney, Hodges's boyhood friend and later fellow member in the Ellington band: " 'I used to enjoy going to Johnny's house because he had a very good record collection, and we used to borrow ideas from records and copy as much as we liked. . . . We had the old Victrola that you wind by hand, with the horn. It gave us the feeling of being sort of big-time musicians, being able to play some of the things that were on records, for instance by Sidney Bechet, who was our idol' " (Dance 6–7). Here is a primal scene of another sort. Less ennobling perhaps than the initiatory moment of personal origins in which the acolyte receives the benediction of the human god; or trial by fire in a jam session; but a story of origins nonetheless. It turns out to be the constant, if mongrel, accompaniment to jazz history from its beginnings. Henry "Red" Allen, who grew up in a New Orleans musical household with all the benefits to be had by personal encounters, testified that even a local fireball like Armstrong cut his figure on recordings: "Louis wasn't an influence to us until he started making records. We got Louis from records, like all the other jazz musicians in the country, I suppose" (Williams, *New Orleans* 260).

And so the lessons at the phonograph go: Ben Webster copying Frank Trumbauer's solo on "Singin' the Blues," and Lester Young ordering Tram's records by mail, arranging for them to be forwarded to locations where his family's band would be playing. As late as 1956 he claimed, "I imagine I can still play all of those solos off the record"[11] (Russell, *Jazz*

Style 150). Charlie Parker used to adjust the speed of his turntable so he could adapt Young's tenor solos to the pitch of his own alto, as he copied them note for note. In a bizarre ventriloquial doubling of the phonograph scenario with the "authentic" scene of instruction, Bird would stand outside the halls where Prez would be playing in Kansas City, silently fingering the solos he heard (Russell *Jazz Style,* 183, 180). Then there is Idrees Sulieman reminiscing how he met the fifteen-year-old Miles Davis in St. Louis, a meeting arranged because both of them had memorized the Dud Bascomb solos off Erskine Hawkins discs (Gitler 79–80). Cecil Taylor, who has always been adamant about Ellington's primacy, concedes that he resisted Duke in adolescence in favor of other bands, and that it was specifically Charlie Barnet's orchestra that enabled him to see "the next step" in Duke (Rusch 56).

Given that the authentification of origins is made suspect by such widespread parasitism of recordings, it is of interest that white players may have been wary of direct copying because their whiteness tended to make them appear potentially inauthentic anyway. Jimmy McPartland recalled that he and his gang "just wore the records out" of Bix Beiderbecke and the Wolverines:

> We copied off the little arrangements, and what was going on in the ensembles. One thing was definite that we would never do—copy any solo exactly.
>
> We didn't believe in copying anything outside of the arrangement. An introduction, ending, a first ending or an interlude, we would copy those, naturally. But never a solo. For instance, if Bix would take a solo, I wouldn't copy that. I would just play the way I felt. (Shapiro and Hentoff 144)

Just playing the way they felt: what does this really mean—given their fanatical refusal to copy a solo, or else to admit they did—but that they were playing the way they felt they should feel? Ralph Ellison describes how as a boy he was caught between the folk tradition which "demanded that I play what I heard and felt around me," and the classical music tradition which required him to "express that which I was *supposed* to feel" (*Shadow* 190). Ellison's perspective helps clarify the extent to which white musicians entering a black musical tradition were invariably in the position of having to approximate and calculate the extent to which their personal feelings corresponded to the *feel* of musical orthodoxy. That is, musical impulses that were presumed to be second nature to blacks were initially apprehended as "cultural" by whites, who then had to assert a commonality claimed as natural by way of "feeling."

Hsio Wen Shih, in his admirable essay on "The Spread of Jazz and the Big Bands," scrutinizes the formation of larger ensemble playing in the 1920s, and after citing such figures as Ellington, Chick Webb, Lunceford, Luis Russell, and Fletcher Henderson, he asks "Where did all these musicians learn to play jazz? Not from records. . . . " While it is true that the earliest giants of the music were almost helplessly swept into their careers without much anticipation or forethought (Hsio's point about the predominantly middle-class origins of these and other figures is well made), and that they were cutting records themselves before they had a chance to absorb much from other records, the peremptory dismissal of recordings as a source is a bit suspect. As Hsio goes on, it becomes clear what his particular angle is:

> After 1920, with the wide distribution of recordings, the tracing of the spread of jazz is no longer necessary; a young musician could "come swingin' out of Chittlin' Switch" without ever having heard live jazz. Unfortunately recordings also make the tracing of musical influence impossible: if Lester Young claims Trumbauer as his principal early influence, it can only be accepted with wonder and doubt. . . . (176)

Here is a vexing double bind: on the one hand, the critic maintaining that recordings render the tracing of influence unmanageable, and on the other hand the musician himself insisting that recordings in fact constitute influence. Hsio's complaint about recordings is that they ruin chronology. Recordings circulate nonsequentially, privately, and defy reliable documentation of their consumption. Unlike verifiable personal encounters, recordings taint the prospect of historical succession. "Influence," a staple of the biographer and historian, is rendered useless. And without a firmly documented pattern of growth by influence, the critic's job of legitimation is imperiled. There is no need to deny the persuasiveness or the usefulness of evolutionary paradigms. In a sense, all stories told are stories of origin, claims for authenticity. This is true whether the storyteller is a critic, a historian, or a trumpet player recounting personal experience. My concern is with the kind of story propagated by the medium of recorded music, for that is the durable domain of jazz. With jazz there are only two kinds of documents: recordings, and testimony (either written or transcribed from oral report). What Hsio (and virtually all other historians of the music) yearn for is access to some stratospheric, indelible transcript of "influence" uncorrupted by recordings or testimony. Something, in other words, like a certificate of pedigree, or a genealogical chart, some guarantee that the story one elects to tell is the authentic version.

The consistent impediment has been the (recorded) music itself, which speaks a disarmingly heterogeneous glossolalia, while at the same time producing tantalizing if unconfirmed traces of actual "influence." Historicist paradigms of development lose explanatory credibility when the evidence is contradictory. Recorded evidence has been reluctantly deployed to conjure hypotheses of what must have "really" been going on—an acoustic scratching at the door from the past that tantalizes Rankean historical fantasies of "wie es eigentlich gewesen."[12] Jazz historians have yet to repudiate the recorded legacy as spurious and irrelevant to their task; but their non- or antitheoretical *use* of recordings prevents them from confronting the actual nature of the activity they seek to describe. That is, the musicians obviously derive their styles from environmental interaction with other musicians, very little of which gets recorded. Since the medium of their exchange is music, all traces of it literally disappear. A positivist history, emphasizing empirical evidence, can come up with little more than playbills, contracts, and a meager trickle of ancillary writing (mostly by nonparticipants). The great exception to this paucity, from the empiricist point of view, is the existence of recordings. We can see, then, how records have had to substitute for an irrecoverable original presence, particularly when overt claims to documentary fidelity have disguised covertly idealist ambitions.

Here I need to emphasize that, despite an avowed reluctance, all jazz historians rely heavily on recordings. Some of the misgivings associated with records have been cited above—the brevity of 78-rpm recordings, for instance—but these are technical impediments. Another common ground for suspicion is the fact that jazz is significantly improvisatory; a recording tends to reify improvisation, converting the extemporaneous into scripture. This is a reasonable objection to the cult of the recording, one that may be seen in grotesque relief in Dean Benedetti's monumental ambition to tape all of Charlie Parker's live solos.[13] In other words, even if every rendition of every tune at every public and private performance were available to the historian, there would be a problem of *selection*. An imponderable bulk of material residue does not make the historian's task any easier. Recordings are of course preselective, and writers like Gunther Schuller and John Litweiler gladly pursue the possibility that the recordings are the latent sketch of a coherent panorama. It would be preferable, I think, to concede a tension between the clean material realm of recorded artifacts and the scattered, rumored, remembered, and intimated "live" (unrecorded) totality of the music. It is a perennial irony that we trace the legacy of an improvised music by listening to "definitive" performances on records. The musicians themselves have been particularly well situated all along to reflect on this irony, realizing in the tensional dynamic that one does not "tell" the truth, for truth is a performance in medias res—just as a solo is always in the middle, surrounded by themes, bridges, inroads to the music from the world of ambient noise, as well as from the obligations of musical form. It is not only curious, then, but a sign of systematic misconception that a music celebrated for its improvisatory character is viewed chiefly as an example of developmental progress. The explanatory conceit fielded as "history" is thereby forced to rely on the very thing it disavows, as records become the numbers between which the historian fills in the dotted lines. The lines are dotted to reflect an incompleteness of material evidence. Material documentation is missing, however, only if one aspires to superimpose aesthetic order on an otherwise heteroglot profusion by the persuasively simple hypothesis of progress.

It is not merely a matter of accommodating the facts to a comely narrative shape, however, since what is perceived as at stake is often an exoneration of the music from the taint of its associations. Jazz critics have traditionally seen their role as justifying and bringing respectability to an entertainment medium, and the ready means of achieving this goal has been to borrow developmental models from classical music, literary studies, or art history. Consequently, jazz is burdened with the obligation to display in a few decades of history the amplitude and irrevocability that literature and the visual arts required millennia to fulfill. Such models vindicate "jazz," but only at the expense of its practitioners, a few of whom are exalted as avatars while the rest are effaced, their voices put on hold. Leo Treitler has skeptically addressed the application of a logic of historical development to classical music history (which is itself considerably truncated in comparison to literature and visual art), noting that "in the mode of historical writing that came to dominate music history, there was no place for individual creation as a factor in history. . . . But it is a weak notion of evolution in the arts that does not regard individual creation as the central factor of historical continuity and change" (166–67). Treitler criticizes the tendency to rescue the individual by positing artistic "autonomy," in which the singular performance may be shielded from the grim vicissitudes of historical accident. The historian of music thus feels justified in isolating and protecting "major figures" in sanctuaries of aesthetic calm, shelter from the storm. The problem as Treitler sees it is precisely what Priestley attacks as "the convenient, but unhistorical, journalistic assumption that as soon as X made his first record, the world of jazz took immediate note and amended its musical habits accordingly" (x). I would call this the *mono-*

lithic fallacy in which the entire constituency of a given history is presumed to be simultaneously attuned to any local modification as holistically consequent. It is monolithic inasmuch as it has no temporal plasticity. The point is, people inhabit different times, if "time" is liberated from mechanism. Jazz is—musically, conceptually, historically—an exploration of the plasticity of time.

There may be a significant case to be made for the simultaneity of attunement by jazz musicians at a given moment, but awareness of innovation does not always conveniently bifurcate into imitation on one hand and repudiation on the other. Explanatory models of "dominant" trends subsume variation, excess, deviance, and singularity into a monolithic tale of progress and destiny. From that point of view, there can be only "influences," never confluences (not to mention divergences). Albert Ayler cannot be factored into a coherent narrative, so his subordination in written histories is clearly at variance with his significance for musicians. The logic of development devalues iconoclasts because they do not fit in with the (narrative) flow. Since that flow is perceived moving in one direction only, the musicians are confined in terms of influence to their "real" historical moment, with no possibility of reprieve. Ayler is one of innumerable instances of musicians venerated by peers but virtually ignored by critics and historians.[14] It would be possible to extract a voluminous register of the subaltern personnel of jazz history from musicians' recollections, oral histories, and interviews. It is presumptuous of the historian to take it as dissimulation when a musician acknowledges influence from a "minor" figure rather than a "major" one, and even more troubling to cast suspicion on accredited influences who are unknown. The retrospective logic of developmental historicism is a sufficient explanation only for the storylines it chooses to follow, not for the entire domain of activity. If we value the legacy of jazz as a tireless pursuit of different ways of playing "Cherokee," among other things, it is heedless to expect the history of that legacy to boil down to some ascertainably "authentic" version.

Must jazz history invariably constitute a sustained arboreal elaboration of seed principles, dominant trends, and major figures? My conviction (clearly shared by Krin Gabbard's view of "The Jazz Canon and Its Consequences" in this volume) is that it need not. We would do well to explore alternative models of proliferating action as a basis for writing jazz history. Deleuze and Guattari's thesis of nomadology and rhizome is clearly relevant, both as a paradigm of discontinuity and as a way of acknowledging the itinerant conditions of jazz lives, "coming and going rather than starting and finishing." "A rhizome has no beginning or end;

it is always in the middle, between things, interbeing, *intermezzo*. The tree is filiation, but the rhizome is alliance, uniquely alliance. The tree imposes the verb 'to be,' but the fabric of the rhizome is the conjunction, 'and . . . and . . . and' "[15] (Deleuze and Guattari 25). In this light, it is not an impediment but a privilege that jazz did not begin with its earliest recordings. Louis Armstrong is an ampersand; the music we hear is always encountered in midstride, rounding a corner, a crowd already gathered, and another already dispersing. Jazz seems especially positioned to dramatize the "ruptures and proliferations" that Deleuze and Guattari associate with musical form, and the cultural heritage it derives from is itself intimately acquainted with "lines of flight" and "transformational multiplicities."

That crowd is a reminder that jazz has a distinct cultural history in that its practitioners hail from a common cultural background. The most diverse social regimes seem capable of producing painters and poets and musicians; and while this may prove to be the case for jazz in the future, its presently abbreviated history links it to the specific social dynamics of black Americans. While jazz cannot be reduced to its social circumstances, it is accurate to say that the music has been a socially provisional practice. Jazz is the ongoing record of an aesthetic ethos; the functional interaction of individual and group is encoded musically in jazz, both as aesthetic design and as principle of social cohesion. In short, jazz must be viewed as the *conscious* self-determination of social order. Jazz is auto-poetic: its history *is* its aesthetics; that is to say, its creative focus is not an accident, and its evolution is not simply purposive but conscious. Any external account of it must admit its own perspectival peculiarity; and any account seeking conceptual parity with the music needs to substantiate itself by means of innovation rather than authority.

It is this specifically cooperative and interactive provocation that makes the jazz ethos so compelling for writers like Ralph Ellison, Ishmael Reed, Nathaniel Mackey, and Michael Ondaatje (among others).[16] *Invisible Man* is not a "jazz novel," but a narrative meditation on History and the complicity it exacts. Ellison's performative enactment, however, bears a consistent if oblique relationship to the improvisational protocols of jazz. Ondaatje's *Coming Through Slaughter* is a vivid realization of the fact that jazz is more keenly imagined than heard, which makes the unrecorded Buddy Bolden a fitting protagonist. Bolden's "brain" is the real hero, extemporized as a fissure not between occipital lobes but between real and imagined, sane and insane. Ondaatje's "novel" is actually a series of floating epiphanies, each radically sundered from continuity while nevertheless contributing to the feel of a cumulative fate, as Bolden's disintegrating mind negotiates the transition from "cornet" to "corner," music to madhouse. Mackey's *Bedouin Hornbook* is also a generic improvisation of its own textuality in the interstices of autobiographical, epistolary narrative, and expository orders. Here the music is always the pre-text in a book that verges on cosmological treatise. Categorized by its publisher as fiction, *Bedouin Hornbook* absorbs the misnomer into its elegant transgeneric fabric with the same performative insouciance displayed by John Coltrane in *Ascension*, where the term "jazz" began to seem not so much inapplicable as inept. Reed's *Mumbo Jumbo* is an even more euphoric carnival of intertextuality than Mackey's book; but both works remind by their vigorous self-examination—provoked by an ongoing indebtedness to the music—that jazz levies a specific challenge to writers. Form and function, work and play, text and interpretation, orthodoxy and heterodoxy, freedom and subordination are some of the antitheses that jazz discloses in the proximity of writing.

The magnitude of such a stylus, needless to say, has not been acknowledged in jazz histories, and it has hardly been intimated as relevant to the *practice* of writing (which is what a history is).[17] Sadly, the establishment of jazz in educational institutions reinforces the dominant cultural shorthand. One would hardly want to object to this sociologically, for it adds to the possible sources of livelihood for musicians and dignifies black culture in a preponderantly white setting. But academia does not inherently encourage compassionate response to passionate creation. In its new academic setting, jazz will continue to be so much raw material for an image of developmental totality. It is the rhetoric of attention (how we "pay" or expend it) that registers the *ethos* of our relation to jazz as social force rather than empirical fact. The sense we make of it should enrich our sensory experience; and further, "we cannot forget that our ways of making sense of history must emphasize the *making*" (Kellner xi).

To say we "make" history is not to say we make it up, but rather that we make it sensible. We give it resonance and significance, pregnant with the psychological need to "find" it there. What we find is shaped in our telling into a made thing, and in the event we should pause to consider what sort of shape gratifies our *fancy* and, to abide with Coleridge's distinction, whether we might not benefit instead from discovering shapes that invigorate our *imagination*. To speak of cultural "evolution" is a fanciful way of disposing of an awkward fact, which is the unresolvable heterogeneity of cultural practices. Aesthetic media like jazz are not collectively stipulated projects; the transfiguration of music through time is not the progressive realization of a goal. It is only retrospectively that a purposive momentum is evident, and that is of course

what is designated as its history. However, "purposive momentum" may
be realized *as music* as readily as history, which is why I am inclined to
think of jazz *as history* inscribed in another register. We need to refigure
narrative function here so that Lester Young, telling a "little story" in
his solo, sanctifies history by disclosing it to us as performance. Likewise, the clangor and rhythmic tension that mark so much of what we
think of as history can be auditioned as tributaries of melodiousness and
harmony in light of jazz. Insofar as history threatens us as a danger-
ously totalizing vehicle, which, in Hayden White's recommendation, we
would do well to get out of, it is only a praxis like jazz that elucidates the
actual nature of our freedom; we may not ever get out of history completely, so it is beneficial to have complex models of what Nathaniel
Mackey (in the title of a book of essays) calls "discrepant engagement."
Jazz tells us a compelling story about getting out of history and getting
back in again, by energetically displaying the euphoric pragmatism of its
ins and outs.

The audible transfigurations that mark each decade of jazz since the
1920s compel a perspectivizing and comparative attitude that is easily
conflatable with *history*. Alain Touraine's distinction between history
and "historicity" is useful here.[18] History, in Touraine's sense, is simply
the inertial accumulation of incident, whereas *historicity* is the social
praxis of actively integrating knowledge and material culture into an
autointerpretive medium of self-reproduction. History is what happens
to a society or group, whereas historicity pertains to what the society
does. Jazz is clearly not lethargic accumulation, but energized self-reproduction. We can discuss the music's changes as inventions, insights,
discoveries, and integrations; but when so much self-consciousness is
involved, of what use is the term "evolution"? Evolution as a conceptual
term is taken from a context in which the norm is measured in millions
of years. It is catastrophic to even attempt to think in evolutionary terms
about jazz—not even a century old in the wildest historical imaginations,
and only surviving in some seventy years of phonographically "fossil-
ized" remains.[19] The problem in film studies has been comparable. Annette Kuhn points out the consequences of the predominant evolutionary model:

> It can be seen that traditional histories of cinema have often con-
> structed the field in highly selective ways which have none the less
> largely been accepted as natural. Once this naturalness is ques-
> tioned, it becomes clear that such partiality has consequences which
> are not necessarily desirable, and can lead to a blocking of the poten-

tial of history to analyse and explain, rather than simply describe. For example, the overwhelming bias, in spite of an apparent diversity of approach, towards describing cinema history as a chronological sequence of progressions towards ever more perfect forms occludes complex relationships between social structures, institutions and forms which do not necessarily operate chronologically. (2)

Film history, like jazz history, invariably sets for itself a dual task—that of presenting founding figures (Griffith, Armstrong) who are regarded as inaugural masters of the medium, then attempting to heroicize the continual improvements of the medium without at the same time implying that these evolutionary ancestors are disposable.

In jazz, for instance, the sectarian vengefulness of Dixieland revivalists in the 1940s was a protest against the evolutionary perspective. The revivalists could declare in a fiat of authenticity (they were there!) that jazz was not an evolutionary form; it was not born, it could not die, and above all it could not "evolve." It could only *be,* and they were there to demonstrate the pure existence of the thing. When Ornette Coleman came to New York twenty years later, the same evolutionary debate raged again. Was this a stillborn development? Was it musically competent? Or was it, as his Atlantic album declared, "The Shape of Jazz to Come"? In retrospect it was not; Coleman was an "original," not a prototype: an engaging counterpoint to which his contemporaries had to adapt, but not subordinate themselves to. Coleman's uniqueness continues unimpaired: he is universally regarded as a major figure, yet he has spawned few followers, and even after three decades nobody else plays at all *like* him. This should logically indicate an evolutionary cul-de-sac, but logic breaks down in this instance, a fitting rejoinder to the mistake of conceiving aesthetic logic as a species of problem-solving.[20] Coleman, like every other jazz notable, solved an individual rather than a collective problem, which was *how to play.*

We have yet to pay adequate attention to what is *lost* in scenarios of advance. Adaptation to a significant predecessor or contemporary does not necessarily mean "imitation." But adaptation does not mean evolution either. In the 1950s Lester Young resisted the opportunity to reprise his swing hits with the Basie band, saying "I don't play that way any more. I play different; I live different. This is later. That was then. We change, we move on." Joachim Berendt quotes this in support of his evolutionary hypothesis. "The most impressive thing about jazz—aside from its musical value—is in my opinion its stylistic development,"

Berendt writes. "The evolution of jazz shows the continuity, logic, unity, and inner necessity which characterize all true art" (4, 3). My concern is with an elision performed by Berendt, for there is absolutely no intimation on Lester Young's part that the music has evolved; quite the contrary, it has simply meandered on: "We change, we move on," says Prez, but Berendt reinscribes this to mean that change is progressive, movement is developmental. The distinction here is between mimesis and kinesis, imitation or motion. In Gaston Bachelard's study of dynamic imagination as applied to air he notes, "With air, movement takes precedence over matter. In this case, where there is no movement there is no matter" (8).[21]

While it is necessary to remain dubious about the presumptions of the evolutionary paradigm, we should resist disposing of its attachment to *kinetic advance,* onward movement. The musicians, for instance, have favored an evolutionary model without adopting the totalizing presumption of superiority. Coleman Hawkins and Lester Young continue to be idolized even as the idiom with which they are most identified, swing, is regarded as obsolete and indeed inferior from the progressive point of view. But the musicians have always kept in mind an uncanny sort of "progress" whereby imitation may, by that alchemic alembic called "woodshedding," be converted into recognizably distinctive personal movement or *style.* In the end, the music as a whole has been transformed by individuals who have either been imperfect imitators or so successfully mimetic that their imitations obliterated recollection of the original. The persistent feature, over the long haul, is not mimesis (which is omnipresent, a part of how music, like language, is learned) but motion, kinesis, *agitation.* Evolution from that perspective is not a thesis that sums up temporal process in a convenient spatialized image but the periodic or rhythmic pressure of change.

Evolution is organic process, then; but what happens when the organic is adapted to explanatory formula as in historical writing? In Stephen Pepper's theory of world hypotheses it is clearly *organicism* that is the paradigmatic basis for evolutionary historicism, and Pepper's account is of practical significance. Organicism, he suggests, "has to deal mainly with historic processes even while it consistently explains time away . . ." (280). With regard to jazz, the implication is that the tale of unfolding organic destiny situates the music in *historical time* but in the process scuttles the plethora of individuated *time signatures* that constitute the kinetic power of the music itself. "The root metaphor of organicism always does appear as a process, but it is the *integration* appearing in the process that the organicist works from, and not the *duration* of the process" (281). The logic of integration is then laid out in seven steps, which will seem all too familiar to readers of jazz history:

> [T]he features of any organic or integrative process . . . are: (1) fragments of experience which appear with (2) *nexuses* or connections or implications, which spontaneously lead as a result of the aggravations of (3) *contradictions*, gaps, oppositions, or counteractions to resolution in (4) an *organic whole*, which is found to have been (5) *implicit* in the fragments, and to (6) *transcend* the previous contradictions by means of a coherent totality, which (7) *economizes*, saves, preserves all the original fragments of experience without any loss. (283)

The great irony, for jazz history, is that the sense of loss, dispossession, opposition, and contradiction that is so much a part of its blues basis is simply erased by the "economy" of this transcendental operation. The denial of mourning implicit in a logic of evolutionary advance is catastrophic for a music *grounded* in the funeral march as a founding social occasion.

Jazz has been a constant testimony to things that will never be known, people that will forever go unheard, words that will remain unsaid. The unspoken of jazz legacy is *not* a matter of all the "unrecorded" epiphanies of live performance (which after all were heard in their own time); rather, its losses and vacancies are the legacy of human lives and not of an archive. The archive, with its dream of a transcendental perspective, a historical overview, is a device for converting song into text, a "magical net" that traps and immobilizes temporality with all of its discomforting abrasions and excesses: "The text is the power of lines that connect. It is akin to drawing sacred, potent, magical figures, like mandala, which are always figurations in both senses—as things and metaphors. The point of figuration, of writing and text is to capture the power (kinesis) of an exterior order through the techne of mimesis, and to defeat time by transforming motion into structure" (Tyler 36). The provocation of jazz confronts writing with two possibilities. One is to explore the kinesis of magical "lines that connect"; the other is to impose an industrial tool, a Cartesian matrix, and assert the necessary conformity of temporality to the plotted coordinates of the grid. It is an *agon* I am evoking here, because by and large those who have written on jazz imagine themselves to be repaying a profound imaginative debt. Having learned from the music how to *hear* the world differently, however, few have been aroused to a corresponding revision of their writing practice, and those purporting to write "history" have never paused to examine the terminological and conceptual presuppositions involved. The specific challenge of jazz's recorded legacy is to admit a broader range of media to the historical pallette of memory.

The institutionalization of jazz, along with its standard heuristic grid of developmental history, compels a question: What has it meant for jazz history to have been written with the ambition to produce a *master narrative* (in Lyotard's sense) of the musical activity of people for whom the term "master" has ominous associations? The white claim to author jazz history, even in its more benign aspirations, has not been able to altogether dispell the aura of the master race. I do not mean to suggest that white jazz historians have intended to perpetuate racism; but I *do* want to propose that we cannot continue to attend to so acoustically subtle a domain as jazz music and plead terminological neutrality. I want to ponder in closing what is projected into that music's history by applying to it the vocabulary of the "classic" and of "masterpieces." How can one suggest that Charlie Parker created enduring masterpieces without at the same time implying that he made himself into a master, and that his followers were thereby enslaved?

We can reflect on this by looking at a significant example, *The Smithsonian Collection of Classic Jazz.* The Smithsonian set is a kind of audiophonic discography, and it is routinely cited in historians' discographies as an essential entry. Textbooks key musical references to it. When original creation is enshrined under the covenant of the Classic, figures that, in the argot of their own culture are the cats, the heavies, become "major figures," as jazz itself is what Martin Williams (compiler of the Smithsonian set) calls "a major contribution of American black men to contemporary culture" (*Smithsonian* 7). The attitude, implicit in this apparent celebration of black music (and quite apart from its sexism), is that jazz is notable *because it contributes* to something else—and what *that* is is the mainstream, the surrounding whiteness, with its master-piece fix, its pantheon, its need for what it admires to be classicized (and cognate with the classic is, of course, *class* as social division). This is the *dominating fantasy* (and let me emphasize the domination) of the *pre-dominantly* white world of jazz criticism and history. Historians like Martin Williams assume that it is all right to convert jazz into a classical order, as long as the blackness of the figures in the pantheon is emphasized. Because the Western cultural heritage is one that is de facto white, any talk of classics is, literally, a whitewash—as it is for Williams to claim jazz as a "contribution." Did any of the "major figures" in *The Smithsonian Collection of Classic Jazz* think they were contributing, and if so, what did they think they were contributing to—contemporary white culture, as he implies, or a black culture which was if anything intent on distinguishing itself, separating itself out, from the rest? The balance of cultural capital prioritizes Eurocentrism precisely by means of its terminological markers. As long as those markers remain in place, a pantheon of major black contributors ominously resembles a precinct lineup.

The figures in this lineup (the usual suspects: Armstrong, Ellington, Parker) are presented as exemplary. From another angle (and to estrange the familiarity of praise) we can say that an example has been made of them. Jonathan Morse, in his book *Word by Word,* designates what it means to become a living example, or to be made an example of: "Example is that which has been taken out of our hands, then displayed to us in the vitrine of a different context. It is always alienated from its subject, because it is always separated from its subject by its speaker's purpose, a telos of discourse which the subject does not possess" (148).[22] The "speaker's purpose" is not necessarily at odds with that of the subject. In the film *Heart Beat* (1980) Neal Cassady (Nick Nolte) warns Jack Kerouac (John Heard) about the price of fame. "Hey, we all gotta serve," he says, "but you get famous, you gotta serve as an example." The implication is that even a gifted novelist might not be able to write his way out of the grip of the paper tiger. For a musician, the odds are even more daunting, since the cultural division of labor disenfranchises the musical subject as speaker. Jazz historians, fabricating display cases of exemplary major figures, are rectifying the voice of the other, *curing* it as it were of some pathological alienation from speech. However, by recognizing the reigning monoglossia of jazz journalism and history, we might begin to detect a different *stance* of speaker and alternate *positions* of speech on the part of the musicians.

From the earliest days, jazz musicians have consistently emerged from the black middle class and have been the beneficiaries of formal musical training and often college education. It is altogether misleading to imagine some kind of constitutional inarticulateness as a component of the musicians' lot. The drama of evasive communication so conspicuous with Monk or Mingus is precisely that: a drama, a staging of paradox, a way of signaling the (white) context as being coercive, while at the same time moderating the counterproductive lure of open *defiance*. What *is* central to jazz is the myth of the musician expending all of his or her creative insight in the moment of spontaneous improvisation, being thereafter semantically spent. The registers of signifying in the music are

indeed semantically rich, but so are the styles and complexities of articulation in jazz musicians' writings and interviews. Because Ellington
was perceived as debonair, his (much noted) strategies of verbal evasion
were regarded as displays of inscrutable charm, where corresponding
strategies on the part of other musicians tended to be seen as dissimulation, insolence, capriciousness, or a simple inability to speak standard
English (or, as in the case of Lester Young, symptomatic of some alleged
mental fatigue). It would be more accurate to see Ellington as the norm
rather than the exception here, practicing a strategically contrapuntal
speech intended to glance off and otherwise evade the dominant code.
Idiomatic expression is the difference intended by those who are not
permitted a simple *indifference* to the dominant discourse.

As it has been practiced, jazz history is closer to anthropology, at least
if we consider Lévi-Strauss's distinction that history attends to the conscious, and anthropology to the unconscious, parameters of cultural
activity. Jazz players are first celebrated as inspired primitives, creating
without benefit of writing (either music or literature); but at the same
time this scriptural vacancy must be treated as a pathological symptom
in search of a cure, with music as a pure performative expression of pre-
(or even anti-) verbal impulses. A legacy of accumulated commentary on
black musicians' purportedly innate sense of rhythm, or irrepressible
animation, or instinctual grasp of harmonic complexities, has generated
the myth of "blacks as presocial, at ease with play" (Frith 88). This is
another way of asserting that their own idioms of communication are
ludic, and therefore semantically deficient. Again, it is not insignificant
that the language we use to describe the activity of this most valorized
segment of black culture is not work, but "play."[23] The situation of jazz
as an object of cultural history is akin to what James Clifford has described in *The Predicament of Culture.* It is precariously situated between a hegemonic monoculture and a "caribbeanized" polyglot dias-
pora. Clifford recommends, along with Edward Said, a wariness of the
"symmetry of redemption" whereby the cultural objects of the disen-
franchised pass from dustbin to museum. The various tragic and comic
plots of a heteroglot culture cannot be so neatly reconciled to a global
history and a master narrative, for that is to subscribe to an "entropic
metanarrative" which boils cultural difference down to a bland stew of
indifference—world culture as a vast museum of neutered objects.

My interest in the constitutive aberrations of jazz history was aroused
in the late 1970s, when Frank Tirro's history of jazz appeared. Tirro
openly avowed a developmental thesis; and while offering a more densely

detailed history than Stearns had in 1955, the music tended to boil down to a roster of stars. It is easier now to recognize the cul-de-sac into which Tirro had driven the vehicle of historicism: his book culminates in tentative affirmation of the predominant style at the time of publication, *fusion*. Tirro seemed uncomfortable that the noble tradition he had outlined had come to this, but the evolutionary paradigm that had provided the historical scaffolding forced him to yield to fusion against his better judgment. In retrospect, it now appears that Tirro had ridden his developmental historicist mule into the ground, for a "tradition" that extended from Jelly Roll Morton and Louis Armstrong to Chuck Mangione and Tom Scott—not to mention Spyro Gyra, the Yellowjackets and now Kenny G—can only be described as an entropic metanarrative (the entropy being concentrated not in the tradition, but in the presumptuous narrativity of History).

And so we have jazz history, as the methodological recuperation of the word from the tantalizing talk of drums. The music itself, as it is inscribed phonologically, is used, cited repeatedly as a spectrum of examples, but rarely *validated* for what it is: the actual historical medium, the style of telling, a vital component in the media of memory of a people's culture.[24] Jazz music *is* black history, and it has been practiced all along as an ongoing medium of memory. It is not a partial or afflicted testimony in search of something else; nor is it a primitive acoustic desire that, with aid, will convalesce into speech. It is history in the American sense specified by Emerson, in which "all public facts are to be individualized, all private facts are to be generalized. Then at once History becomes fluid and true, and Biography deep and sublime" (246). This is the history that Emerson's namesake, Ralph Waldo Ellison, epiphanizes in *Invisible Man* in a climactic recognition; his protagonist, disturbed at the Brotherhood's ineptitude at handling History as if it were a beast to be tamed, suddenly hears a loudspeaker playing music on a Harlem street. He is moved to wonder "Was this all that would be recorded? Was this the only true history of the times, a mood blared by trumpets, trombones, saxophones and drums, a song with turgid, inadequate words?" (433).

The words may be turgid and inadequate, but the music is not. This is a recognition fundamental to Ellison's practice as a writer, for he takes his directives (thematically and linguistically) from the music. *Invisible Man* is a book of black history because of its basis in music, and a book of American history because, in Emerson's sense, it is fluid biography. It is also emphatically the story of a man without a name, a no-man, a nobody, who is in danger of becoming Somebody, a "major figure." But a clue from a turntable comes his way and reminds him that *major* and *minor* can be reclaimed as musical scales, not instruments of domination in the hierarchy of the white marble pantheon.

Notes

1. In Mary Lou Williams's (possibly apocryphal) reminiscences of the Kansas City scene, a musician jamming at night might go home to bed, come back the next morning, and find the same tune still being played by a different set of musicians—a perpetual motion machine, and a community soundscape (Shapiro and Hentoff 291–92).

2. The function of legend in jazz is further complicated by the communal nature of the music, which tends to discourage such legends so prominent in blues, like Robert Johnson's visit to the crossroads to make a pact with the devil. Legend in jazz is closer to rumor and oral embellishment than it is to such primal episodes of *myth*.

3. In my exposition above of "legend" and "legacy" I mean to invoke Heideggerian etymologies of *legein* as "reading" and as "laying out" (as harvest). There are further connotations pointed out by Jim Patrick: "During Bird's lifetime and for several years afterward, much of the Charlie Parker story remained legend in the Latin sense of the word *lego*: to gather, collect, pick through, read out loud, pick up a rumor, or to steal" ("The Complete Dean Benedetti Recordings of Charlie Parker," p. 14 in booklet accompanying Mosaic MD7-129, 1990). Derrida's critique of "logocentrism" is of course relevant to the denigration of recordings as a secondary medium.

4. James Lincoln Collier, following William Kenney, presses the disclaimer that "To study jazz solely through records, as has so often been done, badly distorts its history . . ." (46). But this, it seems to me, is to make a covert appeal to that living tradition unrecuperable by technological means and thus to tacitly glorify it, as in Collier's assertion that "as far as the working jazz musician was concerned, [recordings were] disjunctive: the real business was done in the dance hall, theaters, and cabarets." But, unwittingly, Collier's phrasing is accurate after all: the real *business* was confined to the paying gig, while making records was for most musicians not very lucrative, but it provided a chance to make music outside the (usually racist and classist) constraints of entertainment venues.

5. Priestley pointedly reminds his readers throughout of the distortions inherent in a disco-centric approach. He was apparently asked to write a listener's guide to one hundred top albums and, finding the notion objectionable, chose the route of the historical survey. The result is a very fine book that is unique, not only in jazz history, in its avid pursuit of what is explicitly disavowed. For some cursory remarks on the status of recordings in jazz history, see Martin Williams's "Jazz, the Phonograph, and Scholarship" (*Jazz Heritage* 223–28).

6. See Gioia, *The Imperfect Art*, esp. chap. 2, "Jazz and the Primitivist Myth."

7. This statement is from an unattributed epigraph to the essay that I presume is by Ellison himself.

8. An instructive example of counterhistorical testimony is Miles Davis's account of being upstaged by Kenny Dorham. As he describes it in his *Autobiography*, Dorham asked if he could sit in with the band at Café Bohemia in 1957 and blew

Davis away. "Sometimes you win and sometimes you lose," Davis reflected, "but after you went through it with a great player like Kenny, you had to get something out of that" (215). Dorham figures marginally in conventional jazz histories, which tend to be preoccupied with a figure like Davis as the premier generic representative of bop/cool trumpet.

9   Ogren's work on jazz autobiographies is a welcome and useful exposition of the rhetorical skills at work in the medium; cf. papers presented to the Modern Language Association (New Orleans, Dec. 1988), the American Studies Association (New Orleans, Nov. 1990) and the American Historical Association (New York, Dec. 1990). See also Ogren, "Jazz Isn't." Another resource on which historical surveys have been mounted is the oral interview. Far and away the most enlightening such book is drummer Art Taylor's "musician-to-musician" interviews (1983), which obviously has its own performance agenda, but the performances emanate (as the music does) from insiders rather than from an outsider (journalist, critic) negotiating a conversation with a musician. Books written as studies that are primarily based on interviews are Spellman; Wilmer; and Stokes.

10 See Charters and Kunstadt; Shaw; Russell, *Jazz Style*; Ostransky; Pearson; Ogren, *Jazz Revolution*; Gioia, *West Coast*; and Kenney.

11 Lester goes on to say that what attracted him to those records was that "Trumbauer always told a little story." Curiously, *before* this 1956 reflection, Dexter Gordon had tipped the hat to Prez himself, asserting that "Prez was the first to tell a story on the horn" (Russell, "Bebop" 212).

12 To the fantasy of knowing "how it actually was," we may contrapuntally hear Aaron Neville's "Tell It Like It Is." Knowing something as it is for us now places us in a dialectical relation to the past, which is not the same as being in a time machine. Hans Kellner's insistence on "getting the story crooked" instead of getting it straight is a useful corrective to aspirations of historical omniscience and invincibility.

13 With Mosaic Records' release of *The Complete Dean Benedetti Recordings of Charlie Parker* in 1990 it finally became evident that Benedetti never had the financial wherewithal to follow Bird around the country and become the fan-as-fanatic jazz legend had made him out to be. Benedetti and Jimmy Knepper, the trombonist, were primarily interested in transcribing and studying Bird's solos. The recordings are valuable to us now mainly as a sustained document of a complete club gig, the Hi-De-Ho in Los Angeles, for two weeks in March 1947.

14 Veneration may take diverse forms, of which imitation is simply the easiest to recognize. Critical indifference to a figure like Ayler may stem from hostility to his sound, but just as likely it reflects an insensitivity to the elaborate registration of *differential homage* that is so crucial to jazz playing—and I mean "differential" in its mathematical sense. David Murray's "Flowers for Albert," for instance, anarchically reverses anxiety of influence, since what he is up to is not so much absorbing Ayler as claiming a mutual respect from one who is no longer around to settle accounts with.

15 Significantly, the cited passage is preceded in Deleuze and Guattari's text by lines from "Old Man River." The authors take note of the inherently nomadic and rhizomatic tendencies of music: "Music has always sent out lines of flight, like so many 'transformational multiplicities,' even overturning the very codes that

structure or arborify it; that is why musical form, right down to its ruptures and proliferations, is comparable to a weed, a rhizome" (11–12).

16 The *others* expand almost beyond accounting in the recent anthologies of jazz-inspired prose and poetry, particularly those edited by Feinstein and Komun-yakaa; and Lange and Mackey.

17 The significant exception is Lock, who accompanied Braxton's quartet during an English tour, a factor specified by the title, *Forces in Motion.* The title also points to a series of other "forces" (cosmological, social, political, creative) that Braxton extensively theorizes in his own writing. That Braxton is literally the speaker in much of Lock's book is a credit to the journalist's ethnographic ingenuity, and it accounts for much of the book's force.

18 See Touraine. Also relevant is Brian Stock's distinction between tradition and traditionalism: "Traditional action . . . consists of the habitual pursuit of inherited forms of conduct, which are taken to be society's norm. Traditionalistic action, by contrast, is the self-conscious affirmation of traditional norms" (164). Jazz musicians at any moment tend toward one or the other of these relations to the past. Stock proposes three elements central to discussions of cultural tradition—"pastness, authoritative presence, and the means of transmission" (161). A musician's accomplishment is generally traceable to the tradition in terms of the temporal field assimilated (pastness), stylistic influences (relationship to significant predecessors) and domain of practice (means of transmission, i.e., composition, arranging, leadership, instruments played).

19 This is not to deny the possibility that jazz may figure in theses of historical acceleration, as for instance Ben Agger's "fast capitalism": "Fast capitalism speeds up the rate at which people live out the historical possibilities presented to them" (20). Jazz figures prominently and convincingly in one such exposition of postwar American culture; see Lhamon.

20 Again, Leo Treitler has pointed out that when "musical compositions are regarded as solutions to problems, or even as propositions about how certain problems might be solved," it follows that the critic and historian are *necessary* for the completion of the work, bringing it to its final realization in a sort of Hegelian Absolute Consciousness (99).

21 Bachelard's focus is largely literary, but to read it with music in mind transfigures its occasional pedanticism into revelation. The acoustic and musical import of countless passages then becomes a clamorous counterpoint to Bachelard's intentions: "the dynamic imagination is a *psychic amplifier*" (12); "Breathing is the cradle of rhythm" (239); "Imaginary air, specifically, is the hormone that allows us to grow physically" (11).

22 Morse adds, in a dizzying formulation, "Considered deconstructively, history is a language consisting of an endless regress of exemplary instances."

23 Nor is this unrelated to club owners' notorious parsimony and reluctance to fully acknowledge music as a labor-intensive profession.

24 Given my lengthy critique of the presumptuousness of white historians, I have to register my own acute discomfort with any such assertion as this. I am, after all, yet another white man sounding off about jazz. My initial exposure to jazz—on a Miami radio station, by earphone, after lights-out in a military school dormitory in 1968 at age 15—was an experience not so much of discovery as of personal

liberation from unbearable constraints. That fact may have predisposed me to hear a more subtle dynamic of communication than the strictly musical would have otherwise warranted for a white boy, but I cannot, for all that, discount finding myself now occupying the dubious position of institutional and cultural authority that accrues to the scholarly *text*.

Works Cited

Agger, Ben. *Fast Capitalism: A Critical Theory of Significance.* Urbana: U of Illinois P, 1989.

Bachelard, Gaston. *Air and Dreams: An Essay on the Imagination of Movement.* Trans. Edith R. Farrell and C. Frederick Farrell. Dallas: Dallas Institute, 1988.

Berendt, Joachim. *The Jazz Book: From Ragtime to Fusion and Beyond.* Rev. ed. Westport, Conn.: Lawrence Hill, 1982.

Bloch, Ernst. *Essays on the Philosophy of Music.* Trans. Peter Palmer. New York: Cambridge UP, 1985.

Burke, Kenneth. *On Symbols and Society.* Ed. Joseph R. Gusfield. U of Chicago P, 1989.

Certeau, Michel de. *The Writing of History.* Trans. Tom Conley. New York: Columbia UP, 1988.

Charters, Samuel, and Leonard Kunstadt. *Jazz: A History of the New York Scene.* New York: Doubleday, 1962.

Cixous, Hélène, and Catherine Clément. *The Newly Born Woman.* Trans. Betsy Wing. Minneapolis: U of Minnesota P, 1986.

Clifford, James. *The Predicament of Culture: Twentieth-Century Literature, Ethnography, and Art.* Cambridge, Mass.: Harvard UP, 1988.

Collier, James Lincoln. *Jazz: The American Theme Song.* New York: Oxford UP, 1993.

Dance, Stanley. "Johnny Hodges." *Johnny Hodges* (booklet accompanying recordings). Alexandria, Va.: Time-Life, 1981.

Davis, Miles, with Quincy Troupe. *Miles: The Autobiography.* New York: Simon, 1989.

Deleuze, Gilles, and Félix Guattari. *A Thousand Plateaus: Capitalism and Schizophrenia.* Trans. Brian Massumi. Minneapolis: U of Minnesota P, 1987.

Dussel, Enrique. *Philosophy of Liberation.* Trans. Aquilinia Martinez and Christine Morkovsky. Maryknoll, N.Y.: Orbis, 1985.

Ellison, Ralph. *Invisible Man.* New York: Vintage, 1972.

——. *Shadow and Act.* New York: Knopf, 1964.

Emerson, Ralph Waldo. *Essays and Lectures.* Ed. Joel Porte. New York: Library of America, 1983.

Feinstein, Sascha, and Yusef Komunyakaa, eds. *The Jazz Poetry Anthology.* Bloomington: Indiana UP, 1991.

Frith, Simon. *Sound Effects: Youth, Leisure, and the Politics of Rock 'n' Roll.* New York: Pantheon, 1981.

Gioia, Ted. *The Imperfect Art: Reflections on Jazz and Modern Culture.* New York: Oxford UP, 1988.

——. *West Coast Jazz: Modern Jazz in California, 1945–1960.* New York: Oxford UP, 1992.

Gitler, Ira. *Swing to Bop: An Oral History of the Transition in Jazz in the 1940s.* New York: Oxford UP, 1985.

Gordon, Robert. *Jazz West Coast: The Los Angeles Jazz Scene of the 1950s.* London: Quartet, 1986.

Kellner, Hans. *Language and Historical Representation: Getting the Story Crooked.* Madison: U of Wisconsin P, 1989.

Kenney, William H. *Chicago Jazz: A Cultural History, 1904–1930.* New York: Oxford UP, 1993.

Kuhn, Annette. "History of the Cinema." *The Cinema Book.* Ed. Pam Cook. New York: Pantheon, 1985. 1–56.

Lange, Art, and Nathaniel Mackey, eds. *Moment's Notice: Jazz in Poetry and Prose.* Minneapolis: Coffee House, 1993.

Lhamon, W. T., Jr. *Deliberate Speed: The Origins of a Cultural Style in the American 1950s.* Washington, D.C.: Smithsonian Institution, 1990.

Litweiler, John. *The Freedom Principle: Jazz After 1958.* New York: Morrow, 1984.

Lock, Graham. *Forces in Motion: The Music and Thoughts of Anthony Braxton.* New York: Da Capo, 1988.

Lowenthal, David. *The Past Is a Foreign Country.* New York: Cambridge UP, 1985.

Mackey, Nathaniel. *Bedouin Hornbook.* Lexington, Ky.: Callaloo, 1986.

Meltzer, David, ed. *Reading Jazz.* San Francisco: Mercury House, 1993.

Morse, Jonathan. *Word by Word: The Language of Memory.* Ithaca, N.Y.: Cornell UP, 1990.

Ogren, Kathy. *The Jazz Revolution: Twenties America and the Meaning of Jazz.* New York: Oxford UP, 1989.

———. "'Jazz Isn't Just Me': Jazz Autobiographies as Performance Personas." *Jazz in Mind: Essays on the History and Meanings of Jazz.* Ed. Reginald T. Buckner and Steven Weiland. Detroit: Wayne State UP, 1991. 112–27.

Ondaatje, Michael. *Coming Through Slaughter.* Toronto: Anansi, 1976.

Ostransky, Leroy. *Jazz City: The Impact of Our Cities on the Development of Jazz.* Englewood Cliffs, N.J.: Prentice-Hall, 1978.

Pearson, Nathan W., Jr. *Goin' to Kansas City.* Urbana: U of Illinois P, 1987.

Pepper, Stephen. *World Hypotheses.* Berkeley: U of California P, 1942.

Priestley, Brian. *Jazz on Record: A History.* New York: Billboard, 1991.

Reed, Ishmael. *Mumbo Jumbo.* New York: Macmillan, 1972.

Rosenthal, David H. *Hard Bop: Jazz and Black Music, 1955–1965.* New York: Oxford UP, 1992.

Ross, Andrew. *No Respect: Intellectuals and Popular Culture.* New York: Routledge, 1989.

Rusch, Robert D. *Jazz Talk: The Cadence Interviews.* Seacaucus, N.J.: Lyle Stuart, 1984.

Russell, Ross. "Bebop." *The Art of Jazz.* Ed. Martin Williams. New York: Oxford UP, 1959. 187–214.

———. *Jazz Style in Kansas City and the Southwest.* Berkeley: U of California P, 1971.

Shapiro, Nat, and Nat Hentoff, eds. *Hear Me Talkin' to Ya.* New York: Holt, Rinehart and Winston, 1955.

Shaw, Arnold. *52nd Street: The Street That Never Slept.* New York: Coward, McCann, and Geohagen, 1971.

Shih, Hsio Wen. "The Spread of Jazz and the Big Bands." *Jazz: New Perspectives on the*

History of Jazz. Ed. Nat Hentoff and Albert J. McCarthy. New York: Holt, Rinehart and Winston, 1959. 171–88.

Spellman, A. B. *Four Lives in the Bebop Business.* New York: Pantheon, 1966.

Stearns, Marshall W. *The Story of Jazz.* New York: Oxford UP, 1956.

Stock, Brian. *Listening for the Text: On the Uses of the Past.* Baltimore: Johns Hopkins UP, 1990.

Stokes, W. Royal. *The Jazz Scene: An Informal History from New Orleans to 1990.* New York: Oxford UP, 1991.

Touraine, Alain. *The Self-Production of Society.* Trans. Derek Coltman. U of Chicago P, 1977.

Treitler, Leo. *Music and the Historical Imagination.* Cambridge, Mass.: Harvard UP, 1989.

Tyler, Stephen A. *The Unspeakable: Discourse, Dialogue and Rhetoric in the Postmodern World.* Madison: U of Wisconsin P, 1987.

Williams, Martin. *Jazz Masters of New Orleans.* New York: Macmillan, 1967.

——. *Jazz Heritage.* New York: Oxford UP, 1985.

——. *The Smithsonian Collection of Classic Jazz.* Revised. Booklet accompanying recordings. Washington, D.C.: Smithsonian Institution, 1987.

Wilmer, Valerie. *As Serious As Your Life: The Story of the New Jazz.* Westport, Conn.: Lawrence Hill, 1980.

Young, Robert. *White Mythologies: Writing History and the West.* New York: Routledge, 1990.

THE JAZZ

ARTIST

AMONG THE

DISCOURSES

"Out of Notes": Signification, Interpretation,
and the Problem of Miles Davis

ROBERT WALSER

I played "My Funny Valentine" for a long time—and didn't like it—and all of a
sudden it meant something.—Miles Davis (Hentoff, "Afternoon" 162)

A flurry of posthumous tributes to Miles Davis almost managed to conceal the fact that jazz critics and historians have never known how to explain the power and appeal of his playing. Of course, there has been no lack of writing about Davis, and no shortage of praise for his accomplishments. For example, *Musician* magazine, which covers jazz but is not primarily devoted to it, launched a cover story with the extraordinary statement, "In the entire recording age, no one has meant more to music than Miles Davis."[1] But histories of jazz, biographies of Davis, and jazz journalism often beg the question of *why* he ought to be so highly regarded: there is a curious absence of engagement with Davis's music, and especially with his trumpet playing.

Miles Davis has always been difficult to deal with critically: along with his controversial personal life, and his even more controversial decision to "go electric" around 1969, Davis has long been infamous for missing more notes than any other major trumpet player. While nearly everyone acknowledges his historical importance as a bandleader and a musical innovator, and for decades large audiences flocked to his concerts, critics have always been made uncomfortable by his "mistakes," the cracked and missed notes common in his performances. "The problem of Miles Davis" is the problem Davis presents to critics and historians: how are we to account for such glaring defects in the performances of someone who is indisputably one of the most important musicians in the history of jazz?

Often, critics simply ignore the mistakes. In his history of jazz, Frank Tirro delicately avoided any mention of the controversies surrounding Davis, whether missed notes, drug use, or electric instruments. Joachim Berendt, in his *The Jazz Book* regretfully mentions Davis's "clams" but quickly passes on, and the widely used jazz appreciation text by Mark Gridley, like that of Donald D. Megill and Richard S. Demory, similarly whitewashes Davis's career.[2] When Howard Brofsky and Bill Cole independently transcribed and published the trumpet solo of Davis's 1964 recording of "My Funny Valentine," both chose to leave out the cracks, slips, and spleeahs, enabling them to produce nice, clean texts and to avoid many problematic aspects of the performance.[3]

Critics sometimes apologize for Davis's flaws or try to explain them away. Cole acknowledges that Davis had what he calls "mechanical problems," but he asserts that Davis "used them well to his advantage," building a style out of his weaknesses, forging "his mistakes into a positive result" (127, 129). Gary Giddins similarly credits Davis with "a thoroughly original style built on the acknowledgment of technical limitations." Giddins comments: "By the time of 'My Funny Valentine,' which has one of the most notorious fluffs ever released, one got the feeling that his every crackle and splutter was to be embraced as evidence of his spontaneous soul" (79, 84). But Giddins himself does not seem convinced by this argument, and he remains unable either to embrace the fluffs or to excuse them. The best that can be said of Miles Davis in this light is that he was a good musician but a bad trumpet player.

James Lincoln Collier, as usual, is bolder than most other critics:

> But if his influence was profound, the ultimate value of his work is another matter. Miles Davis is not, in comparison with other men of major influence in jazz, a great improvisor. His lines are often composed of unrelated fragments and generally lack coherence. His sound is interesting, but too often it is weakened by the petulant whine of his half-valving. He has never produced the melodic lines of a Parker or Beiderbecke, or the dramatic structure of Armstrong or Ellington. And although certainly an adequate instrumentalist—we should not overstress his technical inadequacies—he is not a great one. Perhaps more important, he has not really been the innovator he is sometimes credited with being. Most of the fresh concepts he incorporated into his music originated with other men, ironically, in view of his black militancy, many of them white. . . . He has to be seen, then, not as an innovator, but as a popularizer of new ideas. (435)

Collier's complaint is that Davis lacks originality, formal regularity, timbral purity and consistency, and technical facility. But would Davis's playing really be better if his sound were more pure and uniform, or his phrases more regular? By claiming that Davis failed to measure up to presumably objective musical standards, Collier suggests that Davis was not a good trumpet player *or* a good musician, despite the popularity and respect he has earned from fans and musicians. Though he is more blunt in his denunciation of Davis than are most other jazz critics, Collier's assessment is not unique. But when critical judgments become so out of synch with the actual reception of the music they address, it may be time to reexamine some basic premises. Perhaps there are other methods and criteria to use in analyzing and evaluating jazz; perhaps there is a way of theorizing Davis's playing that would account for its power to deeply affect many listeners.

Miles Davis may be the most important and challenging figure for jazz criticism at the present moment, because he cannot be denied a place in the canon of great jazz musicians, yet the accepted criteria for greatness do not fit him well. (The complexity of Duke Ellington's scoring or the virtuosity of Charlie Parker's improvisation, for example, seem to be much easier to explain and legitimate than Davis's performances.) The uneasiness many critics display toward Davis's "mistakes," and their failure to explain the power of his playing, suggest that there are important gaps in the paradigms of musical analysis and interpretation that dominate jazz studies. Understanding Davis's missed notes, and accounting for his success as a performer, may require rethinking some of our assumptions about what and how music means.

Some useful ways of doing so are implicit in the theory of signification presented by Henry Louis Gates, Jr., in his book *The Signifying Monkey: A Theory of African-American Literary Criticism.* I am not the first to notice that this book has much to offer music scholars: John P. Murphy has drawn upon Gates's work in his discussion of dialogue among jazz improvisers; Gary Tomlinson has used Gates's ideas in his excellent essay on jazz canons and Davis's fusion period; and Samuel Floyd has deployed Gates's theory in his insightful analysis of the dialogue of rhythmic relationships and formal conventions in Jelly Roll Morton's "Black Bottom Stomp."[4] But I will argue that Gates's theory of signifying might yet be applied at a finer level of musical analysis, to illuminate the significance of specific musical details and the rhetoric of performance.

At the core of his theory is Gates's delineation of two different ways of thinking about how meanings are produced. Gates distinguishes between two cultural traditions, white "signifying" and black "Signifyin(g)"; I find the latter a rather precious and unwieldy alteration of the vernacular term, and I will refer to these as "signification" and "signi-fyin'," respectively ("signification" also has the advantage of preserving the static, foundationalist character of the theories of meaning to which Gates refers, while "signifyin'" retains the vernacular focus on agency). The two modes contrast sharply. Signification is logical, rational, lim-ited; from this perspective, meanings are denotative, fixed, exact, and exclusive. Signifyin', conversely, works through reference, gesture, and dialogue to suggest multiple meanings through association. If significa-tion assumes that meanings can be absolute, permanent, and objectively specified, signifyin' respects contingency, improvisation, relativity—the social production and negotiation of meanings. We might compare the way a dictionary prescribes meanings with the ways in which words constantly change meaning in actual usage by communities of language users. The difference is like that between semantics and rhetoric: signifi-cation assumes that meaning can be communicated abstractly and indi-vidually, apart from the circumstances of exchange; signifyin' celebrates performance and dialogic engagement.

As Gates himself insists, signifyin' is not exclusive to African Ameri-can culture, though it is in that culture that signifyin' has been most fully articulated theoretically, not only by scholars but also in folklore and song lyrics. In fact, the concept could be compared to literary critic Mikhail Bakhtin's ideas about dialogue in the novel, or to a variety of other twentieth-century philosophical interrogations of the nature of language and meaning, from Wittgenstein to the American pragmatists to the French poststructuralists.[5] But Gates, while certainly influenced by these critics and theorists, means to illuminate African American literature by taking seriously the modes of signifyin' developed within black vernacular traditions.

Gates is not the only African American literary theorist to draw atten-tion to the importance of signifyin', or to attempt to define it. Houston A. Baker, Jr., recently equated signifyin' with deconstruction (183), and Ralph Ellison had earlier defined signifyin' as "rhetorical understate-ment" in *Shadow and Act* (249). Both definitions highlight the richness and slipperiness of signifyin' as a cultural tradition and a rhetorical strategy. Like Gates, Baker and Ellison point to performance, negotia-tion, and dialogue with past and present as features of this mode of artistic activity.

Clearly, Gates's theory of signifyin' is opposed to the perspective of modernism. For the modernists, the artwork had to be autonomous from mass culture and everyday life; it was the expression of a purely individual consciousness, without social content; such art was supposed to be self-referential, exploring the medium itself. Modernist aesthetic theory has long dominated academic study of the arts, and consequently it has seemed attractive to many jazz critics and scholars as a route to academic prestige and legitimation. At a recent symposium on jazz theory and criticism, Gunther Schuller ("Influence") pondered the question of how to judge jazz, coming up with a characteristically modernist dual answer. On the one hand, he says, we must judge jazz performances or recordings on their own merits, based on the composer's and musicians' intentions and study of the work. On the other hand, we can rely on certain standards of performance quality and authenticity, the latter encompassing technical accuracy, appropriateness to the style, and originality. That is, art can be understood as intentional, its meanings owned by the artist; but it can also be held accountable to a set of critical standards that are assumed to transcend particular statements or artifacts.

In a response to Schuller's comments published in *New Perspectives on Jazz*, Olly Wilson pointed out that musical techniques, styles, and procedures are never autonomous; they are organized at a conceptual level, a level of cultural priorities and modes of thought, which must be addressed by criticism. Amiri Baraka argued in the same volume that the critic must understand how the work means; an aesthetic, he pointed out, is expressive of a worldview: "subjective, yet reflective of objective political and economic existence" (60). In other words, reactions to art feel personal, but they nonetheless reflect the ways in which even our most personal feelings are socially constituted.

Some jazz critics, then, resist the modernist attitudes that are so antithetical to signifyin'; such critics are dissatisfied with analytical methods that radically reduce musical activities to formal abstractions that often shed little light on how music is experienced. But overall, academics (and some jazz musicians) seem increasingly drawn to what I will call "classicizing" strategies for legitimating jazz. Now, it seems natural enough that people who are trying to win more respect for the music they love should do so by making comparisons with the most prestigious music around, classical music. But the price of classicism is always loss of specificity, just as it has been the price of the canonic coherence of European concert music (the disparate sounds of many centuries, many peoples, many functions, many meanings all homogenized and made interchangeably "great"). Too often, jazz education and scholarship mimic the elitist moral crusade that created the canon of classical music in the last half of the nineteenth century (see Levine). Audiences are assumed to be passive, the content of jazz is rarely discussed, its relevance to peoples' lives never examined.[6] It is simply presumed that increased exposure to jazz is somehow good for people, and appreciation takes the place of understanding. Moreover, history is distorted when devotees work to separate jazz from the rest of popular music, a move that is meant to put them on the right side of the mass culture/modernism divide (see Huyssen).

The classicization of jazz has even facilitated a nationalist distortion of jazz in the United States. According to such prominent spokespeople for jazz as Billy Taylor, Wynton Marsalis, and Gunther Schuller, jazz is "America's classical music" or "America's one truly indigenous musical art form" (Schuller, "Influence" 10; see also Sales). It "developed steadily from a single expression of the consciousness of *black* people into a *national* music that expresses American ideals and attitudes to Americans and to people from other cultures all around the world," and it makes a single kind of political statement: "in a typical jazz performance each individual performer contributes his or her personal musical perspective and thereby graphically demonstrates the democratic process at work" (Taylor 21). Jazz idealizes "the concept of individual freedom" (Taylor 89).

But characterizing jazz in this way effaces both its complex cultural history, including the myriad effects of racism and elitism on the music and the people who have made it, and the dialogue that is at the very heart of the music. Taylor praised individualism; but what of collaboration: in collective improvisation, in composition, in the ongoing collective transformation of the discourse of jazz? What of the ways in which musicians, as they play, converse with one another, with their audiences, with their forebears? Taylor celebrates the fact that jazz has gotten substantial support from the U.S. State Department and that it has been featured on Voice of America radio broadcasts, without considering why this might be so. The answer is that the sort of reading of jazz articulated by Taylor, which emphasizes individualism rather than collectivism, autonomous statements rather than dialogue and collaboration, helped enable the use of jazz as propaganda for capitalism by distorting the nature of the music, by blurring its variety and its debt to the collective struggles of African Americans, and by effacing the fact that jazz has long flourished outside the United States.[7] The most obvious failing of the movement to classicize jazz, however, is that it has never been able to do justice to the music; for example, it offers no means of accounting for why Miles Davis misses notes, or even of understanding what he is really doing the rest of the time.

This is in part because musicological treatments of jazz have also been chiefly devoted to legitimation, the main argument having been that jazz is worthwhile because even its improvised solos demonstrate organic unity and motivic coherence.[8] Virtually the whole tradition of musicological analysis of jazz, from Winthrop Sargeant on, has been caught between the admission that jazz is different from classical music (and probably inferior), and the desire to legitimate jazz according to the criteria commonly used to analyze classical music. Jazz scholars have long neglected opportunities to learn about the different premises and values emphasized in African American culture from scholars and theorists of that culture. The two writers most often credited as the foremost musical analysts of jazz, André Hodeir and Gunther Schuller, applied the vocabulary of academic musical analysis to jazz, labeling chords and motives without seriously questioning the appropriateness of such wholesale methodological transference. Hodeir's allegiance to the European canon allowed him only a single yardstick against which to measure every musical object, regardless of its history, its discursive premises, or its values (92). And even though Schuller has written an excellent explanation of the sedimented African priorities in jazz, transformed by African Americans in their new contexts, he has also accepted from musicology the idea that Western art music operates in an autonomous domain; his writings on jazz are colored by his desire to prove that jazz is equally autonomous and thus equally worthy of respect.[9]

Both Hodeir and Schuller often referred to the importance of "objectivity"—a common priority among those who prefer not to interrogate their premises. Schuller celebrated "real quality and musical talent" without any reflection on how those categories come to be created and understood by various social groups; indeed, he searched for "purely musical qualities," deliberately stripping away the "historical and social trappings" that enable sounds to be meaningful to people (Schuller, *Swing Era* 199, 63, and passim).[10] In his famous analysis of Sonny Rollins's "Blue 7," Schuller consistently avoided commenting on rhetoric or affect and reduced the force of Rollins's improvisation to the articulation of unity and order. Though it is clear that Schuller, along with everyone else, hears much more than that in this recording, his precise labeling of musical details and persuasive legitimation of jazz according to longstanding musicological criteria caused many critics to hail this article as a singular critical triumph.[11] All it really tells us about Rollins, however, is that his improvisations are coherent; it says nothing about why we might value that coherence, why we find it meaningful, or how this solo differs from any of a million other coherent pieces of music.

The price of such classicizing formalism is always the loss of affect and

history; most jazz analysts and many critics have been modernists willing to make the trade. But Miles Davis, in such terms, would have to be
called postmodern. He refused to be constrained by genre boundaries; his
music embraced and explored contradictions; he dismissed questions of
authenticity or purity; he was unwilling to separate art, life, and politics.
These are the traits that led Stanley Crouch to place the blame for
contemporary jazz, which he sees as being in a colossal mess, squarely on
Davis; he refers to "the mire Miles Davis pushed jazz into" (Crouch 86).
But as Robert Palmer (41) argues, such polemics signal cultural contestation of great import: "Critics and musicians who are still trying to hold
the line against this cultural democratization, mostly from the classical
and jazz camps, are classist bigots fighting a losing battle with musical
and social realities. . . . Davis had a particular knack for getting under
these purists' skins. . . ." As we will see, Davis's consistent and deliberate use of risky techniques and constant transgression of genre boundaries are antithetical to "classicism" and cannot be explained by formalism; from such perspectives, unusual content looks like flawed form.
That is why so many critics have responded to Davis's music with
puzzlement, hostility, or an uneasy silence.

Henry Louis Gates, Jr.'s theory is useful precisely because his goal was
to create the means to deal with cultural difference on its own terms, as
an antidote to theoretical assimilation by more prestigious projects.
Gates does not shy away from questions of value and analysis, yet his
work unmasks the shallowness of attempts to show that African literature is worthy of study because it is fundamentally the same as European
literature, or that jazz is worthy of study because it is just like classical
music (Gates xx). Gates's notion of signifyin' codifies a set of ideas about
processes of signification, and in the process it offers us a bag of new
conceptual tools for musical analysis and challenges us to rethink not
only the tactics but also the goals of such work. I want to illustrate the
productive potential of these ideas through a detailed analysis of Miles
Davis's 1964 recording of "My Funny Valentine." But since audiences
hear Davis's recording up against a long history of other performances of
the song, I will begin with the issue of intertextuality.

Consider a pop vocalist's treatment of the song, such as Tony Bennett's 1959 recording.[12] Bennett's voice is warm, with constant vibrato
throughout; like many singers, he uses vibrato as a component of the
vocal sound rather than as an ornament, so that it projects sincerity and
expressivity evenly over the course of the entire song. Bennett follows
the original printed version of the song closely, but he often slightly

alters the rhythm of the melody to make his delivery of the text seem more natural and intimate; he also changes a note here and there, to suggest even more personal earnestness. A few deft appoggiaturas serve to underline his casual control of the music and to complete his modest customizing. Bennett's rich tenor presents the singer as an ostensibly benevolent patriarch, for when the song is sung by a man to a woman (the opposite of the original context in the Broadway musical *Babes in Arms*), the text's enumeration of faults ("Is your figure less than Greek? Is your mouth a little weak?") becomes somewhat condescending and insulting, however well masked by the tender music. The pianist's nod to "Greensleeves" at the very end completes the atmosphere of poignant sincerity Bennett has worked to create.

"My Funny Valentine" was composed by Richard Rodgers and Lorenz Hart in 1937. By the time of Bennett's recording, Davis had already recorded the song twice himself, in 1956 and 1958; his live recording was made five years after Bennett's. Now can we say that Davis is signifyin' on—commenting on, in dialogue with, deconstructing—Bennett's version? The question is made more complex by the idea that as a performer, Davis is signifyin' on all of the versions of the song he has heard; but for his audience, Davis is signifyin' on all of the versions each listener has heard. What is played is played up against Davis's intertextual experience, and what is heard is heard up against the listeners' experiences. Moreover, Davis is no doubt engaging with the many Bennett-like performances of "My Funny Valentine" he must have heard, but he is also signifyin' on many jazz versions, including his own past performances.[13] This chain of signifyin' spins out indefinitely, though most fundamentally Davis is in dialogue with the basic features of the song itself, as jazz musicians would understand them, and as listeners would recognize them. The whole point of a jazz musician like Davis playing a Tin Pan Alley pop song could be understood as his opportunity to signify on the melodic possibilities, formal conventions (such as the AABA plan of the 32-measure chorus), harmonic potentials, and previously performed versions of the original song.[14]

Davis signifies from the very beginning of his 1964 performance; after Herbie Hancock's piano introduction, Davis understates the first two phrases of the melody (see transcription).[15] His tone is soft and without vibrato, and he has clipped the long notes of the song, making his statement seem idiosyncratic yet restrained. Without a constant vibrato such as Bennett uses, there is no warm surface to hide behind; Davis's statement seems stark and vulnerable. After each phrase, he pauses, and the empty time creates a sense of dramatic engagement as we wait for the continuation we know must occur. On the third phrase (m. 5), Davis deceives us; he begins on the proper note, but instead of ascending to follow the melody, he descends into the lowest register of the trumpet before seeming to gain momentum that shoots him up to almost an octave higher than where he should be, if he were still following the tune. The melody of "My Funny Valentine" was so familiar to his audience that Davis did not need to state it before signifyin' on it; two brief phrases serve to establish the tune. The third phrase not only deceives, but contrasts sharply with the first two (mm. 1 and 3): during this eruption Davis plays loudly for the first time, and adds some vibrato while he holds the final high note. Unlike Tony Bennett, Davis uses vibrato selectively so that its presence or absence is significant; here he uses it to intensify the end of this outburst before he retreats back to a soft note in his middle range.

That next note, in the last measure of the first A section (m. 8), is rich in signifyin'. Davis plays an A♭ in the normal way, with the trumpet's first valve depressed.[16] He then slides down to a G without changing valves. This is a technique that, on the trumpet, is difficult, risky, and relatively rare. Acoustically, the trumpet should not be able to play any notes between A♭ and E♭ with only the first valve depressed; Davis must bend the note with his lips without letting it crack down to the next harmonic.[17] The result is a fuzzy sound, not quite in tune. There is no conceivable situation in classical trumpet playing where such a sound would be desirable. Yet in this solo, it is the audible sign of Davis's effort and risk, articulating a moment of strain that contributes to the affect of his interpretation. If we explain this measure in terms of quarter tones or, as Howard Brofsky does, transcribe it as simply two notes, an A♭ and a G, we gain a neater description but miss the point of the music. Davis deliberately risks cracking that note because it is the only way to achieve that sense of strain. Here, he manages to hold onto the note; at other moments in the solo such wagers are not won. However, it is crucial to appreciate the extraordinary lengths to which Davis goes to make playing the trumpet even more difficult and risky than it already is, and to understand the musical results of his doing so.

For the trumpet, like most wind instruments, underwent a continual process of "improvement" throughout the nineteenth century and, to a lesser extent, the twentieth. In particular, instrument makers sought to adapt the trumpet to the needs of the expanding nineteenth-century orchestra by striving for a smooth, even timbre across the whole range of the instrument, one that would be consistent at all dynamic levels. In contrast, the eighteenth-century trumpet parts of J. S. Bach make use of the inconsistencies of the instrument as Bach knew it. On the trumpets of that time, every note had a different timbre and a different degree of stability. Bach carefully exploited these characteristics, using weaker or fuzzier notes in harmonically strained passages, and returning to cadence with the most gloriously solid notes on the instrument. Players of the time developed a very flexible technique as well, practicing a great variety of articulations, working to make their lines uneven and musically subtle (Walser). All of this was undone in the nineteenth century, as both instruments and pedagogy became standardized for the needs of the symphony orchestra. As a consequence, jazz trumpet players like Miles Davis have had to wrestle with an instrument that was literally designed to frustrate their attempts to produce a wide variety of timbres.[18]

Throughout the solo, Davis uses another risky technique; he half-valves—depresses a valve only part of the way down, which creates a split, unfocused airstream—to create a variety of timbres and effects. In mm. 10 and 11, half-valving is combined with dissonant pitches and halting, fragmented rhythms to create a temporary sense of dislocation. Another half-valved slide blurs the beginning of a reference to the original melody in measure 12. After his unnerving silence during the major seventh chord in the next measure—an important point of arrival in the song—Davis uses a grace note and a slight half-valve to make the high point of the phrase seem delicately virtuosic (measure 14). A quick reprise of the risky bend finishes off the phrase, and we must wait almost two measures for another utterance from Davis.

When it comes, the next phrase contrasts sharply with the previous statement, for its climb is loud and brash, featuring no fewer than three cracked notes in two measures. I suspect that the last of these was done deliberately, to make the other two seem thematic in retrospect. This is not uncommon among jazz musicians, who are free to signify on the music they have played just seconds before. Improvisers can comment on what they have just played by spontaneously repeating, embellishing, and developing their best ideas. But jazz musicians can also engage with their most infelicitous phrases; though they cannot be unplayed, they can be resituated and reinterpreted by subsequent statements. Thelonious Monk was particularly adept at using musical accidents as material for development and elaboration. But of course jazz musicians vary greatly in their attitudes about such things. Many abhor technical imperfections and strive to avoid uncontrolled noises. Some, like Monk or

Davis, play in ways that create such unforseen sounds, though Monk seemed to find them fascinating while Davis simply accepted them as consequences of the way he played.

For I do not mean to suggest that Davis wanted to make mistakes, or that he was not bothered by them. He had absorbed a dislike of technical failings from many sources, including his first trumpet hero, Harry James, who was famous for his stylish phrasing and flawless technique. And when Davis had to choose among various takes after a recording session, he is said to have invariably picked the one with the fewest mistakes.[19] Yet Davis has also been quoted as saying: "When they make records with all the mistakes in, as well as the rest, then they'll really make jazz records. If the mistakes aren't there, too, it ain't none of you" (Gleason 134). Despite his dislike of failure, Davis constantly and consistently put himself at risk in his trumpet playing, by using a loose, flexible embouchure that helped him to produce a great variety of tone colors and articulations, by striving for dramatic gestures rather than consistent demonstration of mastery, and by experimenting with unconventional techniques. Ideally, he would always play on the edge and never miss; in practice, he played closer to the edge than anyone else and simply accepted the inevitable missteps, never retreating to a safer, more consistent performing style.

After the glaring "clams" of measures 17 and 18, Davis returns with a soft nod to the original melody of "My Funny Valentine" in the following two bars. The next lick again goes beyond the classical boundaries of trumpet technique by using an alternate fingering to produce a different timbre and slightly low pitch. Davis plays a lazy triplet of D's, the first and last with the normal fingering of open, but the middle one with the third valve. Another curt nod to the melody sets up a tremendous silence, a charged gap of almost three full measures. Henry Louis Gates, Jr., in one of his few explicit comments on African American music, explains how such a pause can be understood as signifyin':

> [A] great musician often tries to make musical phrases that are elastic in their formal properties. These elastic phrases stretch the form rather than articulate the form. Because the form is self-evident to the musician, both he and his well-trained audience are playing and listening with expectation. Signifyin(g) disappoints these expectations; caesuras, or breaks, achieve the same function. This form of disappointment creates a dialogue between what the listener expects and what the artist plays. Whereas younger, less mature

musicians accentuate the beat, more accomplished musicians do not have to do so. They feel free to imply it. (Gates 123)

To create a pause of such length, during one of the most tense harmonic moments of the song, is, among other things, Davis's confident assertion of his stature as a soloist. Would an audience wait eagerly through such a gap for a lesser musician? Would a lesser musician dare to find out? Davis indulges in that sort of manipulation that is the prerogative of the virtuoso and at the same time illustrates his freedom from having to articulate all of the chords; rather, the chords are there as a field on which he signifies.

In a deviation from the standard 32-bar form, Rodgers and Hart extended the final A section of "My Funny Valentine" with an extra four measures (beyond the usual eight). In the ninth bar of this section (measure 33), we can hear Davis signal, with a single pair of notes, a doubling of the tempo, which is immediately picked up by the other musicians. A high rip, solidly on the downbeat, gets their attention, and the subtle swing of two eighth-notes on the second beat is enough to cue the band to shift tempo. The eighth-notes are signifyin' on the previous rhythmic feel and cannot be contained within it, prompting the change.[20] By starting the new rhythmic feel four measures before the start of a new chorus, Davis cuts against the regularity of the song's formal plan, building momentum at what should be the most predictable point in the song, the turnaround into the next chorus, where the melody relaxes. That he succeeds in sparking increased engagement with the audience is clear from their spontaneous applause here, in the middle of his solo.

Davis begins the second chorus of his solo with a striking contrast, a splattered high note followed by one that is neatly and precisely placed (measure 37). The first note comes across as a scream, particularly since it is on the tense ninth degree (D over C minor); the second note not only resolves harmonically to the tonic but also resolves the gesture of wildness with a demonstration of control. Precise placement of even more dissonant notes in the following measure emphasize Davis's willfulness and strength, as he clashes deliberately with the harmonic context.

The third measure of this chorus (measure 39) is a mess. Clear, distinctly pitched notes are almost wholly absent; what we hear is a raucous, complex ascending gesture. Davis keeps his embouchure very loose and uses breath accents on the higher notes to shape the line. What results is indeterminate in pitch but rhetorically clear. It is a chaotic, almost frantic climb that briefly shoots past the tonic to the flat ninth degree, then spins back to the tonic and down an octave by way of a deft flip into bluesier terrain. Again, Davis is less interested in articulating pitches than in signifyin'; the two halves of this phrase are in dialogue, the messy scramble upward answered by the casual, simple return. Their juxtaposition furthers our sense of Davis's playful, adventurous, multifaceted, sometimes strained but ultimately capable character.[21] Davis does not present his audiences with a product, polished and inviting admiration; we hear a dramatic process of creation from Davis as from few others. And as we listen, we can experience these feelings of playfulness, complexity, struggle, and competence as our own.

For the next seven measures, Davis works primarily with rhythm; his phrases are simple and exquisitely swung, and he places substantial pauses in between them so that the rhythm section can be heard swinging in response. Skipping ahead, we hear him doing something similar at the start of the last A section (measure 61), creating a space for dialogue just before he ascends into a series of stratospheric screeches that must have surprised those critics who have insisted that Davis is a weak trumpet player with a limited range. The solo ends (measure 74) with a series of fading quarter notes on the beat, pitched in Davis's midrange, a dissonant tritone away from the tonic; an appogiatura both blurs and emphasizes each note, making the end of his solo seem enigmatic and inconclusive.

Characterizing Davis's style as "prideful loneliness," Nat Hentoff has argued that Davis's power as a soloist came from his "relentless probing of the song, of himself and of the resources of his horn. There is also the constant drawing of melodic and emotional lines as taut as possible before the tension is released only to build up again. And there is the unabashed sensuality of tone, together with the acute pleasure of surprising oneself in music" (Hentoff, Liner notes).[22] Hentoff's comments are certainly evocative of what I have called signifyin' in Davis's music. And Ben Sidran's book about orality in African American music similarly directs our attention toward the dialogic aspects of jazz, as do LeRoi Jones's *Blues People* and Christopher Small's *Music of the Common Tongue: Survival and Celebration in Afro-American Music.*[23]

Such arguments, however, seem not to have been very influential on jazz scholarship; with the exception of Hentoff, these writers are not often cited in jazz bibliographies.[24] The reason for this, I think, has been the lack of attention within jazz scholarship and criticism to articulating links among the impressions of listeners, the techniques of musicians, and the actual sounds that result. Bill Cole remarked of this solo that Davis "holds his listeners' interest by playing every note as if it were the most important note he would ever play. It is this intensity that is so persuasive in his playing" (Cole 156). This argument is itself persuasive, but how do we actually hear an abstract quality like "intensity"? Gary Tomlinson has nicely described "the technical revolution brought to the trumpet by black Americans, a revolution that toppled the prim Arban methods and military precision of Victorian cornet virtuosos and broke wide open the expressive range of the instrument." Tomlinson goes on to say specifically of Miles Davis: "the power of his vision was such that he could make even his famous cracked and fluffed notes a convincing expressive aspect of it" (Tomlinson 90–91). Like Gary Giddins, Tomlinson is trying to valorize aspects of Davis's performances that escape conventional accounts; like Giddins's attempt, though, it appeals to a fairly misty notion of "vision." But most important, none of these comments are musically specific; jazz criticism has lacked detailed analyses of specific performances that articulate links among reactions, theories, performance choices, and technical details.

My analysis of "My Funny Valentine" is certainly not exhaustive—a more extensive treatment might move beyond Davis's rhetorical choices to examine how the other musicians similarly signify on the conventions of the tune (Hancock's chord substitutions are particularly important). And while I have touched on a few points of dialogic interaction among the musicians, there is much more to be said about that. I have focused selectively on certain aspects of one solo in order to make a number of methodological points and to present an example of a kind of analysis that takes us into the notes but acknowledges the centrality of rhetoric, that leads us into the trees but also sees the forest. The value of a theory of signifyin' is that it can help direct our attention to aspects of jazz performance and reception that have not been cogently addressed, and it helps provide a language for doing so. And by grounding his theory in African American practices, but not limiting its applicability to African American culture, Gates helps us to gain a new perspective on many different cultural practices. Prevalent methods of jazz analysis, borrowed from the toolbox of musicology, provide excellent means for *legitimating* jazz in the academy. But they are clearly inadequate to the task of helping us to *understand* jazz, and to account for its power to affect many people deeply—issues that ought to be central for critical scholarship of jazz. They offer only a kind of mystified, ahistorical, text-based legitimacy, within which rhetoric and signifyin' are invisible. Such methods cannot cope with the problem of Miles Davis: the missed notes, the charged gaps, the technical risk-taking, the whole challenge of explaining how this powerful music works and means.

Why must it be explained? Because it will be, somehow, unavoidably. Artistic experiences are never unmediated by theoretical assumptions, whether positivist or formalist, mystifying or signifyin'. And how we think about Davis's solo on "My Funny Valentine" has implications far beyond our response to this particular performance. The work of Miles Davis seems to repudiate conventional notions of aesthetic distance and to insist that music is less a thing than an activity; his music itself provides the most eloquent argument for analysis to open itself up to issues of gesture and performativity. The problem of Miles Davis is that if technical perfection is assumed to be a universal and primary goal, the deliberate efforts of musicians like Davis to take chances are invisible, and their semiotic successes are inaudible. If individuality and originality are fetishized, signifyin' is lost, for it is fundamentally dialogic and depends on the interaction among musicians, their audiences, and the experiences and texts they exchange.

For example, one of Davis's biographers asserted that the "My Funny Valentine" solo demonstrates "no readily apparent logic" (Nisenson 187), while another waxed enthusiastic about the "dramatic inner logic" of the same solo (Carr 175). Each critic found it a powerfully moving performance, but both lacked an analytical vocabulary that could do justice to their perceptions.[25] Pianist Chick Corea muses: "Miles' solos are really interesting to look at on music paper, because there's nothing to them. On a Trane solo or Charlie Parker solo, you can string the notes out and see all these phrases and harmonic ideas, patterns, all kinds of things. Miles doesn't use patterns. He doesn't string notes out. It's weird. Without the expression, and without the feeling he puts into it, there's nothing there" (Mandel 18–20). Corea's comments dramatize the problems of accounting for the rhetorical power of aspects of Davis's performances that escape conventional notation and theorization.

Davis once said: "Sometimes you run out of notes. The notes just disappear and you have to play a sound" (Burns). The title of this essay takes as a motto Davis's insistence that musical creativity need not be limited by abstractions such as notes, and it signals a call for critics and scholars not to allow such concepts to constrain *their* work. Musical analysts need to confront the challenges of signifyin', the real-life dialogic flux of meaning, never groundable in a foundationalist epistemology, but always grounded in a web of social practices, histories, and desires. Modernism and classicism cannot take us into notes, where choices and details signify; nor out of notes, onto that risky rhetorical terrain Miles Davis never stopped exploring.[26]

Transcription: Miles Davis, Solo on "My Funny Valentine,"
1964 Recording

× — half valved note

~ — swallowed, burbled, or ornamented note

Notes

1   *Musician* Dec. 1991: 5. Other important tributes appeared in *Down Beat* Dec. 1991 and *Rolling Stone* 14 November 1991.

2   Tirro does mention fusion, but without any hint that it was controversial, that it was anything other than natural evolution.

3   *My Funny Valentine: Miles Davis in Concert* (Columbia CS 9106). This is a live recording of a performance at Philharmonic Hall in New York City, 12 February 1964. Davis performed with George Coleman, Herbie Hancock, Ron Carter, and Tony Williams. Ian Carr's (306) transcription is much better in this respect. While most critics refer to "missed notes" or "cracked notes," trumpet players themselves tend to prefer more colorful, onomatopoeic terms, such as "spleeah," "clam," or "frack."

4   Floyd's fine essay actually appeared long after its publication date, when my article had largely been completed; his reading of Gates and his analytical focus differ somewhat from mine, but our goals are similar. See also Gabbard.

5   It might seem that semiotics would be highly relevant to musical signifyin'. But scholars working in the area of musical semiotics have typically assumed that the production of musical meaning is a matter of semantics, following older models developed by structuralist linguistics, or they remain tied to a foundationalist epistemology that is unable to cope with the social and contested production of meanings. See, for example, Nattiez.

6   Has anyone else noticed that *The New Grove Dictionary of Jazz* (Kernfeld) contains no articles under any of these headings: "Analysis," "History," "Historiography," "Criticism," "Audiences," "Fans," "Concerts," "African Music," or "Afro-American Music"?

7   As Martin Williams (*Jazz Tradition* 256) points out, "Jazz not only exalts the individual finding his [*sic*] own way, it also places him in a fundamental, dynamic, and necessary co-operation with his fellows." Compare the individualist, monologic understanding of jazz in Ted Gioia's *The Imperfect Art*. See also the critical review of Gioia's book by David Horn.

8   See, for example, Tirro, "Constructive"; Porter; and Schuller, "Rollins."

9   See Schuller, *Early Jazz*, chap. 1, "The Origins." For an overview of discussions of African retentions in African American music, see Maultsby.

10 Thus when Schuller boasts of listening to more than 30,000 recordings while writing this book, one might ask, "But what was he listening *for*?"

11 Even John Gennari, who criticizes Schuller for stripping away the cultural meanings of jazz, nonetheless credits him with having produced comprehensive and precise analyses of the music.

12 First issued on Columbia CS-8242, this recording also appears in the Smithsonian Collection *American Popular Song* (Smithsonian Institution and CBS, RD-031). Most of the comments that follow could apply just as well to Frank Sinatra's recording on *Songs for Young Lovers* (Capitol, 1954).

13 See Brofsky for a comparison of three different performances by Davis of "My Funny Valentine."

14 We might say that the early bebop musicians were signifyin' on Tin Pan Alley popular songs when they stripped away the melody, doubled the tempo, and explored the harmonic possibilities they found in such tunes as "I Got Rhythm"

and "Cherokee." But bebop practice would have been to give "My Funny Valentine" a new melody and not acknowledge that the tune had any connection with popular song. Davis, when he used Tin Pan Alley songs, almost always said so, making the signifyin' less private and esoteric, more explicit and popular. See Lhamon 172–73.

15 My transcription is provided as a guide to the analysis that follows. The analysis, though, is based on the sounds of the performance, not the sight of the transcription. It should be clear that I have no illusions about the capacity of musical notation to represent musical performances completely or accurately. I have tried, however, to furnish a transcription that acknowledges its own limitations, one that records the existence of aspects of the performance that are not notatable or that are usually overlooked by analysis. Even so, an enormous amount of important musical information is left out, especially nuances of pitch and timbre. Note the key to special symbols that appears at the end of the transcription.

16 Pitches are given in the text at concert pitch, so as to match the transcription. A trumpet player would think of this note as a B♭.

17 Acoustical facts permit a valveless brass instrument, such as a bugle, to play only the notes (or harmonics) of an overtone series, such as A♭, E♭, A♭, C, E♭, G♭, A♭, B♭, etc. The trumpet's valves allow it to switch quickly among various series. Without them, there would be gaps in place of notes that the instrument could not produce.

18 Davis is certainly not the only trumpet player to wrestle with the instrument in this way. For example, Charles Schlueter, principal trumpet of the Boston Symphony Orchestra, has throughout his career struggled to produce a great range of timbres. Schlueter's experiments with equipment and his risky playing techniques and interpretations have made him perhaps the most controversial trumpet player in American orchestral circles. Like Davis, he has often missed more notes than many think he should, but his risks have also paid off in unsurpassedly rich and beautiful performances. On the controversies surrounding Schlueter, see Vigeland.

19 Berendt (84) cites unnamed "recording directors" who agree on this point. On Davis's admiration for Harry James, see Davis (32).

20 It is certainly possible that this tempo change was planned, or that it was at least an option that had been taken in previous performances. But it is made to feel spontaneous, to seem musically cued by Davis.

21 Krin Gabbard (60) cites this solo as a perfect example of how Davis alternated strongly phallic gestures with moments of post-phallic vulnerability.

22 "Prideful loneliness" is from Hentoff, *Jazz Is* 141.

23 See also Baraka, "Davis."

24 For example, Martin Williams's bibliography for the *Smithsonian Collection of Classic Jazz*, rev. ed., ignores Sidran and Jones, as does the entry on "Jazz" in the *New Grove Dictionary of Music and Musicians* (Harrison).

25 The other important biography of Davis (besides Cole, mentioned above) is Jack Chambers's *Milestones*, a tremendous compilation of facts and quotes, but a book that offers little analysis of the music and its meanings. Barry Kernfeld's dissertation uses traditional musicological tools to generate detailed descriptions of Davis's music.

26 Earlier versions of this essay were performed as lecture-demonstrations at the

African-American Music Forum, University of Michigan, 26 Apr. 1990; the IASPM conference in New Orleans, 1 May 1990; McGill University, 31 Jan. 1992; the University of California-Riverside, 11 Mar. 1992; and the University of California-Berkeley, 22 Jan. 1993. This article has benefited from the comments and questions of the audiences at those presentations and from correspondence with Krin Gabbard, George Lipsitz, and Christopher Small. A slightly different version was published in *Musical Quarterly* 77:2 (Summer 1993). I am grateful for the corrections and challenges issued by the anonymous reviewers for *Musical Quarterly* and Duke University Press, and to John Puterbaugh for setting my transcription.

Works Cited

Baker, David N., ed. *New Perspectives on Jazz.* Washington, D.C.: Smithsonian Institution, 1990.

Baker, Houston A., Jr. "Handling 'Crisis': Great Books, Rap Music, and the End of Western Homogeneity (Reflections on the Humanities in America)." *Callaloo* 13.2 (1990): 173–94.

Bakhtin, M. M. *The Dialogic Imagination.* Trans. Caryl Emerson and Michael Holquist. Austin: U of Texas P, 1981.

Baraka, Amiri. "Miles Davis: One of the Great Mother Fuckers." *The Music: Reflections on Jazz and Blues.* Ed. Amiri Baraka and Amina Baraka. New York: Morrow, 1987. 290–301.

——. "Jazz Criticism and Its Effect on the Art Form." *New Perspectives on Jazz.* Ed. David N. Baker. Washington, D.C.: Smithsonian Institution, 1990. 55–70.

Berendt, Joachim E. *The Jazz Book: From Ragtime to Fusion and Beyond.* Westport, Conn.: Lawrence Hill, 1982.

Brofsky, Howard. "Miles Davis and *My Funny Valentine:* the Evolution of a Solo." *Black Music Research Journal* (1983): 23–45.

Burns, Khephra. "Liner notes for Miles Davis, *Aura.*" CBS [rec. 1984].

Carr, Ian. *Miles Davis: A Critical Biography.* London: Paladin, 1982.

Chambers, Jack. *Milestones: The Music and Times of Miles Davis.* 2 vols. New York: Morrow, 1985.

Cole, Bill. *Miles Davis: A Musical Biography.* New York: Morrow, 1974.

Collier, James Lincoln. *The Making of Jazz.* New York: Dell, 1978.

Crouch, Stanley. "Jazz Criticism and Its Effect on the Art Form [response]." *New Perspectives on Jazz.* Ed. David N. Baker. Washington, D.C.: Smithsonian Institution, 1990. 55–70.

Davis, Miles, with Quincy Troupe. *Miles: The Autobiography.* New York: Simon, 1989.

Ellison, Ralph. *Shadow and Act.* New York: Random, 1964.

Floyd, Samuel A., Jr. "Ring Shout! Literary Studies, Historical Studies, and Black Music Inquiry." *Black Music Research Journal* 11:2 (Fall 1991): 265–87.

Gabbard, Krin. "Signifyin(g) the Phallus: *Mo' Better Blues* and Representations of the Jazz Trumpet." *Cinema Journal* 32:1 (Fall 1992): 43–62. Reprinted in *Representing Jazz.* Ed. Krin Gabbard. Durham, N.C.: Duke UP, 1995. 104–30.

Gates, Henry Louis, Jr. *The Signifying Monkey: A Theory of African-American Literary Criticism.* New York: Oxford UP, 1988.

Gennari, John. "Jazz Criticism: Its Development and Ideologies." *Black American Literature Forum* 25:3 (Fall 1991): 449–523.

Giddins, Gary. *Rhythm-a-ning: Jazz Tradition and Innovation in the '80s*. New York: Oxford UP, 1985.

Gioia, Ted. *The Imperfect Art: Reflections on Jazz and Modern Culture*. New York: Oxford UP, 1988.

Gleason, Ralph J. *Celebrating the Duke*. Boston: Little, Brown, 1975.

Gridley, Mark C. *Jazz Styles: History and Analysis*. 4th ed. Englewood Cliffs, N.J.: Prentice-Hall, 1991.

Harrison, Max. "Jazz." *The New Grove Dictionary of Music and Musicians*. Ed. Stanley Sadie. Vol. 9. London: Macmillan, 1980. 561–79.

Hentoff, Nat. Liner notes to Miles Davis, *My Funny Valentine*. Columbia. 1964.

——. *Jazz Is*. New York: Random, 1976.

——. "An Afternoon with Miles Davis." *Jazz Panorama*. Ed. Martin Williams. New York: Da Capo, 1979. 161–68.

Hodeir, André. *Jazz—Its Evolution and Essence*. 1956. New York: Grove, 1979.

Horn, David. Review of Ted Gioia, *The Imperfect Art. Popular Music* 10:1 (1991): 103–7.

Huyssen, Andreas. *After the Great Divide: Modernism, Mass Culture, Postmodernism*. Bloomington: Indiana UP, 1986.

Jones, LeRoi. *Blues People*. New York: Morrow, 1963.

Kernfeld, Barry. "Adderley, Coltrane, and Davis at the Twilight of Bebop: The Search for Melodic Coherence (1958–59)." Diss. Cornell University, 1981.

——, ed. *The New Grove Dictionary of Jazz*. New York: Grove's Dictionaries of Music, 1988.

Levine, Lawrence W. *Highbrow/Lowbrow: The Emergence of Cultural Hierarchy in America*. Cambridge, Mass.: Harvard UP, 1988.

Lhamon, W. T., Jr. *Deliberate Speed: The Origins of a Cultural Style in the American 1950s*. Washington, D.C.: Smithsonian Institution, 1990.

Mandel, Howard. "Sketches of Miles." *Down Beat* Dec. 1991: 16–20.

Maultsby, Portia K. "Africanisms in African-American Music." *Africanisms in American Culture*. Ed. Joseph E. Holloway. Bloomington: Indiana UP, 1990. 185–210.

Megill, Donald D., and Richard S. Demory. *Introduction to Jazz History*. Englewood Cliffs, N.J.: Prentice-Hall, 1989.

Murphy, John P. "Jazz Improvisation: The Joy of Influence." *Black Perspective in Music* 18.1–2 (1990): 7–19.

Nattiez, Jean-Jacques. *Music and Discourse: Toward a Semiology of Music*. Princeton, N.J.: Princeton UP, 1990.

Nisenson, Eric. *Round About Midnight: A Portrait of Miles Davis*. New York: Dial, 1982.

Palmer, Robert. "The Man Who Changed Music." *Rolling Stone* 14 Nov. 1991: 39–42, 47.

Porter, Lewis. "John Coltrane's *A Love Supreme*: Jazz Improvisation as Composition." *Journal of the American Musicological Society* 38:3 (Fall 1985): 593–621.

Sales, Grover. *Jazz: America's Classical Music*. Englewood Cliffs, N.J.: Prentice-Hall, 1984.

Schuller, Gunther. *Early Jazz: Its Roots and Musical Development*. New York: Oxford UP, 1968.

——. "Sonny Rollins and the Challenge of Thematic Improvisation." *Musings.* New York: Oxford UP, 1986. 86–97. (Originally pub. in *Jazz Review* Nov. 1958.)

——. *The Swing Era: The Development of Jazz, 1930–1945.* New York: Oxford UP, 1989.

——. "The Influence of Jazz on the History and Development of Concert Music." *New Perspectives on Jazz.* Ed. David N. Baker. Washington, D.C.: Smithsonian Institution, 1990. 9–24.

Sidran, Ben. *Black Talk.* 1971. New York: Da Capo, 1983.

Small, Christopher. *Music of the Common Tongue: Survival and Celebration in Afro-American Music.* New York: Riverrun, 1987.

Taylor, Billy. "Jazz in the Contemporary Marketplace: Professional and Third-Sector Economic Strategies for the Balance of the Century." *New Perspectives on Jazz.* Ed. David N. Baker. Washington, D.C.: Smithsonian Institution, 1990. 89–98.

Taylor, William "Billy." "Jazz—America's Classical Music." *Black Perspective in Music* 14.1 (Winter 1986): 21–25.

Tirro, Frank. "Constructive Elements in Jazz Improvisation." *Journal of the American Musicological Society* 27.2 (Summer 1974): 285–305.

——. *Jazz: A History.* New York: Norton, 1977.

Tomlinson, Gary. "Cultural Dialogics and Jazz: A White Historian Signifies." *Disciplining Music: Musicology and Its Canons.* Ed. Katherine Bergeron and Philip V. Bohlman. Chicago: U of Chicago P, 1992. 64–94.

Vigeland, Carl A. *In Concert: Onstage and Offstage with the Boston Symphony Orchestra.* Amherst: U of Massachusetts P, 1991.

Walser, Robert. "Musical Imagery and Performance Practice in J. S. Bach's Arias with Trumpet." *International Trumpet Guild Journal* 13.1 (Sept. 1988): 62–77.

Williams, Martin. *The Jazz Tradition.* Rev. ed. Oxford: Oxford UP, 1983.

——. "Suggestions for Further Reading." *Smithsonian Collection of Classic Jazz.* Rev. ed. CBS Special Products, 1987. 118–19.

Wilson, Olly. "The Influence of Jazz on the History and Development of Concert Music [response]." *New Perspectives on Jazz.* Ed. David N. Baker. Washington, D.C.: Smithsonian Institution, 1990. 25–31.

Critical Alchemy: Anthony Braxton
and the Imagined Tradition

RONALD M. RADANO

Tentative, unstable, seemingly betwixt and between, jazz in the early 1970s stood at the crossroads, the space of multiple direction that has identified the character of the blues since Robert Johnson.[1] Yet whereas in down-home blues the crossroads symbolized a confrontation with choice, of an either/or, the jazz crossroads offered varieties of indirection, of negation, of neither/nor. Like a mouse on a playwheel, jazz appeared to be circling endlessly, its diversity of paths offering occasional flashes of brilliance that ultimately traced steps to creative dead ends. Epitomizing this condition of flux was Miles Davis, whose nod to the rarefied sound of free jazz and ventures into rock- and funk-based fusion befuddled former admirers. His blur of sounds and styles that preserved at its core the current "dance rhythms of a dance-beat people" would be dismissed as an act of creative sabotage by those who had once counted on him for mainstream advancement (Murray). In fact, Davis *did* have his finger on the music's pulse, as Gary Tomlinson so skillfully argues in "Cultural Dialogics and Jazz." His vast range of stylistic allusions and words of praise for everyone except the stars of jazz—Karlheinz Stockhausen, James Brown, Krzysztof Penderecki, Jimi Hendrix—gave voice to the condition of sociocultural fracture that countered commonsense beliefs in the immutability of genre and style. For this, Davis would be ritualistically sacrificed by the critical and artistic mass, whose violence may explain more about his six-year silence than the hyperbole about creative, physical, and psychological collapse (Chambers 136, 281).[2]

In the end, the impetus for these criticisms had little to do with the particularities of Davis's transgressions; rather, they were symptomatic of far deeper concerns relating to the integrity of the jazz tradition. If Davis, the consummate trendsetter, the strategist of two, if not three, major styles could find nothing new to say, how would the music proceed? Neither aging mainstream artists nor the emerging generation of fusion musicians could be counted on; similarly, the anarchic expressions of free jazz inspired only the faintest hope, particularly after the death of its mainstream mediator, John Coltrane. As the situation neared crisis, jazz journalists revived a familiar critical theme, advancing worrisome predictions on the life expectancy of jazz. Titles alone voiced their yearning for stylistic center. "Is Jazz Coming Back?" queried Joel Vance, who read the surfeit of releases and reissues as an indication of decline. "Only time will tell," Ian Kendall seemed to reply in his nostalgic look at the successes of the past. And while William Anderson appeared fatalistic as he offered a final "reprise for jazz," others tried to make sense of the aesthetic convulsions by tackling head-on the ontological question, "What Is Jazz?" (Vance; Kendall; Anderson; "What Is").[3]

In the midst of this soul-searching and public rankling, the major promotional institutions worked against the odds to reestablish a sense of coherence of genre and style. The key lay in identifying a figure of consensus, an artist who might consolidate the various streams of innovation and give new legitimacy to the popular teleological theories of musical change and consolidation. While some observers turned to the legacy of Davis's influence—Keith Jarrett, Herbie Hancock, Chick Corea, Wayne Shorter—others ultimately placed their bets on one of the most unlikely candidates, Anthony Braxton.[4] Returning after more than three years in Paris to join forces with Clive Davis's newly fashioned label, Arista Records, Braxton would, in the course of a year (1974–75), be transformed from an obscure jazz vanguardist to the designer of a refurbished mainstream—a star who would recast the uncertainties of the past into a formula for new creative direction. No doubt that Braxton's appeal related, in good measure, to his remarkable skills as an improviser and composer. Yet what really seemed to set him apart from the others was an ability to reflect creatively the uncertainties that typified the postmodern moment. From the expanses of his philosophical system to the details of his saxophone style, Braxton spoke to the puzzling pastiche of 1970s' style and culture. Significantly, he did this while also sidestepping his associations with 1960s' vanguardism, frequently by calling into question the legitimacy of total musical "freedom." As a tradition-centered synthesist, he would, according to the critical view, make sense of the anarchy of the recent past by redefining it aesthetically in the context of the mainstream. To enhance the image of stylistic coherence, moreover, publicists attenuated the radicalism of Braxton's art by shift-ing attention to more superficial matters. Centralizing the most divert-ing characteristics of Braxton's personality and creativity, they would shape a public image that on the surface celebrated pluralistic excess while maintaining the conventions of tradition. The idiosyncrasies of the caricature would, in turn, help to sell a hyperbolic story of "contro-versy" that supported promotional goals while matching claims of his larger-than-life importance.

Since the earliest initiatives in cultural criticism, students of mass culture have recognized that public images regulate, if not determine, artistic meaning: media symbols outline the broad contours of public response as they help to cast the ideological lens through which art is received. Despite their private, real-life personalities, public figures ap-pear in the context of the mass media as little more than images—"signs"—whose meanings can be "read" as the critic reads a text. From this perspective, the interpretation of value becomes less an isolated study of form than an analysis of the way in which pop icons embody culturally symbolic meanings. The most popular and enduring stars—Elvis Presley, Bruce Springsteen, Madonna—appear to be inscribed with a diversity of imagic significance, collapsing into a single figure an as-semblage of views and associations.

In jazz, however, such realizations have, for the most part, escaped serious critical notice, possibly because of writers' assumptions about—and equally likely, identifications with—its marginality and aesthetic "purity." Whether originating on the plantation or field, in the ghetto or after-hours club, jazz seems to have "survived" as a cloistered other whose primitive soul transcends the trivialities of modern mass culture. This myth has endured tenaciously and despite a historical association between artist and media since Paul Whiteman first assumed the throne as "King of Jazz." To be sure, mediated images have helped to popularize many leading artists: Benny Goodman, the severe jazz egghead; Artie Shaw, the rags-to-riches Hollywood charmer; Charlie Parker, the bestial musical savant. With the expansion of corporate control over cultural production, these images grew subtler as their importance increased. En-gaging images not only vitalized the careers of postwar artists (Dave Bru-beck, Ornette Coleman, John Coltrane), but styles as well. Cool became the double-edged sign of forbidden fruits (narcotics, sex) and hip sophisti-cation; soul jazz, the protonationalist challenge to white control; free jazz, the sound of primitive, black rage ("Dope Menace"; Hallock; Race).[5] In the 1970s, moreover, when the integrity of style seemed all but shot, images began to lose the artistic underpinning on which they had been based. As a result, publicists representing Braxton relied exceedingly on image over artistry as they crafted a star whose musical expression played a crucial, albeit secondary, supporting role. Echoing Braxton's own postmodern intermediations, the jazz community constructed a multimediated spectacle that celebrated confusion and fracture couched in the conventionality of a mainstream stylist. Braxton became a homology of discrete images, a centered artist made up of the decentered pastiche of the postmodern. As such, he embodied the fetishized character of the image itself: by playing out the role of the new star in an assemblage of current and historical stereotypes, Braxton, as David Harvey writes, activated the "aura of authority and power" to give official culture a means of "reestablish[ing] the . . . authority of its institutions" (Harvey 287–88).

Braxton's ambitious efforts to draw public notice to the range of his art exacerbated the growth of spectacle and confusion about the true character of his work. On the surface, he seemed to be effectively contributing to his own parody by publicizing the most exotic qualities of his art and aesthetics. Yet beneath the literal comment, his actions suggested a kind of signifying subversion. By assuming the role of the eccentric, of jazz music's cerebral comic or clown, Braxton sought to undermine the interpretive power and, as a result, the legitimacy of official media. Like other "controversial" black artists—Little Richard, Screamin' Jay Hawkins, Jimi Hendrix, Public Enemy's Flavor Flav—Braxton, in the words of Hal Foster, "opted to play the fool, often in a canny way." That role, as Foster explains, can have a riotous effect: "if artful, the court jester is rewarded by the king; and if very artful, he may even conspire against him" (52). By fulfilling the contradictory (yet equally alienated) images of the primitive and intellectual while assuming simultaneously the role of stylistic leader, Braxton helped the community to sell an exciting yet nonetheless aesthetically secure vision of the music in magazines, over the air, and on record. At the same time, by constantly shifting the particularities of his image, he could dance around critics' defining efforts while parodying the supposed "integrity" of jazz as a historical genre. As soon as he retreated musically from this formula, the "noise" of his supposedly mainstream artistry revealed itself, leading to a collapse of images as well as the version of jazz it supported.

II

The falsity of the press characterizations appear most blatant when we look at coverage before Braxton's ascension within the popular ranks.

While known among writers in the early 1970s for his radical decon-
structions of jazz practice, Braxton was hardly at the center of controversy; aside from passing comment in "Blindfold Tests" and polls for
minor talents, he received, at best, occasional notice, and always with
reference to his respectable associations with the Association for the
Advancement of Creative Musicians (1966–69) and Chick Corea's group,
Circle (1970–71). Occasionally, however, the peculiarities of Braxton's
creative complex would confound writers, revealing their potential as
sources of spectacle. In a review of Braxton's 1972 performance at New
York's Town Hall, for example, John S. Wilson balanced references to
Braxton's most visible achievements with glib comment about his unorthodox style and procedures. As "a prominent member of Chicago's jazz
avant-garde," Braxton gained credibility, as he would for his "very capable [skills as a] jazz alto saxophonist in the context of Chick Corea's
group, Circle." Yet as he reinforced the image of the saxophone master,
Wilson also underscored Braxton's ties with the "unmusical" free-jazz
practices taking place in New York's lofts. Equally troubling for Wilson
was Braxton's use of nonverbal picture-titles in the program, which
reinforced the music's already rarefied character. To him, the titular
"diagrams consisting of letters and numbers . . . were as obscure as the
music produced" (Wilson, "Performs").[6] Barry McRae, on the other hand,
sought to limit Braxton's associations with the most anarchic forms of
free jazz by more actively stressing images of continuity and order. After
positioning Braxton against the background of Chicago innovators since
Earl Hines, McRae discussed a recent release, Circle's *Paris Concert*,
with specific reference to Braxton's performance on "Duet." The improvisation, McRae argued, was "very typical of [the style of] the present
Chicago jazz scene," a questionable assertion that nonetheless reinforced continuities with Braxton's Chicago past. Images of continuity
could even appear in the mechanics of the analysis itself. Searching for a
method to a seemingly musical madness, McRae explained in a literary
style evoking Braxton's own album notes how "motivic particles assem-
bled at random [assumed] a logical progression" (McRae, "Avant"). According to Barry Tepperman, however, Braxton, despite his roots, had
transcended categorization. As "the most intensely eloquent alto voice
to emerge from the Chicago pressure-cooker of new jazz," he embodied
the music's new direction. "Each generation in the music produces only
one genius of this magnitude," Tepperman explained, and "Anthony
Braxton is such a genius" (Tepperman "Heard" 1973).

The images appearing in these early reports identify the underlying
themes that would later work to establish Braxton's reputation. As a

saxophonist with undeniable roots in cultural nationalism and free jazz, Braxton played the character of the unpredictable black radical, whose art echoed 1960s' challenges of "primitive" rage. As the inventor of arcane titles and "highly formal . . . chamber performance[s]," however, he assumed the contrasting role of the austere, intellectual other (McRae, "Avant"). At his most spectacular, Braxton would combine images of the clinician and tribal priest, becoming its composite: the mad scientist of jazz (Lynch).[7] As a counterpoint to these sensational images, moreover, publicists promoted the paradoxical claim that Braxton's art held the potential of recentering the growth of jazz. By treating his interests in mysticism and philosophy as the stuff of (black) comedy, they trivialized oppositional elements in order to advance the familiar theme of progress; titles and theories were merely playful antics that cloaked a form of rough-and-ready jazz. The intimidating presence of Braxton's arcane musical theory would, then, be passed off as romantic excess even as it supplied an essential journalistic hook to draw listeners back to jazz.

A key article published in February 1974 served to flesh out the dimensions of Braxton's image while also elaborating on his potential as the new jazz star. In a two-page interview appearing in *Down Beat*, Ray Townley ably worked the exotic extremes of Braxton's creativity in a masterful juxtaposition of oppositional imagery ("Anthony" Feb. 1974). In the lead paragraph Townley set the basis for his essay by establishing the sensationalistic critical formula of a racialist/intellectual homology. Evoking an image of Braxton's stage appearance, Townley described an artist "walk[ing] onto the dimly lit stage, his fuzzy hair evincing the strands of the absent-minded professor." By melding "black" references (ambiance, type of hair) to the stereotype of the academic nerd, Townley constructed a figurative composite of two familiar American outcasts. Moving on, he continued to work this peculiar mix in a series of dramatic juxtapositions: the primitive artist with "prominent forehead" engaged in serious, "thoughtful contemplation"; the alienated, black "intellectual . . . alone on stage, [who] lifts the horn to his lips as *naturally* [emphasis added] as he would take a drag from his [marijuana-filled?] oom-pah [*sic*] pipe." In subsequent paragraphs, moreover, Townley elaborated on these images, which, as oppositions, serve to reinforce the surface theme of musical diversity. Quoting liberally, he described Braxton's account of his "mathematical . . . language system," his work as a musical "scientist," his compositional methods involving "weight shifts," his opinions of various modernist composers.[8] Diverse images of exotica are then counterposed to his potential as a jazz innovator. At once, Braxton emerged as the creator of arcane solo works that could be likened to the masterpieces of Bach; the down-to-earth jazz improviser, who, according to an unnamed critic, would replicate in the 1970s the commanding influence Coltrane had enjoyed in the 1960s. Ultimately, Townley took the images of diversity to a comical extreme by assembling an outlandish pastiche of Braxton's eclectic interests. Parade music, serialism, and his work for one hundred tubas appeared against "pet metaphysical theories" and references to the "notorious" picture-titles, as Townley fashioned an image of a playful, if eccentric, intellectual clown. In a final paragraph, he gathered these images into a lavish display, boiled down to this exotic equation:

> Anthony Braxton's world revolves around three systematic and calculating realms: mathematics, music, and chess. When he not [*sic*] computing or conceptualizing his music, he's sitting alone, across from a chessboard, pondering his next move. He could just as well be shifting weights or cataloging sounds. Or standing alone on a dimly lit stage, manipulating his saxophone keys.

As if to counter *Down Beat*'s parody, *Coda*, a modest, Toronto-based magazine oriented toward free jazz, devoted the bulk of its April 1974 issue to a celebration of Braxton's art. The issue was largely the work of *Coda*'s art director, Bill Smith, whose featured centerpiece, an 8,000-word interview, represented a personal triumph: "the most important document that I have been personally responsible for" ("Braxton Interview"). Smith's enthusiasm clearly stemmed from his unbridled admiration of the artist. According to Smith, Braxton was not just another stylist, but "the new high priest" whose lavish experimentalism would chart the course to the next musical era. Echoing the predictions of Townley's unnamed critic, Smith declared Braxton to be the music's creative savior or perhaps even something more: through his art, "jazz music has reached yet another high plain, a level that lifts it above all else." In the closing paragraph of his review of Braxton's recent releases, Smith presented this litany to the jazz masses:

> He is here, playing, just waiting for you to listen. He knows already what he is, and presents these opportunities for you to discover who you are. It does not matter if your likes are Johnny Hodges, Lester Young, Bird, Ornette or Trane, for Anthony Braxton is the present account of that lineage. He is THE one. So take it now, don't wait like you did with all the others, for ten years to pass. His music is pure and accessible, it's real and if it does not reach your ears/head/heart then it is you who will be the poorer. ("Braxton: Saxophone")

Casting Braxton as both radical iconoclast and the progeny of past greats, Smith created a portrait of the artist in terms that would appeal to mainstream sensibilities as it gave new legitimacy to the beleaguered free movement. Free jazz, in its revised form, would divest itself from an earlier vanguardist agenda in order to reestablish the progressivist impulses of modernism and the swing/bop/hard bop continuity. The oppositional strategies of the "language system" and, indeed, Braxton's own proclamations of resistance—"I'm not a jazz musician"—represented, according to Smith, not so much a departure as a new, improved version of the original ("Interview"). To support this essentialist proposition, Smith gave a detailed account of Braxton's roots in black music, his eclectic jazz and pop background, and his favorite jazz musicians and saxophonists. In an extended discussion of Braxton's music and aesthetics, moreover, Smith challenged Townley's comedic sketch by underscoring the complexity and sophistication of his views of the arts. The accompanying discography further helped to establish Braxton's credibility as a jazz-centered performer, even while the peculiar details of his oppositional art conveyed, at least for some, the impression of a black iconoclast masquerading as an intellectual.

Other essays from the period expressed similar enthusiasm for Braxton's recasting of jazz against the background of an assimilated free style. In a five-star ("excellent") rating of *Four Compositions 1973*, Ray Townley noted that "Braxton has entered a new, and more harmonious phase" marked by "uncommon popular accessibility." As both a saxophonist and a clarinetist, he had become "a leading exponent . . . [to] be reckoned with" (Townley, "Anthony" Apr. 1974). Similarly, Will Smith recognized in the *Town Hall* recording "a tremendous breakthrough" in Braxton's art, for which he was awarded additional kudos. "Gone are the occasional flights of aimlessness" attributable to "his involvement with the European 'new music' syndrome"; Braxton had, in musical terms, come home, "saying things uniquely, directly, and with emotional purity." Coming home stylistically did not, then, hinder innovation. Indeed, Braxton had captured the attention of North American writers precisely because he had managed to strike a balance between freedom and control, thus maintaining the formally conservative nature of pre-1960s' jazz. While posing "a challenge [to the listener] to reconsider all one's tacit assumptions about music," he remained "a major soloist" who had unified jazz from Armstrong to Ayler (Tepperman, "Heard" 1974; McRae, "Lookout"). Put simply by *Melody Maker*'s Steve Lake, "Braxton's an iconoclast, absolutely, but with a love for jazz's tradition and heritage. That's what makes him the giant he is" ("Records").

From the indications on recordings, it certainly appeared as if Braxton had, from a conservative perspective, "gotten serious" about art and finally learned to play jazz the way it is supposed to be played. The bulk of favorable comment focused on Braxton's small-group recordings that featured jazz-oriented (solo/rhythm accompaniment) performance ensembles and the talents of a revolving core of certified jazz artists. The likes of Dave Holland, Barry Altschul, Jerome Cooper, and Kenny Wheeler seemed to have reestablished jazz at the center of Braxton's art, a "breakthrough" about which a fraternity of writers, whose tastes had been shaped during the bop and postbop years, were delighted. From Braxton's perspective, however, the music for quartet and quintet was hardly a center, but merely a means by which he could support his newlywed wife and, later, a family. While he enjoyed the music, he has explained in interviews that he would have preferred to commit his time to composition and music for concert ensembles.[9] This distinction is important, for it reveals a fundamental way in which Braxton's aesthetic would be translated. With the quartet music as the centerpiece, all else—the solo improvisations, concert music, picture titles, theories—could be interpreted as superficial background. Braxton's mediated images had now assumed a hierarchy, with continuity and accessibility positioned front and center and appearances challenging this construct relegated to the rear. By foregrounding accessibility against a dressed-up spectacle of "controversy," mainstream institutions would supply the means for selling Braxton to the public when he literally came home to head Arista's lineup, "The Art Form of Contemporary Jazz."

III

Founded in 1974 by Clive Davis, former president of Columbia Records, Arista was cast in the image of cultural diversity as if to celebrate the fragmentation and stasis of the times. Maintaining his past strategy at Columbia, Davis sought to develop broad stylistic representation at the same time as other labels—including Columbia, which had dismissed him in 1973—were making moves toward consolidation.[10] Arista would gather under its wing an impressive roster of artists who had each forged highly individual expressions. Together they would, in Davis's words, make Arista and its Columbia Pictures' parent "the hallmark of originality" (Fox 221).[11] For Davis, "originality" seemed to mean glamour as much as it did the aura of integrity, as he worked to create a circle of performers who might match the prestige of Janis Joplin, Sly Stone, Bruce Springsteen, and other Columbia celebrities. Former pop icons such as

Eric Andersen and Dionne Warwick (and later, Aretha Franklin) were resurrected to appear alongside the budding stars Barry Manilow and Melissa Manchester; established rock groups—the Kinks, the Grateful Dead—stood in contrast to new FM-oriented bands, including the Outlaws and the more experimental innovators, Patti Smith, Lou Reed, and Graham Parker. Deeply sensitized to the importance of image, moreover, Davis sought to add to this list a jazz component that might enhance Arista's appearance of sophistication while reminding listeners of his past successes as a promoter of black music, notably his publicized backing of Miles Davis's venture into fusion (Albertson, "Avant-Garde").[12] Hiring Steve Backer to manage the label's jazz series, he secured a respected producer and promoter who had most recently refurbished ABC's Impulse jazz line. Granted an unusual degree of autonomy for a producer of jazz, Backer constructed a lineup that matched the diversity of Arista's image: "I'm going to deal with the entire spectrum of modern jazz," he explained, "from bop to avant-garde, including all the current fusions" ("Backer Pacts"). In fact, one suspects that Backer's chief role was that of the promoter and publicist: he would be charged with finding performers who, with limited investment, would help to distinguish Arista from mainline labels while reinforcing Clive Davis's own "controversial" image.[13] Such reasoning might explain why he chose Braxton as his challenger for the title as leader of the jazz world.

Recognizing the inaccessibility of some of Braxton's early recordings, Backer devised a plan that would nurture his star potential by easing his way into the commercial market. He advised Braxton to prepare short, accessible works for his first albums, highlighting his quartet music. He also stipulated conditions that would encourage radio stations to play the recordings. In an interview with Michael Ullman, Backer described the formula that would situate mainstream jazz at the heart of Braxton's developing reputation:

> There are things that not every artist is aware of. For instance, when you record for a major label and play one twenty-minute piece on each side, there is nothing that will be played on the radio. Even the sequencing can turn off a lot of radio people. If you start with more difficult material, the guy who listens to the albums at a station will never listen to the whole album to find the more accessible cut. [So we asked Braxton to] deal with time and meter [on the first albums]. Then we were able to make more people in the jazz community embrace his music. And then we went to the big band album that dealt with time also. . . . From there Braxton went into various

stretched-out, open-ended free improvisational approaches (Ullman 220).

An examination of Braxton's first releases shows that Backer's production guidelines were followed precisely. On the first album, *New York Fall 1974*, Backer, together with producer Michael Cuscuna, positioned six seven-minute compositions—a duration suited for airplay—to highlight his most accessible compositions.[14] On side one, they featured two bop-oriented works that highlighted Braxton's skills as an improviser. The lead track is as rhythmically intense as it is dramatic: good bait for a radio station's music programmer. Positioned in the middle is a "minimalist" composition based on a rich and varied melodic palette. On side two, the producers placed works that require greater effort for the listener to comprehend: a duet for clarinet and synthesizer (performed with Richard Teitelbaum) and a collective improvisation scored for trumpet, violin, contrabass clarinet, and bass. While perhaps a challenge to the standard jazz format, these works, which highlight a pleasant assortment of rich sound colors and inventive textures, most likely appealed to pop-oriented listeners accustomed to the static sound fields of fusion, rock jams, and "New Age" music. And because the tracks are relatively short, they could be tolerated by those who still found them unpleasant. The most accessible track on the side, a piece for saxophone quartet, is predictably the longest, lasting more than eight minutes. The album was packaged inside a jacket graced with a handsome picture of Braxton as jazz professor, smoking his pipe. On the back, picture-titles adorned a whimsical, translucent image of the artist, cast saint-like, skirting along a wooded terrain. Later albums demonstrated similar promotional care: *Five Pieces 1975* is stylistically similar to his first Arista album, employing as a lead track the jazz standard, "You Stepped Out of a Dream." *Duets 1976* with Muhal Richard Abrams, which includes compositions in a free style, highlights more accessible works, such as Eric Dolphy's "Miss Ann," which leads the first side, and Scott Joplin's "Maple Leaf Rag," featured on the second.

Arista's style controls and packaging worked. Gearing the albums for radio by excluding performance practices that listeners might find repellent, the label set the stage for the rise of its new jazz star. Supported by massive distribution and a half-page ad celebrating "Braxton. A new name half the world already knows," *New York Fall 1974* moved quickly up the jazz charts. According to national playlists published in *Radio Free Jazz*, Braxton's early Arista recordings (1975–77) ranked in the Top 10 category five times.[15] These rankings were fueled by the profound increase in press reports—most of which were extremely positive—appearing in North American and British magazines.[16] As critics showered Braxton with praise, his record sales climbed, reaching 20,000—an impressive figure for a jazz-oriented artist (Ullman 219). At that moment, Arista released *Creative Orchestra Music 1976*, which in 1977 won *Down Beat*'s critics' award for best album. After subsequent releases further reinforced Braxton's jazz affiliation, Backer permitted him to expand his offerings with albums—produced, Braxton claims, mostly at his own expense—from his concert-music repertory.

IV

The promotional achievements of Arista's marketing team inspired a closer look at the details of Braxton's personality and opinions. Aesthetics and tastes that had previously received only passing notice, now appeared in full view, to be scrutinized by the jazz public. Two of the most conspicuous commentaries from the Arista period appeared as liner notes to Braxton's initial releases, *New York Fall 1974* and *Five Pieces 1975*. In the first, Bill Smith took advantage of the forum to advance *Coda*'s brand of advocacy journalism (B. Smith, Notes). In a somewhat sycophantic pledge of "privilege to be witnessing" the drama of Braxton's music, he underscored the continuity theme that had appeared in previous essays. Situating the artist against the background of the AACM and the likes of Parker and Coleman, Smith repeated for a mass audience his claim that Braxton "[had] supplied the continuation of the [jazz] lineage." As he encompassed the totality of bop and postbop, Braxton realized continuity in its all-consuming completeness; he was, Smith reasserted, "the most complete musician in this period of American music."

Robert Palmer, on the other hand, applauded Braxton's work without making claims about its ultimate importance. He seemed most concerned with disarming a controversy that had already begun to get out of hand. Mapping out the extremes of the insiders' debate, he began:

> I would like to propose now, at the beginning of this discussion, that we set aside entirely the question of the ultimate worth of Anthony Braxton's music. There are those who insist that Braxton is the new Bird, Coltrane, and Ornette, the three-in-one who is singlehandedly taking the Next Step in jazz. There are others who remain unconvinced. History will decide, and while it is doing so, we should appreciate Braxton's music for its own immediate value.

Attempting to temper the disputes that had animated the jazz community, Palmer proceeded to show that much of the controversy about Braxton had related to misunderstandings about his unusual image (Palmer, Notes). Moving from the difficulties of his rhetoric to the unorthodoxy of his appearance—which mixed contrasting references to the fashions of the street ("mutton chops") and suburb (cardigan sweaters)—Palmer sought to demystify the images "that his detractors love to pounce on," to separate matters of style from the substance of an art that he considered important and accessible.[17] Assuming a casual, informal tone, Palmer described the empirical character of the schematic titles as nothing more than "diagram[s] suggesting the kinds of (improvised) things that can happen in [a composition]." Turning to Braxton's interest in concert music, he showed that what had been mistaken for pretense actually developed from a sound knowledge of the modern repertory. Nor did Braxton's concert-music proclivities negate an ability to match the best at playing straightahead jazz, a feat that Palmer himself witnessed in an informal session. Yet the recording at hand provided the ultimate proof, as he noted with insistence: "the music is original, thoughtfully conceived, brilliantly executed, and not at all difficult. In fact, compared to a number of works of so-called experimental jazz it is downright old-fashioned."

As a reply to Smith's enthusiasm, Palmer's essay represented an impressive exercise in critical analysis. As an attempt to balance perspective, however, it ultimately had little effect. For what seemed especially to annoy Braxton's "detractors" was the attention that this showy Arista artist had been getting. Now the newly established king of jazz, Braxton gained a status at the expense of many equally able, if less adventurous, performers. Worse, his presence might not only redefine the style but perhaps even change the character of the community as a whole. No doubt some observers feared Michael Ullman's speculation that "there are countless teenagers who are cultivating a wide-eyed look, affecting cardigan sweaters, and learning to stutter on the alto sax in order to be like Anthony Braxton" (214). Concerns about the integrity of the genre and its subculture seemed especially to motivate those few who spoke out against him. In a review of a quartet performance at New York's Bottom Line, for example, Scott Albin seemed most upset about Braxton being "overrated and overpublicized"; similarly, John Storm Roberts appeared to object more to what Braxton represented than what he actually played, castigating him for his "decadent . . . flirt[ations] with Europe" and insisting that he "stop Messiaen about" (Albin; Roberts). Furthermore, many of the passing comments that appeared from 1975 until 1979 suggest that much of the confusion stemmed from the observers' vague awareness about what constituted Braxton's music. Recalling the tale of the blind men and the elephant, journalists and musicians seemed to be pointing in different directions when they remarked about the particulars of the artist's highly elaborate musical complex. As Whitney Balliett referred whimsically to Braxton's "ingenuously egoistic mode: by himself," Chris Albertson argued that *Five Pieces 1975* had avoided the "pretentiousness" of those "high on gimmickry and low on talent" (Balliett, "Jazz" 1977; Albertson, "Improvisations");[18] as Art Farmer, in a "Blindfold Test," ridiculed the "musical masturbation" and "abstraction" of "84° Kelvin" (*Montreux-Berlin Concerts 2/1*, 1976) ("[it] sounds like the soundtrack for a Mr. Magoo short subject"), Robert Palmer suggested that *Creative Orchestra 1976* would attract "a wide audience" and ultimately "convince the skeptics" (Feather, "Blindfold"; Palmer, "Creative"); as Gary Giddins criticized the "cute and constipated" indulgences of the second track of *New York Fall 1974*, Michael Zipkin offered high praise for Braxton's performances with Max Roach, which, he argued, "may come as a swinging velvet hammer to his detractors, wont to label him academic, intellectual, dry, etc." (Giddins, "Idea"; Zipkin).

Objections to Braxton's dramatic image and confusion about the true character of a multifaceted art might help partially to explain why the vast majority of writers, while showing enthusiastic support for his highly visible efforts on Arista, continued to refer to a mounting "controversy." As detractors called into question Braxton's obscure, conspicuous experiments, supporters praised the accessibility of works most commonly available to the American jazz public. Yet such a theory does not explain why despite high marks in polls and scores of positive reviews, many still felt compelled to "convince the skeptics."[19] Indeed, confusion alone cannot explain the magnitude of the controversy, whose presence stood in contradiction to the overwhelming praise. It would seem more likely that "controversy," in the end, could be attributed directly to the commentary of the journalists themselves. As part of the spectacle, commentators fueled Braxton's undeniably controversial image by exaggerating the magnitude of the debate about his music. Expressing an irony perhaps fitting for such an elusive artist, the *reports* of "controversy" identified the true controversy, one that had been built on false claims about a "not at all difficult" music. These claims would ultimately shape perceptions of Braxton's art, regardless of style and content, as image and spectacle overwhelmed the reality of form.

V

In his famous essay about the revolutionary potential of mass media and culture, Walter Benjamin identified the source of hierarchical erosion in the elimination of classical art's ritualistic "aura" (Benjamin, "Work"). As an allusion to the sacred, aura defined the mystification of traditional high culture, which, through the processes of mass mediation and mechanical reproduction, had begun to lose its exclusivity, its integrity, and, ultimately, its position of aesthetic superiority. Extrapolating on Benjamin's prophetic analysis—while often siding with the negative conclusions that Adorno had reached—social theorists have argued more recently that aesthetic aura has not been entirely eliminated but rather eclipsed by the potency of the mass-cultural image. Empowered by the status of corporate capital and high visibility, public images of art have acquired a new simulated aura through the "irreality" of the mass-mediated spectacle. The "loss of the real" that critics lament relates to the dominance of commercially generated images, to what Henri Lefebvre calls in his oft-quoted phrase, an "emptiness filled with signs" (Baudrillard 69–76; Lefebvre 71). In the postmodern age, conventional notions of artistic value have been replaced with "image value," a determination of worth as a commodified sign (Foster 92). Rather than emancipatory, the fractious challenge to traditional hierarchies reveals, in its turn, a hegemonic potential. Despite the loss of unity that invigorated vanguardist and popular arts, "spectacle" describes, according to Guy Debord, "the diplomatic representation of hierarchic society to itself." It is a "laudatory monologue, . . . [an] uninterrupted discourse [of] the existing order" (Debord, paragraphs 23–24).

As the celebrated star of jazz, Anthony Braxton seemed to embody a range of images associated with stability. More than a "three-in-one," he occupied a complex of signs that signified artistic innovation (Palmer, Notes). At the core of the complex, however, there existed only, in Lefebvre's term, "emptiness"; peeling away the images of Braxton's mediated projection, one was left with the peelings themselves. For Braxton's true public self consisted of an assemblage of selves that echoed the mutability of his private musical world.

Comparisons between new artists and innovators of the past have been a staple in jazz writing since the genre became prevalent in the 1930s. As in most Western arts, authority in jazz stems from associations with the pantheon, even as artists continually seek to find their own personal voice. Such comparison is perhaps inevitable in any coherent legacy, and particularly in an oral one like jazz, where the musician's artistry is closely linked with innovators of the past. In Braxton's case, however, comparisons appeared with such regularity that associations became ambiguous and confused. Hoisted to the center of attention, Braxton inspired an array of comparisons, creating a vivid collage of the jazz past. In Braxton, Barry Tepperman heard likenesses to Coltrane, Ornette Coleman, Warne Marsh, and Parker, a composite to which John Litweiler added Roscoe Mitchell and Lennie Tristano, Gary Giddins added Lee Konitz, and Chip Stern added Eric Dolphy (Tepperman, "Record" 1975 and "Perspectives" 1977; Litweiler; Giddins "Idea" and "Marches"; Stern). Chris Albertson heard some of the same, while insisting that Braxton had surpassed the innovations of Albert Ayler and Archie Shepp, having created, as his title indicates, "Improvisations as Liberated and Fresh as Louis Armstrong's." For Art Lange, Braxton's duets with Abrams recalled the swing era's Joe Venuti and Eddie Lang, while his clarinet playing brought to mind Pee Wee Russell ("Record" 1978). Whitney Balliett, on the other hand, heard in 1975 an all-encompassing composite: "the best of Coleman and Eric Dolphy and Miles Davis and Benny Carter and Paul Desmond"; by 1977, that composite had foregrounded Carter's influence, now that Braxton had assumed "the same Victorian tone . . . the same high-collared intensity" of the swing composer and multi-instrumentalist ("Jazz" 1975 and 1977). After the release of *Creative Orchestra Music 1976*, moreover, comparisons to big-band composers began to rival the search for Braxton's soloistic precedents. Apart from passing references to Gil Evans and Fletcher Henderson, most writers evoked the name of Ellington as they described Braxton's lush orchestrations (Lake, "I Made"; Mitchell; Balliett, "Jazz" 1977). Evocations of "the Duke" also encouraged comparison between Braxton and Harry Carney, the baritone saxophonist in the Ellington band (Occhiogrosso). As the artist for whom "the conventional critical system of comparisons just doesn't apply," Braxton seemingly had adopted multiple personalities, becoming what Peter Occhiogrosso called "a sort of archetype" of the tradition-centered contemporary jazz musician (Lake, "Curiouser").

The conception of Braxton-as-aggregate identifies the irreality of his public appearance. By acquiring associations with the legacy of innovators, he became an emblem of its history, its mystique, its larger-than-life presence. The grandeur of the jazz legacy, in turn, encouraged the making of exaggerated claims about his stature and influence. Tossing aside Palmer's caveat, journalists translated the spectacle of historical references into hyperbolic signs of innovation and invention. Braxton, the "genius" and "Renaissance man," who must either "play or die," would be "hailed . . . through no fault of his own," Balliett observed, "as the new messiah" (Tepperman, "Heard" 1973 and "Record" 1976; Rothbart; Balliett, "Jazz" 1975). Clusters of accolade, while perhaps meaningful at one level, assumed grand proportions as they piled up one on the other. If Braxton were "one of the most singular and vibrant musical personalities" of the era, or even, as David Less had suggested, "the premier reedman of the 1970s," the intensity and repetition of such claims led to the construction of something more (Hunt; Less). Magnified and exaggerated, Braxton's image grew from one of importance into that of the immortal titan, a jazz version of the mythic romantic artist. He became a creative voice who from the evidence of a single concert held promise of recasting the entire history of jazz; he was the performer who alone "could bring about a more thorough-going reorganization of the Afro-American art improvisational aesthetic than did Parker, or Coleman, or Coltrane in their times" (Hunt; Tepperman, "Record" 1975).

As writers reinforced Braxton's associations with the legacy, they also accentuated his radicalism to distinguish him from the mundane matters of conventional practice. Difference in the form of transcendence ironically served to underscore his importance to what they felt to be a consistent and coherent tradition. At once, Braxton could be the same as and different from (and thus, superior to) the very best in jazz. Drawing comparison to Coleman, he shared likenesses to Paul Desmond; standing beside Coltrane, he seemed similar to Schoenberg. If Gary Giddins found him "academic [and] intellectualized," John S. Wilson had now heard something "much more readily accessible," particularly when compared to his former colleagues in the AACM (Giddins, "Idea"; Wilson, "Nimble"). Sometimes opposing references appeared in a single report. Conrad Silvert, for example, stated emphatically that Braxton was "one of the very best on the instrument since Parker." Yet, on second thought—and apparently with no sense of contradiction—he ultimately stood "closer to Stravinsky and Bartók" (Silvert). For Mikal Gilmore, the saxophonist seemed remarkably "unpretentious" even as he could be "unearthly intimidating," while Peter Occhiogrosso argued that despite "what one reads about Braxton's iconoclastic attitude . . . he appears essentially a traditionalist" (Gilmore; Occhiogrosso).[20] Furthermore, the dramatic reach of Braxton's eclecticism accentuated the ambiguity of his character. Diverting references to his interests in voodoo and hieroglyphics, his following in the Soviet Union, and his theories of a "world music juncture" of Japan, Africa, and India suggested that his "jazz" encompassed the totality of known expression. Ranging across the world musical order, Braxton eventually called into question even the constructs of language and race, all the while "acknowledg[ing] the past" and his place, as his album titles indicated, *In the Tradition* (Henschen; Weber; B. Smith, "Braxton Interview").

Both the insider and outsider, iconoclast and conservator, voice of darkness and light of reason, Braxton as the 1970s jazz star materialized the collapse of certainty that identifies the postmodern. Like his art and the culture in which it existed, Braxton's image slipped through the cracks of conventional categories and identification. Yet the reality of ambiguity could be smoothed over by contradicting the contradiction, by adapting Braxton to advance the theme of cohesion and order. For as both Dick Hebdige and Stuart Hall have observed, officiators of media "not only record resistance, they 'situate it within the dominant framework of meanings' "—in this case, in the theme of mainstream survival (Hebdige 94). As the controversial radical working in the name of the jazz tradition, Braxton would create madness to restore order, as art "cohere[d] in contradiction" of its own message (Hebdige 85). To celebrate Braxton, then, official culture "made sense" of his challenge, his *noise,* by revising it to fit the themes of a mythology to which it was categorically opposed.

Most central to the image would be, fittingly, the most ironic aspect of it: the reference to controversy, which ultimately took on a life of its own as a figure orienting both critical and readerly perception. According to the standard formula, no middle ground existed in the interpretation of the new jazz master: "people seem to love Braxton ardently or shun him completely" (Litweiler). As such, he endured life at the center of a perpetual "storm of controversy," the victim of what might be likened to a critical lynching by an always anonymous group of "detractors" (Lange, "Record" 1979). As a critical formula, "controversy" provided the dominant hook, a tool of public enticement that kept Braxton a safe distance from the conventions of the everyday even as it contradicted revelations about his "downright old-fashioned" music. Indeed, insistence about Braxton's "accessibility" served as a contradictory, secondary theme that provided coherence to the spectacle in headlines announcing that Braxton will finally "explain himself." In this way Braxton could subject himself to the "acidic critical comments from his own community," while remaining a fixture in that same community. As the radical spy playing conventional jazz, he advanced the ebb-and-flow model of progress while his champions condemned "those detractors who choose to evaluate his work in their own backyards" (Hunt; Mitchell).

VI

In her fascinating book *Gone Primitive,* Marianna Torgovnick argues that the idea of the primitive, once a discrete, autonomous concept, has existed in the twentieth century as a composite of the modern and the Other. A powerful trope, it conforms to social need; malleable, it can be crossed to create a "never-never land of false homologies" (10). In the previously cited characterizations of Braxton, two images seemed to stand out: the noble black primitive and the natural intellectual or genius. At once, Braxton embodied two highly disparate and contrasting personae that could attract and repel (and, as a result, attract again) young jazz audiences. What makes this characterization so engaging are the extremes of the imagic contradiction: popular constructions of resistance are successful when they maintain familiarity at the same time as they create foreignness and a sense of distance. As a result, they become, as Dick Hebdige writes, "both more and less exotic than they actually are. They are seen to contain both dangerous aliens and boisterous kids, wild animals and wayward pets" (97).

Close scrutiny of the primitive/intellectual homology suggests that the images do not simply exist side by side but share much in common. In the form of the "natural man" (Tarzan) and the ivory-tower scientist (Einstein), for example, they both exercise control over their environments by taking command of mysterious "natural" forces—the jungle; matter invisible to the naked eye. As the noble savage and laboratory researcher, they operate in the realm of mystery and arcane knowledge, becoming in the popular imagination Yoda of the Star Wars trilogy or Mr. Wizard. At the other extreme, the primitive and the intellectual activate negative imagery, representing the dangerous, unpredictable Other. Here, they demonstrate herculean power that threatens to explode out-of-bounds. They are the Indian Savage and Robert Louis Stevenson's Mr. Hyde, the Zulu "headhunter" and Dr. Frankenstein. And at their most spectacular, they translate into the comic: Dr. Who meets Terminator 2.

In jazz, the construction of the primitive/intellectual juxtaposition coincided with a reconsideration of the character of the black artist in postwar America. Contrasting images of respectability and degeneracy, of noble romanticism and black bestiality came to dominate perceptions as white observers measured the mixed signals epitomizing the jazz artist.[21] Was jazz the classical art of the new "New Negro" or the voice of a subculture built on the illicit and licentious? Was jazz Dave Brubeck or Thelonious Monk? Nat Cole or Billie Holiday? In many cases it seemed to be all of these as leading exponents assumed images that tempered the trivialized characterizations of the past. At the extreme, hokum figures gave way to the likes of John Lewis and Gunther Schuller, as Ellington acquired a new respectability that would ultimately encourage comparisons with European masters.[22] More often, musicians struck a balance between the intellectual artist and the exotic Other, seemingly based on the casting of Charlie Parker as the drug-crazed creative genius victimized by the urban jungle (Ellison 221–32). Likenesses of Parker, the intellectual pagan, appeared in portraits of Sonny Rollins, Ornette Coleman, Art Blakey, Charles Mingus, Randy Weston, John Coltrane, and other artists from the 1950s and 1960s who embodied the homology of the progressive nourished by natural inspiration from "mother Africa."

Braxton's interests and background seemed ready-made for advancing a particularly dramatic version of the primitive/intellectual homology. Balancing interests in the rational and occult, he could perform the roles of the musical scientist and the tribal mystic who kept secret his creative intentions in a set of visual-literary codes. Furthermore, by tempering the cacophony of free jazz while asserting the political potential of music in a semireligious rhetoric, he became the jazz version of the African American social critic, evoking images of Dr. Martin Luther King, Jr., John Coltrane, and Malcolm X. Indeed, Braxton represented the supreme anomaly: while possessing the "calculating mind" of an "intellectual," he reinforced traditional images of jazz through his blackness (Townley, "Jarman/Braxton"); despite objections to the contrary, he remained committed to jazz, for after all, he "look[ed] like a jazz musician" (Zabor). To be sure, Braxton would never be treated entirely as a legitimate intellectual no matter how much he might have hoped for and deserved that attribution. While writers would provide space for him to elaborate on his ideas, his references to mathematics and science inevitably sounded peculiar, if not comical and absurd, when read in the context of popular magazines and against the background of his spectacular image. As Braxton continued to "explain himself," writers incessantly contradicted reason with parody, incorporating rational comment with irrational allusions to Braxton's theosophy, picture-titles, and beliefs in the limitations of language. Clearly, Braxton's intellectualism would be carried only as far as it reinforced mainstream suppositions. Beyond that, it served mainly as spectacle, his "scientific detachment," his "logarithmic loquaciousness," his "arithmetical way of phrasing" exposing what most thought him to be: "the Buckminster Fuller of jazz" (Giddins, "Marches"; Stern; Balliett, "Jazz" 1975).

"Go[ing] back to Africa [to] jump to Mars," as Braxton put it in one of his more outlandish public statements, writers situated the artist at the helm of stylistic advancement by relying on images that seemed to confound the very idea of continuity, (Townley, "Anthony" Feb. 1974). Yet the stereotypes—the primitive as tribal priest, the intellectual as astronomical explorer—served, like the controversy itself, to enhance the theme of tradition and aesthetic hierarchy. Having ascended from the "jungle" of black Chicago and the "fairly militant" AACM, Braxton tempered the savage roots of free jazz as he relied on them for new direction (Lake, "I Made"). Evoking images of primitive mysticism and science, he took control of the crucible of black power—"create, destroy, create"—for a legitimate end: to advance jazz as high art (Mandel). In the archetypal "down-home" of ancient Africa, moreover, Braxton found his true roots in a past that ultimately linked with the other Otherness of the future. As a kind of postmodern noble savage, he resisted primitive desires "to kill someone in the audience," and, restraining the decadent character of the black beast, he operated naturally and freely, "play[ing] by his own rules" in the timeless space that integrated past and future (Chadbourne; Blumenthal). Indeed, freedom became central to Braxton's image despite his commitment to structure as a performing musician. Advancing a radical, "alternative creativity," free from the laws of jazz, of language, of swing, he readjusted rhythmic procedures according to a mystical "vibrational" structure (Occhiogrosso). Braxton's recasting of rhythmical freedom suggested a rethinking of a fundamental impulse of African American music: by freeing swing from present conformities and infusing it both with the integrity of the past and the innocence of the future, he would reinvigorate its lifeblood with the secrets of the ancients and outer space. Attaining the ultimate state of authentic experience, Braxton, like the prototypical primitive artist, "express[ed his] feelings [directly], free from the intrusive overlay of learned behavior" (Price). As a scientist, moreover, he had transcended the limitations of time and space, incorporating the mythic past into forward-looking projections to the point where culture and history stood still (Fabian). *Newsweek*'s characterization of Braxton, the "free spirit," as the modern version of the antediluvean noisemaker captures the mass of stereotypes of "the most innovative force in the world of jazz":

> Braxton is a virtuoso on the saxophone, and the instrument has never been subject to such assault. He squeezes out bizarre sounds and clashing, hitherto unheard tone colors. He plays like a man possessed, in a paroxysm of animalistic grunts, honks, rasps, and hollers. He rends the fabric of conventional musical language as he

reaches into himself—and back into pre-history—for some primordial means of communication (Saal).[23]

Here, the controversy at its most spectacular assumed mythic and coyly racist proportions. And after having been subjected to depictions as a cerebral zombie, as jazz music's mystical black beast, Braxton could hardly have expected to gain respectability as a concert artist, no matter how many interviews he granted. As attention mounted, the spectacle grew proportionately, to the point where Braxton, as jazz music's court jester, subverted his own integrity by shifting jazz recordings to European labels and reserving his concert music for Arista. The release of *For Trio* (1977), *For Four Orchestras* (1978), and *Composition No. 95 for Two Pianos* (1980) finally made fact of the fiction of Braxton's inaccessibility, undermining the formula on which his popularity was based. As critical attention declined, so did his following, which led Arista to withdraw its support, a move that effectively eliminated him from the American jazz picture.[24]

As the inadvertent comic of jazz, Braxton would seem on one level to be its pathetic victim: an artist consumed by institutional machinations as well as by his own ambitions. Yet on another, he appeared more savvy than the victim theory gives credit. In fact, at many points Braxton appeared to handle his image-making deftly, fueling controversy that would increase visibility while baiting and teasing with oblique expressions of oppositional "style."[25] Resisting associations with jazz, concert music, and even at moments the AACM, Braxton transgressed boundaries to remain limited by none. He assumed "the impossible position" that Benjamin attributed to the intellectual's place in the class structure, but he stretched its impossibility in multiple directions (Benjamin, "Author" 261). Celebrated as the jazz star, Braxton retorted, "jazz is only a very small part of what I do"; compared to Bach and Webern, Braxton insisted on the preeminence of the black aesthetic; compared to his Chicago cohorts, he branded the AEC's "Great Black Music" logo as "racist" (Postif; Townley, "Anthony" Feb. 1974; Lake, "I Made"). Perhaps best expressing Braxton's subversive tactics were his explanations of his titles, which from moment to moment, shifted to one of a multitude of meanings. Were they expressions of the absurd or "just titles"? A "cataloguing system" or "outlines of structure"? Mystical codes or alternatives to language? According to Braxton, they were all of these, yet when pinned down he resisted, replying "I could explain [them] to you, but you really don't want to know" (Palmer, "Notes"; L. Smith; Henschen; Lake, "I Made"). From the public view, the picture-titles, like nearly all else in the creative system, seemed like not only one thing but another, calling to mind the child's candy-box hologram whose image changes with a slight turn of the wrist. Braxton's public image, like his private creative world, effects a bricolage of ever-changing signs that signify on the controlling categories of official culture. By extending his art of illusion to the construction of spectacle, Braxton succeeded in "conspir[ing] against . . . the King" (recalling Hal Foster's metaphor) as a way of preserving the integrity of a highly private realm of creative expression.

Notes

1   This essay first appeared in a slightly different form as "Black Experimentalism as Spectacle," a chapter from my book, *New Musical Figurations: Anthony Braxton's Cultural Critique.*

2   Davis's illnesses and resulting complications related to an inherited malady, sickle-cell anemia. Too often, commentators preferred to refer to his early addiction to heroin. Rhythmically, Davis had let the cat out of James Brown's [Papa's got a] "brand new bag," the latter a reconceptualization as profound as Coltrane's *Ascension* (1965). Davis's revitalization of black-vernacular rhythmic impulses, together with his disregard for the historical significance of standard discographical information (replacing personnel information on *On the Corner* with Corky McCoy's cartoon celebration of black street life) represented a powerful expression of resistance against the classicizing, fact-keeping sensibilities of official jazz culture.

3   See also Easter; Feather, "Gap"; Gleason. In 1970 (1): 34–41, *American Music Digest* presented excerpts of several recently published essays referring directly to the sense of loss after Coltrane's death. The essay featured a photograph of the late spirit of jazz (lifted from the cover of his "sacred" album, *A Love Supreme*) positioned catty-cornered to a sketch of a tombstone with the epitaph, "Jazz, Down-and-Out?" In 1974, moreover, the year that Braxton appeared on the American scene, musicians and reviewers were still remarking about a creative decline, usually at the expense of free jazz. See, for example, Hendricks; Schaffer; Ness; and Macek.

4   For an elaboration on Braxton's musical life, theories, and compositional procedures, see Radano.

5   The equation of drugs and jazz musicians appeared commonly in the press during the 1950s. In a 1970 report, references to drugs (Buddy Rich) and violence (Miles Davis) supported a coy, reproving headline, "Days in the Lives of Our Jazz Superstars" ("Days in"). The headline appears below a photograph of Louis Armstrong (supporting the earlier article), whose use of marijuana was well known to jazz musicians and fans. Furthermore, evocations of black power and the noble savage frequently informed free jazz reports, such as Spellman.

6   Wilson's comment about "the ridiculousness of gasping shrieks and squeals" seemed remarkably genteel after a decade of activity in free jazz. Furthermore, it would appear that he was unfamiliar with previously published examples of Braxton's titles on album jackets.

7   Lynch writes: "if a mad scientist ever drank a potion he had concocted to formulate a 'jazz musician,' he would undoubtedly transform into Anthony Braxton."

8   The terms refer to Braxton's figurative linkages of math, science, and musical composition that he has outlined extensively in interviews.

9   The interviews consist of, in the main, twelve formal conversations, together with several informal discussions with Braxton conducted from 1982 through 1990.

10 While Davis was officially dismissed for misuse of company funds, Richard A. Peterson and David G. Berger imply a link with his business approach. The ability to maintain a diverse lineup during a phase of retrenchment suggests a break from an earlier cycle in which major corporate control of the market typically reflected stylistic homogeneity. For the Columbia view, see Flippo.

11 Arista grew out of Columbia Pictures' faltering Bell Records. See Flippo.

12 According to Cynthia Kirk, Manchester and Manilow were holdovers from Bell Records. See also Davis and Willwerth. For a different perspective, see George 141–42.

13 New artists would include the Brecker Brothers, John Scofield, John Klemmer, and Michael Gregory Jackson. Much of the initial material by such musicians as Cecil Taylor, Gato Barbieri, Marion Brown, and Albert Ayler had appeared on Bates's English label, Black Lion/Freedom. For background, see Albertson, "Avant-Garde"; Bouchard; Lake, "I Made"; and Ullman 215–22.

14 Since Braxton employs picture-titles to identify his compositions, I refer to them here as they are positioned on the recording. Their numbers in Braxton's catalog are, in order of appearance, 23B, 23C, 23D, 38A, 37, and 23A. For discussion of these works, see Radano.

15 See the airplay lists published in *Radio Free Jazz* from May 1975, Jan., July, Aug. 1976, Aug. 1977. The ad appeared in the same magazine in Apr. 1975.

16 A count of major articles, reviews, and features from 1967 to 1973 totaled around ten; the total for 1975 through 1977 alone exceeded fifty-five.

17 Bob Blumenthal suggests that Braxton's cardigans challenge the "exotic garb of guru-types in a musical world which celebrates styles of non-conformity." In the context of jazz, Braxton seemed to be the nonconformist.

18 Balliett was referring to his work as an unaccompanied saxophonist. Albertson wrote that "Braxton is not, in fact, a musical revolutionary; what he does is rather tame compared to the output of most of his contemporaries in the field of the so-called 'new music.'"

19 From 1975 to 1979, Braxton ranked from third to fifth in *Down Beat*'s critics' polls for alto saxophone. In 1977 he also ranked second in the "composer" category. In 1976 and 1977 he placed sixth, then fourth in the voting for readers' "Jazz Man of the Year."

20 For Giddins ("Marches"), Braxton was both the one who "plays jazz as though he were a chemist studying it through a microscope" and the representative of a "neoclassical turn to classic forms . . . in a conservative period of retrenchment."

21 Primitive imagery appeared commonly in the early characterizations of jazz and the jazz musician, as evidenced in the texts of Robert Goffin, Hugues Panassié, and Rudi Blesh. Observations of the music against the background of Africa betrayed a questionable association that still characterizes many jazz texts. In Blesh's *Shining Trumpets*, for example, the introductory chapter on "black music" argues that "jazz . . . began not merely as one more form of Negro folk music

in America but as a fusion of all the Negro musics already present here. These . . . all stemmed back more or less completely to African spirit and technique. Negro creative power, suddenly freed as the Negroes themselves were freed from slavery . . . poured these rich and varied ingredients into his own musical melting pot and added his undying memories of life on the Dark Continent and the wild and tumultuous echoes of dancing, shouting, and chanting" (3).

22 Ellington's revival is frequently attributed to the 1956 performance at Newport. Yet the social context of this revival—the ascendancy of a new "New Negro" at the time of integration and the "decadence" of rock 'n' roll—is typically missed.

23 Precedents for such visions inform much of the historical jazz commentary. In *All About Jazz*, for example, the British writer Stanley Nelson equates rhythm with intoxication, primitivism, progress, and the black race: "The Negro undoubtedly has a phenomenal sense of rhythm. In Central Africa are still to be found savages in the last stage of barbarism, but the primitive music of the tom-tom and the reed-pipe will mould these creatures to the plasticity of clay. . . . Right from his origin in the African jungle, through his slavery to his present more or less emancipated condition, the Negro has retained this innate sense of worship of rhythm. Beverley Nichols has described the Negroes dancing in a Harlem cabaret as 'drunk with rhythm.' . . . Rhythm may therefore be said to be the elixir of life. Wherever we look we find it; without it, we cannot satisfactorily exist; because of it, we have widened the gulf between the human species and the lower orders to an enormous width. . . . For rhythm, while not postulating progress, is usually hand in hand with it" (13, 17).

24 Braxton's dismissal also may have been influenced by the company's change-of-hands, sold to Ariola/Eurodisc, a subsidiary of Bertelsmann A.G. in 1979 (Kirk).

25 "The challenge of hegemony . . . is not issued directly. . . . Rather it is expressed obliquely in style" (Hebdige 3).

Works Cited

Adorno, Theodor. "On the Fetish Character of Music and the Regression of Listening." *The Essential Frankfurt School Reader.* Ed. Andrew Arato and Eike Gebhardt. New York: Continuum, 1982.

Albertson, Chris. "Avant-Garde Jazz Finds an Unexpected Outlet on the Arista Label." *Stereo Review* Aug. 1975: 90–91.

———. "Anthony Braxton: Improvisations as Liberated and Fresh as Louis Armstrong's." *Stereo Review* Feb. 1976: 76.

Albin, Scott. "Caught: Anthony Braxton Quartet." *Down Beat* 25 Mar. 1976: 41, 48.

Anderson, William. "A Reprise for Jazz?" *Stereo Review* July 1974: 6.

"Backer Pacts with Davis." *Down Beat* 21 Nov. 1974: 8.

Balliett, Whitney. "Jazz." *New Yorker* 3 Nov. 1975.

———. "Jazz: New York Notes." *New Yorker* 4 Apr. 1977: 84–86.

Baudrillard, Jean. *Simulacres et Simulation.* Paris: Editions Galilée, 1981.

Benjamin, Walter. "The Work of Art in the Age of Mechanical Reproduction." 1936. *Illuminations.* Trans. Harry Zohn. New York: Schocken, 1969.

———. "Author as Producer." Lecture, 1934. *The Essential Frankfurt School Reader.* Ed. Andrew Arato and Eike Gebhardt. New York: Continuum, 1982.

Blesh, Rudi. *Shining Trumpets*. 1946. New York: Knopf, 1958.

Blumenthal, Bob. "Reedman Anthony Braxton Plays by His Own Rules." *Rolling Stone* 2 June 1977: 30–31.

Bouchard, Fred. "Steve Backer Maneuvers in the Front Line." *Down Beat* Mar. 1980: 31–32, 65.

Chadbourne, Eugene. "Anthony Braxton, University Theatre, University of Toronto." *Coda* Jan./Feb. 1976: 45.

Chambers, Jack. *Milestones 2: The Music and Times of Miles Davis Since 1960.* Toronto: U of Toronto P, 1983.

Davis, Clive, with James Willwerth. *Clive: Inside the Record Business.* New York: Ballantine, 1974.

"Days in the Lives of Our Jazz Superstars." *Down Beat* 16 Apr. 1970: 11.

Debord, Guy. *Society of the Spectacle.* Paris: Éditions Buchet-Chastel, 1967; Detroit: Black and Red, 1983.

"Dope Menace Keeps Growing." *Down Beat* 17 Nov. 1950: 10.

Easter, Gilbert. "So, What Is Jazz? A Mainstream View of the Avant-Garde." *Jazz and Blues* June 1972: 25.

Ellison, Ralph. "On Bird, Bird-watching, and Jazz." 1964. *Shadow and Act.* New York: Random, 1972.

Fabian, Johannes. *Time and Its Other: How Anthropology Makes Its Object.* New York: Columbia UP, 1983.

Feather, Leonard. "The Jazz Gap." *Down Beat* 2 Mar. 1972: 1.

———. "Blindfold Test." *Down Beat* 8 Sept. 1977: 43.

Flippo, Chet. "Arista's Clive Davis: From Out of the Muddle." *Rolling Stone* 18 Dec. 1975: 24.

Foster, Hal. *Recodings: Art, Spectacle, Cultural Politics.* Seattle: Bay Press, 1985.

Fox, Ted. *In the Groove: The People Behind the Music.* New York: St. Martin's, 1986.

George, Nelson. *The Death of Rhythm & Blues.* New York: Dutton, 1988.

Giddins, Gary. "Anthony Braxton as Idea Man." *Village Voice* 28 Apr. 1975: 112.

———. "Anthony Braxton Marches As to Jazz." *Village Voice* 30 Aug. 1976: 67.

Gilmore, Mikal. "Anthony Braxton." *Down Beat* 10 Feb. 1977: 20.

Gleason, Ralph J. "Perspectives: Nothing New Under the Sun?" *Rolling Stone* 16 Mar. 1972: 30.

Hall, Stuart. "Culture, the Media, and the 'Ideological Effect.' " *Mass Communication and Society.* Ed. J. Curran et al. London: Edward Arnold, in association with Open UP, 1977.

Hallock, L. "Dope, the Shameful U.S. Jazz Record." *Melody Maker* 20 Dec. 1952: 3.

Harvey, David. *The Condition of Postmodernity.* Oxford: Basil Blackwell, 1989.

Hebdige, Dick. *Subculture, The Meaning of Style.* New York: Methuen, 1979.

Hendricks, Jon. "Perspective." *Down Beat* 17 Jan. 1974: 30.

Henschen, Bob. "Anthony Braxton: Alternative Creativity in This Time Zone." *Down Beat* 22 Feb. 1979: 18–20.

Hunt, Bryan. "Anthony Braxton: A Space, Toronto." *Coda* Jan.–Feb. 1976: 33.

Kendall, Ian. "Only Time Will Tell." *Jazz and Blues* Oct. 1972: 14–15.

Kirk, Cynthia. "Ariola to Buy Arista from Columbia." *Variety* 1 Aug. 1979: 65, 71.

Lake, Steve. "Jazz Records: Anthony Braxton." *Melody Maker* 27 July 1974: 49.

———. "I Made More Money at Chess Than at Music." *Melody Maker* 11 Oct. 1975: 48.

———. "Braxton: Curiouser and Curiouser." *Melody Maker* 29 May 1976: 30.

Lange, Art. "Record Reviews: *Trio and Duet*, Duets 1976." *Coda* Feb. 1978: 18–19.

——. "Record Reviews: *For Four Orchestras*." *Down Beat* 7 June 1979: 18.

Lefebvre, Henri. *Everyday Life in the Modern World.* London: Allan Lane, 1971.

Less, David. "Richard Teitelbaum: Record Review." *Down Beat* 20 Oct. 1977: 29.

Leytes, Nathan. "Braxton, Ganelin Trio Tops in Critics Poll." *Jazz Forum* Feb. 1974: 14.

Litweiler, John. "Record Reviews." *Down Beat* 5 June 1975: 18.

Lynch, Kevin. "Record Reviews: Anthony Braxton, Solo Live at Moers Festival." *Coda* Feb. 1978: 18.

Macek, Karl. "Jazz: Hindsight or Foresight?" *Music Journal* Sept. 1974: 48.

McRae, Barry. "Avant Courier." *Jazz Journal* Dec. 1972: 20–21.

——. "Lookout Form." *Jazz Journal/Jazz and Blues* Aug. 1974: 19.

Mandel, Howard. "Caught: Anthony Braxton/Muhal Richard Abrams." *Down Beat* 11 Aug. 1977: 41, 43.

Mitchell, Charles. "Record Reviews: Anthony Braxton." *Down Beat* 7 Oct. 1976: 20.

Murray, Albert. *Stomping the Blues.* New York: Da Capo, 1976.

Nelson, Stanley. *All About Jazz.* London: Heath Cranton, 1934.

Ness, Bob. "Have You Dug . . . Larry Coryell." *Down Beat* 9 May 1974: 16, 34.

Occhiogrosso, Peter. "Anthony Braxton Explains Himself." *Down Beat* 12 Aug. 1976: 15.

Palmer, Robert. Notes to *Five Pieces 1975.* Arista AL 4064, 1975.

——. "*Creative Orchestra Music 1976.*" *Rolling Stone* 12 Aug. 1976: 59.

Peterson, Richard A., and David G. Berger. "Cycles in Symbol Production: The Case of Popular Music." *American Sociological Review* 40 (1975). Reprinted in *On Record, Rock, Pop, and the Written Word.* Ed. Simon Frith and Andrew Goodwin. New York: Pantheon, 1990.

Postif, Francis. "Anthony Braxton." *Jazz Hot* Apr. 1971.

Price, Sally. *Primitive Art in Civilized Places.* Chicago: U of Chicago P, 1989.

Race, S. "Clean Up the Profession." *Melody Maker* 17 Sept. 1955: 7.

Radano, Ronald M. *New Musical Figurations: Anthony Braxton's Cultural Critique.* Chicago: U of Chicago P, 1993.

Roberts, John Storm. "Anthony Braxton." *Melody Maker* 7 Feb. 1976: 47.

Rothbart, Peter. "Play or Die: Anthony Braxton Interview." *Down Beat* Feb. 1982: 20–23.

Saal, H. "Two Free Spirits." *Newsweek* 8 Aug. 1977: 52–53.

Schaffer, Jim. "Buddy [Rich] Raps About . . . " *Down Beat* 11 Apr. 1974: 12–14, 32–33, 39.

Silvert, "Talent in Action: Anthony Braxton." *Billboard* 1 Nov. 1975: 38.

Smith, Bill. "Anthony Braxton Interview." *Coda* Apr. 1974.

——. "Anthony Braxton: Saxophone Improvisations Series F; Town Hall 1972; Trio; The Complete Braxton" [record review]. *Coda* Apr. 1974: 15–16.

——. Notes to *New York Fall 1974.* Arista AL 4064, 1975.

Smith, Leo. Notes to *The Complete Braxton.* 1971. Arista reissue, AF 1902, 1977.

Smith, Will. "Anthony Braxton: Town Hall 1972" and "Saxophone Improvisations Series F." *Down Beat* 20 June 1974: 18.

Spellman, A. B. "Revolution in Sound, Black Genius Creates a New Music in Western World." *Ebony* Aug. 1969: 84–89.

Stern, Chip. "Kelvin 7666 = Blip Bleep." *Village Voice* 11 June 1979.

Tepperman, Barry. "Heard and Seen: Anthony Braxton." *Coda* Sept./Oct. 1973: 43–44.
———. "Heard and Seen: Anthony Braxton." *Coda* Nov. 1974: 37–38.
———. "Record Reviews: Anthony Braxton New York Fall 1974." *Coda* June–July 1975: 24–25.
———. "Record Reviews: Anthony Braxton and Derek Bailey." *Coda* Jan.–Feb. 1976: 23–24.
———. "Perspectives on Anthony Braxton." *Jazz Forum* Jan. 1977: 34–37.
Tomlinson, Gary. "Cultural Dialogics and Jazz, A White Scholar Signifies." *Black Music Research Journal* 11/2 (Fall 1991): 229–64.
Torgovnick, Marianna. *Gone Primitive: Savage Intellects, Modern Lives.* Chicago: U of Chicago P, 1990.
Townley, Ray. "Anthony Braxton." *Down Beat* 14 Feb. 1974: 12–13.
———. "Anthony Braxton: Four Compositions (1973)." *Down Beat* 11 Apr. 1974: 22.
———. "Jarman/Braxton: Together Alone." *Down Beat* 16 Jan. 1975: 22, 24.
Ullman, Michael. "Steve Backer." "Anthony Braxton." *Jazz Lives, Portraits in Words and Pictures.* New York: Perigree, 1982.
Vance, Joel. "Is Jazz Coming Back?" *Stereo Review* Sept. 1972: 28–29.
Weber, Mark. "Around the World: Ann Arbor." *Coda* May–June 1977: 26–29.
"What Is Jazz? Advent of Rock Puts New Sound in Old Groove." *Variety* 4 Dec. 1974: 56.
Wilson, John S. "Braxton Performs on Alto Saxophone." *New York Times* 24 May 1972: sec. 1:55.
———. "Braxton Is Nimble as Jazz Musician." *New York Times* 9 Oct. 1975.
Zabor, Rafi. "Funny, You Look Like a Jazz Musician." *Village Voice* 2 July 1979: 72–73.
Zipkin, Michael. "Record Reviews: Max Roach/Anthony Braxton." *Down Beat* 6 Sept. 1979: 28.

Ephemera Underscored: Writing Around Free Improvisation

JOHN CORBETT

The already-there-ness of instruments and concepts cannot be undone or re-invented.—Jacques Derrida (138–39)

The analogy with language, often used by improvising musicians in discussing their work, is useful to illustrate the building up of a common pool of material—a vocabulary—which takes place when a group of musicians improvise together regularly.—Derek Bailey (96–97)

The Improviser's Vocabulary: Music Says

Music presents, on the one hand, the problem of a semiotic system without a semantic level (or content plane): on the other hand, however, there are musical 'signs' (or syntagms) with an explicit denotative value (trumpet signal in the army) and there are syntagms or entire 'texts' possessing pre-culturized connotative value ('pastoral' or 'thrilling' music, etc.)" (Eco 10–11). As Umberto Eco explains, music, in general, does not signify in the same sense that verbal language does. A listener does not hear a tone or series of tones and immediately associate it with an object or concept, and, if one does, it is unlikely that the same "content unit" will be evoked for subjects from within the same cultural context. If it is evoked, there are two possible reasons: the establishment of a rigid metalanguage through either repetition or the conjunction of notation and music theory (or, perhaps, in the case of traditional musics, in a "tradition," i.e., cultural memory); and/or the existence of what we might call an "infra-semantic" system.

Musicology serves as the best example of a determinant musical meta-language. In Western classical music a chord change is analyzed as having meaning in relation not only to other music that surrounds it, but to a body of knowledge outside sound, even outside written music—that is, previous analyses. The transparency of terms such as *tension, resolution, harmony,* and *cacophony* is in part a result of their origin as words; that is, they are theoretical terms to begin with—developed in relation to the abstract concept of functional harmony—that are subsequently given legitimacy in their enunciation as music, a process that then erases the writing through which it was produced. Thus, we have a coded system that is given a semantic level through a complex system of denial. Meaning is metalinguistically pasted on; music theory fills the position of semantic referent in the musical language; the words of theory speak through the music they seem to animate.

In this system, meaning is regulated externally. Two written signifying systems—notation and music theory—are given a range of meaning-relations. The musical elements have specific signifying power in relation to one another, and, together, in relation to theory. Theory, finally, has signifying power in relation to "music history," which is the accumulated written knowledge of music. At the moment of its articulation, written music calls on both of these systems to produce intelligibility, while it simultaneously disavows itself of both those (written) referents. This is why tonal music appears to have such an obvious, "natural," internalized signifying system. Atonal, serial, or pan-tonal music also works in reference to the same body of knowledge by constructing a different system, in *relief* of the preexisting one. As improvising saxophonist Evan Parker suggests, perhaps we should "consider score-making as an esoteric branch of the literary arts with its own criteria rather than anything to do with music" (96–97).

Rereading music—listening again—thus allows for recognition of structural elements, presents new analytic possibilities, and reveals the constructed nature of a piece. It "recaptures a mythic time (without *before* or *after)*" (Barthes, *S/Z* 16). However, it also further erases the writing at its base, which the written text in literature or written analysis constantly avows in rereadings. "I've got your memory/Or has it got me?/ I really don't know, but I know/That it won't let me be" (Patsy Cline). While rereading a text lets the reader in on its structure and gives him or her the capacity to navigate through it in ways other than those the author scripted, rereading music serves to naturalize the sound, to make it appear less related to its written structuration, to make its structure more audible but also to make its unfolding seem that much

more *inevitable.* Hence, the written musical text—the score or recording—is a similar, but more complex, form of Roland Barthes's "readerly"
text.

The "writerly" text is improvisation. As Barthes explains: "the writerly text is not a thing, we would have a hard time finding it in a
bookstore [or record shop] . . . the writerly text is *ourselves* writing. . . .
But the readerly texts? They are products (and not productions)" (*S/Z* 5).
We should establish that records of improvised music—available in some
stores—are not the same as improvisation, but are instead a more refined
form of inscription, of composition. To render a writerly text readerly is
to record it; recording involves the post-facto selection, editing, organization, sequencing, titling, and packaging (all compositional, not improvisational considerations) of music that has been made by means of improvisation but is now repeatable and fixed.[1] To render a readerly text
writerly, on the other hand, is to improvise it; for instance, consider the
use of recorded music in improvisation via samplers or turntables.[2]

It may be objected that everyone does not have access to analysis, that
the metalanguage of music theory has a specific readership and therefore
cannot be the basic referent for the mass public that consumes most
music in contemporary culture. Does this suggest that meaning is, in
fact, regulated in another way? Disregarding the dissemination of this
music-theoretical knowledge through channels other than academia, the
traces of which are strategically impossible to map,[3] there are other ways
that meaning may be introduced into music.

First, and related to the metalanguage of music theory, is repetition.
Barthes suggests that rereading "saves the text from repetition (those
who fail to reread are obliged to read the same story everywhere)" (*S/Z*
16). As we have seen, repetition works somewhat differently in music. It
is dependent on the simulacrum[4] (specifically, the "master" recording or
original manuscript; generally, the metalanguage—academic or journalistic—to which it refers), and, with each successive hearing, music further distances itself from those strenuously disowned written sources.
Thus, rereading tends to seal off the relationship between writing and
music—an avowal of which might provide real grounds for a "play of
pluralities"—and it confines that relationship to interpretation and analysis: closure, structure, existence, truth—in short, meaning.

What is essential for this strategy is the fact that more than one of
these meanings can exist for each piece of music. For example, in the
economy of musical repetition a single musical text (or fragment thereof)
could simultaneously have a set of connotative meanings referring to a
metalanguage, a denotative meaning associated with, for instance, capi-

tal (e.g., a film or product, or for that matter, previous articulations of itself-as-recording), and what we might call an infra-semantic meaning. Jacques Attali leaves his use of the word "repetition" ambivalent; it could mean either intertextual repetition (chorus structures, refrains, regular meter) or repetitions of the entire text (regular airplay on the radio or use of the repeat button on CD machines). We should also leave the meaning of repetition unfixed, since the above modes of meaning-making do not constitute a system per se. They do not have formal characteristics. They are illusive, polymorphous. The creation of meaning cuts across textual instances (songs, phrases, genres, styles, modes, formats) and masks itself by forming audible regularities.

The infra-semantic level of music is the unnamed basis of Attali's analysis. It is music's political-economic situation in culture. I hesitate to call it a "function" of music, since it not only indicates music's activity within culture—its effects—but it also suggests the way music is produced, the way that it constitutes its subjects, the way that music can be known about, the manner in which power manifests itself in relation to music—that is, how power is invested *in* music and how power is wielded *on* music. Music. Where can it go? How can it be used? Who can use it? What constitutes *music* at a given point in a given discursive formation? What are its possibilities? What defines its limits, its borders? How are they regulated, patroled? As Attali's analysis reveals, music maintains intimate bonds with other institutions—epistemological as well as material.[5] The noise/music boundary, then, exposes deep, hidden aspects of a given society's political subconscious, its structure, and its means of producing meaning.

These infra-semantics provide music with meaning insofar as they provide meaning with "music." For instance, we can say that in Attali's repetitive society (87–132), improvisation is not possible and cannot be real, but improvised *music* (such as a recording or description of an improvisation) is. The textual economy of hyperreality precludes the existence of the writerly text, or at least its acknowledgment. On the other hand, improvisation can include the repetitive or even the repetitious. In fact, it is arguable that improvisation cannot exist without a surrounding hyperreal. Perhaps improvisation is, in this respect, parasitic rather than "free." Michel Foucault explains: "Rather than speaking of an essential freedom, it would be better to speak of an 'agonism'—of a relationship which is at the same time reciprocal incitation and struggle; less of a face-to-face confrontation which paralyzes both side than a permanent provokation [*sic*]" ("Subject and Power" 221). This is an extremely important distinction, for what is usually associated with freedom in improvisation—anarchy, chaos—thus takes more discernible shape. A group of performing improvisers are not simply *indulging in* freedom, they are creating a power relationship in which a construct of "freedom" is generated by power and simultaneously regenerates that power. As guitarist Davey Williams says: "Life is not free, mankind will not soon be free, and this fact is beside the point. Free improvisation is not an action resulting from freedom; it is an action *directed towards freedom*" (33). Improvisation does not, thus, bypass power. They intertwine. I prefer to figure them dancing rather than fighting, given that no one always leads and considering that no one will conquer.

We may add the third element of our power-freedom-knowledge conjunction, thereby making possible the definition that Williams gives of a philosophy of improvisation as a "creative truth mechanism" (D. Williams 34). Creative = Free. Truth = Knowledge. Mechanism = Power. As such, it is necessary for, and a necessity of, the new set of musical possibilities that are meaningfully present at the infra-semantic level. So, infra-semantics deal less with an interpreting subject than with the signifier "music" and the possible meanings it can possess and support for a range of subjects.

Music is not antisemantic or nonsemantic. It has polyvalent semantics. It fluctuates between *meaning nothing, meaning something,* and *being interpreted as meaning something.* One result of this is a certain exchangeability with other signifying systems such as color,[6] shape, smell, and, as we have seen, language. In improvised music and partially improvised music, for example, titles such as Roscoe Mitchell's "Off Five Dark Six" and Anthony Braxton's intricate diagrams both represent this impulse. The task of naming an improvisation often involves an element of play, sometimes in the form of a joke that refers to the ambiguity or absurdity of assigning titles. For instance, the Music Improvisation Company named a cut "Its tongue trapped to the rock by a limpet, the water rat succumbed to the incoming tide," while German saxophonist/clarinetist Wolfgang Fuchs called an album *So-und? So!,* a play on the question "So and?" (*So und?*) answered by "like this!" (*So!*), at the same time a phonetical construction of the word "sound" and a colloquial reference to the idea of a "so-and-so" as a substitute for a curse word, as in "that lousy so-and-so!"

While other signifying systems can be referenced in the process of evoking musical meaning, they thereby constitute an attempt to endow music with specific denotative power, as if with words: metalinguistically. In the absence of a coherent metalanguage that governs the production of meaning, improvisation can be said to make full use of the polyvalent semantics of music. It can borrow meaning from other idioms' semiotic systems (jazz, blues, gamelan, baroque, etc.), or it can refer to an internal language consisting of a mobile syntax of players, techniques, and contexts that take as their locus the body of the performer.

Wares: The Catalog of Sound

Pat Question: How does an improviser improvise?
Pat Answer: He or she develops and employs a repertoire of possibilities.

If the above was all improvisation consisted of, it would be practically no different from other musics. Its substance would be known, we could construct a definitive history around it, we could record it and sell it. And, in fact, this is where improvisation and other musics appear most similar. It is tempting to view improvisation as a collection of individual idioms (rather than being, as Derek Bailey suggests, *non*-idiomatic), with its parameters determined not by adherence to and divergence from a tradition or style, but in the performer's development of a personal language in practice or solo situations. Thus seen, improvisation is a scaled-down version of the infra-semantic, each performer being the equivalent of a "culture."

Improvisation is not primarily this, however, although these statements are perfectly valid. Two things are missing. First, the essential element of risk involved in improvising and, therefore, its accompanying reliance on temporality; and second, the repositioning of knowledge in relation to the musician and, therefore, history. We should digress a moment to speak about these.

Risk

There are two ways of looking at risk in relation to improvisation. One: improvisation can be seen to *eliminate the risk*. On this level, what is at stake for the improviser is not the same as what is at stake for other musicians. In the sense of "playing incorrectly," of error per se, the improviser need not fear. One cannot "do it wrong." Accidents are permitted, at times even encouraged. So, in terms of written music, improvising presents a no-risk situation. Two: to improvise is to *take the risk*. Since the performer does not *know* for certain what will be played going into the performance, since the music is by definition undefined, the risk of failure, of complete collapse, is everywhere present. As Attali says, "[Improvisation] is thus laden with risk, disquieting, an unstable challenging, an anarchic and ominous festival, like a Carnival with an unpredictable outcome" (142).[7] Danger presents itself as potential inertia: not going anywhere. Evan Parker describes improvisation as a process of exploring unknown territory with three possible results.

> Risk One—*never get out there; can't find the wilderness. The Risk of Stagnation.*
> Risk Two—*never come back; lost in the wilderness. The Risk of Insanity.*
> Risk Three—*go full circle (and take audience with). The Risk of Completion.*
> (Corbett, "Parker")

The first risk threatens the improvisation (with nonexistence). The second threatens the performer (with dysfunction). The third threatens to seduce the other risks (into systematization, gimmicks, the sure thing). Thus, surrounded by codes, improvisation dares to defy codes while it simultaneously runs the risk of becoming fully codified.

If we see improvisation as an attempt to destabilize codes, then we must deal with the problem of knowledge.

Knowledge

Elliott Carter wrote that "a musical score is written to keep the performer from playing what he already knows" (12). Evan Parker's response to this statement is that "improvisation is played to keep the player from playing what the composer already knew" (Corbett, "Parker"). In either case, the always-already. The crucial, unanswerable question: can the improviser play something he or she does not already know?

Regardless of the always-already question that is, it seems, always-already there, another more approachable question is raised by the interrogation of the knowledge/improvisation line. The all-consuming desire on the part of the performer for the unknown, the uncharted, the search for area beyond territory, for "reterritory," as Deleuze and Guattari call it, the nomadic impulse is certain but problematic.

First of all, what does it mean to suggest an "outside"? Does this suggest a privileged space, supposedly exterior to discourse, to which the improviser can aspire? Nonknowledge? Are we not, in this attempt at definition, gesturing toward an impossibility: a discourse without discursivity? Unknown knowledge? How do we mean to use knowledge here? As capital? Law? Codes? "Music"? Simulation? And isn't this essential other—the unthought—simply ushering in a new spiritualism?

Are we not merely replacing the "essence of music" with an "essence of improvising"? Let us allow this question to trouble us a bit and move on to the erotic.

If we see the existing codes as creating (or perhaps constituting) our desire, then where do we locate the erotic in improvisation? How is pleasure possible? On the topic of textual theory, Barthes writes: "Neither culture or its destruction is erotic; it is the seam between them, the fault, the flaw, which becomes so" (Barthes, *Pleasures* 7). In listening, however, there is a different situation of the erotic from that in reading. It is not a private activity, involving only intertextual eroticism. In locating the erotic in improvisation, let us designate two texts: the audience and the performers/performance (inseparable). Thus, we can now read these two texts as elements of a context (the event), both of which we then gather on our lap, to read. The erotic is to be found at the line that divides these two texts: roughly, the edge of the stage. Temporally, it is located at the edge of performances: beginnings and endings. (Parker: "The starts of pieces are very good often because they are impossible to theorize about" [Rusch 11].)[8] The erotic is created in the meeting of these edges: the "obedient, conformist, plagiarizing" audience (culture), and the other edge, the uncoded, "mobile, blank," performance (destruction) (Barthes, *Pleasures* 17).

> Composition [improvisation] thus leads to a staggering conception of history, a history that is open, unstable, in which labor no longer advances accumulation, in which the object is no longer a stockpiling of lack, in which music effects a reappropriation of time and space. Time no longer flows in a linear fashion; sometimes it crystallizes in stable codes in which everyone's composition is compatible, sometimes in a multifaceted time in which rhythms, styles, and codes diverge, interdependencies become more burdensome, and rules dissolve. (Attali 147)

Thus, in the course of improvisation, culture is not destroyed or repeated; it is made pleasurable, invested with pleasure—or perhaps *bliss*. We, the improvised music listeners, become Barthes's "profound hedonist" who "enjoys the consistency of his selfhood (that is his pleasure) and seeks its loss (that is his bliss)" (*Pleasures* 7).

Improvisation does not simply mean the death of language, however, for in the place of the dead language—the disfigured or defiled codes—a new one emerges, more vibrant than the last. Improvisation involves the permanent play of threshold and transgression. In our critical inscription of two texts—audience and performer—we have perhaps wrongly avoided the question that brought us here and the one to which we now return: the improviser's vocabulary. Let us make our way back into the audience and once again read the improvised/improvising text as possessing its own interminable eroticism:

> . . . eath/language/death/language/death/lang . . .
> ware-stew: the potpourri of sound
>
> Old Pat Question: How does an improviser improvise?
> New Pat Answer: By developing and employing a repertoire of possi-
> bilities in order to risk the unknown.

Pat, yes. Provisional, yes. But perhaps satisfactory. These possibilities we speak of are the instruments of the improviser (they include the improviser's instruments, i.e., guitar, trombone, saxophone, etc. . . . but more). They are the springboard for improvisation, and it is through them that an improviser provokes an improvisation from himself and those with whom he plays. The improviser uses his own catalog of sounds, reactions, catalysts, probes, and prongs to get to the "outer sanctum" (D. Williams 33).

A whole rhetoric of "maturity" has been established around the meta-phor of language as applied to improvisation. Bassist Peter Kowald ex-plains: "So it is not like the Jackson Pollock aspect of scribbling that is in the music now, but there are a lot of clear lines happening. . . . That may even be the difference between musicians who have been doing this a long time and those younger ones who are just starting to find their own language, in which case there may be a lot of scribbling" (22–23). For improvisers, this pseudolinguistics never calcifies, however; the lan-guage must never *become* the music. Exposing his nomadic tendencies, Derek Bailey summarized by saying: "One could approach the unknown with a method and a compass but to take a map made it pointless to go there at all" (127).

One must see improvisation as being *arbitrary* in its full range of senses: (a) it necessarily has an *arbiter* in at least three forms: the body of the performer/instrument, the vocabulary of the performer, and the performance context (audience, other performers, atmospheric consider-ations, and the multitude of other imperceptible influences); and (b) on the whole it is given over to the *will* of the performer; it consists of nonrandom utterances—though randomness, passivity, and indecision can certainly be a part of any improviser's vocabulary. Hear, for instance, the brilliantly haphazard music of Dutch pianist Misha Mengelberg. Improvising, in this respect, is particularly violent—it consists in making a decisive statement and at the same time giving oneself over to the situation. Jacques Attali points out the simultaneous self-abnegation and murderous impulse of group improvising:

> This new mode of production thus entertains a very different relation with violence: in composition [improvisation], noise is still a metaphor for murder. To compose is simultaneously to commit a murder and to perform a sacrifice. It is to become both the sacrificer and the victim, to make an ever-possible suicide the only possible form of death inherent in it, in other words, to locate liberation not in a faraway future, either sacred or material, but in the present, in production and in one's own enjoyment. (142–43)

Words. The fantasia of the dictionary. Perhaps "caprice" is more suitable a description than "will," as in "given over to the *will* of the performer." That is, caprice as "whim," which is defined as "a sudden fancy, a sudden unreasoning desire or impulse."

There are three bodies: the body of the performer, the body of the instrument, the body of knowledge. Günter Christmann: "Above all my consideration about free improvisation was developed from the position of this instrument = player" (35). Evan Parker in an interview: Q: "You are your instrument." A: "Yeah" (Rusch 11). Let us now employ two terms from the old regime to cut across these bodies, to violate their apparent unity: *technique* and *instruments*.

Playing with Technique

You may think this is the finest pearl
but it's really only cardboard balls
sheened in glue
overwhelming technique
—Captain Beefheart

As soon as you realize you've made a law out of playing without rule, you've made a new rule and therefore you become interested again in a certain amount of discipline. But what forms those disciplines take and whether you even need to discuss them with the other musicians, these are the questions. . . . I'm not interested in playing without a craft-musicianship.—Evan Parker (Rusch 11)

Attali writes: "Composition [improvisation] ties music to gesture, whose natural support it is; it plugs music into the noises of life and the body, whose movement it fuels" (142). The improviser's technique is thus a reappropriated technique, and it therefore requires a radical redisciplining of the body. Music in both repetitive culture ("mass culture," recorded music) and representation (in which music is dominated by the written score) is largely dependent on correct gesture for its stability.

In classical guitar training, for example, sounds that are otherwise obtainable—through a variety of "extended techniques"—are proscribed by a set of hand positions that cultivate correct and well-disciplined musicianship. These hand positions are painful and by no means "natural," but—like penmanship—they require the development of certain muscles and the contortion of the hand into an optimal playing position to execute the score. Connected to this are correct postures, foot and arm positions. Although the student may play a piece correctly in terms of the sound produced, if it is not obtained through correct gesture it is less economical and more likely to be "missed" in later attempts, thereby foregrounding the presence of the body of the performer and the possibility of musical failure. The training of the hands, their adjustment and alignment to meet the requirements of correct technique, and thus the development of musculature *incapable* of producing "bad" technique, all ensure the reproduction of music outside, off the surface of, away from the performer. Standard technical facility is therefore a strategy by which the instrument and performer are both denied a certain kind of presence in the performance, a strategy by which they are disavowed as the writing of culture and thus a strategy that protects written (preinscribed) music and the discipline of the body against exposure and detection.[9]

Michel Foucault: "A well-disciplined body forms the operational context of the slightest gesture. Good handwriting, for example, presupposes a whole gymnastics—a whole routine whose rigorous code invests the body in its entirety, from the points of the feet to the tip of the index finger" (*Discipline and Punish* 152). Thus, the malleability of the body, its specific disciplining, creates the matrix for efficient gesture, which, in turn, must be aligned with the musical object, the musical instrument. "Discipline defines each of the relations that the body must have with the object that it manipulates. Between them, it outlines a meticulous meshing" (152–53). This disciplined individual (and instrument) can therefore be orchestrated. "The individual body becomes an element that may be placed, moved, articulated on others. . . . This is a functional reduction of the body. But it is also an insertion of the body-segment in a whole ensemble over which it is articulated" (164).

The improviser's task, then, is to subvert this disciplinary action at a number of levels: gesture, the object-body articulation, the orchestrated body, or a combination of these. This does not mean the abandonment of discipline altogether. It requires re-discipline. New techniques, new gestures, new responses. To reposition music in relation to the body of the performer, the player must be willing to stretch, must not be fearful of exposure and detection. Abandoning virtuosity or embracing it: both become possibilities. German saxophonist Peter Brötzmann, for instance, allies himself with the abandonment of technique, or, better described, the adoption of nontechnical techniques of paranormal saxophone playing typical of American free jazz saxophonists such as Albert Ayler, Pharoah Sanders, and Frank Wright.

Brötzmann on fellow reedman and composer Anthony Braxton: "It's a wrong kind of music, that is too much related to technique and that Americans are very open to. Braxton, for instance: I like him, I know him a little, I like his playing, but I think that this over-weighting of technical possibilities is simply the wrong way. . . . Music has never been a matter of technique at least not the music I consider as being important" (Lindenmaier 22). Consider, as well, pianist Cecil Taylor's incisive words in response to Gunther Schuller: "Schuller had made a remark that it would never occur to [Thelonious] Monk to practice and thereby change his technique to improve his music. I asked them, 'Would it ever occur to [Vladimir] Horowitz to practice to change *his* technique?' I said, 'Monk can do things that Horowitz can't, and that's where the validity of Monk's music is, in his technique'" (Spellman 31). Trombonist Günter Christmann: "Part of my playing is to find out new material, new techniques, like playing trombone with water in it, or with a larynx microphone, or to play the double bass with a comb. Doing this it is very important to be critical of yourself. You can find out a lot of tricks and spectacular things to do with your instrument but it is necessary to use only the inventions that really identify with yourself. Otherwise they are only silly effects" (35).

Violinist Phil Wachsmann states it simply: "The real feeling of the music is not in the sound—it's something going on behind it . . . the gestures, which provide the beauty" (Ilic 7). But that physicality makes itself heard. Gesture, movement, body; in short, presence. In vocal music, gesture provides a body for the voice; in instrumental music, it provides a voice for the body. Melody, harmony, and metrical timekeeping are therefore less significant and tend to be elided in favor of surfaces: rubbing, clicking, snapping, overplaying, overblowing, growling, slapping; skin, mouth, tongue, nail, lips, arm, torso, face, hand. The audible possibilities of each player's body are the basis of this language, its "genotext." "As though a single skin lined the inner flesh of the performer and the music he sings" (Barthes, "Grain" 181–82).[10] Structure is not abandoned, it is individualized; it reads the history written on the body of the performer. It exists not at the level of the "score" or the "tradition," but in the friction between the player's body and culture (in the form of the body of the audience, the other players' bodies, or the body of the particular instrument used). The body: a literal point of resistance. Whereas before it had to be sanded smooth by discipline in order to slip imperceptibly through performance, the performer's body now appropriates the sandpaper (any grade you like) and grafts it to its many surfaces.

I am inclined to write this as the ongoing legacy of black music in improvisation. Certainly, it seems that currents in African American creative music (not to mention creative *popular* music) from Armstrong to the Art Ensemble of Chicago, manage to constitute the body in music without necessarily abandoning melody, harmony, and timekeeping. Listen, for example, to Julius Hemphill's composition "Body" on *Flat Out Jump Suite.*

Melody, harmony, timekeeping: tools of expression for romanticism; the lineage to perforate for high modernism. In either case, repressive strategies only insofar as they produce the possibility "music" that denies the presence of the body of the performer.

Melody, harmony, timekeeping: these take on new significance in being improvised. They become the surface of the body of culture, deployable outside their contexts—their rightful homes—without depth. Discipline ("music") sits uncomfortably close to indiscipline (the noises of the body) in improvising.

fart = fugue

Instrumentalizing the Margins

Necessarily implicated in the screen of technical facility is the instrument. If "correct" technique has been formed in conjunction with possible positionings of the performer in relation to the instrument, so has the instrument become complicitous in its very materiality. It is literally composed and manufactured by culture and its possibilities are previously encoded to the degree that the instrument facilitates facility. Implicit in the instrument are techniques for playing it; the knowledge one can have on an instrument is mapped out progressively in terms of a training that allows the musician to move only a certain way and thereby forces the instrument to sound only a certain way. Contained in the very body of the instrument is the power/knowledge juncture capable of producing correct gesture. As a result, improvisers often divide into two groups regarding the question of technique/instrument: those who limit themselves to the instruments of culture and those who deface, deconstruct, and/or reconstruct them. Examples from the first group will allow us to isolate the act of subversion at the level of gesture, the body, and technique, before we are drawn into a discussion of the reconstituted instrument and the object-body articulation.

Evidence

Derek Bailey: "To change the instrument, or to use a found instrument attitude is okay, and it can make some nice music sometimes. I found in my efforts in those areas that the instrument actually lost malleability and permutability. You couldn't fuck around with it as much, you couldn't improvise" (Gaudynski 13). Bailey uses normal, everyday guitars. His vocabulary does not simply consist of the canon of disciplined gestures usually associated with guitar playing, however. For example, when he plays electric guitar he often employs a volume pedal. By turning the volume down completely, the act of strumming or plucking is removed from its pitch-targetedness, and the aural activity literally moves closer to the source of its production; it becomes "smaller," if you will; it focuses attention on Bailey's hand and on the movement of his arm. Rubbing the strings is a similar technique he sometimes employs.

Perhaps the most extreme example of Bailey's rediscipline is his development of techniques enabling "prepared" tones to be called forth without actually "preparing" the guitar. The use of John Cage's term is actually misleading, since the prepared piano is incapable of producing "straight" tones; it is limited to the preparations made.[11] As an improviser, Bailey requires a wider range of material possibilities than these preparations allow, so he has developed his own set of extremely difficult techniques through which he can attain the mute, "non-pitch pitches" associated with preparation, at the same time not compromising other possibilities, like open strings, fretted notes, and harmonics. To do this required active subversion at the level of gesture and the development of alternative techniques through intense practice.

Peter Kowald: In performance, Kowald may choose to weave his bow into the strings of his bass and then flick the bow back and forth creating a random percussive reverberation. In doing so, he allows for sounds that could not otherwise be obtained. Another technique he uses, sometimes simultaneously, consists of pushing three fingers in between the four strings and grasping them together in his fist at a point beyond the end of the fingerboard. This creates a "crude" sound and displays a "lack of technique" in the sense that the action takes precedence over the specific tones or sounds produced. However, once again the gesture is audible. It produces a sound that is the image of the performer's fingers and the inert potential of the bass. In both cases, the instrument is momentarily mutated, penetrated, but in the end it is left unscarred.

Examples such as these are abundant:

> LaDonna Smith rubs a moistened finger on the body of her violin, producing squeaks and sputters.
>
> John Zorn plays his clarinets and game calls into a bowl of water, producing distorted, gurgling tones.
>
> Phil Minton changes the position of his voice in his body, from deep in the back of his mouth with his throat wide open to the edge of his lips with his entire face taut.
>
> Butch Morris might choose to turn his cornet around and press his lips to the bell of the horn, producing wet sounds that betray the presence of both surfaces (lip/metal).
>
> Günter Christmann uses a variety of vocalizing and multiphonic techniques in his trombone playing that range in "technical difficulty" from simplistic and lazy to virtuosic.
>
> Nick Couldry immediately goes inside the piano, to play on the surfaces of its strings with glass, metal, and fingers.

There are several consequences of this emphasis on (re)technique. In the process of improvising, technique becomes unfixed. It can migrate, and other performers can pick up techniques—changing them or leaving them be—and integrate them into their own vocabulary. The body as locus of this music provides for slippage at the level of the instrument; that is, a saxophonist can learn new techniques from playing with a drummer. A constant threat, however, is that of technical reification. If the development of a technique or set of techniques is successful, it may become that which it seeks to avoid: a standard. For the individual improviser this is the danger of the gimmick, of trickery. It represents the petrification of the improviser's vocabulary. "The debacle of a perversion crushed by its own code and no longer able to invent itself" (Barthes, *Pleasures* 15).

On the other hand, when the codes are flexible enough to prevent this petrification, the individual's language can facilitate improvisation. Thus, the emphasis shifts: no longer are sound ideals represented and upheld in the form of written music or recordings, but in the activity of performing. To return to the erotic for a moment, desire is not constituted in the codes themselves—technique, personal and idiosyncratic materials, even in the individual performer's coveted "sound"—but in the implementation of those elements: not in *owning* the codes, the techniques, but in the process of developing them: "in use-time and exchange-time as lived and no longer stockpiled" (Attali 135).

Perhaps, then, improvisation is an act that should be read, as Julia Kristeva suggests *all* acts of signification must, as "the trial of meaning . . . the subject on trial, in process, *en process*" (216). As she explains: "All functions which suppose a *frontier* . . . and the transgression of that frontier (the sudden appearance of new signifying chains), are relevant to any account of signifying *practice*, where practice is taken as meaning the acceptance of a symbolic law together with the transgression of that law for the purposes of renovating it" (217). I can think of no better description of improvisation. The "semiotic" as Kristeva speaks of it is localizable neither in the mechanisms that are said to produce signification (Cartesian structures based on the concept of a unitary subject) nor in the traces of that process (theories of language, or, in our case, musicology in any of its traditional manifestations). The only qualification that Kristeva's notion of the semiotic requires is that it should not be thought of, in relation to improvisation, as access to a pre-Oedipal, prelinguistic space of pure semiosis. This is where the analogy between improvising and language is most useful, since the "trial" is precisely carried out in organized sound, or better, in the process of organizing and disorganizing sound, not in some amorphous nonsense-production. Improvising is not about going *back* to a lost land, but looking for lands yet undiscovered.

Bailey's loaded use of the term "playing" is analogous to Kristeva's "semiotic." "I think most musicians who take part in music are actually interested in playing. It's this business of being involved in the act of music making. That's the attraction of it for me" (Gaudynski 11–12). We might use the word "playing" to open up a comparison between sports, games, and improvisation. They all set up codes for personal interaction that are varied, transgressed (broken rules/world records), observed, and circumvented. New techniques are established and become dated; individuals discipline their bodies in ways enabling them to surpass the codes established for the elaboration of the event. (Of course, this analogy does not take into account the differing political valences of music-making and sports as cultural practices.) Many improvisers have used this likeness in their work; for example the game of Ping-Pong has been widely used as a description of a certain dialogical approach to improvised music. American saxophonist/composer John Zorn (who has written pieces called "Archery," "Pool," and "Jai-Alai") explains his compositional devices in these terms:

In my case, when you talk about my work, my scores exist for improvisors. There are no sounds written out. It doesn't exist on a time line where you move from one point to the next. My pieces are written as a series of roles, structures, relationships among players, different roles that the players can take to get different events in the music to happen. And my concern as a composer is only dealing in the abstract with these roles like the roles of a sports game like football or baseball. You have the roles, then you pick the players to play the game and they do it. And the game is different according to who is playing, how well they are able to play. . . . (Solothurnmann 32)

Thus, sports and games provide a fine metaphor for the constant transgression and reestablishment of codes in the process of improvising. In fact, all musical activity can be seen as containing some degree of this semiotic element that we designate as improvisation. "The aleatory thus rejoins order. Any noise, when two people decide to invest their imaginary and their desire in it, becomes a potential relationship, future order" (Attali 143). What improvisation in its present sociohistorical setting represents, however, is a shift toward that transgressive element, an emphasis on its possibility as "music," a profound decentering of symbolic order: "Not a new music, but a new way of making music" (Attali 134).

In this new environment the musical subject is no longer the audience, but the performer. Improvisation is music to be played. This is not to suggest that it cannot be pleasurable for a listening subject, but that it requires a different kind of listening in which the listener is active, a *participant observer* of sorts, much like the writerly reader, the "writing aloud" reader that Barthes idealizes (*Pleasures* 66). In "The Grain of the Voice," Barthes uses Philippe Sollers's term "gesture-support" to suggest that reading a text could physically involve the reader (183). Thus, we are speaking of two levels of involvement: audience participation at the level of gesture (I think here of the leg-bobbing and head-swaying that I am likely to do at an improvisation, neither of which *necessarily* corresponds or synchronizes with the rhythms or cadences of the performed music), and the play of plural interpretations of the music on stage, the thought-residue of the performance.

Attali says: "The goal of labor is no longer communication with an audience, usage by a consumer, even if they remain a possibility in the musical act of composition [improvisation]. The nature of production changes; the music one likes to hear is not necessarily the same music he likes to play, much less improvise" (142).[12]

In improvisation, history is sped up, but it is also liberated from the desire for a "final state," a utopia, implied by totalizing linear evolution. There are no ends to the means. Improvisation is cut free from its residence in institutions (scores, records [even records of improvised music], standards, idioms) and allowed to exist at a local level, in the microcosmic play of individual subjectivity. To improvise is literally to *make history.* As improvising musician/filmmaker Michael Snow puts it: "In playing totally improvised music one is in a present which is metamorphosing against the wake of the music's recent past, which one is simultaneously trying to categorize while moving into a future over which no one person has total control" (223).[13]

However, if we impose a little "real" history here, perhaps we must see free improvisation in its present form as the uncomfortable juncture of two ages: simulation (hyperreality) and dissimulation (disperse-reality). Obviously, in this context, we could see the audience as a vestige of consumerism—the need to judge the musical text and correlate that judgment with the findings of others in order to produce aesthetic truths and impose economic value. Are we at a strange point between two political economies, a point in which the critic acquires a musical stake (not just a financial or reputational one) in the playing? In such a system, the dissatisfied critic is as much dissatisfied with his or her own performance; the music was not pleasurable because the critic was not creative enough as a listener.[14]

Marginalizing the Instrument

Another possible consequence of the redistribution of technique is produced on the body of the instrument. Those improvisers who do not hold the instrument sacrosanct may direct some of their gestural redisciplining onto the surface of the instrument, with three possible results: defacement, deconstruction, and/or reconstruction. The first two are more likely to occur during the process of performing; the third is usually pursued away from the site of performance.

(1) *Defacement*—This consists of scarring, deforming, or breaking the instrument. Obviously a one-time event, this is generally prohibited by the cost of replacing or repairing instruments, and it is eschewed by improvisers who are suspicious of anything superficially evoking mysticism, exoticism, and the ritualistic. As a result, examples are scarce. Eugene Chadbourne employs an instrument called the "rake" (it is a garden rake with electric pickups affixed to it) that he resonates by sawing on it. Cecil Taylor represents a consistent example of this ap-

proach, infamous for his ability to take a piano out of tune (and often do more serious structural damage) during a single set.[15] He more exactly illustrates the relation between the defacement of the instrument and gestural rediscipline than those who set out to do so in advance, since the destruction and disabling of the instrument is a direct effect of his redisciplined body and not simply the realization of an attempt to deface the instrument.

(2) *Deconstruction*—Many improvisers disassemble their instruments in the process of playing them or before their performance. John Zorn might start a concert with his saxophone in pieces, connecting it with a clarinet or bird call. George Lewis was well-known in the 1980s for playing his trombone in pieces, exploring the possibilities of each piece as an instrument in its own right. Barry Guy has slackened the strings of his bass during a performance, providing himself with a new range and a new set of nonpitched sounds. Andrew Cyrille may remove the cymbals from his trap set and play them on the floor, intermittently lifting them into the air and letting them crash to the ground.

(3) *Reconstruction*—Harry Partch's book *The Genesis of a Music* explicates a theory of new instrument construction and exploration. The elaboration of this theoretical and practical work is continued in the journal *Experimental Musical Instruments*, which often deals directly with the question of reconstituting the body of the instrument. This process of rebuilding can take on the task of either modifying old instruments or dreaming up new ones. Hans Reichel disassembles old guitars and rejoins them in ways that expand their range of possibilities. For example, he built one guitar with two necks pointing in opposite directions, designed to be played on his lap. By striking it with a schnapps glass, he was able to produce a greater number of simultaneous soundings than a normally constructed guitar permits. Another of his guitars provides three ways of producing a tone on one string. By combining this expansion of instrumental possibilities with intense gestural rediscipline, Reichel opens up his lexicon immensely. He does not fetishize the completed instruments, however. He uses them for a time, explores their possibilities, and then discards them or dismantles them for parts. In this, he foregrounds the instrument as a composition of culture, as composing the possibilities of its usage, and he simultaneously works to destabilize that precondition by rendering it a process. Hugh Davies builds instruments to which he attaches electric pickups to amplify their noises. Often his instruments have a radically small "range" in the sense that they are not flexible like Reichel's. For Davies it is more the exploration of a great number of different objects' sound potential than creating

one instrument with an enormous range of possibilities. As Evan Parker recollected of their collaboration in the early free improvising ensemble Music Improvisation Company: "Hugh's virtuosity was expressed more in the building of an instrument than in the playing. Playing most of his instruments was often a matter of letting them speak, but at the right time and at the right dynamic level" (Bailey 112). Hal Rammel builds instruments to his own specifications, such as the "triolin"—a triangular sounding box mounted on a handle with metal rods of varying lengths that can be plucked or bowed—and the "sound palette"—an artist's palette with wooden rods attached, amplified by contact microphones and run through a digital delay unit.

Open Ending—Introducing Paradoxy

Part of improvisation, of the act of improvising, playing with other people, has very much to do with survival strategy. You have, of course, all your expectations and plans destroyed *the moment you play with other people. They all have their own ideas of how the musical world at that moment should be. So there are two, three, five, six composers there at the same time destroying each other's ideas, pieces.—Misha Mengelberg*

It is now possible to maintain a different, more complex image of improvisation as a diverse range of strategies regarding gestural rediscipline and body-object articulation, without a single rallying cry ("Smash the instruments!" "Change the gestures!"). An opposition to the notion of music away from the site of its production, a confederation dedicated to the relocation of "music" in and on the surface of the body of the performer—but one that is not unified at the level of the three bodies (knowledge, performer, instrument) nor at the juncture of those bodies, but in the space between improvisers, at the level of what Attali calls "tolerance" and what we might call *paradoxy*. It exists at the level of the insertion of the performer's body and vocabulary into a playing ensemble, performance context, and musical episteme (infra-semantic). This is not a strategy with an end, but with a process. A new way of generating musical meanings: the heterotopia of a musical steady state.

Perhaps Barthes provides the apt slogan for this level of (dis)unity: "Let difference surreptitiously replace conflict" (*Pleasures* 15). Paradoxy allows for differing strategies, different points of application. It takes as its maxim: there can be no generalizations. It is the harbinger of heterogeneity. It announces the split at all levels. It does not "rule out" orthodoxy; it *outrules* (dethrones) it. Of it, we can give only an indefinite definition: paradoxy is an orthodox use of paradox. If this concept brings us to the level of wordplay, it is because codes are what is at stake; codes, organization, syntax, semantics—such are the fulcrum of paradoxy. We do not pose for improvisation a time outside of codes, away from codification. Nor do we pose for improvisation priority over other musics, or existence away from them. Ours is no primal fantasy, no nostalgia for the tabula rasa of the cave person beating stones and sticks. Free improvisation is not transhistorical, the "oldest form of music making." It is specifically embedded in the political, social, and cultural structures that have incompletely bounded what can function as *music* for the last thirty years, give or take a few. A compromise between order and disorder, improvisation is a negotiation between codes and their pleasurable dismantling. "To express oneself is to create a code, or to plug into a code in the process of being elaborated by the other" (Attali 143). Improvisation is not a revolution that pits itself against codification; it is diffuse. Like ants stripping a carcass, it works from the inside and the outside of codes. In the materials and techniques with which they constitute their provisional language, improvisers enjoy the constancy of their selfhood (that is their pleasure); in experimentation with new materials and in the encounter with other musicians, they seek its loss (that is their bliss).

Notes

1   Alan Williams insists that recording is a signifying practice structured like a language rather than a simple "reproductive" technology in his landmark essay "Is Sound Recording Like a Language?" (51–66). This analysis provides the groundwork for a critique of the notion, prevalent in writings on improvisation, that recordings are nothing more than "documentation" of improvisation. Recordings always rely on editorial and technical decisions that are compositional in nature, such as microphone placement and choice. Whether one uses unidirectional, omnidirectional, multiple microphones, direct line, or some combination will directly influence the way the event is *represented*, and hence how it makes its meaning.

2   Hear the music of David Shea, Matt Wand, Pat Thomas, and Christian Marclay for examples.

3   I mean both that their strategies are impossible to detect, and it is part of their strategy to mask themselves.

4   I mean simulacrum in the Deleuzian, not the Baudrillardian, sense. See Deleuze 45–56. Thanks to Rick Wojcik for this observation.

5   In particular, Attali looks at the way that the specific mode of organization of the symphony orchestra relates to (and makes its meaning in relation to) other forms of contemporary social organization and distribution of bodies in space, on one

hand, and mathematics, on the other. In an earlier musical episteme, Attali locates ritual murder as the deep structure played out in music; for him, this infra-semantic is a vestigial part of the contemporary musical episteme as well.

6   "That's Hokie's famous 'English sunrise' way of playing. Playing with lots of rays coming out of it, some red rays, some blue rays, some green rays, some green stemming from a violet center, some olive stemming from a tan center" (Barthelme 57).

7   Attali perversely uses the word "composition" in sections where he is clearly discussing improvisation, perhaps to undermine any associations of "freedom" one has with the idea of improvising. While his use is not strictly limited to improvisation, I have inserted a bracketed reminder where appropriate, just to keep the idea of improvisation in plain view.

8   Drummer John Stevens: "When Trevor [Watts] and I perform . . . we are seated to enable the drums and saxophone to be approximately on the same level. We face each other and play at each other allowing the music to take place somewhere in the middle. This is very much an outward process. We are trying to be a total ear to the other player allowing our own playing to be of secondary importance, apart from something that enables the other player to follow the same process—the main priority being to hear the other player totally. Both players are working at this simultaneously. At this stage we are not aware of the total sound of the two players. When we arrive at hearing the other player completely and playing (almost subconsciously) for his sake at the same time, we then allow ourselves to bring into focus the duo sound. Up to this point we've let our own personal playing function in an unconscious way. From then on we start to converse naturally, retaining the group awareness we've developed between us. Free group improvisation is our aim, and a preparation piece like this is to aid us to achieve the concentration required for best results. The actual process, loosely described in these notes, may only take a few seconds, but those few seconds are significant in getting us beyond ourselves and into the music."

9   Canadian pianist Glenn Gould is an interesting exception to this paradigm, but an exception that proves the rule, given the overwhelming attention paid to his unorthodox performance techniques, his piano stool requirements (echoed in the omnipresent phone book present underneath fellow Canadian Paul Bley when he plays), and the anticanonical approach he took to canonical piano works.

10   "I shall not judge a performance according to the rules of interpretation, the constraints of style . . . which almost all belong to the pheno-song (I shall not wax lyrical concerning the 'rigor,' the 'brilliance,' the 'warmth,' the 'respect for what is written,' etc.), but according to the image of the body (the figure) given me" (Barthes, "Grain" 188–89).

11   "Just a simple example, sort of a cliché of improvised guitar music. If you put an alligator clip on a string. Now this has assumed quite a high importance in improvised guitar music. In fact, we have a guitar player in England who might be said to actually play alligator clips rather than guitar. But anyway, when you put an alligator clip on a guitar string you get a nice prime sound with two or three subsidiary possibilities. All of which can be obtained without using an alligator clip. What you lose by putting an alligator clip on a string is an enormous range of possibilities. That string is reduced to these things that it can do with this bloody clip on it. It's an exercise in reduction" (Gaudynski 13).

12 Bassist Peter Kowald provides a strikingly literal example of this point. When I asked him to tell me his favorite recordings on the FMP label, for whom he has recorded a vast amount, he remarked that "I just play this music, I don't listen to it." Said in a joking tone, it nonetheless corresponds with the sentiments of certain other improvisers. Of course, there are improvisers who do nothing but listen to improvised music, for whom it is an all-encompassing experience, valid on record just as much as in performance, valid when played by others just as much as when played by themselves. As Derek Bailey told me, contra Attali: "I don't see why anyone would come to hear the music if they weren't attracted to the way it *sounded.*"

13 Snow makes this comment in the course of an argument (in the company of Bruce Elder) that music is not structured like a language at all, that improvised music may provide access to a "prelinguistic" perceptual zone, that visual art is more like language than music (though it, too, is not truly linguistic), and ultimately that language is not strictly cultural, but also based on physiological and genetic predispositions (236).

14 As a music critic, I must insist that in fact this has limits. I do believe, for instance, that there is such a thing as a bad improvisation.

15 It is important to remember that the piano is usually property of (usually white) club owners, and thus, at one time, Taylor's reputation made it difficult for him to secure performances. He now has an endorsement arrangement with the Bösendorfer piano company.

Works Cited

Attali, Jacques. *Noise: The Political Economy of Music.* Trans. Brian Massumi. Minneapolis: U of Minnesota P, 1985.

Bailey, Derek. *Improvisation: Its Nature and Practice in Music.* Ashbourne, Eng.: Moorland, 1980.

Barthelme, Donald. "The King of Jazz." *Great Days.* New York: Pocket Books, 1980.

Barthes, Roland. "The Grain of the Voice." *Image, Music, Text.* Trans. and ed. Stephen Heath. London: Fontana, 1982. 179–89.

———. *The Pleasures of the Text.* Trans. Richard Miller. New York: Hill and Wang, 1975.

———. *S/Z.* Trans. Richard Miller. New York: Hill and Wang, 1974.

Carter, Elliott. *The Writings of Elliott Carter.* Ed. Else Stone and Kurt Stone. Bloomington: Indiana UP, 1977.

Christmann, Günter. "Free Improvisation." *Improvisor* 4 (1984): 35–38.

———. Interview. *Practicing Magazine.* N.p., n.d.

Corbett, John. Interview with Evan Parker. London, 27 Sept. 1985.

———. Interview with Misha Mengelberg. Amsterdam, Oct. 1993.

Deleuze, Gilles. "Plato and the Simulacrum." Trans. Rosalind Kraus. *October* 27 (Winter 1983): 45–56.

Derrida, Jacques. *Of Grammatology.* Trans. Gayatri Spivak. Baltimore: Johns Hopkins UP, 1984.

Eco, Umberto. *A Theory of Semiotics.* Bloomington: Indiana UP, 1979.

Foucault, Michel. *Discipline and Punish.* Trans. Alan Sheridan. New York: Random, 1979.

——. "The Subject and Power." *Michel Foucault: Beyond Structuralism and Herme-neutics.* Ed. Hubert L. Dreyfus and Paul Rabinow. Chicago: U of Chicago P, 1982.

Gaudynski, Thomas. Interview with Derek Bailey. *Cadence* 10.7 (1984): 11–14.

Ilic, David. "Putting the Catgut Out." *Wire* 21 (Nov. 1985).

Kowald, Peter. Interview. *Coda* Feb./Mar. 1986: 22–23.

Kristeva, Julia. "The Speaking Subject." *On Signs.* Ed. Marshall Blonsky. Baltimore: Johns Hopkins UP, 1985. 210–20.

Lindenmaier, H. Lukas. Interview with Peter Brötzmann. *Cadence* 4.10 (1978): 3–7, 20, 22.

Partch, Harry. *The Genesis of a Music.* New York: Da Capo, 1974.

Rusch, Bob. Interview with Evan Parker. *Cadence* 5.4 (1979): 8–11.

Snow, Michael. "On Sound, Sound Recording, Making Music of Recorded Sound, the Duality of Consciousness and Its Alienation from Language, Paradoxes Arising from These and Related Matters." *Music/Sound: The Michael Snow Project.* Ontario: Knopf Canada, 1993.

Solothurnmann, Jürg. Interview with John Zorn. *Jazz Forum* 95.4 (1985): 30–37.

Spellman, A. B. *Four Lives in the Bebop Business.* 1966. New York: Limelight, 1985.

Stevens, John. Liner notes for *Face to Face.* 1973. Emanem Records.

Williams, Alan. "Is Sound Recording Like a Language?" *Yale French Studies* 60 (1980): 51–66.

Williams, Davey. "Towards a Philosophy of Improvisation." *Improvisor* 4 (1984): 32–34.

THE ESSENTIAL

CONTEXT:

JAZZ AND

POLITICS

Double V, Double-Time:
Bebop's Politics of Style

ERIC LOTT

The song and the people is the same.—Amiri Baraka

Fifty years on, the story of how the crash crew made a revolution at Minton's Playhouse is so worn that we forget how disruptive bebop actually was. As Amiri Baraka remarked, the story sounds comfortably like that of the Lost Generation of Americans in Paris, all formal experimentation and narcotic junketeering (*Blues People* 198). But jazz modernism was rooted Stateside, in the roiling New York of the 1940s; indeed, it is impossible to absorb the bop attack without its social reference, as it is difficult to understand New York at that time without consulting the music. Bebop has been claimed by other, mostly unhistorical narratives rather than articulated to its own social history. White-Negro revisionists Jack Kerouac and Norman Mailer to the contrary, bebop was no screaming surge of existential abandon, its makers far from lost. And while bebop said there was a riot going on, it was hardly protest music. Nor was it simply a series of formal innovations, though, as Albert Murray wrote, the musicians' chief desire was to make the music swing harder (166). Bebop was about making disciplined imagination alive and answerable to the social change of its time. "Ko-Ko," Charlie Parker's first recorded masterpiece, suggested that jazz was a struggle which pitted mind against the perversity of circumstance, and that in this struggle blinding virtuosity was the best weapon.

Since the self-conscious advances of bebop so obviously announce themselves, many writers ignore how much those advances belong to a moment, the early forties, in which unpaid historical bills were falling due. Early in 1941, nearly ten thousand black Ford workers threw their weight behind the United Auto Workers in a strike that forced Ford to unionize; wages for blacks in some industries seemed to be on the rise. Later, in 1943, defense plants were finally desegregated under pressure from labor and civil-rights leader A. Phillip Randolph and his March on Washington movement. Black and white together routinely crowded the Track (Harlem's Savoy Ballroom) on those nights when nervous police had not temporarily closed it down. The ranks of the NAACP grew, and in 1942 the Congress of Racial Equality (CORE) was founded. In a still-segregated U.S. Army, there were eight times as many black commissioned officers as there had been in World War I, and though many in Harlem wanted little or nothing to do with what they considered someone else's war, many of those who fought did so in the name of the "Double V"—victory abroad and victory at home. Partly a result of this atmosphere, riots woke up LA, Detroit, New York, and other cities, with politicians like New York's Mayor Fiorello La Guardia denouncing such "juvenile delinquency." Push was coming to shove, and folk were willing.[1]

Amid all this turmoil, a group of young migrants from the South and Midwest was beginning to refurbish the language of riff and accent at Minton's Playhouse and at Clark Monroe's Uptown House in Harlem. The psychological shift they glossed owed largely to another round of black northward movement, a rising threshold of expectation on the part of a generation whose demands refused to be tamed. Such shifts are difficult to pinpoint, but this one came into desperate focus. On 1 August 1943, Harlem exploded—word was that a white cop had shot and killed a black soldier in a scuffle involving a black woman. This was mostly true (the soldier lived), but in the ensuing uprising Harlem's colonialist face got lifted: the youth-wants-to-know flank of the Double V went to work. The inequity of a black military man gunned down by the white Uncle he had protected overseas hit hard, and Harlem hit back, looting businesses and trashing cars to the tune of several millions. James Baldwin later said that Harlem had needed something to smash (93).[2]

The connection between such deeply intended if wasteful militancy and the new youth styles growing up around a radical new music was lost on no one at the time. This was, people said, another "zoot-suit riot," referring to the Los Angeles disturbances. The establishment press in several cities had whipped up a certain hysteria about zooted "gangsters" and "muggers"; white servicemen and some civilians began responding with mob attacks on anyone approaching the color of sharkskin. Despite official denials, these were racial attacks *tout court*. The Harlem riot was an aggressive and hugely collective response to this climate. A zoot-suited participant later declared the zootish disposition to be at odds with the desire to fight a white America's war when conditions at home were the problem: "By the time you read this I will be fighting for Uncle Sam, the bitches, and I do not like it worth a damn. I'm not a spy or a saboteur, but I don't like goin' over there fightin' for the white man—so be it." Psychologist Kenneth Clark termed the new militancy "The Zoot Effect in Personality," but his early attempt to read a subculture proved only that liberal psychologists were as defensive as the new style was dangerous.[3] To stiff-arm the alleged provocateurs—zoots were also in open defiance of the War Production Board's rationing of clothing, a visible sign of antipatriotism—the Los Angeles city council even debated declaring zoot suits illegal (Breitman).[4]

But that did not stop such styles of radical will from flourishing. Zoot-suiters grew in the mid-1940s into hipsters. Encouraged by the ostentatious usages of some bebop originators, black and white working-class bohemia made attitude and appetite signify opposition to routine inequity, and routine generally. Deep-frozen on heroin, they adopted the effrontery displayed by some musicians on the bandstand. And their jargon, itself a kind of improvisation, bucked the regulations of accepted articulateness. These were self-styled ghetto intellectuals, stifled in the kind of ambition that only the musicans were able to fulfill.[5] *Time* magazine, like most, saw it from the other side: bebop people, it said in 1948, "like to wear berets, goatees and green-tinted horn-rimmed glasses, and talk about their 'interesting new sounds,'" while their "rapid-fire, scattershot talk has about the same pace—and content—as their music" ("How Deaf"). LA station KMPC banned the music in 1946; and it is no wonder that when relative old-timer Louis Armstrong went to Paris in 1948, he was given police protection for fear of bebop devotees and their volatile habits.

All of this does merit the spin of subculture theory: zoot, lip, junk, and double-time became the stylistic answer to social contradictions (having mainly to do with generational difference and migration) experienced by the makers and followers of bop.[6] Further, we need to restore the political edge to a music that has been so absorbed into the contemporary jazz language that it seems as safe as much of the current scene—the spate of jazz reissues, the deluge of "standards" records, Bud Powell on CD—certainly an unfortunate historical irony. For in the mid-forties, Parker, Dizzy Gillespie, Powell, Thelonious Monk, and the rest were tearing it up with such speed and irreverence—sometimes so acrobatic as to feel unfinished, often world-historical—that prewar life seemed like a long, long time ago. In hindsight, there may appear to be other more radical breaks with jazz's past, but to an America fed on Bing Crosby and "Marezy Doats," bebop was the war come home. Listen to the fury as Parker roars into "Bird Gets the Worm," or to the way he and Fats Navarro suddenly transpose the head of "Move" to minor on *One Night in Birdland,* or to Monk's 1947 derangement of "April in Paris," and it is clear why many white music writers trying to preserve a sense of professional balance resorted to such denunciatory plum tones as "bad taste and ill-advised fanaticism . . . the sort of stuff that has thrown innumerable impressionable young musicians out of stride" (review of "Billie's Bounce" 15). Brilliantly outside, bebop was intimately if indirectly related to the militancy of its moment. Militancy and music were undergirded by the same social facts; the music attempted to resolve at the level of style what the militancy fought out in the streets. If bebop did not offer a call to arms, as one writer has said in another context, it at least acknowledged that the call had been made.[7] How it translated that acknowledgment into style is the subject of this essay.

New York in this period had an incalculable effect on jazz modernism's big push. Harlem was a magic place, a refuge that lent young musicians, triply alien—migrant, Negro, occupationally suspect—the courage to conquer. Since among the major innovators only Bud Powell, Max Roach, and Thelonious Monk grew up in New York, Harlem offered a rediscovered community of things they had left behind: feasts, talk, home (Ellison, "The Golden Age" 200–201).[8] The phrase of the moment may have been "Harlem is nowhere," but for the musicians it was the logical place in which to coherently combine the various regional styles they had brought with them. Here the Kansas City 4/4 came together with popular song forms and Art Tatum's harmonic ideas, all of it grounded by the blues (skeptics are directed to "Parker's Mood"). "I think the music of today," said Parker, "is a sort of combination of the midwestern beat and the fast New York tempos," another way of saying that it incorporated formally the migratory impulse (Feather 15).

Ralph Ellison remembers turn-of-the-forties New York as a place that itself required improvisation, honing the wits of newcomers to quickness. Beyond "Harlem's brier patch" there seemed to be "no agreed-upon rules of conduct," no sense of the limits the South imposed in the "signs and symbols that marked the dividing lines of racial segregation" (Ellison, *Going to the Territory* 148–49, 152). So homegirl and wonderboy had to make it up as they went along, acquainting themselves intimately with uncertainty the way they did when it came time to stand up and blow their four-bars. Out of encounters in the streets of New York came local versions of the wisdom and agility required of all fleet-footed inventors. "Coolness helped to keep our values warm," says Ellison, "and racial hostility stoked our fires of inspiration" (167). Not even the North could abide the kinds of interracial freedom the musicians cultivated; a palpable dissidence kicks the best of the music.

The shock of relocation was "handled" by the common language that musicians developed—styles of dress, music, drugs, and speech homologous with the structures of their experience. The requisite cool of the northern city dweller was unattainable unless negotiated through style. Malcolm X reports that his transition from Michigan "country" to hip Bostonian was achieved primarily through a new zoot (39–69);[9] South Carolinian Dizzy Gillespie's windowpanes, cigarette holder, goatee, and beret signified on fancy city dress. The hip code sometimes appeared compensatory rather than avant, insecure rather than assured, but it expressed real defiance. As when Gillespie put together a big band in 1945, which later found it had been booked to tour the Jim Crow South. By the time the band got below the Mason-Dixon line, so many players had quit that it had virtually a new lineup (Feather 34). Through secrecy, exaggeration, and wit, self-images were formed, alliances made, strategies of differentiation concocted. Bop style, a kind of "fifth column fashion," was where social responsiveness became individual expression, where the pleasures of shared identity met an intolerance for racist jive (Cosgrove 85–86).

At its hippest (and meanest), such a common language became a closed hermeneutic that had the undeniable effect of alienating the riff-raff and expressing a sense of felt isolation, all the while affirming a collective purpose—even at the expense of other musicians. In preparation for Minton's, Gillespie would work out a complicated sequence of chords for the relatively simple "I Got Rhythm," then call out the tune to cut the uninitiated on the bandstand. The unhip, says bassist Milt Hinton, were "left right at the post . . . eventually they would put their horns away" (Giddins 66). On different occasions, though they knew well to the contrary, the boppers declared they *were not* in the tradition; no "respectable" classicism here. Older musicians were plausibly put off. Johnny Hodges told trumpeter Howard McGhee, "[Bird] don't play nothing," and only later got wise (Giddins 67). Drummer Davey Tough recalled his first encounter with bop: "These cats snatched up their horns and blew crazy stuff. One would stop all of a sudden and another would start for no reason at all. We never could tell when a solo was supposed to begin or end" (Stearns 224–25). Louis Armstrong never really made peace with bebop, "that modern malice" (Stearns 219); more than once Gillespie unfairly dismissed Papa Dip for tomming. Attitudes like these allowed musical youth to make their condition as outsiders meaningful, and whether they intended it to be or not, the stance was scarifying to musicians and audiences alike.

The various elements of bebop style were thus part of a new generational responsiveness to the northern city, particularly 1940s New York, a place distinguished less by its capacity to shock than by its ability to make little seem shocking.[10] What evolved in turn was an aesthetic of speed and displacement—ostentatious virtuosity dedicated to reorienting perception even as it rocked the house. Every instrument became immediately more mobile, everything *moved*. Drummers Kenny Clarke and Max Roach no longer thumped the bass drum four beats per bar, as some other drummers had done. Instead, they extended the work of such innovative swing drummers as Jo Jones and Sid Catlett, substituting for a monotonous bass beat the shimmering pulse of ride and hi-hat cymbals. Bassists like Oscar Pettiford no longer simply walked time, they provided melodic counterpoint to the soloists. Bud Powell, Duke Jordan, and other pianists discarded the full-bodied approximation of an orchestra for a series of jagged chords and horn-like, linear solos (Giddins 68; Stearns 229–36). And the cold, vibratoless edge of Parker's tone, his and Gillespie's high intervallic leaps, their penchant for shifting to double-time at a moment's notice, the breathtaking audaciousness with which they cut up their phrases, dissolved the specious equation of artistic intelligence with respectable European culture. These elements originally made up what Amiri Baraka called the "willfully harsh, *anti-assimilationist* sound of bebop," which at once reclaimed jazz from its brief cooptation by white "swing" bandleaders like the aptly named Paul Whiteman and made any future dilution that much harder (181).

In this way, bebop redefined the tradition, indeed made it possible to keep playing jazz in the face of given musical and social facts without losing self-respect. The sheer velocity of much of the music, ignited by Roach's bombs, shifted the center of gravity from grounded bass to mercurial rhythms echoed from drums to horns; base and superstructure were to a certain extent collapsed. Add the pursuit of the non sequitur to such speeds and such mobility, as in the bridge of Bird's solo on "Klaunstance" (on *The Genius of Charlie Parker*) where disconnected phrases dive at each other until the whole is "resolved" into an arpeggiated drop, and the result is some blues that gleefully critique tradition. So too does Monk's self-portrait/self-parody "Thelonious" (on *Genius of Modern Music*, Vol. 1), its one-note theme riding a lilting harmonic cycle, recalling certain vocal arrangements of Ellington's "It Don't Mean a Thing" while presaging Randy Weston's "Hi-Fly." It riffs self-consciously on tradition—Monk suddenly erupting into stride piano—and depends for its effect on a cool surface continually broken up by jarring piano, the shock of the new. Gillespie once relevantly joked that if it doesn't hurt your ears, it isn't dissonance. For me, this new attitude is captured best on a live recording of Harold Arlen's "This Time the Dream's On Me" (on *One Night in Birdland*): Bird and drummer Art Blakey trading fours, Blakey plays two triplet figures, one on bass and one on snare, one a *half-beat behind* the other. The result is an asymmetrical raucousness that seems to arrest the time as surely as it states its commitment to a caustic groove. Instances of this kind of roughhousing are numberless.

The widespread practice of appropriating the chord changes of popular tunes was another means by which a similar result could be achieved—as in Tadd Dameron's "Hot House," a reworking of Cole Porter's "What Is This Thing Called Love" that lent itself even to Eric Dolphy's out-to-lunch sermonizing fifteen years later. Essentially an old blues impulse that was further refined in the 1930s, writing new melodies for Broadway tunes was nevertheless an intervention into the dominant popular culture of the period—in tunes such as "Hot House" a kind of ritual dismemberment. (Those like David Toop who see similar strategies in rap music correctly grasp the link between bebop and hip hop [18].)[11] Whatever its effect, this was probably not one of the distancing techniques so often ascribed to bebop, but rather a search for harmonic variety and simultaneously a pointed participation in the popular. Charlie Parker, who later flirted with what Martin Williams calls the "spurious challenge" of string formats (*Jazz Tradition* 152), once told an admirer that to understand his music one should listen to the Clovers (Giddins 104); and the course of postwar black music is arguably constituted by the twin refurbishments of bebop and R&B colliding and diverging in mutually enriching ways.[12] Part of bop's force inhered in this involvement in and struggle over the popular.

Bebop, in other words, was one of the great modernisms. Its relationship to earlier styles was one of calculated hostility. It was a soloist's music, despite the democratic ethos of jazz (in which soloists assume a momentary universality in a highly mutual context), and particularly of bop (its dependence on unison riffs, the extreme sympathy required between players to negotiate the rhythms). Its incorporation of elements of the popular (Bird was fond of quoting the "Woody Woodpecker" theme) reminds one of Joyce or Mahler. Its commitment to exploratory rigor amounted to a harshness that many took for ugliness. And its mocking defiance made a virtue of isolation. Moreover, the social position of this modernism—distanced from both the black middle class and the white consensus—gave aesthetic self-assertion political force and value.

Gary Giddins says in his biography of Bird that the chief motive for all this was not to offend but to pioneer, and that by the self-assertion of genius. I would suggest that bebop's context made the two pretty much inseparable; sociopolitical insistence was so available as both source and effect that even a self-consciously arty music could call on it effortlessly. This, together with the recording ban from August 1942 through most of 1943 that made bebop's inception seem sudden, must explain the intensity of the reaction with which the music was first greeted. The small-group format, for example, was given such prominence in part because the music demanded turns-on-a-dime and extended solo space; audiences experienced this as assault. Style wars are not known for taking any prisoners, and critics of the new music were as ruthless as the musicians. Monk's "Thelonious," said *Down Beat*, sounded like the pianist had his mind on "the stock returns or the 7th at Pimlico—anything but his piano" (review of "Thelonious" 19). The further this modernism extended the resources of African American expressive culture, the greater lengths cultural critics would go to miss the point, though (or because, as Baraka ominously suggests) they may have begun to recognize jazz's status as art.

Bebop could not in fact be heard without the alarm registering its birth; if we are to understand its radical implications, we must attend to this alarm. "It was as if," says Martin Williams, "this bop style had swept away almost everything that had gone before it, no matter how well or how badly the writers knew and understood what *had* gone before it ("Bebop and After" 291). To many, the music read as "atonal, futuristic material, produced by the progressive modernists," to quote one of the baffled—so much a departure, as this comment indicates, that there was hardly an available language to describe it (Pease 12). It certainly did not fit into any of the "discursive categories" *Down Beat* used for its record reviews—Hot Jazz (of an earlier kind), Swing, Dance, Vocal, and Novelty—and there is an interesting bewilderment, early on, about where bebop should go. The music generally precipitated an evaluative crisis among the cognoscenti, who responded as though to a breach in the social order. (A notable exception was Leonard Feather's mid-forties work in *Esquire* and *Metronome*.) By mid-1947, polemics raged in *Down Beat* over which was the "real jazz," bebop or Dixieland (a recent reactionary reinvention), and well-known critics battered each others' sectarianism (Leonard Feather vs. Rudi Blesh, Charles Delaunay vs. Hugues Panassié, *Metronome* vs. early *Record Changer*).

Bebop's fearsomeness to many of its contemporaries is suggested not only by the vehemence of the debate, the straining quality of the polemics, but by the language of politics, so often called on to describe, dismiss, or even mock the music and its rivals. Lionel Hampton, not a musician we tend today to associate with political radicalism, said of his music in 1946: "Whenever I see any injustice or any unfair action against my own race or any other minority groups *Hey Ba Ba Rebop* stimulates the desire to destroy such prejudice and discrimination." The writer interviewing Hampton on this occasion (noted Chicago sociologist Horace Cayton, interestingly enough) responded with nervous irony to "Hampton's class struggle" and distanced himself from jazz's claim to "social significance" with a derisive "Marxian" interpretation of "Caldonia" (Cayton 8). Dave Tough, an older bebop convert, in another instance called Dixieland a "Straight-Republican-Ticket kind of music" in some public mudslinging with old-timer Eddie Condon (Gottlieb 4). As a consequence of this kind of talk, much of the forties' music press, per Frank Kofsky, figured as law and order trying to stem the furious tide.[13]

Yet in the postwar cultural formation, beboppers were a black intelligentsia—the other New York intellectuals—only dimly perceived by a myopic left. *Partisan Review*'s commitment to modernism did not extend to black music; its "Music Chronicle" columns were invariably about opera, at best Hindemith. (There was a splenetic dismissal of bop by poet Weldon Kees in its brief "Variety" section, indicative of the music's offensiveness to outsiders as well as their intellectual blindness.[14] Even Harlem Communist party intellectuals had an unsteady enthusiasm for contemporary music still in touch with black cultural roots. Given the huge undertow of protest aesthetic in which the best-intentioned of them had to wade, bebop's transgressive genius was washed aside. Just as the CP had dismissed the "Double V" campaign because Hitler not Jim Crow was the "real enemy," and called with Mayor La Guardia for law and order after the Harlem uprising, so they distanced themselves from the rowdiness of bebop, music far beyond the reaches of the CP aesthetic (James, Breitman et al. 158, 283).[15] While the music generated a following, Beat writers like Kerouac and Ginsberg were the closest bebop came to having visible oppositional champions, a partisanship distorted by the projections of renegade romance.[16]

As it turned out, this was perhaps the only art, with the possible exception of certain painting, that proved fully equal to the moment. In their way, the bebop innovators mapped the time as intelligently as writers like C. L. R. James and George Breitman did in their political commentary.[17] James and Breitman knew the Harlem explosion was no mere hooliganism, and they defended something so seemingly irrelevant as the zoot suit when wearing one threatened to become a misdemeanor in LA. They realized style could be dangerous; and in forcing the connection between Double V and double-time, the people who made music like "Scrapple from the Apple" knew that too. This is, in the end, the importance of the cult of heroin and the eighth note, of the cocked beret and the hip code: a politics of style beyond protest, focusing the struggles of its moment in a live and irreverent art.

Notes

Many thanks to Susan Fraiman, RJ Smith, and Peter Watrous for their suggestions on this essay.

1   For discussions of this political moment, see Anderson 290–346; Jones 232–56; Sitkoff; Cruse; Naison 193–320; Glaberman; James, Breitman, et al.; Baraka 175–207; Kofsky 56, 271; and Cosgrove.

2   Baldwin's powerful account tends unfortunately to psychologize militant energies into an unchanging ghetto mentality.

3   The participant's quote and Clark's analysis are from an article in the *Journal of Abnormal Psychology*, a publication that indicates its perspective.

4   See also Cosgrove 85–88.

5   See Newton 213–22 and Hebdige 46–49.

6   The Marxist subculture theory of the Birmingham Centre for Contemporary Cultural Studies is set forth in Hall and Jefferson and in Hebdige; see also Treichler, Nelson, and Grossberg. I rely on it primarily to think about bebop's "magical" formal solutions to some of the social contradictions outlined here. Cosgrove's "The Zoot-Suit and Style Warfare" goes some important distance toward a reading of the subcultural dress of this period. As far as I know, little writing since Baraka's *Blues People* has taken the music's social and political meanings seriously. Three excellent works that have shaped my thinking are DeMott, "The Future Is Unwritten: Working-Class Youth Cultures in England and America"; Gilroy, *There Ain't No Black in the Union Jack*; and Carby, "It Jus Be's Dat Way Sometime."

7   I am indebted here to Charles O'Brien's argument in regard to black pop in the sixties.

8   Apart from its engrossing meditation on the meaning of Minton's, Ellison's essay can be read as a jazz counterstatement (conscious, I believe) to T. S. Eliot's idea of tradition. "In [bebop] the steady flow of memory, desire and defined experience summed up by the traditional jazz beat and blues mood seemed swept like a great river from its old, deep bed. We know better now, and recognize the old moods in the new sounds, but what we know is that which was then becoming, . . . the best of it absorbed like drops of fully distilled technique, mood and emotions into the

great stream of jazz" (203). Jazz has rarely been treated with this degree of moral seriousness.

9   This was suggested to me by Chibnall 60–61; see also the fine essay by Robin Kelley, "The Riddle of the Zoot." The pressures on those newcomers are typified in Miles Davis's remark that on his arrival from East St. Louis he believed everyone in New York knew more than he did. Davis's response was simply to continue to dress like a fashion plate (Carr 14; Davis 51–115).

10 I am influenced here by Franco Moretti's reading of Walter Benjamin's "On Some Motifs in Baudelaire" in *Signs Taken for Wonders* 116–17. One measure of bebop's close attention to its context is that it spoke largely to northern urban audiences. In the Southwest, Charlie Parker recalled, the music registered as a strange and meaningless noise; "in the middle west the colored audiences liked it but the whites didn't"; and "in New York *everyone* liked it" (Feather 31).

11 "Ornithology," the "national anthem of bop," was of course an appropriation of "How High the Moon." The classic recording of "Ornithology" is Charlie Parker's on *The Complete Dial Sessions*.

12 R&B gained supremacy with the expansion of capital in the sixties, contributing to the exile of many jazz musicians to Europe; jazz lamely but gamely fought back with "fusion" in the seventies, finally stabilizing itself in the currently profitable classicist mode, in whose purer forms R&B has itself been exiled. There are signs, in performers as various as Ornette Coleman, Lester Bowie, Arthur Blythe, Henry Threadgill, and younger players such as Joshua Redman, Geri Allen, and Greg Osby, that the repressed is, healthily this time, returning.

13 For the music press as social control in the sixties, see Kofsky 79–97. Leonard Feather's publisher changed the "cursed" name of *Inside Be-bop* for its second edition to *Inside Jazz*, the name it still carries. See Feather's new introduction to the book.

14 "I can only report, very possibly because of some deeply-buried strain of black reaction in me, that I have found this music uniformly thin, at once dilapidated and overblown, and exhibiting a poverty of thematic development and a richness of affectation not only, apparently, intentional, but enormously self-satisfied. . . . There has been nothing like this in the way of an overconsciousness of stylistic idiosyncrasy, I should say, since the Gothic Revival" (Kees 621–22). The second sentence is probably true and the first absolutely symptomatic.

15 Citing the *Militant*, 4 Apr. 1942 and 7 Aug. 1943. The best response to the CP aesthetic was Charlie Parker's. In 1952 (after he became relatively well-known) Bird was hired to play a CP benefit for embattled activist attorney and city council member Benjamin Davis. During a break, as guest Paul Robeson sang a work song called "Water Boy," Bird trotted scandalously toward the stage with a glass of water (Giddins 113–14).

16 Kerouac in 1940 did praise Lester Young in a Columbia University school paper, for which he himself deserves praise, considering the context. (What might Prez's "hum and buzz of implication" have seemed on Morningside Heights?) Later, however, the romance of the word combined with the distance between cultures resulted in a kind of updated Van-Vechtenism. See Gilford and Lee 23. Thanks to Benj DeMott for his suggestions on the Beats.

17 See particularly James, "The Revolutionary Answer to the Negro Problem in the U.S.A."

Works Cited

Anderson, Jervis. *This Was Harlem: A Cultural Portrait, 1900–1950.* New York: Farrar, Straus, and Giroux, 1982.

Baldwin, James. *Notes of a Native Son.* 1955. New York: Dial, 1963.

Baraka, Amiri [LeRoi Jones]. *Blues People: Negro Music in White America.* New York: Morrow, 1963.

Breitman, George. " 'Zoot Suit Riots' in Los Angeles." *Militant* 19 June 1943.

Carby, Hazel V. "It Jus Be's Dat Way Sometime: The Sexual Politics of Women's Blues." *Radical America* 20.4 (1986): 9–22.

Carr, Ian. *Miles Davis: A Biography.* New York: Morrow, 1984.

Cayton, Horace R. "Social Significance in Jazz Louses Good Stuff Up." *Down Beat* 16 Dec. 1946: 8.

Chibnall, Steve. "Whistle and Zoot: The Changing Meaning of a Suit of Clothes." *History Workshop Journal* 20 (Autumn 1985): 56–81.

Clark, Kenneth B., and James Barker. "The Zoot Effect in Personality: A Race Riot Participant." *Journal of Abnormal Psychology* 40.2 (1945): 143–48.

Cosgrove, Stuart. "The Zoot-Suit and Style Warfare." *History Workshop Journal* 18 (Autumn 1984): 77–91.

Cruse, Harold. *The Crisis of the Negro Intellectual.* New York: Morrow, 1967.

Davis, Miles, with Quincy Troupe. *Miles: The Autobiography.* New York: Simon, 1989.

DeMott, Benj. "The Future Is Unwritten: Working-Class Youth Cultures in England and America." *Critical Texts* 5.1 (1988): 42–56.

Ellison, Ralph. *Going to the Territory.* New York: Random, 1986.

———. "The Golden Age, Times Past." 1964. *Shadow and Act.* New York: Random, 1972. 198–210.

Feather, Leonard. *Inside Jazz.* (Originally *Inside Be-bop,* 1949.) New York: Da Capo, 1977.

Giddins, Gary. *Celebrating Bird: The Triumph of Charlie Parker.* New York: Morrow, 1987.

Gilford, Barry, and Lawrence Lee. *Jack's Book: An Oral Biography of Jack Kerouac.* New York: St. Martin's, 1978.

Gilroy, Paul. *There Ain't No Black in the Union Jack: The Cultural Politics of Race and Nation.* London: Hutchinson, 1987.

Glaberman, Martin. *Wartime Strikes.* Detroit: Bewicked, 1980.

Gottlieb, Bill. "Dixieland Nowhere Says Dave Tough." *Down Beat* 23 Sept. 1946: 4.

Hall, Stuart, and Tony Jefferson, eds. *Resistance Through Rituals: Youth Subcultures in Postwar Britain.* London: Hutchinson, 1976.

Hebdige, Dick. *Subculture: The Meaning of Style.* New York: Methuen, 1979.

"How Deaf Can You Get?" *Time* 17 May 1948: 74.

James, C. L. R., George Breitman, et al. *Fighting Racism in World War II.* New York: Monad, 1980.

James, C. L. R. "The Revolutionary Answer to the Negro Problem in the U.S.A." 1948. *The Future in the Present: Selected Writings.* London: Allison and Busby, 1977. 119–27.

Jones, Jacqueline. *Labor of Love, Labor of Sorrow: Black Women, Work and the Family, From Slavery to the Present.* New York: Basic, 1985.

Kees, Weldon. "Muskrat Ramble: Popular and Unpopular Music." *Partisan Review* 15.5 (1948): 621–22.

Kelley, Robin D. G. "The Riddle of the Zoot: Malcolm Little and Black Cultural Politics During WW II." *Malcolm X: In Our Own Image.* Ed. Joe Wood. New York: St. Martin's, 1992. 155–82.

Kofsky, Frank. *Black Nationalism and the Revolution in Music.* New York: Pathfinder, 1970.

Malcolm X, with Alex Haley. *The Autobiography of Malcolm X.* New York: Grove, 1966.

Moretti, Franco. *Signs Taken for Wonders: Essays in the Sociology of Literary Forms.* Trans. Susan Fischer, David Forgacs, and David Miller. London: Verso, 1983.

Murray, Albert. *Stomping the Blues.* New York: McGraw-Hill, 1976.

Naison, Mark. *Communists in Harlem During the Depression.* New York: Grove, 1983.

Newton, Francis [Eric Hobsbawm]. *The Jazz Scene.* London: MacGibbon and Kee, 1959.

O'Brien, Charles. "At Ease in Azania." *Critical Texts* 5.1 (1988): 39–41.

Pease, Sharon. "Dodo's Modern Style Is Given Pease Analysis." *Down Beat* 16 Dec. 1946: 12.

Review of Charlie Parker's "Billie's Bounce" and "Now's the Time." *Down Beat* 22 Apr. 1946: 15.

Review of Thelonious Monk's "Thelonious." *Down Beat* 25 Feb. 1948: 19.

Sitkoff, Harvard. "Racial Militancy and Interracial Violence in the Second World War." *Journal of American History* 58 (1971): 661–81.

Stearns, Marshall W. *The Story of Jazz.* New York: Oxford UP, 1956.

Toop, David. *The Rap Attack: African Jive to New York Hip-Hop.* Boston: South End, 1984.

Treichler, Paula, Cary Nelson, and Lawrence Grossberg, eds. *Cultural Studies.* New York: Routledge, 1992.

Williams, Martin. "Bebop and After: A Report." *Jazz: New Perspectives on the History of Jazz.* Ed. Nat Hentoff and Albert J. McCarthy. New York: Holt, Rinehart and Winston, 1959. 287–301.

———. *The Jazz Tradition.* New and rev. ed. New York: Oxford UP, 1983.

Discography

Monk, Thelonious. "April in Paris," "Thelonious." *Thelonious Monk: Genius of Modern Music,* vol. 1. Blue Note CDP 7 81510–2 (CD).

Parker, Charlie. "Bird Gets the Worm," "Parker's Mood." *Charlie Parker Memorial.* Savoy SV-0101 (CD).

———. "Klaunstance," "Ko-Ko." *Genius of Charlie Parker.* Savoy SV-0104 (CD).

———. "Move," "This Time the Dream's On Me." *One Night in Birdland.* Columbia JG 34808 (LP).

———. "Ornithology," "Scrapple from the Apple." *The Complete Dial Sessions.* Stash 567-70 (CD).

Ascension: Music and the Black Arts Movement

LORENZO THOMAS

a love supreme.
                    for each
        other
    if we just
lisssssssSSSTEN
—*Sonia Sanchez*

I

If the theme of the Harlem Renaissance was racial vindication, then the Black Arts Movement can be seen as a program of reclamation. The word became popular when it appeared on picket signs of Harlem protesters who renamed a construction site on 125th Street "Reclamation Site #1." The artists and writers of the period also saw their work as a labor of reclaiming the lost souls of black folk. "The black artist," wrote Larry Neal in his 1968 essay "The Black Arts Movement," knows that "his primary duty is to speak to the spiritual and cultural needs of black people. Therefore, the main thrust of this new breed of contemporary writers is to confront the contradictions arising out of the black man's experience in the racist West" (62).

The militant attitude of writers such as Neal was reflected—and perhaps instigated—by jazz musicians whose playing matched the intensity of an entire generation of African American intellectuals who were too young to know much about Jim Crow but old enough to see that integration was, at best, a barely hatched chicken if not a bird in the bush. One of the most interesting projects of this group of young writers was an attempt to control authorship of jazz criticism and, thereby, reclaim the music itself as a central cultural expression of the black community. The story of this effort provides an instructive view of a dynamic within that community that can be traced back to the 1820s and still exerts an important influence today.

Houston A. Baker makes a distinction between that aspect of the international artistic modernist movement of the early twentieth century that was an antagonistic reaction to "replicating outmoded forms" and genteel, class-based, nineteenth-century ideals, and what he sees as the dynamic of the New Negro Movement. For Baker, the Harlem Renaissance represents an embrace of what he calls the "necessary task of employing . . . extant forms in ways that move clearly *up*, masterfully and re-soundingly away from slavery" (101). Though Baker is eloquent, one might just as usefully suggest that his argument depends on accepting the "color line" to the extent that African American culture *must* be seen as essentially different from the coexistent Anglo culture. Reading Alain Locke's *The New Negro* (1925) does not necessarily offer support for this idea. Indeed, when speaking of music and the possibility that African American composers might, as did their eighteenth-century European counterparts, accomplish the "elevation" of folk forms into "high Art," Locke presents ideas that seriously challenge Baker's thesis.

Classical modernism can be seen not only as "an acknowledgment of radical uncertainty" (Baker, *Modernism* 3), but also as an attempt to redirect and revivify Western civilization through a radical reassessment of its traditions. Such a project is explicitly announced in Ezra Pound's writings in 1913 ranging from "A Few Don'ts for Imagistes" to *Patria Mia.* Insofar as Locke and W. E. B. Du Bois—and even the Garveyite cultural nationalists—perceived that African Americans possessed the desire to acquire the benefits of Western civilization, they, too, could be said to have been engaged in a similarly corrective critique. Certainly, artists such as James Weldon Johnson in *God's Trombones* (1927) and Jean Toomer in *Cane* (1923) shared the *stylistic* agenda of other modernist writers. Baker, however, focuses on the Harlem Renaissance as a project of racial self-definition rather than on its equally important goal of using the arts to critique society and ameliorate social antagonism toward black Americans.

Amiri Baraka was certainly heir to modernist poetics and just as aware that the other modernism had failed black people, probably because it was never intended to include them. As poet, playwright, and music critic, Baraka (formerly LeRoi Jones) was a central figure of the times, both for his sometimes notorious celebrity in the "square" press and his genuine popularity among young black readers. He shared with them a somewhat alienated response to both mainstream white and African American mores. "The black poetry circuit Baraka sparked in the 60s," notes Greg Tate, "practically made John Coltrane a national hero in the black community. And if Baraka has been dubbed the Father of the Black Arts Movement it's because, as poet Mae Jackson recently related, he gave young black artists a place to go outside of white bohemia and black academia, a place more open to communion with black working-class culture" (171). It is worth noting that a good many of the black college students who found Baraka's message appealing came from working-class backgrounds. Jazz—an extraordinary edifice of intellectualism balanced on the working-class eloquence of the blues—was seen by this group as the perfect vehicle for expressing and exploring their social reality.

The musicians were also actively involved in the promotion of the ideas so ably expounded by Baraka. In 1965, writes Kalamu ya Salaam, John Coltrane

> consistently loaned both his name and his talents to the blossoming, racially oriented Black Arts Movement of that era.
>
> Furthermore, Coltrane was using his clout at Impulse to champion the recording of artists such as Archie Shepp, Marion Brown and others. Seemingly single-handedly John Coltrane was assaulting the barricades of the music world, leading a battalion of true believers into an apocalyptic and impassioned fray against the forces of traditional musical taste and order. (24)

Along with the Nigerian drummer Babatunde Olatunji, Coltrane was also exploring the possibilities of launching a cooperative concert booking agency and record label (25). As the Black Arts Movement writers spoke of controlling the ideological perception of jazz, so the musicians attempted to exert more practical control over their own careers.

The period during which the Black Arts Movement flourished was full of spectacular public controversies. Beginning with a melee at the United Nations in 1961 when Harlem militants demonstrated to show concern about the assassination of Patrice Lumumba during the transition of the Belgian Congo to the independent nation of Zaire, the streets and television screens of the nation were filled with the clamor of a renewed African American race consciousness. There were protest marches at the 125th Street site of what is now the Adam Clayton Powell State Office Building, a project that resulted in the demolition of Lewis Michaux's famous Black Nationalist bookstore. Michaux's store, established in the

1930s, was revered as a historical landmark, and Harlem humorists acidly noted that the initials of the State Office Building accurately reflected the local taxpayers' opinion of the governor and other members of what was colloquially referred to as the "white power structure." The decade of the 1960s was also marked by the shocking assassinations of John F. Kennedy, Malcolm X, Martin Luther King, and Robert Kennedy; a Selective Service draft system that sent poor black men to fight in Vietnam in disproportionately large numbers; often violent antiwar protests on university campuses; inner-city riots sparked by allegations of police brutality; and the repression of the Black Panther party and other radical political groups by government infiltration and police gunfire.

All of this social turmoil was, naturally, reflected and analyzed in the artistic movements of the time, one of the most vibrant and energetic of which was the Black Arts Movement. The most prominent and accessible artists in the black community were poets who expressed their reactions to such events in increasingly strident tones, which were accompanied by a music (in both jazz and Rhythm & Blues styles) that complemented the intensity of their moods. Even visual artists such as New York's Joe Overstreet and the Africobra group in Chicago produced images that consciously dismantled and defused the racial stereotypes imbricated in both mainstream and African American cultural tradition while promoting an innovative interpretation of African aesthetic values and racial self-respect.

Home to millions of European immigrants since the 1880s, New York's Lower East Side was still a low-rent district in 1960, and it attracted many young artists and intellectuals who could not afford to live in nearby Greenwich Village. They did, however, maintain the artistic atmosphere long associated with the Village. Baraka's work and ideas were directly influenced by other writers, painters, and especially the musicians that he associated with. Howard University classmate Marion Brown, Archie Shepp, Sun Ra, Sunny Murray, and others were close friends or artistic collaborators. It may be that their influence helped to shape Baraka's militant stance of the mid-sixties since it was widely known on the East Side that the black musicians were much more race-conscious and militant than artists in other disciplines. Their attitude went with the territory; and it was not even a new thing. Discussing Louis Armstrong, poet Tom Dent (founder of the Umbra writers workshop) wrote:

> Louis i'm trying to understand what you were
> really like
> in the dark moments away from the stage.

> rumors have it you were not pleasant
> to be around
> the shit-eating grin nowhere to be found

In the bebop era of the 1940s, that old jazzman's grin was not even found on stage. Paul Warren, a white hipster, reported Charlie Parker's 1947 northside Chicago set at the Argyle Show Lounge in these words: "Above the silent crowd in blinding light black musicians masked themselves with insolence, separating themselves from audience by the very music they shared." A similar ambivalence might have been found at Charles Mingus's angry artist-in-residence stint at East 10th Street's Nonagon Gallery. No grins. Miles Davis, who had played with Parker, was well known for playing with his back to the audience and walking offstage after completing his solos. The young black musicians of the 1960s appeared to be just as arrogant and temperamental as the beboppers had been. Some of them preferred not to play for white people at all. Squares *or* hipsters.

Baraka became closely associated with some of these young players and wrote record album liner notes and articles about them in jazz magazines. The musicians themselves were as cleverly articulate in words as they were on the bandstand; some, in fact, were poets and writers themselves. Charles Mingus and Sun Ra, both excellent poets and lyricists, spoke in vast but terse metaphors to those who took the time to listen. Sun Ra clothed his messages in the form of deeply ambiguous philosophical poems such as "The Outer Bridge":

> In the half-between world
> Dwell they, the sound-scientists
> Mathematically precise. . . .
> They speak of many things
> The tone scientists
>
> Architects of planes of discipline.

He would patiently explain that black people were indeed "second-class citizens" in the United States, adding that it was nothing to be ashamed of. "When you first went to school," he would say, "didn't you start out in the first grade? And then you went to the second, right? That's what that's about."

Mingus, for his part, bluntly and beautifully stated the resentments that are shared by all black people who have been on the receiving end of American racism. In 1963 he recorded one of his poems that eloquently expressed such feelings:

This mule ain't from Moscow
This mule ain't from the South
But this mule's had some learning
Mostly mouth to mouth

This mule could be called stubborn and lazy
But in a clever sort of way
This mule could be working, waiting
    and learning and planning

Mingus ended with the words

Your stubbornness is of the living
And cruel anxiety is about to die

As he finished his recitation, the band sang the chorus:

Freedom for your daddy
Freedom for your momma
Freedom for your brothers and sisters
But no freedom for me

Saxophonist Archie Shepp had studied playwriting at Goddard College and published his own poems in literary magazines here and in England. His play *Junebug Graduates Tonight* was produced off-Broadway in 1965. Shepp also composed musical settings for original poems he recited in melodramatic tones at concerts and East Side loft parties. Later, he included them on his recordings. Like Mingus and Sun Ra, Shepp consciously explored the historical styles of earlier jazz in his playing, kept up to date in his reading, and was unequivocally outspoken about his social and political ideas.

After establishing the Black Arts Repertory Theatre/School in Harlem in 1965, Baraka sponsored several concerts there featuring Shepp, Sun Ra's Arkestra, and Albert Ayler. Ayler, recently returned from Europe, had a truly amazing approach to both his instrument and the jazz canon, and his playing exerted a great influence on Baraka.

Albert Ayler and other loft jazz musicians, Baraka wrote in *Black Music* (1967), "have done away with . . . the awe-inspiring popular song [that was the basis for much bebop improvisation]. When Ayler does want memory to furnish him with a fire-source, he uses coonish churchified chuckle tunes" (116). Despite his characteristic signifying irony, Baraka was both accurate and perceptive. Ayler's "Spirits Rejoice," for example, is based on a variant of the anthem "God Save the Queen," which serves as a frame for "free" improvisations bearing little formal relation to the stated theme. The connection of Ayler's approach to church music is apparent on "Angles" where his thrilling vibrato—backed by Call Cobbs, Jr., on harpsichord—recalls George Beverly Shea's "How Great Thou Art" more than it does the blue loneliness of, say, "Harlem Nocturne." Ayler's embellishments of a melody are like a gospel singer's, and his repertoire also included marches that, in their often dissonant ensembles, reflect and comment on the part that New Orleans brass bands played in the origin of jazz itself. At one point Baraka patterned his style of recitation on Ayler's yelping saxophone sound, a style that suited Baraka's allusive poetry and expressing alto voice perfectly.

Saxophonist Marion Brown, however, was probably Baraka's closest link to the young musicians. When Brown came up to New York from Howard University he was better known as a writer than as a musician. He shared a valuable cross-influence with Baraka and was a frequent visitor to the poet's Cooper Square apartment—a running buddy. As a writer and musician, Brown was able to supply a technical explanation of the importance of jazz to African American culture. "In oral societies," Brown wrote in 1973, "the ear interprets what is first perceived visually" (15). A decade earlier he had already perfected the ability to identify by ear the African tribal and African American geographical origins of specific Rhythm & Blues and jazz motifs. He gave a brilliant performance of that skill for Steve Kent and me one afternoon in the black-owned House of Jazz record store on St. Marks Place, down the block from the Five Spot. What Brown suggested in 1964 is that African tribal musics, though distorted by Western instruments and the fickle fashions of the recording industry, can still be recognized in African American music. There is no doubt that some of Brown's ideas influenced the conclusions in Baraka's seminal *Blues People: Negro Music in Black America* (1963), and Brown himself clearly expressed the militant race consciousness implied in his concepts: "Our having made the transition from Africa to America, without the necessary cultural institutions, was a manifestation of a superior adjustment potential and an act of societal improvisation. We brought no books. What we learned of our past was taught orally, and very often in song form" (15). And what was not encoded in the blues was probably expressed in poetic conundrums similar to Sun Ra's explanation of what it means to be a second-class citizen.

"What is seen," Brown wrote, "has little meaning until speech is used to express the emotions that arise from observation." In *Blues People* and other writings from the early 1960s, Baraka carefully weighed the effects of various approaches to the act of opening the mouth. "Speech," Baraka said, "is the effective form of a culture." In "The Myth of a 'Negro

Literature,'" an address delivered to the American Society for African Culture on 14 March 1962, Baraka attempted to identify the authentic speech and culture of African people in America:

> Phillis Wheatley and her pleasant imitations of 18th century English poetry are far, and finally, ludicrous departures from the huge black voices that splintered southern nights with their *hollers, chants, arwhoolies,* and *ballits.* The embarrassing and inverted paternalism of Charles Chesnutt and his "refined Afro-American" heroes are far cries from the richness and profundity of the blues. (106)

Baraka went on to present a discussion fully grounded in Marion Brown's perceptions about jazz. "Africanisms," he said,

> still persist in the music, religion, and popular cultural traditions of American Negroes. However, it is not an African art American Negroes are responsible for, but an American one. The traditions of Africa must be utilized within the culture of the American Negro where they *actually* exist, and not because of a defensive rationalization about the *worth* of one's ancestors or an attempt to capitalize on the recent eminence of the "new" African nations. (111)

The notion of an American identity that cannot be understood without confronting the consequences of an essentially incomplete historical estrangement from Africa is a central feature of Baraka's writings in the early 1960s. His poem "Notes for a Speech" (1961) poignantly stated his sense of loss. "African blues," he began, "does not know me." He added:

> my color
> is not theirs.
> Lighter, white man talk

At the end, he sounds the plaintive cry of a returned prodigal who finds that home is very difficult to reclaim:

> You are as any other sad man here
> American

The problem, of course, is that if the black man is an American in Africa, American racism will not allow him to be an American in America. The unique view of the world that results from this dilemma is what Baraka's work passionately explores.

These ideas were not merely matters of intellectual debate in sidewalk cafés in 1962 but were immediate and local. Despite the artistic energy that surrounded the Lower East Side, the young African American artists felt a sense of personal isolation. The integrated milieu had the effect of foregrounding their racial self-consciousness. As Harold Cruse noted,

> The Negro intellectual has never really been held accountable to the black world for his social role [because] the black world cannot and does not support the Negro creative intellectual. The black bourgeoisie does not publish books, does not own and operate theaters or music halls. It plays no role to speak of in Negro music, and is remote from the living realities of the jazz musician who plays out his nights in the effete and soulless commercial jungles of American white middle-class café culture. (454)

Unconventional musicians like Charles Mingus, not to mention younger experimenters such as Albert Ayler, found themselves unwelcome even in that jungle.

Baraka cultivated a kind of nostalgia for an era when this separation of the African American artist from his community was not as extreme. "The 1940s was revolutionary," he recalled in a 1984 interview, "in terms of the music. I'm talking about Bebop. But the 1940s represents the last time for let's say forty years when the most advanced concepts of the music were worked out in the community" (8). The Lower East Side scene in the early 1960s represented integration as well as a decline in the functional role of African American communities. If there was anything beneficial about segregation, it would be that black communities enjoyed a certain amount of cultural cohesiveness. "It used to be," Baraka noted, "whether you had a million dollars or 20¢, you lived in the same community. I don't give a damn what your class was—the black bourgeoisie, the black no-wasie—you still were in the community" (8). Certainly, such feelings were personal; but Greg Tate is unfair in his judgment that Baraka had a tendency to "confuse . . . his identity complexes with those of all black people" (168). On the Lower East Side in the early 1960s, Baraka's perceptions were not based on paranoia.

II

Only in accordance with a Black value system will the artist be supplied with a means for a correct interpretation of the reality and relevance of the music the music makers make.—Mtume

As an integrationist movement, the Harlem Renaissance did little to encourage the establishment of African American cultural institutions.

Even so, W. E. B. Du Bois issued a "blueprint" for a Negro community theater, and Alain Locke helped to initiate a plan for an art museum in Harlem that never materialized. The fact that the lowering of racial barriers in the 1960s did not fundamentally change the status of African American artists led to a renewed call for black-controlled institutions.

The Black Arts Movement was informed by a class-based, Marxist-influenced critique of American society that did not always state its goals clearly. The Harlem Renaissance, wrote Larry Neal, "was essentially a failure. It did not address itself to the mythology and the lifestyles of the black community. It failed to take root, to link itself concretely to the struggles of that community, to become its voice and spirit" ("Black Arts Movement" 78). These were pitfalls that the leaders of the Black Arts Movement carefully avoided. They did succeed, for a moment, in making an unheard national voice audible. They helped young African Americans open their mouths. The tools available, however, were not adequate to accomplish all of the movement's ambitious goals.

Because he was trying to stimulate black pride and, simultaneously, plead the African American's case to white America, Locke's discussions of jazz often involved mixed signals. Employing the rhetoric of exoticism, mingled with echoes of Emerson and Frederick Jackson Turner, Locke declared in 1936 that jazz "incorporated the typical American restlessness and unconventionality, embodied its revolt against the drabness of the commonplace life, put pagan force behind the revolt against Puritan restraint, and finally became the Western World's life-saving flight from boredom and over-sophistication to the refuge of elemental emotion and primitive vigor" (90). Jazz musicians, however, simply felt that they were being exploited. As with any resentment, this one grew stronger with the passage of time. Locke could announce proudly in 1936 that "jazz, in its more serious form, has . . . become the characteristic musical speech of the modern age" (90). He was correct, but this development did not necessarily mean financial reward or respect for black musicians. Four decades later, singer Jon Hendricks noted an even more ominous development: "Even though we Afro-Americans are still impoverished, still downtrodden, still oppressed, still not yet free, our musical culture is now dominant in the entire Western world. The only thing wrong with the whole picture is that we, in our rush to integration, seem to have thrown our music away" (14–15). What troubled Hendricks was the relative control over the music that was exerted by white critics. In his view, expressed in the militant black journal *Liberator* in November 1969, neither black audiences nor the musicians themselves seemed to be able to control the aesthetic or commercial direction of the music. Here was a very specific example of the loss of a sense of community that Baraka has described.

Hendricks was particularly irked by jazz criticism, noting that "the one field of artistic endeavor where you can walk right in without credentials and become a critic is jazz. All you need is a command of the English language and a lot of opinions, plus access to musicians so they can tell you what to write" (15). Several years earlier, in an essay entitled "Jazz and the White Critic" (1963), Baraka had addressed this problem. "The irony," he wrote,

> is that because the majority of jazz critics are white middle-brows, most jazz criticism tends to enforce white middle-brow standards of excellence as criteria for performance of a music that in its most profound manifestations is completely antithetical to such standards; in fact, quite often is in direct reaction against them. (As an analogy, suppose the great majority of the critics of Western formal music were poor, "uneducated" Negroes?) (182)

This delightful signifying was not objecting to the *race* of these critics. Baraka carefully pointed out that many African Americans were unqualified as well: "Jazz was collected among the numerous skeletons the middle-class black man kept locked in the closet of his psyche, along with watermelons and gin" (179). The issue here was *class* identification. Baraka argued that few white jazz critics of the 1930s and 1940s had been able to either understand or identify with "the sub-culture from which [the music] was issued" (180). In 1936 Locke had argued that jazz was not only universal in its appeal but worthy of technical analysis for its musical sophistication. "In some important way," Locke wrote, "jazz has become diluted and tinctured with modernism. Otherwise, as purely a Negro dialect of emotion, it could not have become the dominant recreational vogue of our time" (90). Baraka felt that, in spite of the music's technical virtuosity, criticism should focus on the *source* of the aesthetic embodied in jazz. "The catalysts and necessity of Coltrane's music must be understood as they exist even before they are expressed as music," he wrote. "The music is the result of the attitude, the stance. Just as Negroes made blues and other people did not because of the Negro's peculiar way of looking at the world" (185).

Baraka's poetically phrased suggestion that the forms of art are derived from preexisting social attitudes is derived from the sort of Marxist analysis, popular in the 1930s, that is brilliantly exemplified in Christopher Caudwell's writings on poetry. Neal's essay "Ethos of the Blues" (1971) gives an even clearer picture of this theory:

> The blues are the ideology of the field slave—the ideology of a new "proletariat" searching for a means of judging the world. Therefore, even though the blues are cast in highly personal terms, they stand for the collective sensibility of a people at particular stages of cultural, social, and political development. The blues singer is not an alienated artist attempting to impose his view of the world on others. His ideas are the reflection of an unstated general point of view.

If Caudwell was able to correlate the styles of English verse to the economic relationships that dominated the centuries during which the poets lived, so Neal was able to suggest that the role of the blues singer in the African American community represented a surviving Africanism. The blues singer, for Neal, is an African griot in North America: "Even though he is part of the secular community, his message is often ritualistic and spiritual. Therefore, it is his spiritual role in the community which links him to the traditional priests and poets of Africa" (113). For Neal, Baraka, and the other writers of the Black Arts Movement, the avant-garde jazz musicians of the 1960s performed exactly the same role. Middle-class white jazz critics, judging performances in nightclubs or on concert stages, could not in any substantive sense employ this extended view of these artists.

"There is a story current in the Black Community," wrote Stephen Henderson in *Understanding the New Black Poetry* (1972), "about a white critic who, after listening to some records by Coltrane and Pharoah Sanders, said with great condescension, 'It's interesting, but you can't dance to it'; whereupon a young brother said with withering scorn, '*You* can't dance to it!'" (55).

If, in fact, most white jazz critics were unqualified because of their truncated view of the music, the question of what black jazz criticism should properly address was yet to be answered. Baraka and Neal both contended that it should be based on an investigation of "socio-aesthetic" features. Among the young people who constituted the national network of what would become known as the Black Arts Movement there were a number of poets working toward a definition of just what all this meant.

Between 1960 and 1970 an outpouring of poems focused on musicians in the role of griots. As Henderson noted in *Understanding the New Black Poetry*: "This is probably the largest category of musical referents in Black poetry" (60). All of these poems issued from the idea that the blues singer or jazz saxophone player is, as Neal pointed out, the contemporary griot—a role the poets had, of course, already accepted for themselves. As a result, these poems can often be read as "praise songs" in the traditional African manner. Walter De Legall's "Psalm for Sonny Rollins" (1963) is an excellent example of this genre:

> In a lifespan-while, I am
> Absorbed into the womb of the sound.
> > I am in the sound
> > The sound is in me.
> > I am the sound.
> I am your tears that you shed for forty days
> And forty nights, Theodore. I am
> Your pain who you accepted as
> Your bedfellow. I am your hunger and
> Your thirst, which purified your
> Soul, Theodore. I am your sorrow that
> You won in a raffle. Pick up your axe
> And let us blow down the Chicago citadels
> Of convention. "You just can't play like that in here."
> Let us blow down the Caucasian battlements
> Of bigotry. "But we don't hire Colored musicians."
> Open your tenor mouth and let
> Us blow into oblivion the insensible
> Strongholds of morality.
> "And I'm sure he's an addict."
> Blow down thunder and lightning
> And White People!! Blow down moons
> And stars and Christs!
> (Henderson 202)

De Legall's collage of biblical language, black hipster slang, and the puritanical voices of middle-class white America is intended to translate into words the preexisting social reality that the poet imagines is expressed in Rollins's music. In fact, the saxophonist's performance is imaged as a ritual, a mass. Like Jesus, or any "brother man," Sonny Rollins has suffered. Like Joshua at Jericho, he is capable of producing a musical sound that will bring down the walls erected by the enemies of his people. De Legall conflates allusions from both the Old Testament and the book of Revelation.

De Legall's poem, like many of the period, is informed by an aesthetic that Eugene Redmond succinctly defined in his "Parapoetics" (1970):

> Poetry is an *applied science:*
>> Re-wrapped corner rap;
>> Rootly-eloquented cellular, soulular sermons.
> (Henderson 371)

"Speech," said Baraka, "is the effective form of a culture." Here, in Redmond's phrasing, one sees the poet's attempt to incorporate the entire range of African American vernacular—sacred and profane—into a poetic diction capable of accurately representing the community's history, ideology, and ("cellular") racial identity. The unspoken assumption, of course, is that such a representation is the proper function of art—whether poetry or music, verbal or nonverbal. Redmond hints that effective art is, indeed, something like a metalinguistics. How it works is suggested by his choice of the prefix *para-* rather that *meta-;* his readers or listeners would have associated that prefix more immediately with its use in words such as "paramilitary" than with "paraphrasis." Indeed, for Black Arts Movement poets, poetry was capable of more than mere representation. As indicated in De Legall's poem, these writers imagined a poetry that makes things happen.

Some poets linked their interpretations of the music to social protest in very specific terms. David Henderson's "Elvin Jones Gretsch Freak" (1965) gives us

> the man elvin behind the baptismal tubs
> that leap like cannons   to the slashing sound of knives
> black elvin knows so well
> the knives the Daily News displays along with the photo
> of a grinning award-winning cop
> the kind of knives elvin talks about
> downtown by the water
> and uptown
> near the park
> (Henderson 267)

Such a poem proceeds from the idea expressed in A. B. Spellman's "Did John's Music Kill Him?" (1969):

> trane's horns had words in it
> (Henderson 261)

The poet had only to decipher those words. This might easily be dismissed as an irrelevant projection of the poet's mood or ideas onto music, except for the fact that many of the musicians were saying the same things. In a brief essay published in *Jazz* magazine, Archie Shepp wrote, "a piece of music is a woman in a foul dress; myriad babies howling, unfed; fat rat slick from the sewer. But what can a piece of music never be? It can never be more than Billie Holiday. But then it should strive never to be less" ("On Jazz" 24).

Again, Shepp's comments could be taken as merely a politically engaged African American's appropriation of nineteenth-century programmatic music rather than an expression of the preexisting "attitude, the stance" that Baraka sought to establish as the source of jazz music. Other musicians of the period, however, were more explicit in sounding their approval of this theory. The percussionist Mtume set forth guidelines for his peers:

> The Black musician must, as any other revolutionary artist, be a projector whose message reflects the values of the culture from which his creation owes its existence. He must be the antennae which receives the visions of a better life and time and transmits those visions into concrete realities through the use of sound and substance (each time must be a lecture via entertainment). (1)

This straightforwardly didactic approach to art was shared by the poets who contributed critical articles and reviews to Baraka's jazz journal *The Cricket*, published sporadically in Newark beginning in 1966. Cleveland poet Norman Jordan, for example, offered a definition of "Positive Black Music" (1969): "Black music, as well as all constructive art, *must be free*, and at the same time it *must contain order* a positive harmony on the physical, mental and spiritual level" (24). Here was the other side of the movement's protest, an urge to accomplish the moral regeneration of African American people who had been victimized and damaged by racism. Taken to an extreme, this impulse led to a rigorous, almost puritanical, concern with order and moral correctness. Mwanafunzi Katibu's nonreview of an Archie Shepp record, appearing in the same issue of *The Cricket*, is a particularly vivid example of this tendency:

> Listening to this album. Makes me tired. Its jive. Shepp hasn't, lost his, soul. *Yet*. But Devil Dogs can make this happen, thing abt it Archie Shepp. You shd know. The elements, you draw near are the ones you become, try to be like. If you around people who smoke, and drink all the time then thats. All you will want, to please, do.

Nothing is said about the music on this recording. Katibu, perhaps ahead of his time, aims his harshest criticism of Shepp at the saxophonist's indiscreet pose with a cigarette in hand: "Archie Shepp thinks, it's *hip* to take an album cover photo w/death air flowin out his mouth. No values" (26). At this extreme, the "critic" is not even interested in the music as an expression of the artist's attitude or stance but claims an ability to critique that attitude through a reading of the semiotics of life-style as revealed by personal habits. Of course, the fact that art is not even discussed disqualifies this article as anything more than a poison-pen letter.

Some writers were growing a bit impatient with the level of writing that was coming out of the movement. *The Grackle: Improvised Music in Transition*, a journal similar in purpose to *The Cricket*, edited by Roger Riggins, James T. Stewart, and Ron Welburn, published four issues between 1976 and 1978. In a letter to contributors, Welburn raised two sharply pointed questions:

> What level of musicological knowledge or skill should we demand of ourselves and each other [as critics]? Shouldn't we know something about music as a musician of amateur, or semi-professional, or professional ability, instead of romanticizing about cult figures and "rapping"?
>
> Isn't it time we moved away from superficial sociology to serious musicological and socio-aesthetic matters about particular artists and periods?

Welburn was not questioning the theory that jazz does, in fact, function as the artistic expression of an ideology. What he was calling for was a more rigorous standard of critical inquiry among African American jazz critics.

No movement, of course, should be judged on the basis of an extreme example of its negative potential; yet it must be noted that the Black Arts Movement, in encouraging an outspoken denunciation of racism, also encouraged the venting of a great many other resentments and the publication of a wide range of prescriptions for reform.

By 1976 the Black Arts Movement had become diffused into the general intellectual culture of black America. Baraka had redefined himself as a Marxist, Neal was directing a municipal arts council. Other angry young "revolutionary" poets had become university professors. Nevertheless, the movement had enjoyed an international range. The critical premises put forth by Baraka and his colleagues in terms of discussing jazz were now eloquently phrased, in England, by Henderson Dalrymple in defense of reggae music:

> Black music is too important a social agent; it fulfills too much of a social function in our lives to be left in the hands of the oppressing class. Culturally, socially and politically black music has an important role to play in the black liberation struggle. The role of our music in the struggle can only be truly revolutionary when black people are making all the decisions that will determine the music's future and direction. Only when we decide how great or how small a part our music must play in our struggle can the music be fulfilling its role as an agent of the revolutionary. (10–11)

The result of the Black Arts Movement focus on jazz was the creation of a socially conscious aesthetic standard that proved difficult for both musicians and audiences to maintain. This does not suggest that the Black Arts Movement, or earlier Afrocentric movements in fashion, failed. A useful comparison might be drawn to the Surrealist movement in its "l'art pour service de la révolution" phase and the enduring impact it has had on both the fine arts and commercial design (not to mention the Black Arts Movement). It is also worth noting that the political/aesthetic problems identified by the Black Arts Movement are still being worked out today on several different fronts, including the controversy regarding rap music.

To posit critical credibility on receptive ability defined by race and culture leads logically to further distinctions. If being African American is the first qualification for a jazz critic, being a practicing musician must be next—as was hinted at by the editors of *The Grackle*. There was, of course, no means of enforcing any of these entrance requirements. Not having any institutions capable of awarding accreditation made institution-building that much more difficult. Nevertheless, the critique of the status quo voiced by Baraka, Neal, Welburn, and others offered a valuable moment of self-reflection in a critical discipline that needs more of it.

Works Cited

Allen, Norm R., Jr., ed. *African-American Humanism: An Anthology.* Buffalo, N.Y.: Prometheus, 1991.

Ayler, Albert. *Spirits Rejoice.* 1965. ESP-Disc/ZYX Music [Germany] CD ESP 1020 (1993).

——. "To Mr. Jones—I Had a Vision." *Cricket* (1969): 27–30.

Baker, Houston A., Jr. "Handling 'Crisis': Great Books, Rap Music, and the End of

Western Homogeneity (Reflections on the Humanities in America)." *Callaloo* 13 (Spring 1990): 173–94.

——. *Modernism and the Harlem Renaissance.* Chicago: U of Chicago P, 1987.

Baraka, Amiri. "Expressive Language." *The Poetics of the New American Poetry.* Ed. Donald M. Allen and George Butterick. New York: Grove, 1975.

——. Interview with Michel Oren and Lorenzo Thomas. 21 June 1984. Houston.

——. "Jazz and the White Critic." 1963. *The LeRoi Jones/Amiri Baraka Reader.* Ed. William J. Harris. New York: Thunder's Mouth, 1991. 179–86.

——. "Notes for a Speech." 1961. *The LeRoi Jones/Amiri Baraka Reader.* Ed. William J. Harris. New York: Thunder's Mouth, 1991. 14–15.

Brown, Marion. "Improvisation and the Aural Tradition in Afro-American Music." *Black World* Nov. 1973.

Cruse, Harold. *The Crisis of the Negro Intellectual.* New York: Morrow, 1967.

Dalrymple, Henderson. *Bob Marley: Music, Myth and Rastas.* Sudbury, Middlesex: Carib-Arawak, 1976.

Dent, Tom. "For Lil Louis." *Black World* Sept. 1975: 65.

Finkelstein, Sidney. *Jazz: A People's Music.* 1948. New York: International, 1988.

Gioia, Ted. *The Imperfect Art: Reflections on Jazz and Modern Culture.* New York: Oxford UP, 1988.

Hart, Philip. *Orpheus in the New World: The Symphony Orchestra as an American Cultural Institution.* New York: Norton, 1973.

Henderson, Stephen. *Understanding the New Black Poetry: Black Speech and Black Music as Poetic References.* New York: Morrow, 1972.

Hendricks, Jon. "Jazz and Its Critics." *Liberator* Nov. 1969: 14–17.

"Jazz and Revolutionary Black Nationalism (Part 3)." *Jazz* June 1966: 28–30.

"Jazz and Revolutionary Black Nationalism (Part 10)." *Jazz* Jan. 1967: 38.

Jones, LeRoi. *Black Music.* New York: Morrow, 1967.

——. "The Jazz Avant Garde." *Metronome* Sept. 1961: 9–12, 39.

——. "The Myth of a 'Negro Literature.'" *Home: Social Essays.* New York: Morrow, 1966.

Jordan, Norman. "Positive Black Music." *Cricket* (1969): 24–25.

Katibu, Mwanafunzi. "Archie Shepp, AS-9162, Three For A Quarter, One For a Dime." *Cricket* (1969): 26.

Lang, David. "Archie Shepp—Jazz Playwright." *Jazz* Jan. 1966: 26.

Locke, Alain. *The Negro and His Music.* 1936. New York: Arno P and New York Times, 1969.

Mingus, Charles. "Freedom." 1963. *Charles Mingus, Reevaluation.* Impulse AS-9234-2 (1973).

Mtume. "Trippin'—A Need for Change." *Cricket* (1969): 1–2.

Neal, Larry. "The Black Arts Movement." 1968. *Visions of a Liberated Future: Black Arts Movement Writings.* Ed. Michael Schwartz. New York: Thunder's Mouth, 1989. 62–78.

——. "The Ethos of the Blues." 1971. *Visions of a Liberated Future: Black Arts Movement Writings.* Ed. Michael Schwartz. New York: Thunder's Mouth, 1989. 107–17.

——. "New Grass/Albert Ayler." *Cricket* (1969): 37–40.

Rutter, Larry. "The animal loves you, wear it in your eyes." *Jazz* Jan. 1967: 26–29.

Shepp, Archie. "On Jazz." *Jazz* Aug./Sept. 1965: 24.

Tate, Greg. "Growing Up in Public: Amiri Baraka Changes His Mind." 1984. *Flyboy in the Buttermilk: Essays on Contemporary America.* New York: Simon, 1992. 168–77.

Warren, Paul. "Holding Up All Sorrow for Heaven to See." *Village Voice* 6 July 1972: 32.

Welburn, Ron. Letter to Lorenzo Thomas. 2 Jan. 1978.

Ya Salaam, Kalamu. "The Man Who Walked in Balance." *Coda* Sept./Oct. 1992: 20–26.

Contributors

JOHN CORBETT teaches at the Art Institute of Chicago. He has written *Extended Play: Sounding Off From John Cage to Dr. Funkenstein* (1994).

STEVEN B. ELWORTH has taught at Fiorello LaGuardia Community College in New York City. He is completing a dissertation at New York University entitled "The Garden and the Machine: Pastoralism and Post-War American Film."

KRIN GABBARD is Associate Professor of Comparative Literature at the State University of New York at Stony Brook. His most recent book is *Jamming at the Margins: Jazz and the American Cinema* (forthcoming).

BERNARD GENDRON, who is Professor of Philosophy at the University of Wisconsin-Milwaukee, teaches courses in aesthetics, cultural theory, and popular music. He is presently working on a book entitled *Between Montmartre and the Mudd Club: Popular Music and the Avant-Garde.*

WILLIAM HOWLAND KENNEY is Professor of History at Kent State University and the author of *Chicago Jazz: A Cultural History, 1904–30* (1993). He is at work on *"Circles of Resonance": The Phonograph in American Life, 1877–1945.*

ERIC LOTT teaches in the English Department at the University of Virginia. He has written *Love and Theft: Blackface Minstrelsy and the American Working Class* (1993).

NATHANIEL MACKEY teaches Literature at the University of California at Santa Cruz. He is the author of *Bedouin Hornbook* (1986) and *Discrepant Engagement: Dissonance, Cross-Culturality and Experimental Writing* (1993). He has coedited *Moment's Notice: Jazz in Poetry and Prose* (1993).

BURTON W. PERETTI, who teaches History at Middle Tennessee State University, is the author of *The Creation of Jazz: Music, Race, and Culture in Urban America* (1992) and the forthcoming *Jazz as History: An American Music in Twentieth Century Society.*

RONALD M. RADANO is Professor of Afro-American Studies at the University of Wisconsin. He is the author of *New Musical Figurations: Anthony Braxton's Cultural Critique* (1993).

JED RASULA teaches English at Queen's University in Kingston, Ontario. His most recent book is *The American Poetry Wax Museum: Literary Effects, 1940–1990*.

LORENZO THOMAS is Professor of English at the University of Houston-Downtown. His several volumes of poetry include *Fit Music* (1972), *Dracula* (1973), *Chances Are Few* (1979), and *The Bathers* (1981).

ROBERT WALSER is Assistant Professor of Musicology at the University of California at Los Angeles. He is the author of *Running with the Devil: Power, Gender, and Madness in Heavy Metal Music* (1993).

Index

Several chapters in this volume have appeared in previous publications and are reprinted with permission.

Krin Gabbard: "The Jazz Canon and Its Consequences," *Annual Review of Jazz Studies* 6 (1993): 65–98.

Bernard Gendron: "Moldy Figs and Modernists: Jazz at War (1942–1946)," *Discourse* 15, no. 3 (1993): 130–57.

Eric Lott: "Double V, Double-Time: Bebop's Politics of Style," *Callaloo* 11, no. 3 (1988): 597–605.

Nathaniel Mackey: "Other: From Noun to Verb," *Representations*, no. 39 (Summer 1992): 51–70, © 1992 by the Regents of the University of California.

Ronald M. Radano: "Black Experimentalism as Spectacle," in *New Musical Figurations: Anthony Braxton's Cultural Critique* (Chicago: University of Chicago Press, 1993).

Robert Walser: "Out of Notes: Signification, Interpretation, and the Problem of Miles Davis," *Musical Quarterly* 77, no. 2 (1993): 343–65.

Library of Congress Cataloging-in-Publication Data
Jazz among the discourses / edited by Krin Gabbard.
Includes bibliographical references and index.
ISBN 0-8223-1581-5 (cloth : acid-free paper). — ISBN 0-8223-1596-3 (paper : acid-free paper)
1. Jazz—History and criticism. 2. Musical canon.
I. Gabbard, Krin.
ML3507.J36 1995
781.65'09—dc20   94-41051 CIP   MN